ONTOLOGY AND DIALECTICS

ONTOLOGY AND DIALECTICS

1960/61

Theodor W. Adorno

Edited by Rolf Tiedemann

Translated by Nicholas Walker

polity

First published in German as *Ontologie und Dialektik (1960/61)*, © Suhrkamp Verlag, Frankfurt am Main, 2002

This English edition © Polity Press, 2019

The translation of this work was funded by Geisteswissenschaften International – Translation Funding for Work in the Humanities and Social Sciences from Germany, a joint initiative of the Fritz Thyssen Foundation, the German Federal Foreign Office, the collecting society VG WORT and the Börsenverein des Deutschen Buchhandels (German Publishers & Booksellers Association)

Polity Press
65 Bridge Street
Cambridge CB2 1UR, UK

Polity Press
101 Station Landing
Suite 300
Medford, MA 02155, USA

ISBN-13: 978-0-7456-9312-5
ISBN-13: 978-0-7456-7946-4 (pb)

A catalogue record for this book is available from the British Library.

Library of Congress Cataloging-in-Publication Data

Names: Adorno, Theodor W., 1903-1969, author.
Title: Ontology and dialectics : 1960/61 / Theodor W. Adorno.
Other titles: Ontologie und Dialektik, 1960-61. English
Description: English edition. | Cambridge, UK ; Medford, MA, USA : Polity Press, [2018] | Originally published: Ontologie und Dialektik, 1960-61. Frankfurt am Main : Suhrkamp, 2002. | Includes bibliographical references and index.
Identifiers: LCCN 2018010019 (print) | LCCN 2018021553 (ebook) | ISBN 9780745694900 (Epub) | ISBN 9780745693125 | ISBN 9780745679464 (pb)
Subjects: LCSH: Ontology. | Dialectic.
Classification: LCC BD313 (ebook) | LCC BD313 .A3613 2018 (print) | DDC 111–dc23
LC record available at https://lccn.loc.gov/2018010019

Typeset in 10.5 on 12 pt Sabon Roman
by Toppan Best-set Premedia Limited
Printed and bound in Great Britain by CPI Group (UK) Ltd, Croydon

For further information on Polity, visit our website:
politybooks.com

CONTENTS

Aristotle • Experience of being is not 'prior'; being as
product of abstraction • Being and thought in Parmenides;
abstraction and vital powers not distinguished for archaic
thought; the most ancient not the truest • Philosophy and
the particular sciences; dialectic of enlightenment; residual
character of being • Two kinds of truth

Prehistory of the new ontologies: Franz Brentano; ontology
as counter-Enlightenment • A double front against realism
and conceptualism • Fundamental ontology as hermeneutics;
being and language; nominalist critique of language •
Analysis of the concept of being; positivism and language •
Conceptuality as domination of nature; inadequacy of
concept and thing; thing in itself and being • Functional
understanding of concepts; double sense of being as concept
and anti-concept

Ambiguity of the concept of being (I) • Arbitrariness in
concept formation; Kant versus Spinoza • Ambiguity of the
concept of being (II) • Ambiguity of the concept of being
(III) • Subjectivity as constitutive for ontology • Substantial
character of language; borrowing from theology • On the
analysis of language; obligations regarding linguistic
form • The wavering character of being

Examples from antiquity; on Aristotle's terminology; the
priority of the *tode ti* • Genesis and validity; Heidegger's
being as third possibility; on Heidegger's concept of origin •
Archaic dimension of Heidegger's ontology; against genetic
explanation; phenomenology and history • Phenomenological
method; red and redness; the inference to being-in-itself in
Scheler and Heidegger • Husserl's return to transcendentalism

'Priority' as *petitio principii* • Critique of the possibility
of ontology; on Cartesian dualism • Phenomenological
reduction of the subject; objectivity of the second level;

shutting out beings • Philosophical compulsion for
cleanliness • Allergy towards beings; an aura borrowed
from theology; the story of Snow White • Ontology as
counterpart to nominalism and positivism

The subject–object division not permanent; fundamental
ontology and the loss of tradition; the 'unintelligibility' of
Heidegger • Oblivion of the numinous; material stuff and
abstraction in the pre-Socratics • Ontology or dialectics;
'being' as 'the wholly other' • Critique as differentiation;
original non-differentiation; Heidegger's
anti-intellectualism • Against postponement • Heidegger's
trick: ontologizing the ontic

Conceptualizing the non-conceptual; philosophy of being
and idealism, Heidegger and Hegel • Ontologizing
existence • Spurious appeal of the new; fascination through
ignorance • Subreption of the nominalized verb 'being' •
Dasein as being and a being • 'Be who you are!' • Eidetic
science and ontology • Subjectivity as the site of being

Heidegger and Kant; Kant's ultimate intention •
Heidegger's thought as the site of being; a diminished
concept of subject: absence of labour and
spontaneity • Initial observations on the ontological
need • A sociological interjection • The 'elevated tone';
Heidegger's language and Adorno's great-grandfather;
fundamental ontology as index of a lack

On the sociology of the ontological need • Philosophy and
society; distracting effect of Marxism; the relevance of
morality • Philosophy and the natural sciences; philosophy
and art • Kant's abdication before God, freedom and
immortality • The 'resurrection of metaphysics'; impotence
of philosophy in the face of the essential • Schelling,
Schopenhauer, Nietzsche

'Existence' as authoritarian • 'Historicity' • Against the
ontology of the non-ontological • History as the medium of
philosophy • Critique

'Peep-hole metaphysics' and negative dialectics • Left
Hegelianism and the ban on images • Priority of the
object • Reversing the subjective reduction • Interpreting
the transcendental • 'Transcendental illusion'; against
hierarchy

EDITOR'S FOREWORD

Adorno had once considered employing the title 'Is Metaphysics Possible after Auschwitz?' for the section of *Negative Dialectics* which undoubtedly formed the heart of the work and was eventually entitled 'Meditations on Metaphysics' (NaS IV.13, p. 462). And this initial formulation, which alluded to the central question posed by Kant in the Introduction to the *Critique of Pure Reason*, could well be applied to the book as a whole: the idea of a negative dialectic searches after some kind of answer to the question of whether philosophy can be pursued at all after all that has happened in the meantime. Whereas the traditional notion of a critique of reason could once ask *how* truth in an emphatic sense is possible – Kant himself had spoken of synthetic a priori judgements – without having to put this very possibility into question, for the philosopher who had returned to Germany after the era of fascism, and after everything that a German mass industry of destruction had unleashed upon the world, it was anything but self-evident that one could simply carry on the business of philosophy as if nothing essential had changed. In the *Dialectic of Enlightenment*, written in the 1940s under the immediate impact of the events in Germany, Adorno and Horkheimer admitted that what 'we had set out to do was nothing less than to explain why humanity, instead of entering a truly human state, is sinking into a new kind of barbarism' (GS 3, p. 11; *Dialectic of Enlightenment*, trans. Edmund Jephcott, Stanford University Press, 2002, p. xiv). This question, in relation to which the traditional problems of philosophy had come to appear irrelevant, would never cease to haunt Adorno and constituted the centre of his thinking to a degree that was paralleled only in the case of Günther Anders. Towards the end of *Negative Dialectics* Adorno asks 'whether after Auschwitz one can go on living'; rather than a simply rhetorical question, this was actually the gravest question of all, and Adorno specifically asked in relation to his own life 'whether one who escaped by accident, one who by rights should have been killed, may go on living. For his mere survival calls for the coldness, the basic principle of bourgeois subjectivity, without which there could have been no Auschwitz' (GS 6, pp. 355f.; *Negative Dialectics*, trans. E. B. Ashton, Routledge, 1973, p. 363). After he returned from exile to Germany, Adorno composed numerous essays and investigations which addressed a whole range of different themes and subjects, yet they were all basically concerned with deciphering what he called 'the basic principle of bourgeois subjectivity'; and in the seven years between 1959 and 1966 he was principally engaged with the composition of *Negative Dialectics*, which represents a kind of summation of all his specific material studies. Here Adorno undertakes to traverse 'the frozen wastes of abstraction' (GS 6, p. 9; *Negative Dialectics*, Ashton, p. xix) to see what has become of the traditional philosophical categories under the conditions of society after Auschwitz. With reference to specific 'models', Adorno provides a substantive indication of how moral philosophy and the philosophy of history have to be transformed if they are to remain possible for us at all. Thus *Negative Dialectics* had no ultimate 'pronouncement' or definitive solution to offer beyond the exposed and vulnerable doctrine that something resembling philosophy could only be salvaged if it can make itself good in materialist terms. Just after the book was published Adorno wrote to Gershom Scholem in the following terms:

> What I describe in an immanent epistemological context as the priority of the object, and what can actually only be conceived in an extremely delicate way rather than simply as a crude assertion – or only in a dialectical way – is precisely what does justice to the concept of materialism, so it seems to me, once we have escaped the spell of identity. The convincing arguments which I believe I have brought against idealism thus appear, beyond this spell, and indeed stringently I think, as materialist in character. But this implies that such a materialism is not simply fixed or conclusive, is not some kind of world-view. It is this path towards materialism, quite remote from all dogmatism, which seems to harbour that affinity to metaphysics, or I might almost have said to theology, which you have rightly recognized as the central motif here. (Letter to Scholem dated 14 March 1967)

It is this concept of materialism, the centre around which Adorno's *Negative Dialectics* turns, that prevents philosophy from stopping its ears against the cries of the victims, a concept which attempts, on the contrary, to think with such ears. For this approach 'the need to lend voice to suffering is a condition of all truth' (GS 6, p. 29; *Negative Dialectics*, Ashton, pp. 17–18). It is only in this context that the final sentence of Adorno's book acquires its full significance: 'There is solidarity between such thinking and metaphysics at the moment of its fall' (GS 6, p. 400; Ashton, p. 408).

Adorno generally pursued his academic commitments as a teacher without constant or direct connection with his own activity as a writer, but in the case of *Negative Dialectics* he proceeded in a different way. Between 1964 and 1966 he presented three successive lecture courses on the subject matter specifically treated in this book, which, for all the author's critical reservations about the idea of a masterpiece or the 'genre chef-d'oeuvre', still surely represents Adorno's own masterpiece. The first of these lecture series was offered in the winter semester of 1964/65 under the title *The Doctrine of History and Freedom* and addressed the complex of issues that would be taken up in the chapter on Kant and Hegel in *Negative Dialectics*. In the summer semester of 1965 Adorno went on to deliver the lectures on *Metaphysics: Concept and Problems*, which was concerned with the last of the 'models' presented in *Negative Dialectics*, namely the 'Meditations on Metaphysics' which we have already mentioned. The last series of lectures, delivered in the winter semester of 1965/66, undertook to develop, in close connection with the recently composed 'Introduction' to his book, the idea of a dialectic of negativity which provided Adorno with the name 'negative dialectics', and this was the title he gave to the lectures in question as well as to the published book. What the three lecture series have in common is the fact that each was delivered at a point of time well before the corresponding sections of the published version had assumed their definitive form. Thus the lectures arose while Adorno was still working on the book and emerged from what he liked to describe as 'work in progress', and when it was still unclear what precise form the resulting work would take. Adorno's intention in these lecture series was to develop 'something like a methodical reflection with regard to what' he was 'fundamentally doing' (Theodor W. Adorno Archiv, Vo 10813) – an observation which corresponds to his remarks about 'the methodology of the author's material works' in the Preface to *Negative Dialectics* (GS 6, p. 9; Ashton, p. xix). It is quite possible that this methodological aspect, the immanent categorial analysis which holds the book at least partly in the regions of what Benjamin called 'the frozen wastes of abstraction', has contributed to the reputation which soon attached to *Negative Dialectics* as a particularly difficult work. It may be that the author anticipated this and hoped through the freely improvised

form of the corresponding lecture courses to make things a little easier
for his future readers, at least amongst the students involved – even
if the primary intention, as Adorno himself repeatedly pointed out,
was the different one of avoiding the need to prepare entirely new
lecture material and thus giving himself enough time to complete the
book. Anyone who reads the lecture course on negative dialectics
today will be able to confirm what the present editor has pointed out
in connection with another lecture course:

> To accompany Adorno along the roads and the byways of his thought
> is to find oneself in situations in which the sense of the fully rounded
> and conclusive form that always predominates in his writings is con-
> stantly broken up, and possibilities emerge that Adorno was unable to
> resolve in his authoritative works ... But it is only the record of his
> lectures that allows us to see the effort of thought that went into them
> and gives us a glimpse of the workshop in which the philosopher hones
> his concepts like Siegfried forging his sword in Mime's cave. (NaS IV.4,
> pp. 420f.; *Kant's Critique of Pure Reason*, trans. Rodney Livingstone,
> Polity, 2001, p. 285)

It is clear at any rate that the lectures on negative dialectics provide
a welcome propaedeutic to a work which is indeed hardly easy to
approach, which made a name like no other work of the time, and
which could also help us to understand the present time precisely 'as
critique, as a form of resistance to growing heteronomy, even as a vain
attempt on the part of thought to keep hold on itself' (GS 10.2, p. 464).

The three lecture courses we have mentioned were in fact preceded
by a fourth one, the series of lectures on *Ontology and Dialectics*
which is published here. They were delivered in the winter semester
of 1960/61 before Adorno had conceived the plan for *Negative Dialectics*, an idea which crystallized in his mind only as a consequence
of these lectures. We might almost say that *Negative Dialectics* derived
from a specific occasion, namely a conversation with the French Ger-
manist Robert Minder, who at Adorno's invitation had given a lecture
at the Frankfurt Institute for Social Research on 25 July 1959. Minder
had spoken from a sociological angle about issues connected with the
cultural history of Swabia and had coupled his discussion with some
reflections on Heidegger (which Minder himself apparently did not
regard as particularly successful). Adorno and Minder had long shared
a similar antipathy to the ontological grumblings emanating from the
Black Forest and to its fatal political implications. Minder, who held
the chair 'de langues et littératures d'origine germanique' at the Collège
de France, invited Adorno to Paris in return. In his letter of thanks
for this invitation Adorno wrote:

I hardly need to tell you what a great honour and satisfaction that would be for me. Now I believe that it would be good, for certain intellectual and strategic reasons which also emerged clearly enough in the course of our conversations, to expose the cult of Heidegger for once in its principal character. In order not to accord Heidegger an objective honour which in my deepest conviction he does not deserve, the discussion should not of course be centred upon him and his person but be formulated more in terms of principle, while leaving enough room to say what is necessary about him. I would therefore suggest 'Ontology and Dialectics' as my topic. (Letter to Robert Minder dated 25 March 1959)

Immediately after he had written the letter Adorno began writing down his initial thoughts on the theme of ontology and dialectics in his notebook. And it was these thoughts which then resulted in the lecture course of 1960/61 as well as the three lectures which Adorno delivered at the Collège de France in March 1961. His earliest notes on the subject, the embryo as it were from which the book on *Negative Dialectics* would eventually emerge, are reproduced here.

The main issue: that ontology cannot be regarded as divorced from history and is not divorced from history.
 We cannot just *overleap* nominalism.
  It is to be transcended from within (as already in Kant)
  The *compulsion* towards ontology is to be understood.
  1) the self-dissolution of reason, its crisis
  2) overcoming the reification of s[ubject] and o[bject]
  3) the impossibility of idealism, of grounding in spirit
 But o[ntology] falls back into all this: arbitrariness, rigidity, hypostasis of spirit (abstract being = spirit)
 O[ntology] is correct false consciousness, i.e. appropriate to a (pre- or post-) fascistic situation, yet as untrue as the latter
 The ontologization of history: what persists is transience – already in Hegel. Difference. But this needs criticism in both [i.e. Hegel and Heidegger].
 The abstract character of ontology. What is decisive here not the abstractness as such but its function. The original *pseudos*: that a lack, an omission is supposed to signify a *greater* truth.
 O[ntology] as idealism in disguise, unconscious of itself, and thus all the more malignant idealism. Being, without any further determination, *is* the same as thought. Hegel is right here.
 Bring out the aspect of arbitrariness. The talk of the forgetfulness of being corresponds to the worst features of the idealist tradition: anyone who *names* what is base is base. 'The kind of philosophy one has depends on the kind of human being one is.'

Ideology in the strictest sense: a necessary false consciousness. Transferring the *closed character* of the administered world onto metaphysics. [Inserted here:] (To be developed. Principal thing is deception: but it is posited as *necessary* by unreflective dominatory thinking.)

Duplication of what is as being amounts to its justification.

In Hegel too transience = historicity is ontologized in a certain sense. Showing up difference: negativity. (going much further here: in H[egel] no 'being'.

Hegel's doctrine of the dialectic of self-undermining essence to be applied critically to ontology.

If ontology really wishes to get back before the split between s[ubject] + o[bject] – why should it have to exclude content.

After Hegel every philosophy that lacks content is regression. O[ntology] conceals this. Pseudo-concreteness, when it passes into the substantive, becomes arbitrary, as with all idealism. (Existentialism).

Semblance of 'destruction'.

Archaism dressed up as modernity. The objectivism is subjectivistic … [Added later:] subject/object to be criticized but no going back behind them!) en attendant, 27. VI. 59.

(Theodor W. Adorno Archive, Notebook E, pp. 59ff.)

The fact that *Negative Dialectics* could spring from such beginnings may remind us of Adorno's interpretation of Beethoven, where he attests that the composer's themes and motifs often arise from 'the insignificance of the particular and the arbitrary character of first thoughts' (NaS I.1, p. 34). Just as the composer of the Eroica, in a thoroughly Hegelian way, frequently 'develops its musical being out of nothing' (GS 12, p. 77; *Philosophy of Modern Music*, trans. A. G. Mitchell and W. V. Blomster, Sheed & Ward, 1987, p. 77), so in Adorno the theoretical whole not infrequently emerges out of barely developed things which in their disparate state may strike us as irrelevant or unpromising. The initial remarks on ontology and dialectics which we have just cited were followed in Adorno's notebooks over the succeeding weeks and months by numerous further observations, most of which were also not particularly helpful or illuminating at first sight. When Adorno began to deliver the corresponding lectures a year and a half later in Frankfurt, at the start of October 1960, it seems that he had not yet composed the three lectures to be given in Paris. It was only on 19 December 1960, when ten of the Frankfurt lectures had already been delivered, that he reported in a letter to Minder that 'I am deep in the midst of writing the original German version of the three lectures for you which I shall be presenting in March. The first one is finished, and the other two have already been largely sketched out.' The corrected version of the first lecture, on 'The Ontological Need', is dated 18 December, the day before. On 2

January Adorno wrote again to Minder in relation to the second lecture, on 'Being and Existence', the manuscript of which was completed on 9 January, to tell him: 'In the meantime I am basically finished with the second of the Paris lectures, which just needs some clearing up so that it is ready to be translated in the middle of January, and that only leaves the last one to be done, which would need to arrive in Paris by the middle of February.' At the moment it is not possible to provide a precise date for the completion of the last Paris lecture, on 'Negative Dialectics'. Once the lecture course in Frankfurt was concluded at the end of February, Adorno set out, on 13 March, on a lecturing trip to Paris and then Italy, which lasted until 17 April. In a report to the German Research Council, which had provided financial support for the trip, Adorno wrote:

> In Paris ... I delivered the three lectures on ontology and dialectics at the Collège de France under the respective titles of 'Le besoin d'une ontology', 'Être et existence', and 'Vers une dialectique negative'. Numerous members of the Faculty of Philosophy were present ... including the academic colleagues Minder and Merleau-Ponty. The lectures gave rise to some extremely fruitful discussions ... From Paris we flew on to Rome. There I delivered two lectures which were concerned with the aesthetics of music ... and, at the invitation of academic colleague Lombardi, I repeated two of the Paris lectures at the university. (Report to the DFG dated 18 April 1961)

In his diary Adorno entered only a few sparse remarks on the Paris lectures; thus he writes on 15 March: 'Gave my lecture, too difficult, Merleau-Ponty shocked. God and everyone was there'; on 18 March: 'Lecture was packed; went much better'; on 21 March: 'Final lecture went very well, roared like an ox. Merleau-Ponty and Jean Wahl were present but didn't say anything' (Theodor W. Adorno Archiv, Notizheft J, pp. 5, 12f., 17). Maurice Merleau-Ponty (who from 1952 onwards held Bergson's chair at the Collège de France), the friend and later something of an opponent of Sartre's, was clearly the natural and, as it were, ideal addressee for Adorno's Paris lectures; in fact Adorno was unable to establish a real dialogue with him, and it proved too late to do so since Merleau-Ponty died only a few weeks later. It is certainly not particularly easy to imagine precisely how a conversation might have unfolded between this student of Husserl's, intent as he was on developing a kind of 'indirect ontology', and the proponent of a 'negative dialectic', yet it should not have been impossible in principle. In an impressive testimony to his humanity, Adorno subsequently wrote to Minder, on 16 May 1961, regarding the death of Merleau-Ponty:

Let me just add how much the death of Merleau-Ponty has deeply disturbed me. When you were kind enough to introduce us nothing would have led me to think that I was talking to a man on the brink of death. Without question he revealed a quite remarkable intellectual power – especially in view of the deep theoretical differences between us, as I believe I can justifiably and am also duty bound to say. And in view of this irrevocable loss I do feel a certain guilt in his regard insofar as, so shortly before his death, I attacked in very fundamental ways positions which were essential to him. Yet how we are entangled in life; if we wish to speak the truth, this also turns to the worse; Ibsen already saw all this so clearly.

Adorno repeated the three Paris lectures on several occasions, although he never published them as such. But they formed the initial basis of the new book that was now germinating in his mind and that would take another five years to reach completion. The first outlines which he considered in this connection (see Theodor W. Adorno Archiv, Notizheft E, p. 59, and the letter to Stefan Burger of 18 April 1961) do not yet reveal that much similarity to the plan which ultimately provided the structure for *Negative Dialectics*. In the final book the two Paris lectures on 'The Ontological Need' and 'Being and Existence' were reworked to form the first part of the text, which bears the title 'Relation to Ontology', while the third Paris lecture, on 'Negative Dialectics', was incorporated into the second part of the book, which is entitled 'Negative Dialectics: Concept and Categories'. But the Frankfurt lectures which are presented here must stand – and can stand – for the book on Heidegger that Adorno neither wrote nor wished to write. They represent the belated realization, as it were, of a project which Brecht and Benjamin had already begun to pursue around 1930, not long after the appearance of Heidegger's *Being and Time*, but had never completed, namely the project of 'demolishing Heidegger' [*den Heidegger zu zertrümmern*] (Walter Benjamin, *Gesammelte Briefe*, III: *1925–1930*, ed. Christoph Gödde and Henri Lonitz, Suhrkamp, 1997, p. 522; *The Correspondence of Walter Benjamin, 1910–1940*, trans. M. R. Jacobson and E. M. Jacobson, University of Chicago Press, 1994, p. 365). Adorno hardly needed to be reminded of this plan on the part of his friend who had fallen victim to the Nazis, amongst whom Heidegger belonged. When one of Heidegger's students, anxious to establish some kind of communication, contacted Adorno directly after the publication of his book *The Jargon of Authenticity*, the latter replied that he had 'already reacted in exactly the same way as today immediately after the appearance of *Being and Time*, thus long before Heidegger's open commitment to fascism' (Letter to Hermann Mörchen dated 13 September

1965). This attitude is also documented in Adorno's inaugural lecture of 1931 (GS 1, p. 329 passim) and in the lecture he gave at a meeting of the Kant Society in the following year (ibid., p. 351), as well as in his *Habilitationsschrift* on Kierkegaard, which appeared in 1933 (see GS 2, pp. 100, 119). After his return to Germany from exile, Adorno was widely regarded as the pre-eminent intellectual opponent of Heidegger, and indeed he concerned himself more intensely with Heidegger than with any other contemporary philosopher. The index to Adorno's *Complete Writings* turns up almost 600 references to the name of Heidegger, exceeded in number only by those to his friend Benjamin. But that certainly does not imply that Adorno overestimated Heidegger's significance, for he actually regarded his gifts as far more modest in character, yet as a thinker who was all the more dangerous for that. Heidegger's *Holzwege* [Forest Paths] came out in 1951, one of his first publications to appear after the end of the Third Reich, and it created something of a furore in philosophical circles at the time. Adorno was not slow to read the book in which the philosopher, who, along with Carl Schmitt, Arnold Gehlen and others, had formed the intellectual avant-garde of the Nazi state, chose to announce his continued presence, as it were, in the re-established democracy. But this was not actually the first occasion in this regard, for in 1949, when Heidegger was still subject to the teaching ban imposed at the end of the war, he had already uttered the unspeakable statement which seemed the only thing he could think of to say about Auschwitz: 'Agriculture has now become a mechanized industry of food production, in essence the same as the fabrication of corpses in gas chambers and concentration camps, the same as the blockades and the starvation inflicted on countries, the same as the fabrication of hydrogen bombs' (quoted in Wolfgang Schirmacher, *Technik und Gelassenheit: Zeitkritik nach Heidegger*, Alber, 1983, p. 25). And in 1953 he was even prepared to publish the other statement about National Socialism in which he speaks of 'the inner truth and greatness of this movement' (Heidegger, *Einführung in die Metaphysik*, Niemeyer, 1953, p. 152; *Introduction to Metaphysics*, trans. Gregory Fried and Richard Polt, Yale University Press, 2000, p. 213).

Before the publication of *Jargon of Authenticity* in 1964 and that of *Negative Dialectics* two years later, Adorno had already frequently engaged with Heidegger and his writings. He never did so in the form of political denunciation, however, but always in an attempt to reveal the relationship between the philosophical and the political content. If the first part of *Negative Dialectics* took its point of departure from 'the situation of the ontology which still prevails in Germany' (Typescript 53504), we cannot really say that much has changed today as far as this domination on the part of ontology is concerned. On the contrary, despite the insistence of Adorno's philosophy on remembering the implications of the recent past, we witness the triumph of a renewed interest in chthonic origins, of the ideology of another 'new' mythology which finds expression in the combination of a misunderstood Nietzsche and a renaissance of Heidegger which had long seemed inconceivable, so that 'Brother Heidegger' is finally brought home in this new empire to join other comrades and brothers from Ernst Jünger to Carl Schmitt. On all fronts, whether right, left or centre, ontology seems to have triumphed over dialectics. The return of philosophy to a kind of pre-Socratic irrationalism corresponds to a retreat from actual history which extinguishes memory and eliminates experience: a ratification of tendencies which contemporary society is already effectively following. Given this state of things, the publication of the only lecture course which Adorno dedicated to the thought of his antipode in philosophy may not prove to be entirely obsolete and perhaps not even without a certain advantage – as a plea for reason and enlightenment, which – to adapt a formulation of Benjamin's – clearly look small and ugly today and thus have to make themselves scarce.

This edition of Adorno's lecture course is based on the transcripts from tape recordings produced in the Institute for Social Research in Frankfurt, usually in immediate connection with the particular lectures as they were delivered. The tapes themselves were then wiped in order to be reused. The transcripts in question are now lodged in the Theodor W. Adorno Archive with the classification numbers Vo 5688–5972.

In preparing the text the editor has attempted to follow Adorno's own example in editing the texts of lectures that he had given extempore if he subsequently agreed for them to be published. A particular effort has been made to preserve the informal character of the lecturing situation. The editor has intervened in the text as little as possible but as much as seemed necessary. After his previous experience in editing Adorno's lectures the editor felt freer in the case of the present lectures to retouch the transcripts here and there, materials which did not come directly from the hand of Adorno and were not authorized by him in their present form. Anacoluthons, ellipses and grammatical slips have been corrected. In addition to the cautious deletion of over-obtrusive repetitions, occasional attempts have been made to disentangle particularly obscure syntactical constructions. Adorno tended to speak relatively quickly and individual words not infrequently became garbled in the process; corrections have been inserted whenever it was possible to ascertain his meaning precisely. Filler words, especially particles such as 'now', 'so', 'indeed', and a somewhat inflationary use of 'actually', have been cut where it was clear that he was searching for the right word or thought. The frequently repeated address to Adorno's audience – 'Ladies and gentlemen' – has often been omitted when it merely sounded redundant. Since the question of punctuation naturally had to be decided by the editor, he felt most at liberty to impose his own practice here to achieve maximum clarity and comprehensibility without regard to the rules Adorno followed in preparing his own texts. No attempt has been made to 'improve' Adorno's lectures; the aim was always to present *his* text to the best of the editor's abilities.

In the editorial notes the quotations occurring in the lectures have been identified where possible, and the passages to which Adorno alludes or appears to allude have been cited and references supplied. Wherever English translations of the works quoted by Adorno, or of Adorno's own writings, are available, the relevant details and page references have been provided (although the translation in question has sometimes been adapted or not employed at all). In addition parallel passages from Adorno's other writings have occasionally been added or referred to wherever they can shed light on something mentioned or discussed in the lectures. These also help to underline the varied and abundant connections between the lectures and the published works. As Adorno writes: 'One needs to develop a capacity for discerning the emphases and accents peculiar to that philosophy in order to uncover their relationships within the philosophical context, and thus to understand the philosophy itself – that is at least as important as knowing unequivocally: such and such is metaphysics' – or indeed ontology, or dialectic (see NaS IV.14, p. 81; *Metaphysics: Concept and Problems*, trans. Edmund Jephcott, Polity, 2000, p. 51). The editorial notes aim likewise to facilitate a reading that takes Adorno's injunction seriously. It is hoped that the notes in their entirety will help to furnish some idea of the cultural sphere, the *univers imaginaire*, within which Adorno's activities as a lecturer unfolded, a world which can no longer be taken for granted today.

All that remains for me here is to express my thanks to Hermann Schweppenhäuser and Michael Schwarz for their assistance in the work of editing the text of these lectures.

October 2001

LECTURE 1

8 November 1960

Ladies and gentlemen,[1]
  It is well known that Gustav Mahler was passionately interested in Dostoyevsky, who stood for something quite different in the years around 1890 than he does in the age of Moeller van den Bruck.[2] On one occasion, during an excursion with Schoenberg and his pupils, Mahler is said to have advised them to spend less time studying counterpoint and more time reading Dostoyevsky. And Webern is supposed to have responded with heroic timidity: 'Pardon, Herr Direktor, but we have Strindberg.' The story is probably apocryphal, but it may aptly be applied to the relationship between ontology and the dialectic. For the last thing we want to say here is 'We have Strindberg', or 'We have the dialectic'. It might be tempting to adopt this approach in attempting to offer some initial orientation for those who are not professionally involved in the study of philosophy. But in these lectures I specifically want to get beyond anything resembling a 'philosophy of standpoints'.[3] In other words, I want us to relinquish the idea that we can endorse the position of ontology on the one hand or that of the dialectic on the other. For then we would already feel as though the task were to choose between such standpoints. Yet amongst the philosophers who have anything to do with the specific directions of thought we have indicated – and I believe I can say this without exaggeration – no one on either side has ever had any time for the concept of a philosophical 'standpoint', or, as we could perhaps also put it, for philosophy as a 'world-view'. Indeed all those who have given any serious thought to these things have always rightly

scorned the idea of a world-view that could be selected from a range
of others or be regarded as a sort of supplement to life, and have
abandoned this approach to the dilettante. Yet this attitude is actively
encouraged by the cultural climate in which we find ourselves; and
the power of this cultural climate is so great that it is perhaps advis-
able for you to stop and think about it for a moment. In other words,
to think about the way in which everything between heaven and earth,
and most certainly everything in the realm of the mind, is constantly
presented in such reified and congealed forms and simply laid out for
you to choose from. This is what I generally describe as the reified
consciousness that is expressed in such commodified brands of thought.
As it happens, I read only recently about a discussion about the radio
where someone with a supposedly theoretical interest in the role of
radio in contemporary culture – his name is Maletzke[4] – claimed that
people emphatically have a right to be presented with a range of
images which they can proceed to choose from. And, God knows,
that all sounds very democratic – sounds as though we had a free
choice between high and low. But in reality this already presents the
world of mind and culture like a range of cars for sale, where you
can get something cheap, like a tiny Volkswagen (if any are still to
be found), or something extremely expensive, like a Cadillac imported
from America. I think it is a good idea for you to reflect upon these
things so that you will have some idea in advance about what these
lectures will really be concerned with. On the one hand, I certainly
do want to satisfy your curiosity about what stands behind the alternative we are talking about here; in other words, I want to address
this need in the sense that you may really learn why it is that I and
my friend Horkheimer assume such a critical position towards ontology and attempt to defend a dialectical philosophy. That is precisely
what I want to show in the lectures that follow. But at the same time
I also want to show you that the opposition between these two philosophies is not itself an unmediated one – in other words, that we
are not talking about two brands of thought between which you are
supposed to choose, in the way that you might choose to vote for the
Christian Democratic Party or the Social Democratic Party. For the
approach I am offering you here is intended as a well-motivated and
well-grounded approach rather than one that is based in an arbitrary
fashion on a so-called decision. For the approach presented here must
be understood as one that springs from the matter itself. Thus, instead
of a choice between what are merely world-views, you may get a
genuine sense – if I succeed in what I am trying to do – of what we
might describe as philosophically motivated thought, in contrast to
the kind of thought that is interested merely in establishing a

'standpoint'. But let me also qualify this somewhat straight away, since I certainly have no desire to rouse any false expectations amongst you. For the rigour which the following considerations may claim for themselves is not the same as that with which you are familiar in the field of the positive sciences, for example, or of the mathematically oriented natural sciences. The structural rigour which belongs to philosophy, and which allows philosophical thoughts to acquire their own plausibility and justification, is very different from that of the natural sciences. Above all, for the kind of fundamental philosophical controversies with which we shall be concerned in the coming months, we cannot presuppose or appeal to the structure of the positive sciences because the form and character of scientific thought itself is something that is first constituted by reference to those constitutive questions of philosophy which need to be addressed in their own right. We would therefore fall victim to a ὕστερον πρώτερον [husteron prōteron][5] if we tried to turn science, and the procedures associated with science, into the criterion of those considerations which for their part also precede science and are supposed to provide a critical investigation of science itself. And this is a point, incidentally, where I may say at once – although this may well astonish many of you – that I find myself in agreement with Heidegger.

First of all I would just like to outline the path which I hope to follow in these lectures. In general, of course, I am not very sympathetic to such announcements in advance. But since we shall have to concern ourselves here with what are indeed essentially systematic – that is to say, essentially interconnected processes – of thought, which are often by no means simple in themselves, it may be as well for you to know how I intend to proceed; and the way I shall proceed derives from the fact that I have no intention of presenting one position in an external manner in counter-position to another; on the contrary, I wish to show precisely how this position necessarily emerges for its own part out of the treatment of the other. In other words, the path that is meant to bring you to dialectical thinking, to the consideration of certain dialectical models, is the path of immanent critique (as it is generally called in the dialectical tradition).[6] I begin, therefore, from the need for ontology that appears in the present. And there is surely no doubt that ontology would not prove as influential as it is unless there was some corresponding need for it amongst thinking individuals and indeed more generally. And I would like to consider this need in both positive and negative terms. In other words, I would like to try and present for you both the justifiable and the questionable character of this need, or rather of these needs. For I shall attempt to resolve this complex of ontological need into its various aspects; and I shall try, through immanent critique, to lead us beyond certain of the motivations behind ontology; and I shall undertake to show you, precisely by taking ontology at its word, by measuring it against its own claims, that it fails to redeem this claim. And what is known as dialectic, fundamentally speaking, is nothing more than this very procedure. We could also express this by saying that, in our present situation, dialectic is mediated by ontology; and the analyses which lead us towards dialectical statements are, in a certain sense, by no means unrelated to the kind of phenomenological analyses which originally led towards ontology. I could reveal this affinity by direct reference to Hegel himself, and specifically to his *Logic*. Later on in the course of these lectures, once I have said at least something about the texture and structure of Hegelian thought, we may be able to go into this point in a little more detail. This is dialectic: that the transition to dialectic consists precisely in the self-reflection of ontology. Or, to rephrase this in more Hegelian terms, dialectic is mediated in itself precisely through ontology. That I am not simply declaiming empty words here, or simply indulging in idle speculation, and that these very considerations emerge from the philosophical tradition itself, is something you may readily and trenchantly confirm for yourselves. For one of the most fundamental texts of dialectical thought, Hegel's *Greater Logic*, namely the *Science of Logic*, opens with the doctrine of *Being*, and the dialectical movement itself only gets going through an analysis of the concept of being – that is to say, through an analysis of what 'being' really means. Yet it is entirely characteristic that modern ontology, inasmuch as it is a philosophy of being, specifically ignores this dialectical movement which is involved in its own concept. Once I have unfolded this transition to dialectic in what I hope is a fairly convincing manner, I shall then attempt, in the closing lectures, to develop and present certain categories and models of dialectical thinking itself.

But before I begin to talk to you about the ontological need,[7] about its justifiable or unjustifiable character, I think I ought first to say something about what 'ontology' actually is. But that is easier said than done. For the concept of ontology – like every philosophical concept, which is never just an arbitrarily stipulated piece of terminology – only really unfolds its wealth in and through the investigation of the matter itself. Now it is particularly difficult in this case to begin with a universally accepted definition of ontology, since (as people like to say) there is no scholarly consensus regarding the meaning of this concept. You will probably know that there is a whole range of supposedly 'ontological' approaches in philosophy, of which Nicolai

Hartmann[8] was one of the first representatives in Germany. And if you read the writings, and especially the later writings, of the most famous ontological philosopher in Germany, namely Martin Heidegger, you will find that what Hartmann understands by ontology, namely a return to 'realism', the doctrine which affirms the existence of the external world independently of consciousness, is rejected as an authentic criterion of ontology by Heidegger, at least implicitly, and is described as a far too superficial view of the matter. And again Heidegger is quite right here. Now in these lectures I have no intention of offering you a history of philosophy, or providing an overview of contemporary movements in philosophy, but want simply to bring out the substantive questions involved, so I shall not go into all this in any detail. But I wish at least to make one thing clear to you here. Ontology, in the first and simplest meaning of the word, is the doctrine of being. I am asking, therefore, what 'being' properly means. Now it is evident (and I think this hardly requires further elucidation) that nothing is served by a merely verbal definition of being, by simply staring as it were at this single concept. It is quite true, in the later phase of Heidegger's thought, that it is often difficult to avoid the impression that the somewhat richer vein of existential ontology which he started has actually increasingly contracted to the single concept of being, has turned into an insistent meditation upon this one concept, has become something that can now hardly be described as a thinking through of this concept, but resembles a kind of obsessed and fascinated staring at the same. Remarkably enough, this attitude to the concept of being was anticipated and scorned by Hegel himself. For he had already recognized and sharply criticized this attitude to the concept of being in the work of Jacobi.[9] But if we ignore all that for the moment, and for the purpose of our introductory observations today simply consider what has been influential under the name of ontology, then it is clear we are not merely talking about, or not *simply* about, what Heidegger pointedly calls the question or the problem of being, the question concerning being which seems to require a conclusive answer. For we also find an attempt to unfold a structure in which this very 'being' presents itself – I am thinking of the way that the older traditional forms of ontology, especially the ontology of Aristotle and that of Aquinas which was so closely connected with it, presented ontology as an articulated structure of fundamental concepts. In the earlier, original stages of ontological thought there was also talk of the 'articulation of being', something which served only to magnify the pathos of the concept of 'being'. For this concept cannot simply be pinned down at a stroke, as if it were just like any other concept. In order to get a hold upon the concept of being it was also necessary to develop an entire network of concepts which alone was capable of yielding what the concept of being really signifies. When Heidegger introduced the concept of 'framework'[10] in one of his later texts, something which sounds terribly concrete but also reveals the same ontological intention, you can see that this attempt to answer the so-called question of being, the question of what being really is, by reference to some kind of structure is just as clearly at work in the ontological schools of today as it was in the past.

Ontology, then, is meant to be the doctrine of being. I am well aware that such an assertion, which looks very much like a definition – and which can indeed be derived from certain passages in Aristotle to which I shall return later on[11] – will not initially be very helpful. But this is just how it is with philosophical concepts and doctrines: when we encounter them in this isolated form, above all without that characteristic difference that marks them off from what they are actually challenging or contesting, from what they are responding to, then they say very little to us. And I can imagine that, when you hear that ontology is the doctrine of being, or the doctrine of those structures which together constitute being, you may well react by saying: Well, then, these are simply the concerns of philosophers, and of course they want to tell us a story about being, but what is the point of this talk of being as such? I shall turn more closely to what I should like to call the historical significance of this entire problematic when I come to talk about the 'ontological need' in the next few sessions. But I should like at least to open up this perspective for you here and point out that the ontological philosophy that arose in response to Husserl's phenomenology was first expressly formulated as ontology by Max Scheler and then became especially influential through Heidegger – that this ontology owes its effect and possesses its force through opposition to neo-Kantianism in particular and the position of idealism in general. If I remember correctly, Heidegger says in his essay *On the Essence of Ground* that the difference between ontological thinking and idealism is not the decisive thing.[12] And let me say right away that the relationship between ontology and idealism is an extraordinarily complex one, and that the thesis which I myself shall present to you in this regard is directly opposed to the usual views, at least, which place idealism in straightforward opposition to ontology. But first it is necessary to understand the pathos which belongs to the so-called question concerning being, why people become so enormously excited about the problem of being, why this whole issue has proved so influential, and terms such as 'attunement', 'situation' and other such expressions[13] have almost seeped down into radio announcements and toothpaste advertisements. But in this connection it is good for you to realize what lies behind this entire philosophical movement, which is by no means internally unified and whose representatives are constantly at one another's throats, and that is the thought that the question concerning being is emphasized or prioritized over the question regarding the status of knowledge. Indeed I believe that we can identify this as the fundamental motif of ontology, and thereby recognize its essential distaste for a philosophy that had basically become nothing but methodology – had been reduced, in other words, to the question of how we think, or of how objects are constituted by thought or consciousness. And such thinking no longer seems to redeem what philosophy is there for, namely to discover something, if I may put this quite simply, about the things that are really essential.

Now this tendency which ontology specifically rebels against is very evident in Kant. And when Heidegger emphatically claims Kant *for* ontology, it certainly has to be admitted – and we shall come back to this in detail later[14] – that there are indeed ontological aspects in Kant, and that Kant was anything but a simple subjectivist. Yet in the first instance Kant specifically *prohibited* us from making absolutely binding claims about being, God, freedom and immortality – in other words, about the ultimate objects of metaphysics. And the need to say something really binding about these essential things, rather than just abandoning them to some kind of Sunday world-view, is surely one of the essential needs that have motivated this question concerning being. Ontology is thus a philosophy concerned with being in pointed opposition to a philosophy which remains essentially dedicated to a preliminary question, namely the question of how knowledge is possible at all, but which generally no longer gets to what is supposed to be known, to what knowledge is essentially concerned about. Now at one point in *Being and Time* Heidegger expressly defines ontology as the 'explicit theoretical questioning concerning the meaning of beings'.[15] This formulation is difficult and in a certain sense is also easily misunderstood. And I believe you should not simply take this statement (which will surely be familiar to all of you who have read Heidegger) as naively as it may here appear – as if we were talking about any beings you care to mention and were supposed to try, in a kind of mystical speculation, to interpret their *meaning* in terms of some secret divine meaning of creation or of metaphysical processes somehow hidden or concealed within the creation. For the expression 'meaning' – and I should say this right away, since we will have a lot to say about this – is ambiguous in all the ontological schools of today. And any critique of the concept of ontology must pay particular attention to this concept of meaning. On one side it derives from phenomenology, which is essentially the analysis of meaning, an attempt to clarify and determine the meaning of concepts. But it also possesses a certain metaphysical quality: What is the meaning of all this? What does this really mean for us? But even this is not the decisive thing here. If ontology is defined by Heidegger in this context as the question concerning the meaning of beings, this actually already harbours the answer which those of you who have not yet specifically engaged with all this will hardly expect – namely that the *meaning of beings* is precisely supposed to be *being*. And here I come right to the central complex of issues which is essential for the whole problem of being, namely the question of the relationship between being and beings. Or, to describe this opposition in the Greek terminology from which indeed it derives, the distinction between τὸ ὄν [to on] where the neuter singular form of the participle corresponds to our 'being', and τὰ ὄντα [ta onta], where the plural form corresponds to the concept of many and various individual beings. Now you might initially think (and grammar only encourages this) that 'being' is nothing but the most general concept that covers all beings; so that all ὄντα, taken together, would specifically comprise 'being'. But what is decisive here, and contains the entire problematic of ontology in a nutshell, is that at least the leading formulations of the programme of ontology expressly contest this. Thus, for ontology, 'being' is not simply the most universal concept that subsumes all particular beings, for 'being' itself is alleged to be something qualitatively other than what it covers.

That may all sound rather mystical to you. But it is relatively easy to understand what it means when you reflect on a concept which in an everyday context is expressly opposed to the concept of being, and which is expressly opposed to it in Hegel too, namely the concept of *essence*. Essence signifies that which first really allows any and every being to be what it is in accordance with its concept. Whatever has being is supposed to have an essence. Thus when we perceive all the items of clothing in this room which exhibit shades of red, then the relevant essence is the red itself, which reveals itself in its various 'adumbrations', as the phenomenologists say, in these particular items.[16] The distinction between the two – and it is imperative that you understand this from the start, if only terminologically, if you are to grasp what is involved in this discussion about being – is supposed to be this: τὰ ὄντα [ta onta] are the beings that exist in fact, namely that which is individuated in space and time, as Schopenhauer and indeed Husserl would put it. That which is individual and particular in space and time is therefore what corresponds to the expression τὰ ὄντα [ta onta]. Then, in contrast to this, there is the purely conceptual essence that is supposed to possess validity as something abstract that is

independent of such individuation. This essence, at the very highest
level of abstraction, is supposed to be τò ὄν [to on]. This is therefore
the concept of being that you are dealing with here. And I have elu-
cidated this concept of being quite simply in the way you may encounter
it in everyday consciousness, namely through abstraction: there is an
essence 'red' independently of the particular individuations of red
that are to be found.[17] And in a very similar way we can also form
the highest possible abstraction 'being' independently of the individual
beings which are grasped under this concept in each case. At least
from the genetic point of view, this is the path we take in order to
form this concept of being, which (as I believe I have shown here)
has much more to do with the concept of essence than what you
would generally tend to understand by 'being'. Yet it is no accident,
as I also want to point out, that ontological philosophy in its most
consistent form calls this 'something' that we are talking about 'being'
rather than 'essence'. And this already brings us to a key thesis that
is distinctive of modern ontology at least in its most radical form, for
this philosophy claims it is a mere illusion or misunderstanding on
the part of abstractive, organizing, classificatory and scientific thinking to suppose that we first derive this concept of being from all the
individual beings there are, that it is something secondary in relation
to the latter, that it is a false reflection of what is the case in a consciousness that is 'lost to being', as Heidegger would say, or no longer
capable of sustaining the concept of being. Indeed today Heidegger
would go so far as to say that, *sensu strictissimo*, being is not actually
a concept at all. In other words, being is not supposed to be the
highest abstraction that we reach by omitting all particular individuation on the part of spatial and temporal beings. On the contrary,
being is actually supposed to be that which is utterly prior and primary,
that which is highest and most constitutive, and in relation to which
it is individual beings that are secondary. Or that which has particular
and individual existence is also supposed to be nothing but a 'mode
of being', as Heidegger puts it, rather than 'being' itself.

LECTURE 2

10 November 1960

In our last session we introduced certain elementary considerations about the meaning of the word 'ontology' and the so-called question of being – all of this in order to give you a really precise idea of what is actually at issue here. I drew your attention to one of the fundamental themes of ontological philosophy, and one which is by no means peculiar to the ontological philosophy of our own times, namely the relationship between 'being', τὸ ὄν [to on] (though that is hardly a literal translation of the Greek), and 'beings', τὰ ὄντα [ta onta], the particular things that actually exist, the realm of fact that we are accustomed to contrast with that of essence, that which is individuated in space and time. I have already pointed out that the question of ontology not only involves the doctrine of being in the purest sense, namely in the sense that radically distinguishes the concept of being from that of beings in principle. For ontology also understands itself as the question regarding the being of beings – and this expressly implies that the theme of ontology is concerned not simply with that pure being that you read about in the later writings of Heidegger in particular, but also with the relation between this remarkable category of being and the beings that are interpreted so differently with respect to the former. And in this sense the question of being, according to a quotation from Heidegger that I read out and interpreted for you, is actually supposed to be the question regarding the meaning of beings, or the question regarding the being of beings. Ontology in the usual sense, in this extremely radical and critical sense of something that precedes all beings, is understood to include the 'ideas', for example, the highest concepts of all possible particular regions – in other words, the structural categories which serve to constitute particular fields as such. In this sense we could speak of an ontology of ethics as the epitome of the highest ethical principles or, again, of an ontology of physics (even if natural scientists would understandably resist this language) as the epitome of the axiomatic principles of theoretical physics, if it actually has such principles. I drew your attention to the problem of the relation between ontology and these highest regional unities when I claimed that ontology generally involves a double perspective: the question regarding the so-called structure of being and also the question regarding the concept of being itself. In the form which ontology has assumed in Heidegger, and which most of you will almost certainly associate with the concept of ontology today, this very relationship between the structure of being, between the fundamental categories of beings in general or the particular realms of being, and the concept of being itself is problematic and is indeed the real issue. When Heidegger describes his ontology as 'fundamental ontology', this involves the distinctive claim that there is a further fundamental question to be addressed with respect to the ontologies of the particular sciences and particular fields of knowledge – or as I would put it with respect to the ontologies concerned with beings, a fundamental question upon which these particular ontologies themselves depend. It is therefore specifically characteristic of the metaphysical and philosophical claim mounted by contemporary forms of ontology that the so-called ontological question regarding the *meaning of being itself* is prior to the question regarding the *being of beings* which ontology also understands itself to be. This priority ascribed to the question regarding being – over against the highest regions, the highest and most universal concepts of all possible classes of beings – is what is decisive here, as you will see, precisely because it really involves the problem of the possibility of ontology as such – namely whether such a pure doctrine of being can be thought as such independently of the doctrine regarding the order of beings. That is why you must clearly recognize this distinction – between ontology as a question regarding the meaning of being and the equally ontological question regarding the specific regions of beings – because the central critical considerations we shall raise about ontology depend precisely on this heightened or intensified concept of ontology. In other words, they depend on whether the question regarding being as such does indeed precede the investigation of the being or the mode of being that belongs to beings. For the question regarding the possibility of ontology itself ultimately depends on this

question, on the possibility of this question, and on the answer that
is so intimately bound up with it.

Before I attempt to clarify this for you with reference to an important passage in Heidegger – and I know this is rather challenging, but
there is no way round it if you seriously want to understand the basic
ontological problem and are unwilling to accept mere chatter in this
regard – before I explore the question more closely to help you understand what we are talking about here, for you can reflect critically
on these things only when you have actually grasped what is at stake
– before all this, I would just like to correct a small terminological
omission for which I was responsible in the last session. I was trying
to clarify the distinction, fundamental for all ontology, between τὸ ὄν
[to on], 'being', and τὰ ὄντα [ta onta], 'beings', or also between εἶναι
[einai], or 'to be', as it is expressed in a particularly famous passage
in Aristotle,[1] and particular beings. In this context, since Heidegger,
it has become quite common to talk, in what is a rather helpful terminological innovation, about the problem of this difference between
being and beings, which is reflected in our language in the apparently
simple and seemingly almost arbitrary difference between an infinitive
(*sein*) and a participle (*das Seinde*); in other words, it has become
common to speak of this difference, or the problem of this difference,
as the problem of *ontological difference*.[2] Ontological difference is
therefore understood to mean the difference between being and beings.
Now this difference signifies a distinction but also, in the view of
ontology, a connection between the two moments precisely because
beings are supposed to possess a special and significant character for
ontology. On the other hand, according to Heidegger, without the
'understanding of being' we cannot come to any understanding of
beings, and therefore of the so-called particular regional ontologies.
Thus, whenever I use the expression 'ontological difference' in what
follows, we are talking about this difference between being and beings
in the concept of being itself, in the framing of the ontological question itself. I would ask you to bear this carefully in mind throughout.
For you will be able to understand what is at issue for us only if you
are quite clear, from the start, about this specific – though in itself
rather arbitrary – terminological point.

Now let me turn to that particular passage in Heidegger where
so-called fundamental ontology, in the sense of the question concerning being or the question of being, is distinguished from other kinds
of ontology in the sense of the doctrine of the highest concepts and
propositions that can be applied to beings, of the highest domains of
objects – such as the concept of ontology that in recent times was
reintroduced into philosophy by Husserl.[3] I shall come back to this

pre-ontological concept of ontology (if I might put it like this) in much more detail shortly, so that here too you will come to understand the relationship and the difference between Heidegger's philosophy and phenomenology in particular. The passage I mentioned comes near the beginning of Heidegger's principal work, *Being and Time*, and you will find it on page 11 of the sixth edition (of 1949). I shall read it out for you: 'But such inquiry [and here he means ontology as an inquiry into constitutive truths, rather in the way that Aristotle or Aquinas ask after such truths] – ontology taken in its broadest sense without reference to specific ontological directions or tendencies – itself still needs a guideline. It is true that ontological inquiry is more original than the ontic inquiry of the positive sciences.'[4] Now I would clarify this for you as follows. You must clearly distinguish between three levels here. First, there is the level of ontic inquiry. Put simply, this is the level of naive immediate scientific questions about what is the case: what law governs the duration of sound; what particular mathematical propositions hold or perhaps hold only with specific qualifications; what historical events can be said with certainty to have transpired at what time. These are the kinds of questions which may initially be described as ontic in character. Then there is the level of ontological questioning in a rather naive sense, if you want to put it that way, namely questions concerning the highest principles that are constitutive in each case for a particular science or form of inquiry. Here, for example, we ask questions such as these: What are the fundamental principles that hold for history in general? What is history itself? What do we mean by motivation in history? What is causality in history? What do we mean by relevance in the context of history? Or, again, what principles or regularities are operative in philology? Or, to take an example I mentioned earlier, what are the immutable axioms of theoretical physics, if indeed there are any? This is what Heidegger calls ontological questioning in the naive sense: the question concerning the basic truths that, as truths about beings, are supposed to underlie all beings or entities that are investigated by particular disciplines, and here we are thinking specifically of scientific disciplines. This ontological questioning, according to Heidegger, is certainly more 'original' than the ontic questions of the positive sciences – the simple questions about what is the case which I mentioned before. He continues: 'But it remains naive and opaque if its investigations into the being of entities leave the meaning of being in general undiscussed.'[5] Thus, according to Heidegger, you can certainly ask about the being of beings in the context of the particular sciences. In other words, instead of simply asking about historical facts, you can ask about what historical change means, about what history itself is. Or, to put this really simply and to set aside the elaborate terminology, you can ask any of these kinds of questions within the context of science or systematic knowledge itself. As a scientist or researcher you can reflect internally upon the knowledge you possess; you can think about what such knowledge means and about the highest and most general propositions which it presupposes. But, according to him, if you do actually think in this way about the being of beings, if you ask, for example, what makes a historical datum into something historical as such, and even if this question is, for him, more original – i.e. is constitutively deeper than any particular historical questions – this questioning is itself still naive. It is still unreflectively caught up in the business of particular scientific knowledge, or in the business of everyday consciousness, unless you also specifically think about the concept of being that is bound up with it – about what is constitutive for history, or what is constitutive for physics – and do so in such a way that you confront the meaning of being in general – in other words, what being in general actually means.

Heidegger continues: 'And precisely the ontological task of a genealogy of the different possible ways of being (a genealogy which is not to be constructed deductively) requires a preliminary understanding of "what we really mean by this expression *being*".'[6] I would draw your attention to the fact, as I have already pointed out, that the concept of 'meaning' in this philosophy is ambiguous: while it sometimes refers to metaphysical meaning, it is sometimes used in a simply semantic-analytical sense, or is supposed to tell us what a technical term means. In this sense, at least according to the method, the semantic interpretation of being enjoys priority in the context of fundamental ontology. In other words, the question concerning the meaning of being here really implies nothing more – according to the good old phenomenological rules of the game – than that you should understand what is actually meant by the expression 'being'. Yet in Heidegger we can see in the most remarkable way how all these categories begin to fluoresce, as it were, and in a certain sense always mean more and something other than they do in the place they occupy. This is very characteristic of the atmosphere of this philosophy and something which, from a dialectical perspective, is by no means simply a shortcoming. On the contrary, there is also, if I may say so, something positive and very deep here, for every individual concept that we employ, unless we are speaking according to the established scientific rules of the game, means more than it can mean simply in terms of its specifically defined place. Heidegger continues as follows: 'The question of being thus aims not only at an *a priori* condition of the possibility of the sciences ...' As I have already pointed out, our understanding of the meaning of the word and the concept of being in general in this sense is prior to the fundamental categories and axioms, or the fundamental principles, which we find in the particular sciences, and therefore belongs to a sphere which, for this philosophy, is itself supposed to constitute the sciences and scientific thought in the first place. And not only the sciences 'which examine entities as entities of such and such a type, and, in so doing, already operate with an understanding of being, but also for the possibility of those ontologies themselves which are prior to the ontical sciences and which provide their foundations.'[7] We could thus describe this as a distinction between the ontologies of the ontic, that which makes particular regions of beings into what they are, and the *genuinely* ontological questions which are addressed to the concept of being itself. Heidegger goes on: 'All ontology, no matter how rich and tightly knit a system of categories it has at its disposal, remains fundamentally blind and perverts its innermost intent if it has not previously clarified the meaning of being sufficiently and grasped this clarification as its fundamental task.'[8] Thus the clarification of the meaning of being, of what being really signifies, is the essential task of ontology under-stood in this radical sense – and this is precisely what fundamental ontology is. This is the difference between fundamental ontology and the individual concretely conceived ontologies that we find so abun-dantly represented, for example, in Nicolai Hartmann or the modern neo-scholastic tradition.

And here I should already like to draw your attention to a problem within this particular passage from Heidegger, a passage which may have helped to clarify for you the distinctive approach that we are dealing with here. I have attempted to bring out certain principal themes of this approach and why they appear so plausible. But with regard to this approach as I have presented it to you, I must say right away that I simply cannot swallow it in the form in which it has been set forth. But here there are two questions I should like you to think about: when he says that ontological questioning is more original than the ontic questioning of the positive sciences, then to some extent this already implies – and you should pay very careful attention to this here if you are to become familiar with the atmosphere of this kind of thinking – already implies that the decision about the question Heidegger himself regards as the central question, as the so-called *question of being*, as the task of fundamental ontology, has itself been made. For it already implies that the ontologies of the individual positive sciences and their axiomatic systems are more 'original' than the empirical findings they comprise. Now one might respond to this with a genetic account – and I think this is just what every thoughtful scientist would do – and say that the path involved in these regional ontologies, these supposedly fundamental truths of the individual sciences, is generally in fact the reverse. In other words, in concrete scientific work, in actual investigation, they emerge as a structure that is subsequent to the findings about what is the case and from which they are then derived. From the genetic point of view, therefore, this question concerning the 'origin' looks very questionable at the least. We could also put this in a quite simple and straightforward way and say that most of the ontologies concerned with what concretely exists are actually abstractions which are themselves abstracted from the field of concrete beings. Now Heidegger, and every follower of Heidegger, would respond with extreme irritation at this point and vehemently insist that this is not at all what they mean by really original questioning. In other words, what is 'original' here is not to be understood as what is 'earlier' in any temporal or genetic sense. On the contrary, it means that what is more original is that which is *ontologically* more original – that is to say, is nearer to this enigmatic and remarkable 'being', is more immediately concerned with this being than anything else is. Yet if you try and escape this historically genealogical or genetic interpretation by tearing the concept of the 'original' away from time in this way, by referring it to ontology as something which is itself more original, then you have actually prejudged the very theme of the ontological problematic – in other words, precisely the priority of being with respect to beings. Thus at this central point in this philosophy we already find a *petitio principii*.[9] What really needs to be shown – namely the priority of being with respect to particular regions of being, and pre-eminently with respect to particular beings – is presupposed as already harboured in the concept of what is truly 'original'.

Now Heidegger, who is an extraordinarily acute thinker, has naturally seen this problem too; and he has found an extraordinarily inspired expression for it in saying that the task for philosophy is not to escape this circle but to enter into it at the right point.[10] I would concede that there is something quite right about this. In other words, the idea that one could simply start from scratch, or provide some absolutely first principle in contrast to anything merely derived – the idea that underlies this constant worry about circular arguments and *petitiones principii* – has something chimerical about it and leads ultimately to total subjectivism: the notion that an absolutely first principle can be derived from the pure determinations of thought. To this extent, therefore, I would accept Heidegger's argument, which I shall now present directly. But I also think there is a distinction or difference here: between the necessary qualification of continually asking back, and back, and back – something more characteristic of Heidegger, incidentally, than it is of dialectical philosophies – and a thinking which defends the concept of origin as utterly true and primal being. But such thinking basically already helps itself to the *thema probandum*, namely the priority of being with respect to beings that bestows its distinctive savour, through its *definition* of what originality in this context means. I want you to understand precisely what I mean here: I want to say that the counter-objection that Heidegger brings against the purely logical objection that I have raised at this point may well be valid in general but is not valid precisely here, where the content of philosophy itself that is at issue is presupposed in this way as something already given. This view of things, namely that philosophy is ultimately tautological, that it can only explicate what it already simultaneously posits – this is precisely the essence of the idealist philosophy from which, as we shall see, ontology seeks so emphatically to distance itself. This is why the thesis of the more original character of ontologies with respect to the merely ontic, and again of fundamental ontology with respect to individual ontologies, is so very problematic. Quite apart from this, I would also like to point out here that this cult of the concept of originality also suggests that the primal source to which everything else is led back in some kind of non-temporal manner involves a claim that is hardly unproblematic in itself. This is the claim – and here ontology really shows its rather traditional character despite its protestations to the contrary – that *prima philosophia*, that which is primary and originary, the ἀρχή [archē], is truer and better and deeper than anything which issues from it. It is the kind of thought that Nietzsche once ironically characterized as the superstition that truth cannot possibly have arisen, that what has not arisen, what is utterly original, must also inevitably be truer.[11] I believe that the really decisive difference between ontological and phenomenological thought on the one side and dialectical thought on the other is to be discovered here. In other words, this primacy of the First, or, to put it paradoxically, this 'Firstness', this priority of the First, this idea of tracing everything back to what is 'fundamental', cannot be accepted in the way it is proposed by ontology. And I believe the nerve of any critique of ontology in general, of an immanent critique of ontology, is intrinsically bound up with the critique of this dogmatically posited concept of what is allegedly 'original' – a concept, moreover, with certain overtones which only a highly prejudiced perspective could regard as entirely unconnected with specific social and political tendencies.

It is tremendously important to me that you should see the things we are dealing with here very clearly and really understand what is involved, so let me restate the issue like this. Heidegger says: I do not deny that I am arguing in a circle, since all of the considerations and demonstrations that I present in order to show the more original character of being with respect to all individual ontologies, with respect to anything of an individual ontological or ontic character, already presuppose the project of fundamental ontology. But what I start with is that grain of the arbitrary and contingent, as it were, without which human thought cannot begin. And I would reply that Heidegger's argumentation is quite legitimate in principle but is too broad to capture what is really at issue here. As if Kant were to say: Of course, that there are categories and forms of intuition is prior, as it were, to the whole *Critique of Pure Reason*, and in the deduction of the pure concepts of the understanding and the transcendental aesthetic I cannot basically demonstrate anything but what I am really already presupposing. In one place Kant says that the fact that we have these categories and these forms of intuition rather than others is something that ultimately escapes the deduction itself – in other words, we are here confronted with something ultimate, something irreducibly given, something that has to be accepted. But this does not relieve him of the extremely arduous task of actually showing, if we just stay with Kant here, that space and time neither simply subsist nor inhere in the phenomena of our experience. Philosophy here assumes the serious task of clarifying and rigorously defending its own fundamental conception of the problem in intellectual terms. Yet this sort of commitment is essentially negated by Heidegger's approach. When you constantly read and hear that Heidegger's philosophy has gradually turned into a kind of mysticism, this should not be interpreted merely as the symptom of an aging philosopher increasingly mesmerized by the concept of being. For this turn to what is dubbed mysticism is indeed already implicit in that dimension which I have tried to describe for you. We could perhaps also express this by saying that this philosophy harbours an inner flaw, a moment of untruth, which it struggles to escape. On the one hand, it avails itself of language, of all the means of discursive logic, makes all the claims that thought, for God's sake, must ultimately make; yet it also constantly indulges in the esoteric gesture and implicitly utters a kind of abracadabra. While it acts as if it wants to be thought of as philosophy or, as Heidegger would rather say, to invite be-thinking, it actually suggests that thinking is ultimately inadequate – that, if you don't feel it, you won't get it.[12] And even that mode of expression would still be far too ordinary. If being doesn't 'unconceal itself' or 'illuminate itself' for you, then it just stays in the dark. Now everyone has a right to esoteric doctrines, and I am the last person to deny this right, as long as these doctrines are honestly presented in the character they implicitly claim for themselves. What is so questionable here is just the way in which this esoteric aspect is fused with the rational claim that is necessarily bound up with philosophy and its conceptual language, with its method of drawing conceptual distinctions, above all with its fundamental method of analysing meaning.

And now, ladies and gentlemen, I would just like to say a few words about the historical dimension of the so-called question of being. I have no intention of offering you anything resembling a history of the concept of being, although this would be a rather tempting proposition, and one could indeed unfold the dialectic of philosophical thought itself in terms of the history of the idea of being. The emphatic question of the problem of being, as we find it in Heidegger, derives from a philosopher who plays a distinctive and decisive role for this whole way of thinking. Yet, while this way of thinking relates directly to this philosopher, it also repudiates the position in question from the start because it is not deep, radical and 'original' enough. I am talking about Aristotle, who posed this question of being in the famous formulas of τὸ τί ἦν εἶναι [to ti ēn einai] and τί τὸ ὄν [ti to on].[13] These expressions are usually translated in terms of the question as to 'what being really is', although there are two striking things to be observed here: what we find in the second formulation, instead of the infinitive εἶναι [einai], is the nominalized participial form ὄν [on], which is commonly understood to refer to the individual being or entity that is. This is something remarkable that fundamental ontology tends to pass over, since it hardly appears to confirm the idea that the less reflective ontology of the ancient philosophy neglected to thematize the ontological difference in the way that this appears in Heidegger. I shall say a few words later on about the particular way in which the ontological difference is a thematic issue in ancient philosophy as well. But what is even more remarkable in the first formulation here is the presence of the word ἦν [ēn], which, literally translated, means 'was' rather than 'is'. I do not want to go into the philosophical problems involved here, for these are certainly very difficult questions. This word ἦν [ēn] naturally tempts us to interpret the question concerning being as what Goethe calls 'the truth of old'[14] – in other words, as that which has allegedly always and immemorially been what it is, with the notion of ἀρχή [archē] in the background. Indeed in very early Greek philosophy, in the pre-Socratics, the concept of ἀρχή [archē] already possesses this remarkable double meaning: on the one hand it means 'the origin', 'the first', 'the most ancient', and the adjective ἀρχαῖος [archaios] just means 'very old', while on the other hand it also means the highest and most general principles of whatever particular conceptions of the

world we are talking about. It seems likely that this ἦν [ēn] has exerted
a certain influence here. And not enough attention has seriously been
given to the question of whether this particular temporal construction
of Aristotle's does not involve a regressive mythological aspect – i.e.
one that has not been reflected upon philosophically – although in
the Heidegger school these very features, these archaic aspects even
of so-called classical Greek thought, have been opposed, and opposed
in expressly positive terms, to the modern and enlightened character
that is already so strong in Plato and certainly in Aristotle. The question as to what being really is, this famous and indeed fundamental
question of Aristotle's *Metaphysics*, the question around which metaphysics in Aristotle essentially turns, goes back to Plato and the Eleatic
tradition. And it ultimately only reflects the kinds of problems that
had already emerged amongst these thinkers. For when Plato distinguishes that which possesses true being, or the Idea, from τὸ μὴ ὄν
[to mē on], or non-being – in other words, from the individuated
world and the world of space – that is basically a very similar distinction to that between τὸ ὄν [to on] or εἶναι [einai], namely being, on
the one side and the τὰ ὄντα [ta onta], namely beings, on the other.
This thematic of ontological difference is therefore already implicit
in Plato, as it also is, in a very similar way, in Aristotle. And this
seems to confirm what I was saying in the last session. In other words,
the emphatic concept of being which you find in the new fundamental
ontology is actually, *sensu strictissimo*, not the concept of being at
all but rather the concept of *essence*. For this concept of being – as
you can see precisely from the distinction between what truly is and
the realm of non-being, space, τὸ μὴ ὄν [to mē on], the world of δόξα
[doxa], of appearance – derives from the world of Ideas as conceived
by Plato. Thus you will only properly understand the concept of being
in modern ontology when you see it as an attempted reconstruction
of the metaphysical concept of the idea that exists absolutely in its
own right, as we find it in Plato, and which Plato himself inherited
from the Eleatic tradition.

LECTURE 3

15 November 1960

Before we go any further I would just like to return to something from the last session, since I have heard that I may not have made myself sufficiently clear on the point in question, and it is very important to me that you really understand the quite fundamental considerations that we need to introduce in this connection. And it concerns what I am saying about the problem of circular reasoning in philosophy, and specifically about Heidegger's claim that the task in philosophy is not to avoid such reasoning but to get into it at the right place. You may recall that I conceded this proposition in the general terms in which Heidegger formulates it[1] and that I pointed out to you that there is indeed no philosophy which actually fails to acknowledge this. The idea of a philosophy *ex nihilo*, a form of thinking which produces itself simply from its own resources, an *actus purus* – this is not a demand, as some may naively imagine, that we should make of any philosophy. For this presupposes a very specific philosophical standpoint that deserves to be criticized in its own right. This is the standpoint of an absolute identity philosophy which claims that being and beings can be grasped adequately and completely by pure thought without remainder. And this particular thesis, which is indeed the basic thesis of idealism in the strict sense, is one which is extraordinarily controversial in philosophy generally. On the contrary, one must admit that philosophy begins somewhere – and I would add that philosophy cannot establish its beginning purely from itself. I would also concede that, to a certain extent, there is something circular about this, for the demonstrations that philosophy offers in its own distinctive way are demonstrations which generally lead to what in a certain sense has already been posited as a thesis from the beginning. Thus when we begin – and once again I turn to Kant to illustrate what I mean – in the *Critique of Pure Reason* by assuming that there are synthetic a priori judgements – in other words, that there is such a thing as pure mathematics and pure theoretical physics – then the argument of the work amounts in large measure to showing that there are indeed such synthetic a priori judgements. For the question *how* synthetic a priori judgements are possible – where indeed Kant himself admits their givenness, the *thema probandum* itself – is developed in the demonstration provided by the first *Critique* in such a way that the *possibility* of synthetic a priori judgements is thereby meant to be proved; what is at issue is the substance of synthetic a priori judgements and not merely the modus of such judgements, as the question itself might initially suggest.[2] Yet the procedure of Heidegger's philosophy, by comparison, is different in one rather essential respect. Perhaps we could put it like this. When he affirms the general thesis of the priority of what he likes to call the question of being over against all particular beings – *and the answer to this question or this thesis will be the heart of what I am trying to say in this course of lectures* – then he would have to incur a certain obligation if he really wants to enter into the virtuous or legitimate circle, as he says he does. This is the obligation, once the experience that basically sustains this thinking has been presupposed, to unfold all this in a way that does full justice to the sustaining experience. Now the methodological objection which I raised at this point – and this is the methodical difference between the dogmatic existential ontology of today and every critical or dialectical philosophy – is precisely this: that Heidegger never fulfils this obligation to unfold his argument but, rather, sets up what we might describe psychologically as a taboo, or describe politically as a kind of 'terror', so that any approach which does *not* involve this priority of being with respect to beings is already rejected *ab ovo* and defamed as inferior, as a failure, as a betrayal of the real question. His paradoxical claim that philosophy should attempt not to avoid the circle but to enter it at the right point is indeed quite right, yet he falls short of his own thesis to the extent that he actually remains caught up in a merely circular argument. In other words, we are constantly presented with the same invocation, variation or repetition of this premise, namely the priority of being with respect to beings, while the premise itself is not explored in terms of genuine argumentation at all. And this approach is methodologically encouraged by a contempt for argument as such, and ultimately a contempt for thinking in general, which is so highly characteristic of this particular thinking. This is actually the fundamental objection that I would have to raise here. And this will also already suggest the method which I shall pursue throughout the following discussions. For I shall make good, or try to make good, what this kind of thinking withholds from us. And in encouraging, so to speak, the self-reflection of this very premise regarding the priority of being with respect to beings, I hope to show you that the premise does not actually hold – to put it bluntly, is not true. This is the task I have set myself here. And I hope I have perhaps already indicated, at least in this particular regard, something of the difference between thinking of this Heideggerean type and thinking of the Kantian type, which I introduced all too briefly in the last session. As for the *substantive* implications of this difference, this is something about which I shall perhaps have more say today, or certainly in our next session.

But let me return to the historical aspects which I went into last time with a very specific intention in mind. Let me come back, in other words, to the point (to repeat this in one sentence) that the so-called question concerning being, often dubiously expressed by Heidegger simply as 'the question of being', in the form in which it has come down to us actually goes back to Aristotle. It goes back to the question raised in the *Metaphysics*: What is 'being', properly speaking? And behind this Aristotelian formulation there stands the Platonic problematic of the doctrine of the Ideas, namely the distinction between that which truly possesses being and those beings which are consigned to the realm of mere 'opinion' and identified with the sensible world, a world that is ultimately characterized by Plato as simply that of non-being, as τὸ μὴ ὄν [to mē on]. This Platonic view itself (if you will allow me to take the historical account a little further back) presupposes the Eleatic tradition which indeed Plato basically took up into his own philosophy and thereby liberated, so to speak, from the abstract universality that formerly belonged to it. And that was the thesis – already found in Xenophanes but fully developed only in the great poem of Parmenides – that nothing really exists but being, and that all specific and particular beings, by contrast, ultimately belong to a purely deceptive world that does not properly exist at all. This doctrine of Parmenides, whom Heidegger indeed declares a pre-eminent thinker, underlies all ontology and is repeated by Heidegger in this archaic form, in a form, we might say, that has not yet been differentiated through enlightened reflections or conceptual determinations of any kind. Now it is important to me that you should be quite clear about the achievements of the Eleatic tradition – which incidentally finds its direct contrapuntal response in Heraclitus and his own universal and comprehensive principle of becoming – since the Eleatic doctrine actually involves an unparalleled advance in philosophical consciousness. And the progressive aspect here is this: in the context of older Greek speculation, amongst the first of the pre-Socratics – for Parmenides and Heraclitus already belong to the last pre-Socratic generation – and thus *before* these two, the earlier thinkers had always posited various more or less arbitrarily conceived fundamental principles at the basis of everything. These principles had initially assumed the form of something like primal 'life forces', although they subsequently tended to undergo a kind of rejuvenation, as it were, becoming ever thinner but also more comprehensive in the process. Thus the ancient doctrine of the ἀρχή [arche] was supplanted by the doctrine of being itself as the ground and essence of all things. Now the word ἀρχή [arche] already enjoyed a double meaning, one which returns again and again in ancient ontological speculation and in later ontological philosophies as well. On the one hand the word relates to the concept of 'origin'. For ἀρχή [arche] means 'the First', what is there first of all, the immemorially old. This is the archaic sense of the word. But ἀρχή [arche] also means 'principle' in the specific sense of the most universal and all-embracing principle on which the constitution of any beings whatever, or indeed any particular realm whatever, is supposed to rest. And the same double meaning returns in the Latin translation of this word as *principium* and prevails throughout philosophy in the sense it assumed with the Aristotelian expression, or the expression perhaps introduced by the Aristotelian scholiasts, namely πρώτη φιλοσοφία [prōtē philosophia] or 'first philosophy'.[3]

I referred to the extraordinary advance achieved by consciousness in arriving at this concept of being as the utterly original principle in contrast to the particular and relatively arbitrary principles that were posited before – whether it was the 'water' of venerable Thales, the 'air' of Anaximenes, or again τὸ ἄπειρον [to apeiron], the unlimited space of Anaximander. But of course, in saying that the newly acquired concept of being was an extraordinary advance for consciousness, I have already turned against a thesis of fundamental ontology itself. I have not offered this entire rather cursory account of what we might call the primordial history of ontology out of a merely historical interest in the story of philosophy. For the interest that governs these lectures, if we follow the usual dichotomy, is a systematic interest, one concerned solely with the truth of the matter in question rather than with how something or other has come to be. Nonetheless, I cannot avoid pointing out how enormously fruitful and helpful it would be for the understanding of the so-called ontological problematic if someone did undertake to write something like a history of the concept of being in the grand style. I presented this little historical excursus for substantive reasons, and specifically in relation to a Heideggerean thesis which I think can be challenged in the very field where Heidegger has established a kind of dictatorship, namely in that concerned with the connection between philosophy and classical philology or with the history of ancient philosophy. If, as the history of early Greek philosophy genuinely appears to me to show, the concept of being is indeed the product of reflection rather than what lies at the beginning, then this implies in any case, historically speaking, that the experience of being is not prior with respect to the experience of particular beings in the way that Heidegger associates this with ancient philosophy, and especially with the earlier pre-Socratics. Much obeisance has now been paid to the idea that in every ancient philosophy, whether we are talking about Parmenides or Heraclitus, or indeed, as I have recently learnt, about Empedocles, we invariably encounter nothing but the same thing: being, being, and being. In his famous address *What is Metaphysics?*, which is amongst the first of his texts that enacts a radical turn to the question of being independently of its relation to *Dasein*, a famous piece that was republished in 1949, Heidegger says, and I quote: 'By recalling the beginning of that history in which being unveiled itself in the thinking of the Greeks, it can be shown that the Greeks from early on experienced the being of beings as the presence of what is present.'[4] And here he can certainly appeal to certain passages in the poem of Parmenides that speak of 'presencing', although I do not wish to go into these points now. I do not cite this passage from Heidegger because we already have to decide about concepts such as 'perceive' and 'perceivability' and 'presencing', about whose alleged concreteness I hope to say something later on. I cite it simply in relation to Heidegger's thesis that the history of philosophy, the beginning of the history of philosophy, is just the question concerning being, and indeed that everything that comes later is a kind of decadence, as they would say in the East. I want to say that this thesis is untenable precisely because the concept of being itself has only been attained through a process of reflection stretching over centuries, or, let me say directly, through a certain abstraction, a process that for its part arises from the manifest inadequacy of earlier more or less arbitrary particular principles or kinds of stuff (whatever they may be) that the earliest thinkers invoked in order to explain everything that exists. For what we are talking about here are indeed attempts at explanation in the face of the variety and multiplicity of phenomena. And the unity of

Western consciousness, if there is such a thing, lies precisely in this kind
of explanatory principle. In other words, it is an attempt to discover
a unified ground for the multiplicity of appearances. And the greater
the multiplicity, the greater the need for an explanatory ground that
is ever more universal and all-embracing. And the concept of being
now steps in to provide the requisite universality. I should add in
parenthesis that the concept of ground that is deployed here naturally
has something very problematic about it. In other words, the more
universal these principles of explanation become, the more they end
up as a mere synthesis, a mere summary description, a mere form for
what they encompass. And throughout the history of philosophy we
may repeatedly observe how the most universal form of that which
is to be explained in each case is conflated with the ground through
which it is meant to be explained. One of the greatest achievements
of Hegel's *Science of Logic* – the second volume of which, contrary to
common assumptions, actually belongs within the context of the entire
European Enlightenment – is precisely that it provides a particularly
stringent critique of this conflation of the most general or universal
concept of things with the ground that is supposed to explain them.

Now the Heideggerean school, of course, would strenuously object
to the account of early Greek philosophy as I have just presented it
to you. Here I would simply remind you that the celebrated dictum
of Parmenides – which does not play that much of a role in Heidegger,
since it hardly fits in with his own conception, and which he constantly
tries to reinterpret through one device or another – namely the dictum
that being and thinking are the same,[5] actually confirms what I was
saying earlier. It confirms, in other words, that the concept of being
we are talking about is, we could say, a result, a historical result,
something that was attained only through a process; that this concept
of being in the first instance is nothing other than the highest abstraction, as we would describe this today in language very alien to antiquity; and this abstraction, precisely because it turns away from all
particular beings, is no longer anything more than pure thought. Thus
pure abstraction, as it appears objectively in the concept of being, is
supposed to be identical with the thinking which has produced this
abstraction, and which is all that is still present, all that still remains,
in this abstraction. To this extent, therefore, I believe that this decisive
dictum of Parmenides, which essentially provided the ground for the
subsequent identification of the Ideas or the highest ontological categories with Reason, with the λόγος [logos], fully supports the interpretation which I have suggested – namely that the concept of being
itself was attained by philosophy, that this concept is something mediated (in the first instance historically mediated, namely through an

ongoing act of abstraction). I am well aware that the interpretation I have offered here can only be anathema in orthodox Heideggerean circles, that they will say that I am still caught up in the European rationalist tradition which was never able to understand the pre-Socratics and their central 'concern' – and this is indeed the word people like to use here, and it is certainly the right place for it. In this connection Heidegger or his adepts would claim it is a misunderstanding to connect these vanished ἀρχαί [archai] with elemental material forces or substances, or with universal concepts. For what they mean, what they allegedly must have meant, is, of course: being, being, being – even though the concept of being is not yet found here. For the question of being, at least implicitly, is what is prior. Now I certainly do not want to make things too easy for myself with regard to this question, although the undifferentiated way in which any particular questions that philosophy might raise repeatedly provoke the same response should surely make us extremely sceptical about the form of the question itself. I have already pointed out that such an interpretation is contradicted by the historically rather late emergence of the so-called question of being in a period which can already be described as one of demythologization, of an advanced Greek 'enlightenment'. But the thesis which might be raised in objection to me here would be right to claim that, with the ἀρχαί [archai] in their older form (in Parmenides and the Eleatics themselves we are already talking about something else), no distinction whatsoever is drawn between beings and being, between τὰ ὄντα [ta onta] and τὸ ὄν [to on] as the power at work in things. I would also draw your attention to the fact that this interpretation of being – that is, of the highest abstraction, as at once the effective power or original cause of all beings – a notion which looks very mythological to us, is still at work in Plato's thought, which can certainly no longer be described as archaic. For in Plato the Ideas are clearly conceived both as universal concepts and as effective powers, as powers which actually and originally generate the phenomena that are grasped under these concepts. In the ancient conceptions of the ἀρχή [archē] there is still no distinction between what I might call its ontological meaning – what it signifies as being, as an essential nature, independently of the beings that it includes – and its interpretation as the highest and most comprehensive category of beings, namely as some kind of material stuff. The earliest speculations of Western thought owe their distinctive aura to this fact that essence and being are here inseparably involved with each other, that the highest conceptions applied to particular beings appear at the same time as the essential natures that lie beyond all beings. This aura consists in the way these speculations are meant to be metaphysical and transcendent in character, to be more than merely factical description, while yet possessing something of that welcome concreteness that strikes us in such ideas and conceptions as water, air, the four elements of Empedocles, or whatever it happens to be. But to say that such distinction is still absent from the ἀρχαί [archai] implies that the reflection which actually yields the concept of being (what Heideggerean philosophy calls the question of being) has not really yet been accomplished in such philosophy. It implies, in other words, that, in such philosophy, the question of being did not actually precede, in a supposedly more 'original' fashion, the question concerning beings, that the distinction between being and beings is not yet made at all, that a tentative consciousness in search of explanation has not yet distinguished between being, as that which lies behind appearances, and the comprehensive categories that apply to particular beings. It is only when both of these moments have been differentiated, or only through a process of reflection, that the concept of being itself can arise at all. So let me formulate one of the fundamental theses which I have developed here in a basically historical rather than a systematic way: the concept of being itself is not the 'original' question that Heideggerean philosophy would have us believe that it is. It is a concept of reflection in the sense of those concepts that Kant subjected to criticism in his 'Amphiboly of the Concepts of Reflection' when they are hypostasized – in other words, when they are treated as an expression of true being as such. On this view of things, the concept of being is not, as we are encouraged to believe, something that is very ancient but something rather late – and here too I cannot help advising some scepticism towards the dogma that what is oldest, what has been there from the first, must inevitably therefore be what is more true. I believe I have already said something about this, and I should simply add here that I can hardly think of anything more fateful in our cultural and intellectual tradition than what Goethe in old age expressed in one of his last letters when he spoke of the ancient truth that we can allegedly never lose.[6]

But there is another aspect to this question of being, apart from the need for a more comprehensive explanation of the manifold character of experience than can be provided by simply plucking out particular features or characteristics of that manifold experience. And I would further like to draw your attention to this aspect because I believe that it is also relevant, in a very analogous way, to the modern ontology and the modern philosophy of being. For you must not simply isolate philosophy as one realm in the world of the mind. Even if, like Heidegger himself, we reject the idea of philosophy as a kind of particular science or discipline, we must not for that reason effectively detach philosophy from its relationship with the totality of conscious experience. Now it seems to me that the early history of philosophy, which ended up in questions concerning being in the Eleatic tradition and then in classical Greek philosophy itself, was motivated, for its part, by the history of science. Heidegger speaks very contemptuously both of the history of science and of the accompanying insight that these ancient principles, or ἀρχαί [archai], could no longer be reconciled with advances attained in the course of the Greek enlightenment. Thus it is as if the original questions, the pure questions that belong to philosophy, were now being conflated with merely scientific questions. But you must not forget that the separation of sciences from philosophy itself, just like the transition to the concept of being, is a relatively late result. And I would say that these two processes – the detachment of philosophy from science and the concentration of philosophy on the question of what being really is or what true being is – are the same processes. One cannot simply deny, *ad maiorem gloriam philosophiae*, that the limitation set upon the material claims of philosophy is drastically connected with the way that more and more fragments are wrested from the clutches of philosophy by the individual sciences. Nor that the individual sciences have taken control of ever more numerous areas and emancipated themselves from the primacy of free and unfettered explanation and speculation. Whether this process is a blessing or, as the Heideggerean school certainly seems to think, ultimately a curse is not something I would like to decide on here. I would think that what we are dealing with is a model of the *dialectic* of enlightenment, where the advance in one decisive respect, namely in the progress of scientific knowledge, is paid for by an equally great loss as our awareness of the whole is splintered by the division of labour in the particular disciplines. In any case, this so-called question of being is actually a kind of residue: in the first instance, historically speaking, being is what is left over for philosophy. I would almost say, if you forgive the frivolity, that it is the one branch left to philosophy once the others – medicine, geography, or whatever other branches there were in antiquity – have robbed it of their specific claims with regard to particular beings. In the end, all philosophy has is 'being', which it now has to deal with. That may seem somewhat impoverished and monotonous, but at least its claim to being is not something that can be denied to philosophy. And, even today, amongst the most serious of scientists and the most advanced of physicists there are those who solemnly declare their agreement about the residue of being that is left for philosophy.[7] This

residual character of being, historical as it is, is remarkably concordant
with the fact that the concept of being, in its logical genesis, is indeed
what remains once we set aside all particular beings, namely everything
that the sciences have arrogated for themselves. In one place, in a
rather famous passage of special pathos, Heidegger says that 'thinking
has descended into the poverty of its provisional essence.'[8] Now I
believe that this 'provisional essence' is one thing we could talk about.
But he is certainly quite right about the 'descent into poverty'. This
descent into poverty lies in the way that philosophy has been ever
more deprived of its concrete content, has become a kind of residual
philosophy. And our subsequent considerations will show that the
question concerning being, even in its internal philosophical structure,
reveals itself again and again as a residual philosophy. In other words,
that the question concerning what is utterly 'first' is actually the question concerning what is supposedly left once the subjective production
costs of thought have been subtracted from thought itself. The new
ontology finds itself in a very similar position. For it stands, as I have
already suggested to you, in pronounced opposition to scientism, and
to the positive sciences, for the reason which you will already have
understood from our earlier sessions: all of these sciences unfold in
relation to beings that are already constituted and can therefore only
be regarded as 'forgetful of being', as Heidegger puts it. In other
words, they would always fail to remember being as that which is
prior to anything else – which is very much what came to pass with
the philosophy of being in ancient thought.

But I believe – and this is where I wish to close for today – that
there is a kind of correlation between ontology on the one side, as
that which is left once science has invaded philosophy at almost
every corner and quarter, and the positive sciences on the other side.
In other words, the ontological dimension, in that all-encompassing
purity with which fundamental philosophy presents it to us, is itself
quite impossible without the pressure exerted by scientism. Thus the
relationship that obtains here is somewhat analogous to that between
the process of abstraction in art and the rise of photography, without
which this process is inconceivable and which this latter simultaneously negates. A student of Heidegger's – I am thinking of Bröcker in
Kiel[9] – has recently defended the claim that logical positivism, namely
the most advanced method of the positive sciences, is the truth for
the first level of consciousness, as it were, for the sphere of facticity,
but that over and above that, as in the Christian paradox, there rises
a sphere of pure being,[10] as this is expressed by fundamental ontology. Now this is indeed a rather strange and absurd view of things
which looks as if it is trying to resuscitate the old idea of a twofold

truth, the doctrine of two kinds of truth, yet I have to say that there is a certain consistency here. If I may put it crudely, this rather lets the cat out of the bag and clearly reveals the thought that the mere facticity of reified consciousness, on the one side, and the extravagant and vacuous purity of ontological consciousness, on the other, do indeed correspond to each other, but that the one cannot be conceived without the other, that both belong together in a correlative fashion.

LECTURE 4

17 November 1960

In our last session I said something about the elements of the doctrine of being as we find them in antiquity. However, in keeping with what I am trying to do here, I did not undertake to present even a rudimentary historical account of the concept of being but chose instead to discuss the elements which I introduced solely with reference to the problematic of the philosophy of being as we encounter it today. And we shall address the new philosophy of being solely with reference to its continuing relevance – in other words, with regard to whether it is true or is not true and with regard to the conclusions which such a critique may prompt. But I think I should remind you that the new philosophy of being, these new ontological approaches of the most various kinds, do stand in a quite specific relationship with the old ontologies. The turn which has led to the philosophies of being, as is generally assumed, should indeed probably be traced back not so much to Husserl, the teacher of Scheler and Heidegger, as to Husserl's own teacher Franz Brentano. Now Brentano was originally a priest who came straight out of the scholastic-Aristotelian tradition, and his philosophy represents a rather remarkable combination of scholastic-ontological themes and issues associated with the tradition of empiricist and enlightenment thought. And here I would like at least to mention the most important work which in a sense effectively inaugurates this ontological approach, since I know that some of you are certainly interested in the historical origin of these things. Now it is significant that the word 'origin' actually occurs in the title of the book in question: *On the Origin of Ethical Knowledge*.[1]

The work does not attempt to develop the fundamental categories of ethics from some formal principle of reason but treats them instead as possessed of intrinsic being in their own right, as a form of being *sui generis*. And the orthodox followers of Brentano, Oskar Kraus in particular,[2] argued against Husserl, with some justification, that what phenomenology proclaimed as a completely new turn in philosophy really goes back to the philosophy of Brentano, which is directly bound up with the scholastic and Aristotelian tradition. It was Scheler who took up ontology as initially conceived by Husserl – in no bad sense – merely in terms of certain logical categories, and extended and reoriented it as a so-called material ontology. Scheler was thus the first to introduce that concept of being-in-itself on the part of substantive intellectual elements which finally terminated in the concept of being. Now to a significant extent he too was indebted to the Catholic-Aristotelian tradition. And the same is true for Heidegger, who also originally intended to become a priest. Thus this entire philosophy is connected in various ways with a theological-philosophical tradition which in a certain sense is very different from the later general European concept of the Enlightenment, and which has also maintained its distance from the latter. Nonetheless – in spite of the remarkably ancient and archaic moment which you may say is already involved in this ontological approach, and which has finally been openly confessed in the Heidegger school – you must not overlook the fact that we are not talking simply about a philosophical tendency which remains untouched by the Enlightenment or, more precisely, by critical philosophy. On the contrary, we are talking about a tendency which does indeed take up those earlier themes but has itself arisen out of an entirely new situation. Namely from the situation in which there *is* something such as autonomous reason, in which, therefore, whatever we say about real or intellectual objectivities of one sort or another, the moment of reflective reason is already inevitably involved. We could say that ontology – in relation to the critical philosophy, in relation to transcendental philosophy in the context of idealism in the broadest sense – has something in common with what certain movements of contemporary philosophy declare themselves to be, namely a form of counter-Enlightenment. In other words, this is a thinking which employs the means of autonomous thought and exploits the entire armoury of philosophical culture and philosophical critique in order to restore or re-establish a kind of view of the world or a kind of experience which had been dissolved by the Enlightenment and by critical philosophy. It is a kind of thinking, to put this more crudely and more generally, which would use autonomous intellectual means to restore something like *heteronomy* – just as in the totalitarian political movements of our time we may clearly observe a tendency not to derive forms of heteronomy in simply immediate terms from established relations of a social kind, but to deduce them instead from rational categories which actually presuppose autonomy, as in the concept of elites for example. I shall develop this notion of heteronomy on the basis of autonomy in more detail later on, and all I want to say here is this. What seems utterly impossible to me in all these ontological efforts – impossible in a very weighty sense, not just in the way we easily say today 'that's impossible', but impossible in a quite objective sense – is precisely the idea of getting back to some position where we are bound by categories replete with being, to being itself, from a position where consciousness is not bound at all. But it will be some time before we come to all this.

Here I would just like to say instead that the so-called question of being that we are talking about in these ontological approaches does indeed have a lot to do, substantively speaking, with the older problematic that I spoke to you about last time. This is so even though the question of being, as I shall also show you, is anything but a pre-critical return to naive realism. Even though Heidegger himself has specifically distanced himself from Hartmann, whose turn to ontology is effectively a turn to a very solid or, if you wish, pre-critical realism,[3] and has emphasized that his own existential ontology is not ultimately motivated by the desire, for example, to defend some kind of realism, whether critical or naive, against idealism or the phenomenalism associated with it. The concept of ontology is indeed somewhat complex and ambiguous. And amongst those of you who have not specifically engaged with Heidegger's thought, there will probably be some who take the naive and straightforward view that ontology is precisely a philosophy of being that is simply opposed to a philosophy of consciousness. In other words, that it is a realist philosophy in opposition to one that is grounded in self-reflection. Now there is also something right about that, and we shall return to it in due course. But, since we are trying to address ontology in its most consistent and differentiated form, it must already be said that the conception of so-called naive realism is not what is most decisive here, for the concept of being or being as Heidegger describes it attempts to escape – whether it succeeds is another question – both from any mere conceptuality and from any reality simply or immediately accepted as such. This double approach, this double front against a philosophy of concepts and against a philosophy of reality, is precisely what characterizes the efforts of ontology in its most rigorous and consistent form, namely its Heideggerean form. And, if I am not mistaken, it owes its very considerable influence to this distinctive double perspective and the wavering character associated with it. I have thus already suggested that, in ontology of the Heideggerean kind – in the most consistent and in a certain sense, by its own measure, most radical form of ontology – we are not dealing simply with the concept of being. And this touches on a thematic that is indeed directly connected with the ancient philosophical tradition. We are talking about ontology as the doctrine of being – and we want to concentrate on this so-called question of being as much as possible, since it really is the crucial point on which this philosophy turns, and since we can do critical justice to the claim it makes only if we really think through this point where everything is finally 'secured', as Kant puts it[4] – and Heidegger's philosophy of being is caught up in a most curious and wavering alternative. For it is by no means clear whether we are talking here merely about the meaning of the *concept* of being, what the concept of being means when we think, when we say the word 'being', or whether we are talking here directly about *being itself*. Now the answer we would receive in this connection is undoubtedly the latter. A convinced Heideggerean would immediately object – and would imagine this to be a very powerful objection – that we are indeed dealing with being itself rather than the concept of being. But then we would already encounter certain issues which really have a lot to do with what in modern philosophy we have generally come to describe as the 'analysis of meaning'.

Here I should already point out that Heidegger himself, or at least the Heidegger of *Being and Time*, expressly confessed his allegiance to phenomenology as a method, and that he regarded himself as a student of Husserl's methodologically speaking. And the phenomenological method of taking up the phenomena of mental life precisely as they are given amounts effectively, to a considerable degree, to the careful analysis and differentiation of meanings. And when you look at Heidegger's texts you will discover just such analyses of meaning all over the place. Indeed an entire discipline within fundamental ontology – one which plays a very important role there, although its cultural and historical origins point in a rather different direction, namely to Dilthey – actually consists precisely in the analysis of meaning, namely the much discussed discipline of hermeneutics.[5] Now, if you think about Aristotle, we find that the question we were just talking about, whether we are concerned with being or the concept of being, is in one sense put very simply. This is because, for Aristotle, language is quite simply the guiding thread by which we can make something out regarding being. The expression κατηγορία [katēgoria], or 'category', itself signifies nothing more than 'in accordance with speech'. And if

you wish to characterize Aristotle's *Metaphysics* in a very crude way
as a doctrine of categories in an admittedly meta-logical sense, that
is, in a material rather than a merely formal sense, then you would
find that all the categories that Aristotle provides – a list which, as
you all know, is taken over in the *Critique of Pure Reason* with a
few modifications as the relevant categories plus the forms of intuition[6]
– simply comprise the totality of syntactic forms already identifiable
through an analysis of language in Aristotle's time. In other words,
the pure forms of speech themselves are supposed to be the forms
that also say something about being itself, without explicit reflection
on the difference between language and object being required. Now
we could say that one of the decisive steps which has shaped modern
thought since Bacon, and the whole movement of Western nominalism in particular, consists in the fact that this canonic character of
language is no longer recognized. Reflection on the difference between
language and its object did eventually emerge, and in a certain sense
critical thought is nothing but the investigation of this difference
between language and object, namely – to employ the classical expression which Kantian philosophy has lent to this problem – the attempt
to explore the *possibility* of concepts themselves rather than simply
philosophizing 'from concepts'. And this possibility, this reflection on
the possibility of concepts, in Kant means nothing other than reflection on the fundamental sustaining relationship between the concepts
and their object, that is to say, on their *meanings*. In this way language
is actually displaced from its once dominant and unchallenged position. In this sense the refusal to think in terms of mere concepts, the
critique of rationalism, is actually one with the critique of scholasti-
cism insofar as it is implicitly but essentially a critique of language.
Indeed the word 'nominalism' implies as much, since it treats concepts
as mere *nomina* for what they designate rather than as something
substantial, as a kind of being in itself. Let me say that the concept
of 'being' also belongs amongst the hypostases of language, inasmuch
as a method which believes that every typical and exemplary linguistic
state of affairs we can accomplish must also possess a corresponding
objectivity of its own, and actually proceeds in a hypostasizing manner
– irrespective of whether we are dealing with a mental state of affairs
or some factical or empirical state of affairs. The linguistic form which
is supposedly substantiated in the concept of being is the copula.[7]
The copula is simply nothing but the 'is' in the predicative judgement
A is B. It is this 'is' which is commonly called the copula. And the
concept of being as we find it in Aristotle in the first instance is nothing
more than this: when we investigate the state of affairs that is supposed to stand behind these linguistic forms, then the state of affairs

which is also supposed to stand behind the 'is' is just 'being' – just as in grammar an εἶναι [einai] or an ὄν [on] stands behind the copula ἔστι [esti] or 'is'. To that extent, the concept of being, in terms of its origin and its legitimacy, is also directly bound up with the categorial structure of language. In one sense, therefore, this entire tradition hypostasizes concepts by tacitly assuming that some constitutive state of affairs must also correspond to everything which is constitutive for language – and 'being' has also largely fallen victim here through the process of philosophical critique. As I believe I have already pointed out,[8] Kant has formulated this in a particularly emphatic manner in his 'Amphiboly' chapter, where he says that concepts of reflection (concepts which have no immediate application whatsoever since they are essentially posited merely by consciousness in general) are treated as if they possessed intrinsic being in their own right. As far as this question is concerned, Heidegger's new ontology basically proceeds in a similar way, and indeed precisely by appealing to Husserl's method, which holds that philosophy can essentially be grounded through an analysis of meanings. And Heidegger's ontology, as I said before, is to a large extent founded in the theory of meaning – even though this is not *entirely* the case.

Now I think it is time that I should try, with you, to get closer to the problem we are talking about here through a rather more specific analysis regarding the concept of being – although I would ask you at first not to press me too much if, in what I am saying, I do not distinguish strictly between being and the concept of being. I believe that you will soon understand why this alternation between these two ways of speaking is so extraordinarily difficult to avoid. In order to understand the possibility of the ontological approach in an emphatic manner, you must clearly realize that this word 'being' involves a very specific problem which does not arise in the same way with other concepts. Thus, if we simply tried to apply the critique of concepts of reflection or the critique of rationalist conceptual dogmatism to the concept of being, we would really be making things all too easy for ourselves, or celebrating a great and joyful triumph when, as is so often the case with such triumphs, we have simply occupied a battlefield on which our opponent is nowhere to be found. In other words, and I apply this warning to myself as well, you must by no means make things too easy for yourselves in this critique of the concept of being, for there is indeed something quite distinctive with regard to this 'being'. On the one hand, it is impossible to speak about being directly without reference to the concept of being. Sometimes, when we find ourselves in this sphere, we must, in order to expose its own triviality, be ready to descend into the sphere of triviality ourselves – we cannot actually avoid this, since here in particular the most extreme triviality and the most extreme insight exist together in a most remarkable symbiosis that needs to be teased apart somewhat. Thus when I say the word 'being', when I speak about being or think 'being', then this 'is' not indeed *being itself*. And the thought that I have in this connection – what I mean here – is not immediately the same as being, for it is mediated by the word. And this word – I do not believe I need to expand on this: just think about the copula that I mentioned to you earlier – this word is not of course something isolated but is an element of language, something that could not be characterized at all outside the context of language. It thereby mediates what is meant, what is to be said, with language itself. We are presented here with a *mediation of being*, as I tried to suggest before in genetic terms by reference to the history of philosophy. I spoke of the extent to which the concept of being was due to abstraction, to the transition from more specific ἀρχαί [archai] to principles of an ever more general character. The word 'being' is not being, for there is something else between what we say and what we mean. And to that extent we can say that what we talk about is conceived in terms of something: it is itself a concept. We cannot get round this conceptual dimension. With the word 'being' we think something that is not being itself – for otherwise it would be precisely the kind of immediate revelation that we do not have. Yet this very word 'being' also points towards thought, if I may put it this way. Here, incidentally, you can readily understand the tremendous significance which belongs to language and the idea of language in Heidegger's philosophy, a significance which I would certainly also be inclined to ascribe to language, albeit in a rather different way. And it is a significance, I might add, that the most extreme counter-position to the Heideggerean school, namely logical positivism, especially in the case of Moore but to some extent also in Wittgenstein,[9] ascribes to language as well. We could even say that so-called neo-positivism is distinguished from good old positivism in the style of Mach and Avenarius precisely by the way it no longer talks simply of the immediately given or the context of the given but has come to see that the given itself is not ultimately immediate, since in thinking about it we are already treating it as something linguistically mediated. Thus if we really wish to reach the so-called ultimate data, we are still reliant on language, and this explains the extraordinary importance of protocol sentences for positivist philosophy.[10] Thus, with regard to this thematic of language as a constitutive dimension of philosophy, I would say that this is by no means limited to modern ontology since it is essentially involved in all philosophical reflection, and that philosophy that is not also philosophy of language is not even

conceivable today. I emphasize this here since it is only on the basis
of this admission, of this shared conviction, that we will be able to
understand the very real differences which I shall try and unfold for
you in relation to Heidegger's own philosophy of language.

Now, on the other hand, and this confirms what I said about the
distinctive character of the word 'being', where I would certainly not
challenge Heidegger's view: for the word 'being' reminds us of that
which is not exhausted in a merely subjectively instituted concept,
in other words, of what was described in the language of ancient
and archaic philosophy, in the Ionian philosophies of nature, with
a relatively unusual expression, as ὑποκείμενον [hypokeimenon], as
'that which underlies'. The concepts that we employ all have something instituted or 'superimposed' about them, as they say in English,
something foisted upon things. They basically serve the domination
of nature and are generally acquired *more scientifico*, through a
process of definition, in accordance with scientific procedure. And
they are retained as long as they confirm these so-called definitions,
without decisively touching what they refer to. They are mobilized as
chips or counters and deployed for technical ends – in the broadest
sense of the word – although what they mean does not actually find
expression in language here. This is something that has often been
recognized by philosophy. I would simply remind you historically
that Hegelian philosophy rests upon the idea that every *individual*
concept is false, or that there is no actual identity between any finite
concept and what it is meant to designate. It does indeed designate
it, but in being imposed on the heterogeneous by the subject it also
always differs from what the thing is in its own right. And the driving
force of the whole Hegelian philosophy is an attempt to make good
this difference, to produce that identity between thought and thing,
between subject and object, which is bankrupted by every individual
concept, precisely through the *totality* of the developed system as a
whole. In a less emphatic way, though one that is therefore also much
easier to grasp, Nietzsche expatiated at length in a relatively early
piece on the philosophy of language upon the incommensurability
of concepts and things.[11] And Nietzsche's irrationalism – if we can
really put it like that: the priority of life over spirit which Nietzsche
himself proclaimed – finds its ultimate epistemological justification in
the recognition that concepts are inadequate to the living reality they
would encompass, that all that is living, as people repeat ad nauseam,
is mortified and life perishes in the medium of concepts. Now this
moment of inadequacy is removed from every individual concept and
finds itself indefinitely postponed, as it were. We do not reflect thoroughly upon any individual concept as it is usually deployed – unless

we think dialectically, which certainly cannot be presupposed here – to see how far this concept is fully adequate to its object. Yet we will still have some awareness of this inadequacy in the background, as it were, and will finally transfer this awareness to the totality or to that ultimate concept which stands behind it. Thus in Kant, for example, this will be the highest concept of all those objectivities which are not exhausted in our concepts of them, namely the concept of 'the thing in itself', that transcendent unknowable thing which certainly stands in some obscure relation to the particular knowledge and thus to the concepts we do have, yet is supposed to be unreachable as such. It would do no violence to Heidegger's thought, and I believe he himself would not particularly object, if we claimed that the position of the concept of the thing in itself in Kant's transcendental philosophy bears an extraordinarily close relationship with that dimension of being that, as Heidegger believes he has shown, eludes conceptuality. The peculiar thing about the concept of being lies in its twofold character: on the one hand, it is a concept, the comprehensive concept not only of all beings but also of every idea, of every essence, or the ultimate concept, the concept par excellence; on the other hand, it is also an expression of the opposite, it is a non-concept insofar as it is meant to identify, retain and preserve what cannot for its own part, in principle, be conceptual – in other words, it is the concept which is the intrinsically contradictory concept κὰτ' ἐξοχήν [kat'exochēn], the concept as anti-concept. It is both at once. And this is what motivates – to return to the thought expressed earlier – the distinctive significance of the philosophy of language in Heidegger.

Perhaps I may just repeat here something that I have already mentioned in various contexts during these lectures. And this is that you will find it helpful for comprehending difficult philosophical theses if you understand the thoughts and concepts that arise in these philosophies in a *functional* manner or, to put this even more bluntly, if you understand the *cui bono* question. Here I am not thinking specifically of social interests or the like, for example, but quite simply of the function which thoughts and concepts possess in the overall philosophical structure or edifice itself – in other words, of what the concepts are meant to be good for. Thus the idea of language not merely as a semantic or signifying structure that serves to express beings, but as a realm in which, Heidegger constantly assures us in his later writings, being itself allegedly resounds, is something that emerges precisely from that distinctive double character of being. For on the one hand, of course, being qua concept is referred to language, since 'being' is a word; on the other hand, however, being is just what cannot be expressed through mere meanings – inasmuch as it cannot be exhausted

BEING AND LANGUAGE (I)   41

in conceptual terms, or, let me put this more precisely, inasmuch as it *points* towards what is not exhausted by concepts, what is cut off from concepts. And Heidegger tries to deal with the whole thing by immediately conceding that language does indeed mean or signify, while claiming at the same time that language itself is something other, something more, than meaning in this sense.[12] Now this peculiar construction of language in Heidegger, which is ultimately there only to do justice to this double character of being as concept and anti-concept, allows you to recognize, in a nutshell, the structure which actually gives shape to this entire philosophy. That is why I have already drawn attention to this aspect at this point: to the way in which contradictions such as that of concept and anti-concept, or the concept of the non-conceptual, are not actually unfolded or developed, and the way in which we find, instead, an attempt to master these contradictions by a kind of sorcery, by magically invoking or summoning them through the Word. Now the difference, if I may anticipate the basic theme of these lectures, between dialectical thinking and fundamental ontological thinking, considered from this perspective, is just this: fundamental ontological thinking remains with such contradictions, believes them to be overcome through the immediacy of the Word of language, whereas dialectical thinking takes up the challenge that is harboured by these contradictions and attempts to unfold the contradictions themselves. Let me simply add here that there is certainly also a truth moment to Heidegger's conception of language as something which is not simply exhausted by what it means. The problem is that he absolutizes this moment in a one-sided way in relation to being and emphasizes the *mimetic* moment of language[13] – as we would call it – in a one-sided way over against its semantic moment. He thereby brings the dialectic to a standstill in the very sphere which gives the dialectic its name – precisely in the sphere of language which, *ex definitione*, is nothing other than a διαλέγεσθαι [dialegesthai].

LECTURE 5

29 November 1960

Now I think I should just say a few more words in relation to what we were talking about last time, since it has been almost a fortnight now since our last session. We had pointed out that the concept of being – or our talk of being, for the concept of being is not an entirely accurate way of speaking about what I am trying to express – is intrinsically marked by a most remarkable ambiguity. On the one hand, being is a concept, the broadest concept for everything that can possibly be brought under the highest conceptual unity – that is how we would have to define being if we do indeed wish to treat it as a concept. On the other hand, however, being evokes also something else, namely the aspect which a philosopher such as Heinrich Rickert once described with the expression 'heterogeneous continuum'[1] – that moment which is not itself conceptual, which is not exhausted by our subjectively instituted concepts, which for its part underlies all conceptuality. That we are justified in speaking in this way is evident, as I have already indicated, from a certain arbitrary character that clings to every process of concept formation, despite all of the later Plato's efforts to escape this very problem.[2] In other words, the way we cut up our concepts always has something arbitrary about it; any individual thing can be embraced under countless concepts, and there is no absolutely compelling necessity within the thing which demands that it be grasped under this and *only* this concept or under these and *only* these concepts. Again, every concept reveals an enormous degree of vagueness with respect to its possible forms of realization, given that the concept identifies only one feature or only certain features of what it embraces, leaving others free in turn. It is precisely by virtue of this freedom in relation to those dimensions not defined by the concept that so much more already finds its way into the concept, so much which for its part appears contingent or indifferent to the latter. These points may help briefly to remind you that the order which our concepts procure for us (especially in a scientific context) is not immediately identical with the way things are, with the constitution of that to which these concepts are directed. It is for this very reason that the fundamental thesis of Spinoza's metaphysics and theory of knowledge, according to which the order of ideas and the order of things is identical,[3] can rightly be described as the leading principle of rationalist philosophy in general. And the entire critique of Western rationalism, especially as it derives from Kant, has in fact destroyed this conception of knowledge, although the basic question involved goes back much further and is none other than the old problem which was discussed under the name of nominalism in the wake of late medieval philosophy. Now the truth is that – if I may point out the relevant structure (to put this benevolently) or the relevant trick (to put it less benevolently) – in fundamental ontology or the philosophy of being, this moment of ambiguity, between being as concept and being as what is beyond the concept, this deficiency or inadequacy which lies in language here and indeed points towards something deeper, is not acknowledged by fundamental ontology or the philosophy of being as a deficiency at all. On the contrary, it is chalked up as a positive and accounted as credit. In the course of our investigations we shall find again and again that, whenever such deficiencies of thought or the concept are encountered by this philosophy, they are exploited in a distinctive way and used to lend a particular dignity to its own claims. Now I am trying in these lectures to immunize you with a certain resistance to these philosophical tendencies that continue to be so influential in Germany. And I believe it is no bad advice if I encourage you, when confronted with the basic theses of fundamental ontology, always to ask whether some moment of insufficiency, of inadequate knowledge or concept formation, or whatever it may be, is not perhaps being used in just this way. In other words, whether a concept's *failure* to accomplish what it is specifically meant to accomplish serves only to prove and reveal its peculiar profundity or its 'priority', to use a Heideggerean expression, over against the 'labour' and 'exertion' of the concept, to use a Hegelian expression.[4]

But I do not want to make it too easy for us either. Things really stand on a knife edge, as is usually the case where truth is concerned, for truth is something extraordinarily fragile. And, if philosophy can teach you anything, it's that you should perhaps lose a little of your faith that truth clings to the massive differences, that it's something you can just take home in your great big folders and notebooks.[5] But the matter is not that simple. Thus that wavering indifference of the word 'being' which we talked about – the way it is at once concept and non-concept, namely the concept of what cannot for its part become a concept – also announces something of constitutive significance. And I would even go so far as to agree with Heidegger and say that it is not even the least of the criteria of philosophy, or certainly not the most contemptible, that it be able to explore such ambiguous matters which hardly unfold in accordance with any established rules of play. For this ambiguity reveals something which can never be eliminated by deliberate definitional procedures, or could be eliminated only in the most superficial manner for specific organizational purposes. It reveals, on the one hand, to emphasize this once again here, that we can only ever think in conceptual terms, that conceptuality is the prison in which our thought finds itself enclosed; but also, on the other, that what we strive to grasp in thought, what we intend to think, is by no means exhausted in this structure, that the task of thought is to recognize its own limits through self-reflection. In this sense at least, the old Aristotelian demand that thought should think itself remains in force, even if we no longer feel authorized to regard the νόησις νοήσεως [noēsis noēseōs][6] as a positive given or some kind of transcendental fact. But, even if we concede all this, there is still an enormous difference between recognizing the aporetic character of the word 'being' and what this aporetic character shows us, or turning this aporia itself into a prerogative and acting as if the concept of being (as Heidegger once put it in rather questionable German) were the *einmaligste*, or 'most unique', concept that we have. And this is the limit that we are concerned with here. Since the word 'being' in itself also marks a limit with respect to the conceptual, since the intention of this word is conceptually directed at what is not exhausted in the concept, it is illegitimate to appeal to this word, given that it is nonetheless *still* a concept, as if it were somehow immediately beyond the concept at the same time.

This is a very fine distinction, I will readily admit, but there is no way round this subtlety, for it actually harbours something quite decisive for our problem. When a concept points towards something that is not for its part conceptual, you may say that conceptuality itself is thereby limited or qualified in some way. Conceptual thought is quite capable of becoming its own warning, its own 'writing on the wall'. Yet it is a delusion to imagine that such self-reflection, in which thought recognizes that it does not exhaust what it thinks, would already imply that thought enjoyed some positive access to what is beyond thinking – merely by belabouring the kind of words that expose this limit. You can understand why this is impossible if you remember, from our last analysis, how we showed that 'being' not only aims conceptually at that non-conceptuality but also *is* itself a concept. But this strange double meaning that is harboured in the word 'being' is exploited by the Heidegger school as if the distinctive character of the word itself allowed its conceptual dimension to recede behind something quite Other than this, precisely because that Otherness is what is conceptually *meant*. Yet, in spite of this intention directed towards the non-conceptual, the word still does not cease to be a concept. In other words, to come back to this point, in the word 'being' we do not immediately have being in our mouths, so to speak. For something is meant by this word, as with every concept, and this limit over against what lies beyond the concept also needs to be respected in our talk of being – although the philosophy of being rides right over it. What the philosophy of being makes out of this non-conceptual moment of the concept of being, out of this conceptual 'remembrance' of the non-conceptual, is deployed by this philosophy in a very particular way. Thus 'being' is supposedly distinguished from two aspects or moments: on the one hand from the abstraction or pure universal concept of being, and on the other from anything determinate included under a general concept, namely from its correlate, or the particular beings from which abstraction is made. The profit (if I may put it this way) that the philosophy of being derives from the wavering character of its 'most unique' concept is precisely the way it allows this philosophy to retain this wavering word on both sides. Thus on the one side, as I have already indicated on various occasions, 'being' is not supposed to coincide with 'beings', and nor is it supposed to be a summary concept for all particular beings. It is supposed to be something quite other than all this. In the first place we have to say that this otherness of being with respect to beings is nothing but conceptuality itself. In other words, being is distinguished from all particular beings that are included within it in the sense that it is the *concept* of those beings, rather than being immediately the same as the latter. Now the philosophy of being eagerly cashes in on this conceptuality, even while it insists at the same time that being is *not* itself a concept. And this gives rise to that curiously indeterminate and wavering structure which (if you will forgive the vulgar expression here) manages to draw the cream off both sides at once, namely from the concept and from particular beings. The cream of the concept consists in the fact that we are talking here not about some arbitrary or contingent particular being but about something which, as they like to say, is prior to that, something that is allegedly higher and more dignified with respect to beings. At the same time the cream of beings is supposed to consist in the fact that what we are talking about here is not something conceptual but something concrete, namely something substantial that already underlies conceptuality in the first place.

I believe that this quid pro quo that I have tried to analyse for you is indeed the mechanism through which the dignity of all this talk of being arises. But this process should not be understood – and I hope you grasp the actual methodological point of what I have been saying here – simply in social or psychological genetic terms. For it is something which arises out of the economy of the concepts in question, that is necessitated by the constellation of the relevant elements concept/non-concept and being/beings. Let me remind you that the two moments from which being – now written by Heidegger as 'beyng' or even struck through as being[7] – is persistently distinguished, namely the concept and the given, are also those moments in being where subjectivity, a thinking subject, is involved as a constitutive factor – in other words, that thinking subject which was not subjected to reflection in the ancient form of ontology, while such reflection cannot be avoided in the context of modern ontology. For the concept is indeed the subjective intellectual contribution, the result of abstraction; and beings, as givenness, at least in the sense of traditional philosophy, are what remains in the hyletic givens, the primary materials of consciousness, which can no longer be eliminated. And to that extent one of the essential features of all ontology – one of the features to which it most emphatically owes its influence – is to be found precisely here: its anti-subjectivism, or the appearance that philosophy had somehow escaped its imprisonment within subjectivity through this ontological 'project'. This apparent overcoming of subjectivism in conditions where nothing has actually changed regarding the presuppositions of subjectivism is intimately bound up with that quid pro quo that I have tried to lay out for you. This apparently higher dignity of ontology as something prior to subjectivity is actually grounded in this: that those deficiencies of reflection regarding what being means are chalked up to the philosophy of being, so that the so-called overcoming of subjectivism – as an essential consequence in my view – which is surely one of the strongest seductions of this philosophy, arises only from that wavering, negative and inarticulate character of this talk of being itself. And just as we should mistrust the word 'overcoming' in general, so too we should certainly mistrust any philosophy which has nothing with which to replace the positivity of its pathos except the ambiguity of the medium within which it moves.

In spite of these moments that we have just discussed, it is very characteristic of modern ontology that it stays within the domain of language, as I think I have already pointed out to you. Yet I want to re-emphasize this here, for you may want to object that these rather subtle distinctions, as Kant would call them, in our own fundamental critical investigation of being have basically all been oriented to the meaning of the *word* 'being', and that the ultimate intention of fundamental ontology, what it is actually defending, is getting rather short shrift here. Now I think I have in principle already responded to this objection when I pointed out that fundamental ontology too cannot become aware of the other or the beyond of language, of that which is not exhausted in the concept, except by virtue of the concept. In other words, fundamental ontology cannot possibly sustain the claim through which it would counter conceptual thought. But, even if we disregard this here, I believe that fundamental ontology cannot seriously raise any objections to the method which I have employed in these last analyses of ours, since this ontology emphatically presents itself precisely as a philosophy of language. You will recall how I said that the word 'being' is a concept, for when we say the word – irrespective of whether being has a particular range, as other concepts also do, or whether this range is intrinsically problematic – this word 'being' is not immediately being itself. In other words, as I put it somewhat drastically before, we do not thereby already have or feel being in our mouths. For in God's name we actually just have the word itself. Now Heidegger's philosophy is extremely consistent and acute in this regard and never even supposes the absurdity I have just suggested, namely the idea that we ever *could* have being itself in our mouths. In other words, Heidegger knows perfectly well that I am also compelled by conceptuality itself to call being a concept, and that this moment of mediation has thus already found its way into any attempt to philosophize about being, even though he strives to suspend it for the sake of his own ideal of original thought. And the conclusion he draws from all this is indeed that language must here be immediately one with what language expresses. In his very fine dissertation, Schweppenhäuser[8] has shown how Heidegger effectively began as a theorist of linguistic meaning in a more or less traditional Husserlian sense but was subsequently driven to ascribe some kind of immediate and substantial being to language. And this is duly reflected in his famous remarks that being 'illuminates' or 'unconceals' itself within language, and in all those speculations where comrade Heidegger[9] even found himself remarkably close to certain theses of the Cabbalistic philosophy of language, as it subsequently turns out. After what I have just explained here, you will perhaps understand

– and I really want to help you grasp the inner structure, the force field, of this philosophy – precisely why Heidegger arrives at the eccentric claim that being *immediately* unveils itself in language, rather than simply saying that language *expresses* being. For, if he is in earnest with this intention, with the claim that being is in principle neither conceptual in character nor indeed a being, even though it is only in language that we have being at all, then this can only be sustained if ontological dignity is already bestowed on language itself. In other words, language must be approached as if it were the manifestation of what is meant in it, as if language immediately coincided with the latter, rather than standing in various intentional relations of tension towards that which it expresses. Here too I am following my methodological principle that does not allow me to eliminate or simply cavil about the difficulties involved in particular philosophies, and I regard both such approaches as equally unworthy. For the task is to develop these philosophies out of the urgency and aporia of the thinking in question, out of the difficulties in which it finds itself entangled – in short, out of its own internal dynamic. And this is what we have found with Heidegger. Let me just add that the kind of philosophy of language we encounter here is at home in the theological domain and is one that becomes intelligible, assumes a meaningful context, inasmuch as it proceeds from the idea of a true language, that of the revelation of the divine Word, a language which corresponds, as it were, to the *intellectus archetypus*[10] in which thought and intuition actually coincide with each other. The whole problem of this philosophy of language in Heidegger seems to me to be the way that it is borrowed from theology while nonetheless being detached from this theological ground, so that this approach is now just freely ascribed to language as such – completely ignoring the historicity of language and the particular historical features of language – without showing in any convincing way where the dignity thus afforded to language comes from. This is all only done for the sake of a rime[11] – in other words, in order to fulfil the function which the exemplary word 'being' is called upon to fulfil in this philosophy. But this doctrine of language thereby assumes a merely mythological character. In other words, language is simply and magically furnished once again with all those qualities which were once criticized as problematic by nominalist reflection, or at least as something that did not necessarily have to attach to language.

I would just like to draw two very brief conclusions from what I have said in this attempted deduction, this critical deduction of the philosophy of language that is bound up with fundamental ontology. The first thing, given precisely what I have said about the burden of language, indeed the *inevitable* burden of language, is that one cannot object to the specific arguments or reflections that I have presented here simply by claiming that they are concerned with semantic problems, namely the problem of the meaning of being, rather than immediately with being itself. I have already tried to show you that this objection is beside the point, since we do not encounter being directly or immediately; we encounter it only in the form of language. After what I have tried to explicate for you here, all I have to add is that, even if language is indeed the medium, the organon, the complexus of truth, rather than simply a body of signs, just as Heideggerean philosophy claims, then it is only right and proper for philosophy, and especially critical philosophy, to engage with such thinking specifically in terms of the philosophy of language. It is right and proper for us, in other words, to explore the kind of language where that which is highest of all, the *summum bonum*, namely 'being', claims to dwell. One cannot on the one hand set language and the philosophy of language in the place of theory of knowledge, or even of metaphysics, while objecting on the other hand when we actually proceed to analyse the language in question, as if to say: Well, you are just doing philosophy of language here, whereas what we are ultimately concerned with is not language but being ... This is a trick, a quid pro quo – and I want to tear this veil open, and I hope you will follow me in the procedure I have undertaken here and avoid participating in this kind of shadow-boxing. The second thing which follows from our reflections – and this is a moment that I would like to pursue further in this lecture if time permits, although I already offer it here as a programmatic hint at least for engaging with this philosophy – is this: if any philosophy of language betrays the kind of pathos we have just been talking about, then it surely implies an incomparable obligation with regard to the language involved here. If language claims to be more than simply a matter of signs, if it takes itself to stand in an absolutely essential relationship to the real question – and in a certain sense I would indeed agree with Heidegger regarding our responsibility for finding the appropriate form of language for what is at stake – then it follows that the specific linguistic articulation we adopt must answer to the greatest rigour, the greatest exactitude, and the greatest sense of responsibility we can summon. Now if a detailed analysis of language – which I probably cannot deliver in these lectures, but which I can promise you in some form or other for the future[12] – could demonstrate that the language which appears in this philosophy cannot, and immanently by virtue of its own form, do justice to the claim such language announces as the content of philosophy, this would be a fatal objection to a philosophy which can ultimately be critically addressed only in terms of its language precisely because it has cast the entire burden of its truth upon language. Now if I have taken advantage of various occasions, as some of you may know, to speak of 'the jargon of authenticity' in critical connection with the entire structure of this philosophy,[13] and have repeatedly analysed certain figures of language encountered in this field, this was certainly not for the sake of deriving merely literary pleasure from a polemic against a philosophy which acts as if it drew its inspiration from the Castalian spring[14] while talking the most professorial German. That might well be an enjoyable pastime, but it would hold very little interest for me. For these excursions into the analysis of language which I repeatedly allow myself, and with regard to which I hope to undertake a thorough expedition into the jungle one day, touch the nerve of the whole. In other words, they touch the point where the whole of fundamental ontology is 'secured', as Kant would say,[15] where its own truth claim is to found, and where at the same time its own solidity and substantial character can be discerned.

Let me just say a few words here which we may be able to consider more closely in the context of our preliminary discussion of the relation between being and beings (we shall need to address this much more carefully in its own right later on in the lectures). It belongs to the curious wavering character of being, which I discussed with you in terms of conceptuality as a model, that this same implicit and wavering character is also assumed in relation to the domain of beings (as I have already suggested). On the one side, being is meant to be prior to beings, to be that original dimension in whose pathos the old Platonic and Aristotelian notions of true and enduring being, in contrast with ephemeral and illusory being, still survive. On the other side, however, being – and once again this recalls being as concept, as the comprehensive concept of everything it encompasses – is also the totality of beings as such. In this conceptual sense, being would just be all beings. And this second wavering effect, this interference (if I can describe it that way), in the word 'being' also arises from the history of philosophy. In Plato it is implicit in the way that true being essentially consists in the Ideas, while the merely scattered and particular beings are supposed to be τὸ μὴ ὄν [to mē on], non-being, or that which is utterly nugatory and delusory. But, then again, philosophy is also compelled to take up this μὴ ὄν [mē on], to describe it as space – or indeed finally to grasp the Ideas as the highest possible universals for the individual things which they encompass. And even earlier than this we recognize the same ambiguity in the concept of being in the structure of the great didactic poem of Parmenides, which remains of course an extremely enigmatic and, in many ways, contentious text. The first part of the poem declares the concept of being in that emphatic purity that Heidegger basically endorses and ascribes to Parmenides. Now although whole libraries have been written about the connection between the two parts, and I hesitate to express an opinion of any kind here, since it would almost certainly be challenged by the classical philologists in one way or another, the second part of the poem specifically addresses that realm of δόξα [doxa], or opinion, the realm of particular, scattered and merely apparent beings that was so conspicuously excised from the first part. If we really wish to take Parmenides seriously, we can recognize here the need to give expression to that double character of being within philosophy itself. In other words, on the one hand being as that which is not concept, and on the other hand being as the concept par excellence, as the concept of all beings. And the same problem returns in a certain way in Aristotle, as I shall discuss next time, when we shall also say more about the problem of τὸ ὄν [to on] and τὰ ὄντα [ta onta].

LECTURE 6

1 December 1960[1]

Last time I talked about the peculiar ambiguity that belongs to being, on the one hand, as a concept, covering all of the beings that it encompasses, and, on the other, as an abstract and merely negative expression for what is not itself conceptual. And I traced this ambiguity briefly in relation to one or two models from ancient philosophy where this double sense – and not simply the so-called problem of being as such – was also to be found. In this context I briefly discussed the problem of being in Plato, namely the being of the Ideas which stood in such contrast to non-being, τὸ μὴ ὄν [to mē on], even if, with various concessions, the latter still had to be addressed after all. And here I should just mention a structure which did not come up explicitly in Plato last time but which is so familiar from the history of philosophy that I am sure I hardly need to draw your attention to it. I am talking about the concept of μέθεξις [methexis], namely the 'participation' of the many disparate things in the Ideas, a doctrine which only makes sense of course if the realm of beings is not simply defined as utter non-being in relation to genuine being. And I pursued this back even further to the enigmatic fracture or duality, or however you want to describe it, within the didactic poem of Parmenides. Let me just add here that, even in Aristotle – who effectively provides the model for the philosophy of being in the emphatic sense, namely for the question of what being really is – this peculiar alternation between being and beings can be found in his concept of πρώτη οὐσία [prōtē ousia], or 'primary substance', as that which pre-eminently has being. For this πρώτη οὐσία [prōtē ousia] appears in Aristotle in two quite different and, we might say, entirely contradictory senses. And the contradiction would appear so flagrant that we should have to charge the first great teacher of logic with an elementary error in this very field if this same ambiguity did not actually reveal the much deeper problem of the concept of being or of being itself. For, on the one hand, in Aristotle, this πρώτη οὐσία [prōtē ousia], the first or primary being that exists, is supposed to be the same as the τόδε τι [tode ti], the 'this there', the individuated singular thing that is immediately given to me here and now in space and time. We should point out, incidentally, that this expression τόδε τι [tode ti] for the 'this there', for 'thisness', as it were, is a fundamental expression for the entire history of philosophy. And those of you who are just beginning to study philosophy, for whom these lectures may also serve as a kind of introduction to the subject, would do well to familiarize yourselves with these terms, which, like all of Aristotle's terminology, effectively represent a model of philosophical terminology in general. Thus the concept of *haec cei*, 'the this there', in scholastic philosophy is a direct translation of τόδε τι [tode ti], and the famous Scotist expression *hacceitas*, or 'thisness', namely the *principium individuationis* in addition to essence and existence, is actually nothing but the hypostasis of this Aristotelian concept. Needless to say, this concept of the τόδε τι [tode ti], the specific individuated 'this there', the individual thing or appearance that presents itself before our eyes, refers to beings or entities and not to being. For what lies closest, as it were, actually corresponds to τὰ ὄντα [ta onta], to the individual and specific things that exist, not to any underlying structure of being as such, whatever it may be. In view of the emphatic concept of being which I have talked about, you will naturally ask how it is possible that Aristotle initially introduces being in the form of beings or entities in this way, and that this kind of being is even presented as constitutive. Now this is actually not that hard to understand if you just recall for a moment how I tried to show you that the concept of being is itself mediated – in other words, that it is an abstraction with respect to the particular beings from which it derives. But please do not misunderstand me here, for I was not trying to claim that being is nothing but such an abstraction. I was trying to show that this very moment of the non-conceptual, which is indicated by the concept 'being', actually points towards something which, precisely because it is not conceptual, cannot itself be abstract either. On the other side, however, we have already described the mechanism of abstraction as constitutive for the possibility, for the meaningful constitution, of 'being'. And, if that is so, beings would indeed, in this sense, be prior with respect to being, just as we find with the τόδε τι [tode ti] in Aristotle.

Now you can see here how the distinctive Eleatic and Platonic dualism, or the Eleatic and Platonic ambivalence with regard to being, still reaches into the purest philosophy of the Greek enlightenment. For in addition to this interpretation of τὸ ὄν [to on], or beings, of πρώτη οὐσία [prōtē ousia] as the τόδε τι [tode ti], we also find a doctrine that is directly opposed to it: the authentically Platonic doctrine of the priority of the Idea, the priority of the concept, over against the individual things that are encompassed by it. These two opposed conceptions of what is first or primary, of the πρῶτον [prōton], in Aristotle are possible – and Aristotle's philosophy is certainly *prima philosophia*, a philosophy that attempts to discover what is utterly primary – precisely because they are grounded in that peculiar ambiguity which belongs to the talk of being itself. For, on the one hand, being is meant to be the comprehensive concept for all the beings that are, so that beings are primary, and being is derived from that. On the other hand, being is what is meant to recall what stands behind any and every conceptuality, what is not exhausted in concepts, what, in the language of ancient thought, exists φύσει [phusei] rather than θέσει [thesei]. In other words, that which is not itself the result of our classifying operations of the mind, and to which priority can in turn be ascribed over against the τόδε τι [tode ti] or over against particular ὄντα [onta]. It is only this ambiguity in Aristotle's question concerning the concept τὸ ὄν [to on] that really explains this strange turn in the argument. The explanation which Aristotle himself offers for this ambivalence, as it happens, is remarkable because it sounds incredibly modern. This is because it is the kind of explanation which effectively prevails throughout the subsequent history of Western thought wherever the philosophical problem of genesis and validity is involved. For in one place Aristotle says that the πρώτη οὐσία [prōtē ousia] in the didactic sense, the first thing we become aware of, is precisely the τόδε τι [tode ti], whereas in itself or objectively, according to the *ordo rerum* – independently of the way we come to it or rise to it by way of experience – it is the actual ontological concept of being that enjoys priority. This distinction is in fact that of genesis and validity;[2] it is the distinction which attempts to deal with aporetic concepts, with the difficulties involved in such a central concept as being, by specifically distinguishing the process through which we come to form such concepts in the first place from the validity of these concepts as such. This is a conception that was emphatically revived by Husserl, for his theory of abstraction expressly maintains that the prior ideal unity of the species has nothing to do with the processes of abstraction through which, as thinking individuals, we actually arrive at them. Max Scheler in particular then took up this distinction and turned it into a dualism by going on to construct two worlds, a genetic-empirical one and a pure ontological one, which are supposed to have nothing to do with each other – until this rather disconcerting philosophical division of labour in relation to origin and truth finally dissatisfied him so much that he turned to the vitalist metaphysics of his later period.[3] I draw this to your attention here only because this distinction between genesis and validity implicitly plays a certain role in Heidegger as well. For his work always shows a tendency to separate the nominalist moment of thought – the moment which produces concepts as abstractions from the facts which they cover – from the properly ontological level and present it as something pre-ontological. And this in spite of the fact that the point of Heidegger's project – and it is good to remember this if you wish to understand the specific difference of Heidegger's thought as the most influential form of ontology today in comparison to earlier ontological approaches – is precisely this: what Heidegger believes he has discovered in his region of being, in what he expressly addresses as being, is not a dimension of validity, a dimension of the logical in itself, which as pure logic would enjoy priority over any process of genesis. On the contrary, in one extremely perceptive passage[4] he has even clearly shown that logical absolutism on the one side – which turns this dimension of validity into an absolute – and psychologism along with the positivist theory of genesis on the other are essentially complementary and fit perfectly with one another. So you must actually try and understand the specific character of Heidegger's approach if you really want to understand the nature of my argument with it. For he specifically believes not only that the concept of being provides him with the ontological counter-pole to the ontic domain but also that his concept of being is indeed ἀδιάφορος [adiaphoros], that it is effectively indifferent with regard to both of these dimensions: that of an absolutely fixed and objectified conceptuality and that of beings or entities included under concepts. For it is supposed to be a third perspective, though not of course a third and different sort of principle in addition to others. It is supposed to refer to an order of thought which resides in principle beyond – or, if you prefer, this side of – that dichotomy between the concept existing in itself and some mere ultimate given. Now you will sometimes encounter in Heidegger (in contrast to Husserl or to Scheler in his ontological phase) certain ways of speaking which do not really seem at home in the ontological domain, which you would sooner expect in the domain of genesis. I am thinking, for example, of the concept of origin, which plays an extraordinarily central and important role in his thought, although 'origin' here does not refer to anything temporal within time itself.

On the contrary, it is an emphatically metaphysical concept that refers
to time itself as a temporalizing principle – in other words, to time
itself as an ontological structure rather than to any concrete, specific
or particular temporal relationship of any kind. Here too, however,
it has to be said that these things remain shrouded in a kind of
overwhelming ambiguity. Thus, whenever he talks about origin and
originality, this also always seems to evoke the suspicion that what
lies much further back in time is somehow also more original, and
therefore closer to the truth. However strongly he resists such a doctrine, his whole attack on what he later calls 'metaphysics', namely
subject–object thinking with its objectification of thought and thing
alike, can be understood only in terms of some such archaic turn in
his thinking as a whole – and I believe we can say this without doing
much injustice to him.

If I draw your attention to this archaic moment in Heidegger's
ontology here, this involves a thesis which only confirms the essential
priority of such thinking over all carping, argumentative and merely
rationalistic thought in the eyes of the Heidegger school – which has
transformed the technique of avoiding or withdrawing from certain
questions into one of consummate depth. But it is just here, in this
aspect that I have tried to point out, that you can see, if you consider
this philosophy in its fully developed form, that it would clearly never
endorse anything like the Platonic priority of being qua Idea over the
domain of beings qua τόδε τι [tode ti] or τὰ ὄντα [ta onta]. But at the
same time you can also see, if you really consider the matter in
earnest, that the pathos of this philosophy lies essentially in the contrast between being and beings. In this sense, then, it is really archaic,
for the way in which being is related back to beings, as found in
Aristotle's genetic explanation, is expressly repudiated by Heidegger.
I would like to quote him directly here, since I regard it as an
extremely important thesis, and I shall read you a relevant passage
from *Being and Time* to substantiate this point. Now of course I am
quite sure that an orthodox disciple of Heidegger – though I have no
idea how he himself might respond in this connection – would argue
that he has almost certainly moved beyond this way of putting things.
But then the question how far the text of *Being and Time* can or
cannot be regarded as binding for existential ontology is something
that remains rather unclear. At any rate, on page 27 we read the
following:

> The task of ontology is to set in relief the being of beings and to expli-
> cate being itself. And the method of ontology remains questionable in
> the highest degree as long as we wish merely to consult the historically

transmitted ontologies or similar efforts. Since the term ontology is used in a formally broad sense for this investigation, the approach of clarifying its method by tracing the history of that method is automatically precluded. [*Being and Time*, Stambaugh, p. 26]

Now the concluding and purely phenomenological remarks here are just good old Husserl. For there is the same negative attitude to history in any phenomenological philosophy which is dedicated to the description of essences, like that of Husserl, who once formulated one of the highest principles of his philosophy in the first volume of his Ideas for a *Pure Phenomenological Philosophy* in these terms: 'No stories will be told here.'[5] In this sense, Heidegger certainly belongs to the phenomenological tradition, although that is not the point that I want to explore here. I just want to say en passant that the whole school of Husserl, Scheler and Heidegger showed an eminently justified interest in these issues. For in the kind of socio-cultural historical investigations that built on the work of thinkers such as Wilhelm Dilthey and his school[6] the substantive questions of philosophy were marginalized or replaced by cultural-historical questions as to how certain phenomena came about. In this way the question of how concepts arose, developed and passed away in turn, and the accompanying transformation of philosophy into a kind of philology, eventually came to prevail, until philosophy felt the justified need to resist this and rightly attempted to provide some kind of answer to the questions that have been inherited by philosophy itself. It may have been unnecessary for Heidegger to present these things, which were the subject of polemical debate fifty years earlier, with such tremendous pathos as if this amounted to a wholly new discovery, yet the interest that he was responding to here seems to me quite legitimate. On the other hand, the first sentence we have just quoted demands rather close attention, and I would ask you to consider it very carefully with me. If the later Heidegger has declared[7] that we should do less philosophy and stay truer to the word itself than is usually the case today, then perhaps I may apply this principle to Heidegger himself and explore his very words in the passage in question. Thus he states that the 'task of ontology is to set in relief the being of beings and to explicate being itself ...' Now, if we assume with the tradition that ontology is the science of being, then this sounds entirely plausible. For such a science of being must distinguish its true object, namely being, from beings themselves. But once you postulate that distinctive character which Heidegger ascribes to being, this apparently quite sound methodological demand on the part of the ontologist is by no means as self-evident as it first seems. For if being

itself is neither a pure concept nor any specific being, then the relationship of being to beings belongs thematically to this concept of
being itself as what is intrinsically involved in it. But if instead it is
already decided, or pre-decided, that being is absolutely different
from beings, or is separated from beings by an ontological gulf, then
this is 'begging the question', as they say in English, or committing
a *petitio principii*, to use the apt Latin phrase. In other words, it
actually assumes what is supposed to emerge from the ontological
analysis in the first place, namely: in what way being relates to beings;
whether it is essential to being to become beings; whether being is
mediated with reference to beings or is wholly other than beings;
whether being constitutes a unity with respect to beings or is something else again. All of these problems – which would really have to
form the serious content of any philosophy of being – are already
decided, as if by decree, with this seemingly reasonable and plausible
statement of Heidgger's before the analysis has actually been undertaken. In other words, we are informed in advance that the task is
to explicate being and to set the being of beings into relief. Now this
is all very well and good, but what if part of the meaning of being is
that it *cannot* absolutely be set off against beings? What if, on the
contrary, beings as such *belong* to the meaning of being, as is clearly
suggested by the predicament of ancient philosophy that I have
already outlined for you? How can I then establish in advance the
methodological principle that being must be separated from beings?
For in effect this anticipates, and indeed with a somewhat threatening
gesture, what can only result from the analysis we have been promised, namely the contrast of being and beings. And this postulate,
incidentally, implies a kind of ontological objectification or solidifica-
tion of being over against beings of the sort that Heidegger specifically repudiates in his critique of metaphysics. Indeed this critique
insists that we should not understand the concept of being in this
way merely as a counter-concept to beings and should recognize
instead that it lies outside or beyond this alternative. I have presented
things in the way that I have in order to show you how this kind of
thinking, if we take what it asks of us really seriously – that is, if we
just try to think along with it – certainly lacks the rigour and plausibility it claims and faces the most serious methodological objections. And I believe that we have shown as much.

Now I would like to point out that the question of the relationship
between τὸ ὄν [to on] and τὰ ὄντα [ta onta] is a principal theme in
Husserl's thought, and that Heidegger shows himself to be a faithful
student of Husserl in this regard, for the whole priority of the doctrine of being, the doctrine of universal concepts or the 'ideal unity

of the species', as Husserl puts it, is also something taught by Husserl. Here too the individual fact as the τόδε τι [tode ti] (he even uses this Aristotelian expression), as the actual individuated being presented in the context of time and space, is contrasted with what he calls 'essence', although this is not interpreted in terms of its highest concept. Now Heidegger's method actually reflects this shared outlook, and I think it is really important for us to be clear about this, for I neglected to mention this point before and it needs to be emphasized here. For the method of Heidegger, at least at the level of *Being and Time*, professes to be a phenomenological one. Here I quote from *Being and Time*: 'Ontology is possible only as phenomenology.' And he continues: 'The phenomenological concept of phenomenon, as self-showing, means the being of beings – its meaning, modifications, and derivatives.'[8] If you translate that into Husserlian terms, you have a proposition that Husserl would probably endorse. The task of phenomenology in Husserl's sense is to address the thing purely in its own right, precisely as it presents itself, and ignore as far as possible any further contribution or ingredient (if I may put it like that) on the part of thought. In other words, we must cultivate a passively receptive or intuitive mode of comportment and abandon ourselves completely to the things themselves, thereby discovering a source of indubitable certainty such as we find in the realm of immediate sensory givenness. Now I cannot go into the problems of this theory here but must simply refer you (if you will allow me) to a book which I once wrote about these issues and which I have no desire to go over again right now. I am talking about the *Metacritique of Epistemology*, which, especially in the final chapter, challenges the possibility of categorial intuition in this sense.[9] When Husserl talks of the being of beings, what he means is nothing more than this: when I see an instance of red, such as the red blouse of the lady in the third row, what is given to my intuition is not just this specific red blouse but redness as such. In other words, this intuition of a particular colour exemplifies the species 'red' itself, even if I cannot see any other red blouses in the room which would allow me to recognize redness as a common feature here.[10] I hope you will forgive the triviality of the example. The fact that phenomenology must always appeal to such banal examples is rather symptomatic, as I see it, for this sort of philosophy itself, and I would therefore ask you not to lay this at *my* door. Thus to become aware of the being of beings, for Husserl, is quite simply this: when I see a given red I elevate the redness from this red, as it were, instead of restricting my attention to this limited individuated case of red. But the really decisive twist that Heidegger furnishes here is this: whereas Husserl treats this redness in an entirely innocuous logical fashion, namely as the quintessence of all conceivable shades of red, it is now turned into something independent, is made into a kind of being-in-itself that 'gives itself to me'. Now up to a certain point – and these things are very subtle – this is already prefigured in classical phenomenology, whose method is indeed accepted by Heidegger, as the passage I have quoted indicates. For Husserl says that, if I look at the red blouse, even if, God forbid, there were no other red blouse in the entire world, and no other case of red either, I would still be able to intuit the essence red or redness from this single instance. Now if that were really true – and this is the reason I have been so emphatic on this point against Husserl and expended so much effort on all this – then Heidegger's thought that some form of being *sui generis*, of being in its own right, namely the form of being 'redness', is prior to any particular given red would be plausible. For if there is no such redness in itself, how could I speak of this redness and immediately perceive this redness when I have only a single example in front of me? The move from the immediate perceptibility of this redness towards the being-in-itself of redness, and then, by extension of this method, the move towards the effective independence of being itself with respect to particular beings, is an extraordinarily tempting conclusion. But then, as I would say, it was not really all so bad in Husserl, if you will excuse this rather crude way of putting it. It is certainly true that Husserl liked to talk about ontology, and indeed frequently did so, but what he meant by ontology was basically nothing but the attempt to epitomize the highest regions of specific fields and determine their internal structure. Thus if I consider the highest concepts to which mathematics can aspire, or those of theoretical physics, of pure grammar or of pure logic – and he was always fundamentally interested in pure logic and pure mathematics – and bring these concepts together and determine their structure, their interconnection, their mutual dependence, and so on, then for Husserl that would be the relevant ontology. And this ontology is located in each case within the domain of an already established and developed science which can be related, through reflection on its logical structure, to a certain number of ultimate general concepts, those concepts without which it is allegedly impossible to conceive of the region in question. But it would never have occurred to Husserl that these general logical principles or logically articulated material regions, for which he already introduced the term ontology, would enjoy any sort of absolute independence or would possess a truly ontological character – in other words, that they represented anything more than the structures of the individual sciences and needed justification as ontologies in their own right. And, as soon as Scheler attempted to reinterpret these formal-logical elements that pertain to individual fields into an ontological doctrine of being-in-itself,[11] Husserl was utterly mortified. As in the story of the sorcerer's apprentice, he now exerted all his efforts to quell the spirits he had himself unleashed. And he did so by referring the question concerning the constitution of the individual sciences, and thus also the constitution of the relevant ontologies, right back to the transcendental subject. In other words, Husserl subjected this question to the judgement of reason and thus effectively returned to traditional idealism – while his successors went on to turn the ontology he had conceived in a merely provisional way into ontology in the emphatic sense.

If you are to understand more clearly the transformation involved in the more recent history of the concept of ontology, it is important to see how this talk of ontology, how the recourse to ontology through the analysis of meaning within already constituted regions, was accomplished by Husserl, but also how he ultimately referred the *question of constitution*, of the derivation and justification of these regions and ontologies, back to reason in a quite traditional Kantian way. But this relationship between ontology and subjectivity is subsequently reversed. In Husserl these ontologies, these provisional expressions of the highest classificatory concepts for the particular domains they encompass, are still referred to critical reason, that is, to subjectivity. In his successors, on the other hand, we find the exact opposite. In other words, the categories of subjectivity and constitutive reason are now supposed to depend on the relevant ontologies, namely on the ontological structures which for Husserl were merely secondary and derived in character. And it is this transition that actually defines the turn to ontological philosophy. Though we have to say, and I want you to be really clear about this, that the doctrine of categorial intuition, the notion that we can become aware of something categorial or conceptual in an *immediate* way, already suggests that being-in-itself could also belong to something as categorial, as conceptual, as being ultimately is. And that is why Husserl, with complete consistency, came to subject this idea of categorial intuition to increasing restrictions and effectively demoted it to a merely transitional stage within experience. If we look closely at Husserl's doctrine of categorial intuition, on which the whole of the ensuing ontological development depends, we see that it actually leaves little trace in his own thought.

Ladies and gentlemen, I showed you that, in spite of an attempted original return to the question of being, ontology treats being as what is prior with respect to beings. Let me just close today by offering a thesis which I shall develop in the next session. This is that, once again, we discover here a necessary aporia in this philosophy. For if the priority of being with respect to all beings is *not* defended in the way that ontological philosophy undertakes to do, then a doctrine of being is not actually possible at all. A pure ontology, a doctrine of being as such, is only possible if being is taken to be independent of particular spatio-temporal beings. This doctrine of pure being, at this level of universality, cannot possibly be carried through in any other way, for otherwise it would inevitably have to refer back to something determinate, particular and individual for its significant content. And it would thereby expressly forfeit that character that belongs to it of the χωρίς [chōris], of that separation from all individual, random and finite things. This seems to me the really decisive issue which has led to the hypostasis of the concept of being. And that is precisely what I shall try to show in detail in our next session.

LECTURE 7

6 December 1960

You will recall that last time I read out a passage from the beginning of *Being and Time* and undertook to interpret it for you. I hope I was able to show you how the text already assumed that priority of being with respect to beings that could properly be a *result* only of an analysis such as that provided by fundamental ontology. So I think we are now in a position to approach the problem that I already identified fairly early on in these lectures[1] as the really crucial one in the context of contemporary ontology, namely the problem of so-called ontological difference, and to get a much clearer view of its implications than we were able to do before. If Heidegger does commit the *petitio principii* which I pointed out – in short, if this philosophical approach already anticipates what it claims it will accomplish – that is not merely the consequence of some intellectual blunder or inattentiveness on the author's part. Rather, as in all such logical configurations in philosophy, this reflects a certain need or compulsion rooted in the matter itself. For ontology in the emphatic sense, namely a doctrine of being as such, is impossible unless we can show that being – whatever we may understand by this – is independent of any beings, or is 'what is prior' to any beings, to use the language of *Being and Time*. I should also point out that such a linguistically unattractive expression as the one I have just used – 'what is prior', or *vorgängig* – is not simply the result of an arbitrary decision. On the contrary, the violence that is done to language in such cases reveals something of the aporia of the matter itself. For temporal modes of speech must be avoided here since intra-temporal relations belong to the domain

of beings, and the priority of being with respect to beings is not meant
to be understood as 'the earlier' rather than 'the later' – although
Heidegger's philosophy does change somewhat in this regard, and at
least hardly excludes these suggestions and overtones of *temporal*
priority as rigorously as we might have expected in terms of the argument itself. On the other hand, this priority – or, we could say, this
apriority – of being with regard to beings is not to be taken as a
merely logical one, as this is usually understood in philosophy. For
we are not supposed to be talking about logical or conceptual necessities here but rather about what precedes them, about what can only
be expressed precisely as 'being'. And this difficulty – the problem
that the priority of being is supposed to be neither temporal nor
logical but ontological in character, without its being clear what we
are actually to understand by that – is precisely what compels recourse
to such linguistic formulations as *Vorgängigkeit*. I believe this is really
one of the cardinal points for the entire philosophy of being, for a
doctrine of being is only possible if the priority of being with respect
to beings can itself conclusively be shown. Now when I said that the
problem of 'being and time' is already shaped and anticipated by the
approach of *Being and Time* itself, this was perhaps not entirely fair,
or at least not entirely correct, for this anticipation is based not actually on the arguments that are developed in the work as such but in
the desideratum of ontology itself. To enquire into any ontology as
the doctrine of being already implies the priority of being with respect
to beings, for no such doctrine of being as πρώτη φιλοσοφία [prōtē
philosophia], as a philosophy that precedes and bears everything else,
would otherwise be possible. If even the barest hint of a particular
being, if any determinate being whatsoever, is allowed into this sphere
of being, as a necessary condition of the latter, then we have effectively
conceded what is anathema to this philosophy. For it would make
the doctrine of being itself dependent in a certain way upon beings,
and thus upon something particular that is temporal and spatial in
character, thereby impugning the very priority of the structure of
being which for its part constitutes the claim of ontology as such.

Thus ontology is bound, by definition, to teach the priority of being
with respect to beings. And, given this necessary relationship, the
point of any criticism of a developed ontology cannot be that of
altering certain ontological features or trying to replace them with
different ones. Rather, the point of such criticism in my eyes, a criticism which would investigate the construction of ontology in immanent
terms, already invariably involves – even where the smallest details
of argumentation are concerned – the question regarding the possibility of ontology as such. Any incoherencies, confusions, or mistaken

lines of thought which may arise in particular instances here can only be referred back to the possibility of this discipline itself – instead of attempting to correct them in some way, for the immeasurable and overweening ambition of such a philosophy of being inevitably regards whatever challenges the very concept of being in its purity as an intolerable attack upon itself and must repudiate this in principle. Now it is a remarkable thing that this overweening claim for the priority of being with respect to beings, and which certainly accounts for the distinctive atmosphere of ontology at least in its most influential contemporary form, is something that ontological philosophy has inherited from phenomenology – although its inner consistency has allowed this philosophy to go far beyond what Husserl accomplished. I have already pointed out[2] that all of these philosophies are really heirs to Plato rather than to Aristotle, even though it is actually Aristotle who talks much more about 'being', while Plato speaks more about the Idea or the paradigm of things. And we have now come to the point where you can most clearly recognize the inherent Platonism of the philosophy of being. I am referring to what is known as the problem of $\chi\omega\rho\iota\sigma\mu\acute{o}\varsigma$ [chorismos], or 'separation', in Plato, and which returns in Husserl when he speaks about the 'abyss of meaning',[3] about the utterly unbridgeable difference between the domain of essences on the one hand and that of facts on the other. Now I am sure all of you, or at least many of you, will know that Heidegger's teacher Husserl, in his later period, composed a text, or actually presented a series of lectures, that was subsequently published under the title of 'Cartesian Meditations', or in the original French edition as *Méditations Cartésiennes*.[4] And this serves really well to capture the thematic[5] we are talking about here, namely a certain return to the kind of fundamental reflections on the first principles of philosophy that formed the substance of the seminal text by Descartes.[6] The difference between the Husserlian and Cartesian conception here will give you an extremely clear idea of the infinite expansion of $\chi\omega\rho\iota\sigma\mu\acute{o}\varsigma$ [chorismos] which has since emerged, namely of the gulf between essence and idea on one side and the domain of beings on the other. You all know that the Cartesian philosophy was dualistic in character. And this very dualism has often been taken as a key to basic problems connected with modern thought in its entirety – the dualism between *res extensa* and *res cogitans*, between extended substance and thinking substance, between things in space and the conscious subject. Now there is certainly a *chorismos* in Descartes, and it has frequently and convincingly been shown that the overcoming of the gulf or dualism in question was only possible through the most artificial and somewhat grotesque baroque expedients such as the *influxus physicus*,[7]

namely the special influence of one substance on the other by means
of the pineal gland. The degree to which this rigid Cartesianism, in
spite of the rather scholastic-theological solution that Descartes imagined he was able to maintain, was still regarded as the crucial question
can readily be seen from the history of post-Cartesian rationalism
that we all know. For right up until Kant the rationalist tradition was
nothing but a series of different attempts to mediate between these
rigidly and immediately opposed spheres or principles, between the
reified sphere of real spatio-temporal being and the sphere of thought
itself, or the sphere of pure subjectivity. I do not think I need to
recount these various attempts at mediation in any detail here. The
most well known of these are the pantheistic solution of Spinoza,
which simply proclaims the unity of the one and only substance, and
the 'occasionalism' of Geulincx or Malebranche, which requires recourse
to divine intervention to ground the ongoing relationship between
the two substances in every particular case. Or finally we have the
approach which Leibniz defended in the *Monadology*, namely the
doctrine of the infinitely many substances and the pre-established
harmony as the a priori coordination of these same substances.

Now if you really think about all these approaches, you can see
that what phenomenology has contributed here is an infinite intensi-
fication or radicalization of the claims of *res cogitans* in relation to
res extensa, or, in other words, not so much a mediation between the
two as a deepening of the rupture between them. And one of the
central motivations here is that the consciousness which Descartes
and his successors, including Kant, opposed to everything else as an
essentially intellectual principle – insofar as it unfolds in time and
belongs to individual consciousness – becomes drawn into the sphere
of facticity and factuality. What is more, as factical consciousness, as
concrete, empirical and singular human consciousness, we can only
be conceived as bound to particular spatio-temporal persons. Thus
what in Descartes is still ingenuously described as *res cogitans*, as
something removed from the arbitrary and contingent character of
the merely factical, now in a sense finds itself firmly attached to – and
made dependent upon – that same empirical reality which according
to these idealist and rationalist philosophies is supposed to be constituted by pure mind in the first place. We can say that an enormous
part of what is described as subjectivity, or as the transcendental
sphere in Kant, is to some extent swallowed up in the course of Husserl's logical reflections by that which merely is, by mere spatio-temporal
existence, and that it thus forfeits something of its essential character
as pure thought. We could say that all that remains of subjectivity
– something already implicit in Kant's doctrine of reason qua logical

faculty and quite explicit in Husserl – is just that which is entirely abstract and indeterminate, namely the objective regularity of thought itself. While all the other determinations that also belong to this subjective dimension in Kant, such as a unified personal consciousness in space and time, are then turned, consistently enough, into a piece of the empirical reality which is supposed to be grounded in that subjectivity in the first place for Kant. Thus you arrive at a rather paradoxical point here, a point of *Umschlag* or reversion, to which I particularly wish to draw your attention, since to some extent I believe it offers an illustration of the distinctive objectivity which gets ascribed to being in ontological philosophy. For if everything that is individuated in time and space is written off by the concept of constitutive or transcendental subjectivity, then whatever remains on the side of *res cogitans* – namely pure possibility and the logical regularity to which this possibility is subject – is no longer really anything subjective at all, but nothing more than a kind of objectivity. The subject finds itself so reduced, so divested of all those aspects and features through which it becomes an 'I', through which we can give any rational meaning whatsoever to the word 'I', that it eventually forfeits its I-hood altogether and becomes an objectivity at the second level. And it is only because it has been made into just such an objectivity that it can take on that exaggerated purity which allegedly allows it to furnish a priori or, with Heidegger, ontological structures. In his later period Husserl struggled to overcome the difficulty involved in the idea of pure essence as a pure thought from which any actual process of thinking has been removed by recourse to the doctrine of the *eidos ego*.[8] Thus he now attempted to bring transcendental subjectivity, or the constitutive subjectivity of idealist thought, into specific relationship with the realm of pure essence, albeit by means of a highly elaborate philosophical construction. And his motivation is understandable here, for so much of the transcendental in Kant is actually bound up with the realm of factual existence, and the primacy of thought itself is also threatened if every trace of subjectivity is simply eliminated. But Husserl does not actually succeed in justifying this philosophical construction. I cannot undertake here to analyse precisely why he fails in this regard but must simply (if you will forgive the professional gesture) draw your attention to the fact that I have already tried to develop a detailed argument to this effect in the final chapter of my book *Metacritique of Epistemology*.[9] In any case, Heidegger's philosophy tacitly presupposes the radicalization of the χωρισμός [chorismos] that I mentioned before, along with that reversion of a transcendentally grounded subjectivity into something quite objective which transpires once the subjectivity in question

is deprived of the last trace of the object, namely of the object in the
subject.[10] And what Heidegger calls being, and what we can indeed
actually grasp only in this extremely tentative and, as I would say,
dynamic way, namely through the force field of philosophical concepts
rather than by immediate recourse to some drastic claim – this is
ultimately nothing but a pure state of affairs which is presented independently of all actual existence, including the actual existence of
thinking and personality, and as utterly prior to all this. But in contrast
to the good old subjectivity we know, this state of affairs can no
longer be defined or determined at all, for any determination we might
try and ascribe to it would simply be redirected in one way or another
to the realm of beings. And this philosophy is indeed extraordinarily
touchy and sensitive in this regard – and rightly so, I have to say. For
it clearly realizes that the barriers are down once I bring any particular
being, however slight, into consideration – once I attempt, in other
words, to determine being itself by reference to anything that would
be reducible to beings. For then we cannot just stay with this one
particular spatio-temporal being but would basically have to take up
– as the great philosophers from Plato to Hegel have indeed taken
up – the entire realm of beings, in all its objective riches and abundance, into the content of philosophy itself. And that is what this
whole philosophy from Husserl to Heidegger most fears in all the
world.

Let me repeat the point: this kind of trans-subjectivity, which is all
that remains of the subject once it is reduced to pure essence, furnishes
the model for Heidegger's concept of being. The abandonment of the
empirical dimension in phenomenology – which actually goes so far
as to ascribe all substantive content whatsoever, and not just psychological phenomena, to this dimension – is what leads to a kind of
allergy towards beings in general where fundamental ontology is concerned. And if you really wish to understand what motivates fundamental ontology, and if you also wish to reflect personally on what
it is that many of you surely find so tempting about fundamental
ontology – or at least once found so tempting about it before you
were prompted to pursue these somewhat unwelcome reflections along
with me here – then I believe we must look to this distinctive allergy,
as I have called it. For it is a philosophy, if you will permit me this
psychological image, which rather reminds us of those people (and
they are not that uncommon) who feel a constant compulsion to wash
their hands. It is a philosophy which is terrified at the thought of
getting its hands dirty, which would dearly like to exclude from itself
all that is ephemeral, all that might be otherwise, all that reminds us
of what is somehow base or lowly, of the merely material character

of the senses. Now you will constantly hear that this philosophy is essentially quite different from all 'idealism' – and I am myself the last person to minimize the differences in relation to idealism here; and indeed I think I amply recognized this aspect when I pointed out how transcendental subjectivity reverted to a kind of objectivity of the second level. But in this marked sensitivity or allergy towards beings, which regards them as some sort of contamination, here at least we discover a complete unanimity between fundamental ontology and idealism in its Fichtean or Schellingian form. On the other hand, if I may just mention this by way of anticipation, since it properly belongs to our subsequent reflections when we turn to the question of dialectics, it is one of the decisive distinctions between Hegel and the other idealists that he does not actually share this allergy. If I may return to the psychological analogy, it is as if Hegel already knew what Karl Kraus would say when he was accused of getting his hands dirty all the time by hanging around with blackmailers and low-minded journalists. Kraus replied that, if we get our hands dirty, we can always wash them again.[11] It is better to become involved in things than to hover above some lower reality at the cost of refusing to engage with it or to expose ourselves to it. And something of the atmosphere which is evoked in these words of Karl Kraus can already be found in the Hegelian dialectic. This is exactly what is captured by the idea of *Entäusserung*, or self-exposure, of venturing out beyond the pure Idea for the sake of its own realization.

Now we could certainly engage in lengthy speculation about what has produced this allergy in the face of beings. I am assuming something here – though I wouldn't want you to write this straight down, for otherwise you will reproach me with showing my hand too early and with rushing all too precipitately into the midst of beings myself, whereas the actual transition to the domain of beings, or the demonstration of the necessity for such a transition, still lies before us. What I mean is that this peculiar allergy which pervades philosophy, but which has probably never been as acute as it is in these ontological philosophies, arises from the memory that our existence depends upon bodily labour and actually lives from such labour. But, in spite of this, up until very recent developments, bodily labour was itself looked down upon as something demeaning or even base. And anything that might recall this distinctive involvement on the part of labour with the level of mere being, with the merely natural, is repressed in the medium of thought. And the priority of what we call mind or spirit over the material world on which it lives and depends is once again consolidated and transfigured through this allergy, which now effectively decrees the absolute purity of all that is mental or spiritual as the domain of true being in contrast with the mere domain of beings. For that ideal of purity on the part of being, which grounds the pathos or, as I would call it, the religious or theological aura of fundamental ontology, is something *borrowed*. And here I would ask you to take this thought in full seriousness and continue to think about it carefully. For it is the thought of a sphere of mind or spirit which fundamental ontology has allegedly left behind and already consigned to speculative metaphysics as a kind of intellectual aberration. Now there is something about this particular attitude that I would describe as mythical,[12] a certain fear lest the slightest hint of something beyond our own principle might already suffice to threaten or dislodge the entire authority or dominion of what we are, namely the authority of the mind, of the mind as 'in-group', if I may express this in sociological terms. Thus fundamental ontology relates to the domain of beings in like manner to the wicked stepmother in the story of Snow White. For while the queen is indeed the fairest one of all 'here', in her own immeasurable kingdom, somewhere else far away, beyond the mountains with the Seven Dwarfs, there lives one who is fairer than she.[13] And this little thing proves unbearable for fundamental ontology, precisely because such thinking, in a kind of manic or even paranoid extremity, is driven again and again to expel any trace of anything that might recall the realm of beings, to eliminate anything of the kind and run the danger of becoming so abstract in the end that no such trace remains. At the same time I have no desire whatsoever to dismiss or belittle that aspect which largely accounts for the pathos and the passion of this philosophy. For there is indeed something right about the anxiety in question here, one which actually reveals the crux of this whole philosophy at this point. For as soon as we pass on to beings in however inconspicuous a manner – and this is the tremendous significance of that radicalized χωρισμός [chorismos] that is accomplished by Husserl and Heidegger – and as soon as we relate the determinations of being to any aspect or feature of beings, we are at a loss to answer the question as to why we should stop with *this* being in particular, and why we should not take up beings into philosophy in all their fullness and abundance as well. In other words, Snow White from beyond the mountains, unless she is done away with, can step into the carriage with her prince the very next day and enter into the city, while the stepmother can dance herself to death in red-hot shoes, or meet whatever pleasant fate mythology has decreed for such cases. And something of this feeling prevails in fundamental ontology. In other words, if I may put this in a very extreme form, at the very moment when philosophy acknowledges beings *as* beings – in place of the abstract category of beings in general – we have already renounced the form in which all traditional philosophy appears. There is no longer any such thing as *prima philosophia*.

In terms of the history of philosophy, this excessive χωρισμός [chorismos] and essential purity, which has ultimately led to the concept of being, is the response to positivism and nominalism. For positivism and nominalism alike, if I may put this in a rather exaggerated form, all that is left now is beings, while the concept has been dropped. Of course I am well aware that this is an exaggeration, although the old nominalist definition of the 'word' as *flatus vocis*, as a mere flutter of the voice, gave the game away in this regard right at the beginning of this philosophical development. For even nominalist and positivist philosophies, of course, cannot manage without concepts, and the fact that they cannot do so reveals both the impossibility of reducing concepts entirely to beings and that of reducing beings to being. But we can still say that concepts thereby forfeit the independence they once enjoyed, that they eventually become nothing but counters which no longer possess any content in their own right. In this way they effectively become little more than pointers to specific cases of sensuous experience, to whatever actually happens to come along, although this is treated as redundant once it is cashed in and factual experience furnishes sufficient material to decide on the validity of concepts and judgements that simply appear to belong to the conceptual sphere. It is very important to realize here that this positivist development has proved tremendously influential, and indeed far more so than is really recognized in Germany and the general consciousness that prevails here. Nonetheless, I would suggest that this attitude will actually change soon enough. For this is all bound up with what people like to call the integration of the West, and in a very short time we shall see that positivism will spread and emerge triumphant in Germany as well, very much as it has already done in other Western European countries. But I simply make these remarks in passing here. I would be more than happy if my reflections could at least manage to throw some sand into the machine, although there will soon be far too many professors of analytic philosophy around for this to work for long. But, whatever happens in this regard, the attempt to preserve that which has been forgotten, that which has been suppressed by the tremendous power of positivism – namely the independence of conceptual thought itself – will be as isolated and neglected in a philosophy, such as Heidegger's, which fails to mediate thought with the domain of beings, as it is in positivism, which fails to mediate the domain of beings with thought. I believe it is really important for you to recognize, if you wish to do justice to the depth of reflection

which drove Heidegger to adopt this approach, that this polemical
emphasis upon the aspect of χορισμός [chorismos] prevents the essential dimension of what was once called the mind from simply disap-
pearing from view, but also isolates it at the same time. And this very
isolation turns it into something immediate, and through this immediacy, I am tempted to say, once again into a kind of material stuff.
Now the concept of being in this new ontology does have a rather
peculiar and almost material character, or I would even say a kind
of hylozoic character.[14] For being is indeed what is not subject, what
would not be subject at any cost, yet acts in all kinds of ways and
has all kinds of things ascribed to it. Thus being is said to 'illuminate
itself' and 'unconceal itself', and God knows what else, in language
that we usually apply only to a subject. And this whole structure of
thought closely resembles the kind of archaic thinking which ascribes
various activities or teleological tendencies of one sort or another to
certain material substances precisely because such thinking has never
isolated the concept of stuff as such. The ψεῦδος [pseudos] or actual
untruth of ontological philosophy is not that it maintains the independent aspect of conceptual thought with respect to what it subsumes.
On the contrary, this philosophy is true precisely as a corrective, to
use Kierkegaard's language,[15] in relation to positivist thought and has
rightly grasped something essential here. The ψεῦδος [pseudos] consists
in the way that this aspect or moment ceases to be a moment, that
the necessary mediations are forgotten, and that the principle in question is itself turned into something immediate. We could therefore
say, once again in a rather paradoxical fashion, that, while Heidegger
constantly challenges reification by warding off any contamination
of beings with being, or rather of being with beings, the thinking
itself is a reified and fetishized consciousness insofar as it establishes
the intrinsically mediated concept, which points ineluctably towards
the non-conceptual, as an absolute, and struggles laboriously to repudiate and forget these aspects of mediation.[16] At the same time – and
here I would like to close and carry on with this next time, so that
you will be able to appreciate the whole of the complex landscape
involved – this pure being is not supposed to be an issue of essence,
a question of *essentia*, for that would only presuppose the very divorce
of essence and fact which is contested as anathema here. And the
peculiar paradox which brings this philosophy to nothing lies in the
way that being is supposedly neither a being nor an essence, but a
third possibility beyond both. Yet if we were to describe it as such a
third, we would roundly be told it is not that either – so that we can
eventually come to no other conclusion than that it is indeed precisely
nothing.

LECTURE 8

8 December 1960

You will recall the analysis of the problem of ontological difference which I attempted to present for you earlier. I explained why, in spite of the doctrine that being or the concept of being is allegedly prior to the conceptual and the domain of beings, we actually find that ontological difference is already decided in favour of being in the sense of concept or idea. And I explained the way in which this claim to priority turns out to be unjustified. I should say that, at this point of course, as in all these matters, we discover something of the most tremendous significance, which is that the fundamental division of subject and object which appears as the last word in all congealed or reified thinking cannot actually be the last word at all. And this is something that Kant repeatedly acknowledged in all those passages in the *Critique of Pure Reason* where he alluded to the need to discover a common root both for the sphere of intuition which is concerned with existing things and for the conceptual sphere of the categories. We have good historical reason for regarding the separation into subject and object, and thereby all the dualisms and rigid antitheses with which consciousness typically likes to work, as something which has actually come to be. We know there have been whole strata of thought in which these dualisms have never occurred. And the difficulties encountered by Western thought in even trying to understand the speculations of the Far East are surely bound up with the fact that Far Eastern thought, and perhaps all non-occidental thought, is not couched in terms of this dualism, of this fixed structure of subject and object. If this division or separation itself has emerged historically, we have some reason to think it may not be permanent, that this gulf might yet be closed – though it is an open question whether that can only happen once it is closed in reality, once reality is reconciled with itself, or whether philosophy can somehow anticipate this. And it is certainly true that fundamental ontology recognizes something of this. It also has to be said that this realization that dualism should not be regarded as definitive or absolute is precisely what motivated those tendencies of idealist philosophy which often prove most offensive to the contemporary mind. Here I am thinking for example of Schelling's doctrine of intellectual intuition as an immediate unity of subject and object, or also of Hegel's dialectic insofar as it always takes the object to be subjectively constituted and the subject to be objectively constituted at all levels. And I would just add that the extraordinary influence that has been exercised by fundamental ontology is surely connected with a certain loss of cultural continuity in relation to the philosophical tradition. Or, to put this less grandiosely, we could say that certain ideas – like the notion that 'being' somehow has to reach back behind the division between the concept, that which is merely thought, and the concretely material – could come to exert the enormous effect that they have only because, in the general wake of modern Western positivism, earlier philosophies had rather fallen into oblivion beyond the extremely narrow circle of what we like to call 'professional' philosophers, amongst whom this whole problematic is still alive. And it is surely not the least attractive feature of fundamental ontology that it manages to talk about these things without assuming any significant background knowledge. In other words, this ontology acts as if the relevant problematic could be addressed in an immediate fashion if thought simply immerses itself in 'being' – and underestimates the historical dimension of all these things in the process. And if I take the view – as I have made emphatically clear in another context – that what is ancient, what is handed down to us from the historical past, can only be understood from the perspective of the substantial and compelling experience of our current situation, then the reverse is certainly also true. In other words, this intensified form of the philosophical problematic that is expressed in the word 'being' can only really be understood, can only amount to more than a kind of verbal magic, when we see how the problematic of philosophy already leads in this direction in terms of its own rigorous and internal logic. And it is also one of the tasks of these lectures to draw your attention to this point and help you to realize its full significance. For it also implies, amongst other things, that certain vulgar objections which have been raised against fundamental ontology and Heidegger in particular – and here I would

simply mention Carnap's famous critique as a typical example[1] –
essentially reflect the charge that this philosophy is unintelligible.
Now if we actually take this philosophy as it presents itself in the
first instance – and that is what I was alluding to when I spoke of
verbal magic here – that is, if we take this philosophy as if it promises
in an utterly immediate fashion to reveal certain mysteries purely in
and of itself, then we cannot evade this apparent aspect of unintelligibility. In other words, we shall be confronted with a whole pile of
concepts with regard to which we no longer know what we are actually supposed to picture or 'represent' to ourselves, to borrow an
expression from Hegel's polemic with his contemporaries. But when
we really recognize these difficulties in their internal and necessary
relationship to the problematic that has been handed down by philosophy, to the continuing process of thought itself, I will not exactly
say that we can instantly fulfil, as it were, all of the concepts in question. For where philosophical concepts are concerned that is often
quite impossible. In Kant too there are many concepts where we have
to ask what precisely it is that we are supposed to think when we
use them. And when we look for whatever it is that corresponds to
them we find again and again that this eludes us. Yet in many cases
we also discover that philosophical understanding is not a matter of
translating concepts into corresponding facts or states of affairs at
all; rather, it is a question of translating concepts into *problems*. In
other words, it is a matter of realizing what has driven us to formulate
a specific concept, of recognizing what is effectively postulated in the
formulation of a specific concept such as, in this case, that of 'being'.
And here I would like to help you by attempting – as I tried to do in
the last session – to bring a specific historical dimension, in this case
the epistemological problematic of phenomenology, into the heart of
our discussion of fundamental ontology.

Now, after all that I have just explained, you may be tempted to
say: Well, if you yourself assume the possibility of some such unifying
moment, which you have criticized so much in Heidegger, then why
don't you actually permit this in Heidegger's case? And I believe the
answer to this question, which you have every right to expect, is
indeed the central issue here. For we can indeed recognize the limited
and provisional, and even illusory, character of a certain intellectual
tendency or tradition, such as the dualistic or dichotomous mentality
which has existed since antiquity, just as Heidegger has done. Yet
since the process which has led to this mentality also has a rigour of
its own, we cannot simply conclude from the problems involved in
this dualistic separation that, to put it very crudely, we can just try
to turn the wheel or the clock back. We can certainly argue that this

emphatic opposition, let us say, between material stuffs or substances on the one side and principles on the other – as this was played out in the intellectual labours of the pre-Socratic thinkers, in the archaic hylozoistic philosophies of the Ionians – did actually lead to the loss of something. For the dimension of the numinous, the element of mana,[2] the awe bordering on horror which was experienced in the face of the world as a whole – or however we put it, since these are all rather kitsch expressions, and the fact that we really have no other expressions at our disposal is extremely telling in itself – has effectively been expelled from the world, and this does entail a certain loss. And this loss is registered in Heidegger's expressions about the loss of being and the forgetfulness of being. But this still does not allow us to regress to such archaic theses. Now, of course, if Heidegger were confronted with the claim that we can no longer sustain the idea that the whole world consists essentially of air or water because the natural sciences have taught us otherwise, he would undoubtedly reply that we would thereby simply be misrepresenting the ancient Ionians, such as Anaximenes or Thales, about whom we really know so little. For far from making the kind of claims we associate with the natural sciences, they were saying something about 'being' as that which is allegedly prior to any split between conceptual principle and the particular material character of things. But I would say in response that the change in human consciousness that we associate with the rise of science, and which had already led thinkers in antiquity to postulate something as abstract as the 'being' of Parmenides or the 'becoming' of Heraclitus rather than some material stuff as the most universal principle of all, had made itself felt long before the explicit emergence of developed scientific thinking and had already forced philosophy itself to look for a new principle. And this was simply because the material dimension in the hylozoistic philosophies had shown itself to be limited and limiting, and in a sense capricious, in character. Thus one thinker appealed to 'water' and another to 'air', while Empedocles invoked all of the four 'elements', and one could carry on like this in a basically random way. And the arbitrary aspect of all this rightly motivated the really bold and radical speculative minds amongst the ancient philosophers to develop those much more abstract unifying principles which for their part now specifically furnished the model for the concept of being. Now I believe these things are very important if we are to grasp the situation in which this thinking arises. For they reveal that what fundamental ontology treats as if it constituted a kind of ontological Fall or original sin is not something that is arbitrarily or externally visited upon being, or the thinking of being, by an intellectual process of reflection, but is something that was motivated by what those concepts essentially touch upon. In other words, if we suffer today from this division, from this rigid separation of dualistically opposed moments, whether we call them subject and object, or conceptuality and actual beings, or however we describe them, if we suffer from such ossified antitheses, and become aware at every step of their own inadequacy – in the inadequate character of the business of science itself, for example – then the possibility of any reconciliation here surely cannot lie in a forced attempt to restore a stage of consciousness that has already effectively been abandoned. Rather, if the distress of this separation continues to be felt, this can only encourage us to think this dualism through to the end, to overcome these rigidly opposed moments by reflection upon the very reflection that has produced them.

In terms of the problem we are talking about here, that is precisely what defines the problem of dialectics. And in this connection I have already allowed myself to develop a fundamental line of thought which will show you why it is necessary to contrast dialectical thinking with ontological thinking. I should also add, however, that so far I have indicated only the necessity for thinking dialectically rather than ontologically in a merely formal way or, we might say, merely in terms of certain philosophical reflections on history.[3] But I have not yet really begun to provide what I promised you at the beginning – something which I certainly intend to do in what follows. For I need to show you precisely how the necessity for dialectical thinking itself arises specifically from the substantive problems and concerns, from the inner problematic, of the philosophy of being. But we can only accomplish this once we have entered into this philosophy much more deeply. And let me just say that 'being' really remains hanging in a rather indefinite relationship to the domain of conceptuality here – for let me remind you once again that being, for reasons I already analysed in some detail last time, must not be regarded as a being or entity of any kind. Thus in the *Introduction to Metaphysics*, one of Heidegger's later texts, we read the following on page 31 (and although he puts this in a hypothetical fashion here, you will clearly see where this is leading. I could easily have found other more direct textual evidence as well):

> But now the question is whether the assessment of being as the most universal concept reaches the essence of being, or whether it so misinterprets being from the start that questioning becomes hopeless. The question is whether being can count only as the most universal concept that is unavoidably involved in all particular concepts, or whether being has a completely different essence, and thus is anything but the object of an 'ontology', if one takes this word in its established meaning.[4]

It is very clear from this formulation that Heidegger certainly inclines
to this latter way of putting it – that is, to the idea, as he says, that
being has a 'completely different essence' from any concept whatsoever.
And right there you actually have the whole aporia that I have tried
to present to you as the essence, indeed as the dynamic essence, of
this conception of being. For you have now recognized the specific
character of this concept of being in both of its aspects: on the one
side it cannot signify beings regarded as a whole, cannot simply be
taken as an objectification of the 'is', of *existentia*; on the other side
it is not to be regarded as a concept or as mere universality either.
For, in contrast to the realm of conceptuality, it is supposed to enjoy
the wealth of significance and the kind of objective character that we
generally ascribe only to what actually exists. Thus we see how one
side effectively lives off the other here, how one always borrows
something from the other, although the debt is never paid back. In
other words, it is precisely from beings themselves that the concept
'being' borrows that concreteness, wealth and objective character
which concepts otherwise lack; while this moment that is borrowed
from beings now borrows in turn from being, thus helping itself to
that essential, universally binding and unforfeitable character which
contrasts with the contingency of the things that simply exist. Now
if these two moments are inseparable, and if in such inseparability
this mode of thinking emphatically, deliberately and archaically resists
the differentiating movement of thought, this even serves a good
functional purpose. For the inseparability of both elements here already
means, whenever we try and pin one of them down on either side,
that such thinking can always claim that this is not what it meant to
say at all, and that we are thereby simply failing to enter the dimension of being in the first place. One is thus secured on every side, and
this very inseparability, this lack of articulation, already affords pro-
tection to such thinking, allowing it to spurn everything that does
not bow to its claims. For the separation into being and beings, into
the domain of the conceptual and the domain of beings – which is
maintained throughout the history of metaphysics, for which indeed
Heidegger shows such disdain – would already open up this concept
of being to critique.

Critique is actually nothing but a process of distinguishing, a process
of confronting different aspects or moments in order to see whether
the conceptual moment is genuinely fulfilled in its respective objects,
whether it is an empty or a legitimate conceptuality, namely one to
which something corresponds; and, on the other hand, it is a confrontation of the realm of beings, of what is there, with the concept. In
other words, we must ask, like Hegel, how far something that exists

corresponds or answers to its concept, namely whether that which merely exists is actually what it purports to be. This process of distinguishing varying and contrasting aspects or moments is the critical element par excellence. And if Heidegger's philosophy in its entirety is essentially anti-critical – rather in the sense that certain contemporary sociologists describe their orientation as anti-Enlightenment[5] – then we can even trace this back to the philological roots of the concept of critique itself. Now I do not actually share Heidegger's fondness for invoking philological considerations in order to elucidate issues supposedly connected with 'being'. And we shall certainly come to my reasons for eschewing this approach in due course. But it is a very remarkable thing, and I cannot resist reminding those of you with a knowledge of Greek in this connection that the etymology of the word 'critique' refers back directly to the idea of separating or distinguishing things, specifically to the verb κρίνειν [krinein] – thus κρίνω [krinō] means 'I distinguish'. And insofar as the thinking of being basically brands such distinguishing thought as the original sin of thinking, it sets its face, even in explicitly philological terms, against 'critical' thinking itself. Indeed, as far as I can see, the concept of critique has no place in Heidegger's philosophy at all. And this particular philological reflection is never pursued in his thought. Thus 'being' is neither τὰ ὄντα [ta onta], the domain of beings themselves, nor that of the concept. When he says in the passage we have just quoted that being has a 'completely different essence', he certainly does not want us to think that it is some additional third or distinct term. For it is supposedly prior to any and every distinction, in accordance with archaic thought where the distinction of being and beings is not yet reflectively established. Thus being would be a kind of essence in which being and beings are as yet undistinguished. This naive and unreflective character of archaic thought is then equated with what is original and thus also higher in kind. If Heidegger's philosophy actually reveals itself in countless variations as anti-intellectualist in character, and to that extent takes up the legacy of all those irratio-nalist tendencies in philosophy which have emerged from the most varied quarters, such as Nietzsche, Bergson, Simmel and Dilthey, this irrationalism or anti-intellectualism itself is also, if I might put it this way, still systematically motivated. In other words, since this philosophy repudiates the separating and distinguishing aspect of thought precisely because, as a function of the intellect or the reflective understanding, it fails to do justice to the concept of being, the devaluation of this dimension inevitably leads to the devaluation of the very capacity for making such distinctions. And if the concept of being manages to elude any closer definition or determination through its various infinitely elaborate techniques of defence and avoidance, and thereby also any real confrontation with the question regarding the truth or falsity of any pronouncements about being, we also discover on the subjective side a corresponding defamation of the kind of approach which is capable of drawing such distinctions. Yet there is an exceedingly high price to be paid for all this. And it is exceedingly high even when measured immanently in terms of this philosophy itself. For the determinations which correspond to this substrate or this absolute – and I believe that the expression 'absolute', drawn of course from German Idealism, is still the best word of all to capture what is ultimately at issue here – or, rather, the way in which this substrate or absolute is effectively exempted from any determination – something which would merely limit it or prevent it from being absolute at all – leads only to its complete impoverishment. In other words, it can lead only to what I already intimated to you earlier when I said we end up with something which in an emphatic sense can no longer actually be thought at all. And indeed the highly elaborate and sophisticated apologetic techniques developed by this kind of thinking reveal only how it lends this poverty and indeterminacy a certain dignity of its own. Thus, in the *Letter on 'Humanism'*, Heidegger talks expressly about how thought must descend into the poverty of its provisional essence[6] – as if the poverty in question were the fruit of a salutary renunciation by which thought might escape every merely reified, superficial and illusory conceptual determination in order one day, perhaps, in the monastic cell to which it has withdrawn, to recover its earlier abundance, even if this very recovery is then always postponed indefinitely. But what is so troubling here is just that this promise – the promise that being will discover that abundance within itself only once it has endured this poverty – remains unfulfilled. And indeed it must remain unfulfilled, for every attempt actually to determine this being on one side or the other would only compromise it, either through contamination with conceptuality or through contamination with beings themselves, which is also unacceptable.

I would like to take this opportunity of warning you about something in particular, both in your academic work and in your intellectual life more generally, and this not just in the context of fundamental ontology but also in the immediately contrasted realm of the special or positive sciences. What I mean is that you should beware when people defer everything and say that what really matters about something is not what it has achieved so far but what it will surely accomplish one day. I believe that, whenever you encounter a postponement of this kind, you will find that certain aporias or structural impossibilities that are already prescribed by the matter in question are simply being cosmetically disguised, that what cannot be accomplished by virtue of the matter in question is simply being put off to the future. Thus in empirical sociology we are constantly assured that we must naturally go out and gather an enormous amount of average material data, of an average conceptual level, but that finally, once we have spent long enough gathering it, we might just arrive at a *theory* of society.[7] It is basically very similar to the 'poverty of being' into which thought must allegedly withdraw if it is to partake, God knows *how*, in the undiminished abundance of being. Now precisely that approach which presumes to piece society together from innumerable individual observations and the way they are classified cannot actually get to the concept of society at all, for it already excludes the idea that there is such a thing as a concept of society. Now it is characteristic of this whole way of thinking that it makes a virtue out of necessity. In other words, precisely what thought has failed to accomplish, the defects and negative features that it involves, everything that it cannot resolve, all of this, in an extremely bold and clever move, is now reinterpreted as if it were actually a higher form of positivity. We might almost say, from this point of view, that fundamental ontology is a parody of the dialectic, for it pursues a kind of positive negation in the sense that, if this philosophy is deficient or lacking in something, this very lack becomes a mark of distinction, becomes something positive and, above all, even an emblem of higher dignity. The abstractness to which being is aporetically condemned is stylized and transmuted through the supposedly concrete character of this monastic life of thought as if it represented some greater immediacy and proximity with respect to what 'authentically' is.

Let me simply add to these preliminary observations something that I may in principle have mentioned earlier – and we are now rapidly reaching the end of these observations before we proceed to an analysis of what I call the ontological need[8] – but which can be expressed again more precisely at this point. I mean that, in spite of that return to the origin which Heideggerean thought claims to accomplish, it cannot actually escape its own historical situation; in other words, that the very reflection in terms of subjectivity which it presumes to overcome as an immediate proclamation from the heart of being nonetheless still makes itself felt in its own method and mode of thought. And in fact Heidegger has not really attempted to deny this. Here I would merely draw your attention to two decisive categories at work in this philosophy where this is rather evident. In the first place I am referring to the analysis of the meaning of words, which, precisely as *intentio obliqua*, implies reference to the realm of consciousness. For the meanings of words also always necessarily involve something which is subjectively instilled in them, and, by pursuing the philosophy of language as emphatically as Heidegger does, the idea of a speaker is also necessarily implied here. Heidegger is driven to grant absolute significance to language as such precisely because he has to abolish by force this moment of subjective reflection that creeps into his own philosophy at the hands of language. And that is precisely what leads him simply to hypostasize language – in other words, to say that being speaks directly and immediately in language itself without being mediated by human beings. And the second way in which subjectivity comes into play is the pre-eminent position accorded to man. Heidegger expresses this in the *Letter on 'Humanism'* by saying that being is 'illuminated' in man, and that man is the 'clearing of being'.[9] This ultimately suggests the old and quite traditional philosophical claim that everything that exists is inevitably mediated by consciousness. And this mediation here appears as the self-illumination of the matter itself. But once again we are presented with a kind of trick, since the character of subjectivity is itself interpreted as if it were something objective and is now, in a certain sense, thrust back into 'being'. This subjective character is thus turned into a determination of being, and being is reflected within itself in terms of that moment we otherwise describe as subjectivity. And here, of course, is where we encounter a difficulty within this philosophy, for the ontological interest which (as I have tried to explain for you) is basically *objectively* directed – and I specifically use this word here, although it would certainly be offensive to Heidegger – is actually incompatible with subjective reflection itself. And insofar as we can talk of a history of Heidegger's philosophy, it consists precisely in the way that these subjective moments, which in *Being and Time* still appear emphatically and almost independently, with recourse to Kierkegaard and others, in the concept of 'existentials' in contrast with 'categories', now increasingly begin to withdraw into being itself, so that subjectivity itself is subordinated to this objectifying tendency. When Heidegger says that his original intention had always been essentially ontological in character, that is certainly quite true. What he effectively undertook to do can be seen only as an attempt to take up that moment of reflection and subjectivity which is directly opposed to the ontological approach and integrate it into his original project by turning it into a mode of objectivity, turning 'existence' into a *Seinsweise*, or 'mode of being', that belongs to essence, that belongs to being itself. This fundamental tendency of Heidegger's, which I have already talked about and about which I shall have more to say in our next session, consists in turning a defect into an advantage, in trying to address and overcome a basic philosophical problem by a particular kind of conceptual sleight of hand which makes it impossible to draw the required distinctions. We might also express this fundamental tendency in this way: if archaic thought never actually separated the ontic and the ontological, Heidegger now finds that his own concept of being is fashioned in such a way that, without separating these dimensions either, it also harbours ontic moments. For we cannot ultimately make any ontological claim at all, not even the later Heidegger's rather impoverished claims with regard to being, without ontic modes of speech cropping up in one form or another. Thus Heidegger's famous formulation that talks about man as the 'shepherd of being'[10] is an ontic mode of speech. In other words, the attempt to capture something of primordial metaphysical significance here takes us back to primitive pre-agrarian conditions of a cattle-rearing society, and thus to something that belongs very much to the realm of beings and the temporal historical world. Shepherds, as we know, have essentially disappeared, and even in the Black Forest one would now be very hard put to discover one. The whole fundamental structure that underlies this thinking, which you will recognize when you read these things with an alert and critical eye and attempt to withstand their fascinating appeal – if they can still exert such an appeal – is effectively always fashioned in accordance with a certain schema or model. And indeed with most of the theories which have proved so influential in the world we actually find, as Schopenhauer admitted with regard to himself,[11] that they really involve only one thought, and this single thought or single motif is then endlessly repeated. And this endless repetition, this constant self-advertisement, which is also of course the secret of commercial advertising, seems to be what sustains the influence and effectiveness of these claims. The fundamental structure we find here consists in the constant and repeated ontologization of the ontic moment – which we cannot evade whenever we try and determine being or articulate the ontological in an emphatic sense. In other words, the ontic itself is turned into a way of 'being ontic', beings themselves are turned into a 'mode of being' that belongs to being. And this tendency to ontologize the ontic, to take *Dasein* and facticity itself, which represents a *universal* structure, and use it precisely to resolve everything factical into the relevant conceptuality and universality – this is actually the trick, the universal procedure, of this kind of thinking. And once you have really seen through this approach, once you have inured yourself against it, I believe that the compelling fascination of such things will ultimately evaporate.

LECTURE 9

13 December 1960

Ladies and gentlemen,

In our last session I had begun to say something about that basic structure of fundamental ontology which, along with its general method, seems to me to justify the critical approach we need to adopt in relation to it. I am referring to that aspect which I provisionally described as the ontologization of the ontic. And this structure, as I pointed out, permeates the whole of Heidegger's philosophy and that of his followers. The trick, as it were, of this entire philosophy basically operates as follows. We are confronted with an opposition between the concept and the non-conceptual dimension which every concept tries to grasp. But insofar as I now form a concept of the non-conceptual, the non-conceptual that is subsumed by this concept in a certain sense itself becomes something conceptual. In other words, if I grasp all manifold beings together, which is what happens when, to use Greek terminology, the things that exist are gathered under the expression τὰ ὄντα [ta onta], then this non-conceptual and material dimension, heterogeneous to thought, is itself subjected to conceptuality. And this moment, through which the non-conceptual is subjected to the conceptual, and with it the universal expressions employed to capture the non-conceptual, are now ontologized – that is to say, are themselves elevated to structures of being. The transition consists precisely in this: since every being, everything non-conceptual, is mediated, as we would put it, or is referred to some concept, the domain of beings, or of what is, is at the same time supposed to be more than what it is, more than the beings themselves – is supposed to be ontological, as Heidegger puts it. Now, when I speak of a trick here, I beg you not to misunderstand me, as if I were thereby casting suspicion upon the subjective bona fides of the thinker Heidegger or that of his followers. That is very far from what I mean. What is more, I regard the particular character of private individuals as irrelevant as far as the critical reflections I am offering are concerned, for I consider the existentialist thesis that any form of thinking should be measured against the one who thinks it to be extraordinarily questionable in itself. And, apart from that, I think I have already indicated in these lectures that the problematic aspects of Heidegger's philosophy which I have pointed out do not arise on account of subjective insufficiencies of any kind. On the contrary, such errors of thought are, if I may put it very strongly, aporetic in character. In other words, they are inevitably brought about by the way this form of thought possesses and pursues a quite specific intention, deliberately undertakes to express a specific kind of experience – or however you wish to describe it – but in the very attempt to realize this intention comes up against certain internal substantive problems, which lead to the sort of manoeuvres we have described if the original intention is to be maintained. Now I believe that it would simply be dishonest of me if I refused to admit that this very aspect which I have criticized and held against Heidegger at this point is also to be found, strangely enough, in that thinker who I myself would say, in the words of Tristan or rather Isolde, 'for terrible poisons hold a counter-poison'[1] – namely Hegel. And this applies, also strangely enough, at a point which is remarkably analogous to the problematic we are discussing right now. Of course, I cannot assume any real familiarity with Hegel here, but for those of you who have studied some Hegel I would just say that I am thinking of the transition from 'essence', or, more precisely, from 'ground', to 'existence' in the second book of the *Science of Logic*, where existence is also resolved into pure thought in that existence itself is taken to be conceptually mediated as such.[2] This may already allow you to glimpse a certain profound affinity between Heidegger's philosophy and idealism, something which Heidegger himself also occasionally points out, at least in contrast to materialism. Just as idealism must try and resolve everything into consciousness, so Heidegger too must try and resolve everything into being. And 'being' here, as this pure and absolute objectivity, is precisely nothing other than a subjectivity that is concealed from itself, that is held over itself – in other words, pure thought. And in both cases, in absolute idealism, or German Idealism generally, and in the Heideggerean philosophy of being, the transition from absolute thought or pure being to the domain of beings leads to endless difficulties, which can only seemingly be mastered by mobilizing the kind of approach we have indicated. And this certainly explains why even the most significant philosophical conceptions – and here I am really thinking of those of Hegel in particular – in their specific execution are saturated with fallacies and sophisms. In Hegel's case, I believe, this is often directly connected with the fact that these conceptions are ultimately more programmatic in character, that the conception of what he has seen and what he wants to show goes beyond any intellectual procedures that he was actually able to develop and deploy in order to demonstrate this. And that is why these strangely sophistical leaps sometimes find their way into the text as a sort of substitute in this regard, something which is a constant source of irritation for those who wish to engage directly with Hegel's *Logic* in particular, even in the most sympathetic spirit. With Heidegger the situation is rather different. What we find at these points in Heidegger is not so much a desperate attempt to capture something merely 'conceived in thought' as an attempt, as I hope I have shown, to present something that cannot be thought at all or again, and this amounts to the same thing, to present thoughts to which nothing effectively corresponds, as if they could indeed claim a kind of self-evidence in the realm of thought. But, as we have said, these are all developments which certainly belong to the objective problematic of this philosophy, if not of philosophy in general. And you will have completely misunderstood these lectures if you just go back home and report, Well, there you have it: Adorno has told us that Heidegger is a charlatan. I no more actually claim such a thing than Nietzsche actually claimed that Wagner was a charlatan. For insight into the objective untruth, into the objective aporias of specific cultural and intellectual forms, is something that cannot be reduced to some admittedly fallible and contingent subjectivity. And you can believe me that thinkers and philosophers are generally far too vain to let themselves be accused of deliberate lies when they must be fully convinced that more or less intelligent people will one day come to think the same as they do.

And now that I have presented this thesis, this 'subreption' or trick, as I have called it, in very general terms, I certainly need to substantiate this with reference to *Being and Time*, which in the final analysis is the most influential text of Heidegger's, and one which he himself has never effectively revoked. I now have to show what I have claimed through detailed interpretation of specific passages. And I would just like to say in advance that this tendency to ontologize the ontic relates not only to the highest category of all, namely 'being', but also specifically and in precisely the same way to the realm which is emphasized more than any other by the philosophy of being. I am talking about the sphere of history which in fundamental ontology is immediately sublimated into the *Befindlichkeit*, or 'state of mind', that belongs to *Dasein* – in other words, into *Geschichtlichkeit*, or 'historicality' – and indeed in such a way that concrete history, and the wholly concrete distress and problematic of history with it, actually falls through the gaps in this concept of historicality and is thus repudiated as something unworthy of philosophy.[3] In the form which it assumes in Heidegger, this ontologization of what is not ontological refers in the first instance to the 'existence' of *Dasein*. This is the point – at least with respect to the early work *Being and Time* – where fundamental ontology and the philosophy of being connects with what you would perhaps call existentialism, which ultimately goes back to Kierkegaard and his doctrine that existing subjectivity is truth. The transformation that has taken place in Heidegger's thought – and I do not wish to give you the impression that I would necessarily hold the Heidegger of today to views that he no longer endorses – involves a certain change of emphasis. For the analysis of *Dasein* – and to make things easier to grasp here I would suggest that you understand *Dasein* simply as subjectivity in an extremely broad sense of the word – is already essentially taken in *Being and Time* as the key or appropriate mode of access to the domain of being. The construction that I describe as the ontologization of the ontic serves precisely to facilitate this transition. In other words, *Dasein* is meant to be the key to being because existing subjectivity is the place in being, as it were, where the being that exists becomes aware of itself as being. Existence or *Dasein* or subject thus constitutes the place where ontology enters into subjectivity or subjectivity enters into ontology – a construction which indeed is hardly alien to the history of philosophy. Already in Schopenhauer, for example, the theory of motivation as one form of the principle of sufficient reason, which initially relates specifically to the world of 'representation', to the world of appearances, is at the same time the little window through which the absolute, namely the will, peers in to the realm of representation.[4] In other words, this is the place where representation is mediated in relation to will, where beings (as Heidegger would say) are mediated in relation to being. I should just try and clarify the historical context of the change in Heidegger's thought which has taken place here: the philosophical intention which was in fact already emphatically announced in *Being and Time* – namely the idea that the analysis of *Dasein* or of 'existence' was only supposed to open up the way to being as such – has only become all the more obvious and pronounced in his later writings. It is equally evident that, in order to avoid the conflation of his own analysis of being with the 'philosophy of existence' in the

narrower sense associated with Kierkegaard or Jaspers,[5] he has effectively moved further and further away from his earlier recourse to
Dasein. Yet we are still justified in appealing to that analysis of *Dasein*
as the ψεῦδος [pseudos] which I am talking about, since the intention
behind the analysis of *Dasein* in no way involves the reduction of
truth to human existence, given that the analysis of human existence
itself is only supposed to open up some kind of access to the problematic of being as such.

Now I have made these preliminary observations,[6] I would like to
read you the decisive, or some of the decisive, and prototypical passages from *Being and Time*. Thus in the sixth edition of 1949 you
will find one of these passages on page 12. I would ask you to listen
very carefully here, for we are dealing with some fairly difficult issues
which you really need to grasp if you are to understand what I hope
to get over to you, and which you will be able to understand properly
only if you pay the same attention to the precise wording, which
Heidegger himself quite rightly recommends us to do in relation to
other philosophers. Thus he writes: '*Dasein* is a being that does not
simply occur amongst other beings.' I have already said that you
should translate the term *Dasein* in terms of the subject, in terms of
man – not indeed in any particularly individual sense, but in the sense
of the human essence – if you wish to get a preliminary understanding
of what *Dasein* means in this connection. 'Rather it is ontically distinguished [i.e. as a specific being] by the fact that, in its being, this
being [i.e. *Dasein*, the specifically individual and existing being] is
concerned *about* its very being.' This is the decisive claim. You should
try and translate it directly into what it is supposed to capture: namely
what really 'distinguishes' the human being and its consciousness
'amongst other beings' that are known to us from all these other
beings (and human consciousness, the actual consciousness of human
beings, is indeed also a 'piece of world', as Husserl would say, is also
in the first instance a being). And this is what philosophy in earlier
periods would simply have described, if not as 'consciousness', then
certainly as 'self-consciousness', an expression that Heidegger avoids
only in order to confer a semblance of absolute originality upon
reflections that are actually already encountered in the philosophical
tradition. Perhaps I may just add here that this is something where
the strategy of Heidegger's philosophy shows a certain fatal conver-
gence with the current state of consciousness in general. In other
words, this form of thinking, with all its related aspects, actually
stands right within the tradition of philosophy, though God knows
this is hardly something I would hold against it. There is no problem
in this thinking – just as it is quite difficult to discover what are called

really new problems in philosophy generally – that would not be directly related to the inherited problems of philosophy in quite manifest and usually extremely tangible fashion. But since this philosophy claims to be one of 'radical questioning' and of absolute originality, these historically mediated problems always also appear as if they were being asked for the very first time, as if entirely new ground were being broken. And this effect is encouraged above all by the nomenclature which is deployed and the way it specifically avoids terms such as 'subjectivity' or 'consciousness' or 'self-consciousness'. But in our own time philosophy is no longer a kind of ether which permeates the whole of cultural and intellectual life, as it did in the age of German Idealism, and has now become such a specialist and professionalized subject that it holds very little interest for many people. As a result we can no longer really expect any significant knowledge of the historical continuity of philosophical thought, and this increases the chance of immeasurably overestimating the claim such thinking makes, through its particular linguistic formulation, to genuine originality, to an ability to think what has never been thought before. But this claim gets taken *à la lettre*. And it is this aspect which accounts in part for the quasi-religious relationship which so many people adopt in relation to Heidegger. We can say, therefore, that the fascination which is exerted by this thinking is, to a certain degree, a product of ignorance. And I believe that when, in God's name, we really get to know the tradition, and therefore once we realize the continuity which connects these allegedly primordial experiences with what is indeed historical, much of this fascination will dissolve – unless, of course, we *desire* this fascination and anxiously cling to it as a possession we would not lose.

Now when Heidegger says so pompously that this particular being, namely *Dasein* – in other words, the human being in general or in its essence – is concerned *in* its being *about* this very being, this initially means nothing more than that human beings think or reflect about themselves, that they ask themselves questions such as: What am I ultimately? How did I come into the world? What did I come into the world for? What is the meaning of my existence as such? The comprehensive form or general horizon of all such questions which arise through self-reflection, through self-consciousness – and which are actually limited, as far as we know, to human beings – is formulated here as the claim that this being in its being is concerned about its very being. You must try and make very clear to yourselves precisely what 'being' means in the situation which is captured here, and which is indeed quite real, in this situation where, as human beings, we do think about questions such as: What is it to be human?

What am I ultimately? Why am I in the world at all? I think I have already indicated my view on this. This concern, this being-concerned-about-something, as it is understood here, actually means that what this being is concerned *about* is what this being is. In other words, the human being wants to know what it ultimately *is*. But the concept of the 'is' here is at first completely ambiguous, or completely vague, and it certainly does not already imply the idea that, when we think about what Fichte still calls 'the vocation of man',[7] we must think about the being of man in distinction from *Dasein*, as that which is particular and individuated in space and time. But the substantivized verb to which the actual verbal form 'is' belongs is none other than *Sein*, or 'being'. Yet 'being' in Heidegger's philosophy is of course an eminently laden expression. For 'being' is precisely that which precedes both any particular being and any conceptual universality, as I hope I showed you when I explicated the concept in some detail in the last few lectures. The subreption or illegitimate move that is involved in this decisive claim of Heidegger's can be described as follows. Since this *Sein* is also the infinitive of 'is', yet on the other hand is identical with the hypostasized metaphysical entity that Heidegger calls 'being', it now appears as if the question about what man ultimately is, that the traditional question from the history of philosophy about the essence and vocation of man, is presented as if man qua man is characterized by the specific way in which he relates to that entity (if I may put it that way) that bears the name 'being' in Heidegger's philosophy. And this quite minimal ambiguity, for the detection of which we require the literally microscopic linguistic analysis that I have just employed, then has tremendous consequences for the entire approach which is adopted by this philosophy. I have not pursued this point simply for pedantic reasons – I beg you to believe me here – and certainly not for the sake of scoring points against Heidegger for his use of language, but solely to show you precisely how this leads to what I have called the ontologization of the ontic.

The text continues as follows: 'Thus it is constitutive of the being of *Dasein*' – the entire separation of *Dasein*, being, and beings is already presupposed here – 'to have, in its very being, a relation of being to this being [*in seinem Sein zu diesem Sein ein Seinsverhältnis hat*].' In terms of the history of philosophy I would just point out here that this passage, as it stands, is effectively a loan, a variation, a duplication of a particular passage in Kierkegaard. You can all easily look it up, and I have no wish to explore it philologically here. You will find it in the opening pages of *Sickness unto Death*,[8] where existence itself is grasped as a relation which the human being has to itself, as a kind of internal 'reflection', but with the difference that

Kierkegaard has here taken over from Hegel certain concepts such as
existence, being, and so on – whatever they may be – which involve
immeasurably complex presuppositions of their own,[9] whereas Heidegger presents the idea of the twofold character of *Dasein* as at once
'being' and 'a being', as some kind of primordial relationship. In other
words, *Dasein* is supposed to be that specific being which, through
its mere existence, possesses a relationship to that absolute which is
known in Heidegger's philosophy as 'being'. And here you can also
readily see that the famous remark from the *Letter on 'Humanism'*,
which I have mentioned once or twice before,[10] that being 'lights up'
as it were in man, is actually already implicit in the far less provoca-
tive formulations of *Being and Time*. As Heidegger continues: 'And
this in turn means that *Dasein* understands itself in its being [*in seinem
Sein*] in some way and with some degree of explicitness.' And there
you have it. It is already evident that what really constitutes man as
man, for Heidegger, what constitutes *Dasein* as *Dasein*, is precisely
that it is a particular being that stands in a relationship to that *absolutum* which is singled out by the honorific name of 'being' in this
ontological philosophy. He goes on: 'It is proper to this being that it
is disclosed to itself with and through its being.' In other words,
according to Heidegger, it is the distinctive characteristic of man that
Dasein, as a being, possesses the quality, the admittedly rather enigmatic quality, of being open to that *absolutum*, namely 'being' which
is itself neither a concept nor a being. What he calls 'the understanding
of being' [*Seinsverständnis*] stands in contrast to 'the forgetfulness of
being' and must therefore be understood in the emphatic sense which
I have explained in the last few sessions. Thus he goes on: '*Understanding of being is itself a determination of being of Dasein. The
ontic distinction of Dasein* lies in the fact that it is ontological.' The
transition here consists specifically in the fact that something determinately ontic, namely man, by virtue of possessing self-consciousness,
is itself ontological at the same time. In other words, it is something
like the consciousness of being as such. Something determinately ontic,
on account of its own conscious awareness, thereby immediately
becomes the bearer of ontology, or, as we might also put it, is utterly
ontologized. At a slightly later point of the text, a page or so further
on, Heidegger formulates this as follows: '*Dasein* accordingly takes
priority in several ways over all other beings. The first priority is an
ontic one: this being is defined in its being by existence.' Now that
is effectively a tautology. It means that the particular being that we
call 'man', that we are as existing human beings, as *Dasein*, is just
what an existing human being is *ex definitione*. Thus the predicate
hardly adds anything new to the subject.[11] But now comes the decisive

claim, and it is one to which I effectively appeal as a literal confirmation of my thesis about the ontologization of the ontic: 'The second priority is an *ontological* one: on the basis of its determination as existence *Dasein* is in itself "ontological".' In other words, by reference to a universal determination of *Dasein*, such as the possession of self-consciousness, it follows that *Dasein* is itself ontological. This is the special and exemplary case of that far more universal claim that we could formulate as follows: every being, all that exists, precisely by virtue of existing, is itself subject to universality, to the category of existence, so that in its being it has existence 'as its ground', as Heidegger would say, and that within it which is precisely not being, namely its character as a being, the particular qualification of its being, is itself specifically supposed to be a particular ontological characteristic, and thus again something ontological.

And here I would just like to draw your attention to another formulation. For you can also recognize the hypostasis involved and see right here, in the following remarks of Heidegger, how existence is indeed identified with being, and thus how the ontic, the actually existent, is identified with the ontological. He writes: 'We shall call the very being to which *Dasein* can relate in one way or another, and somehow always does relate, *existence*.' I should add that this concept of existence is defined by Heidegger as its own possibility to be or not to be itself – which confirms a thesis which I hope I shall be able to substantiate in detail, namely that the concept of 'existing' which plays such a significant role in existential philosophy ends up with the mere self-identity of what exists. In other words, of all the imperatives which philosophy, as long as it still possessed a meaning, addressed to those who genuinely engaged with it, one alone has finally emerged almost as parody: Be who you are! Since, in the world in which we live, human beings cannot be anything more than what they are, namely what they have been condemned to be by the way in which life is currently arranged, they are now encouraged with tremendous palaver and truly vatic gestures to take up what is already unavoidably imposed on them and freely identify with it. Now they can be themselves – because we cannot actually be anything other than what we are condemned to be. This is a thesis which in some of the ideas of Jean-Paul Sartre has actually, in spite of himself, been taken *ad absurdum* in a rather parodic manner.

You will hardly have failed to notice that Heidegger appeals to this structure – that a particular being is itself 'ontological' – as the defining and distinctive feature for the doctrine of *Dasein*. But it is necessary to justify in more detail the claim that this subreption actually provides the schema for this thinking as a whole. In other words, to show how this is not merely limited to *Dasein*, to the fact of self-consciousness, but that we also constantly find the same move at work in relation to 'attunement' [*Befindlichkeit*] and all the other theoretical analyses. Here too, of course, there is a precedent in the philosophical tradition, and especially, as with most of Heidegger, in the form in which this tradition was directly passed on to him by his teacher Husserl. For in Husserl every particular discipline – including the factual sciences which are concerned with specific beings, such as psychology – is coordinated with a so-called eidetic discipline, namely a pure science concerned with the fundamental structures of the psyche, which is ultimately distinguished from the former discipline only because it does not instruct us directly about the actual spatio-temporal existence of the relevant objects but 'brackets' the latter by means of the *epochē*. These Husserlian 'ontologies' which correspond to the material disciplines relate to the relevant empirical disciplines in much the same way that, on Aristotle's view of things, the Platonic 'ideas' relate to the actual things in the world. In other words, they ultimately simply *repeat* the latter. And this repetition – where the pure essences repeat or duplicate what actual beings are, but precisely without the moment of individuation – already of course effectively implies that these beings themselves ought to be one with their corresponding ideas or, to put this in Heidegger's terms, that the ontic ought to be ontological. If we just abandon the methodological scientistic separation between the material disciplines and ontology, as it were, then, if we are concerned solely with essences, we already find that a discipline such as psychology, taken as a mere doctrine of essence, is at once both ontic and ontological. The ontic, namely the elements of psychology which are confirmed in the field of experience, then becomes the ontological as an eidetic science, as a pure doctrine of the psyche, as ideal possibility. Heidegger's doctrine of the universal ontological character of the ontic simply draws the required conclusion from this tension within Husserl's phenomenology. And here, incidentally, Heidegger's thought also has the advantage of dispensing with that burdensome duplication, that suspicious parallelism between the eidetic disciplines and the factual sciences. For in this way he directly ascribes ontological dignity only to the highest ontic concepts, the highest universals of the ontic realm, whereas with Husserl we can naturally always ask the same question that Aristotle asked in relation to Plato: That is all very well, but if, apart from this purely formal index, your eidetic disciplines and factual sciences are the same after all, what is actually the point of this entire separation in the first place? And what is the point of the enormous effort expended in order to attain something such as pure phenomenology?

But the passage which I have just read out and interpreted for you
also implies something else, and perhaps I should say at least a few
words about this here. For this interpretation of the subject, of *Dasein*,
as that which possesses the ontic priority of being ontological, involves
a remarkable turn of thought. And here you can surely still recognize
the legacy of that earlier idealism which regards the self-consciousness
of man, and the analysis of mind or spirit, as the key for the understanding of everything – the key for 'the understanding of being'. But
the turn of thought here, and it is presumably this which explains
the considerable influence of Heidegger's philosophy, consists in this:
the realm of being or objectivity, or however we may describe it for
the moment, is not constituted from the perspective of the subject,
since the question concerning the subject is subordinated to the question concerning being. And this is abundantly clear from everything
I have told you about the superiority or the priority of being in his
philosophy. And when he defines *Dasein* precisely as that being which
also enjoys the particular advantage of being open to being and receptive to being, then you find that this immediately implies, in contrast
to the critical philosophy, that it is not being, namely the concept of
being, which is brought back to subjectivity in a critical manner but,
rather, subjectivity, which almost becomes, to recall the terms I have
used before,[12] the stage or scene of being. But that too has a tradition
behind it and has not just fallen straight from the heavens. I do not
know whether any of you heard the inaugural lecture which Herr
Liebrucks[13] delivered recently. For he showed with reference to one
of the most crucial passages in Kant, namely the 'Deduction of the
Pure Concepts of the Understanding', that this deduction which is
presented in such emphatically subjective terms is nonetheless always
governed by an objective interest. I would just add to this that Kant's
basic interest, as we can see above all from a passage in the Preface
to the *Critique of Pure Reason* – a passage which I shall read out to
you in one of the coming lectures[14] – is actually *always* an objective
interest. What sets Kant apart from empiricism is that he was not
really interested in studying the mechanisms of thought or consciousness as such, although he does do this; rather, he was interested in
studying and understanding how, through these processes, something
like objective cognition, validity and objectivity are possible at all.
And to this extent, that aspect of objectivity, which I have spoken
to you about in Heidegger, or that turn through which subjectivity
becomes a stage or scene, is also prefigured in Kant – albeit with a
crucial difference.

LECTURE 10

15 December 1960

In the last session, after discussing the problem of the ontologization of the ontic at some length, I also spoke about the moment of objectivity that is involved in subjectivity. And in this regard I would call your attention once again to the way that here fundamental ontology in a sense unfolds something that was already implicit in subjectivist and idealist philosophy. For all the approaches which were concerned with analysing the so-called mechanism of knowledge (of what Kant calls 'cognition'), even that of the British empiricists, were not primarily interested in this field from the perspective of what we would describe today as cognitive psychology. Rather, what they really wanted to do was to discover how we get to knowledge at all and, by more or less assuming the validity of objective knowledge, to learn something about how objective valid knowledge comes about in the first place. Or we could put this the other way around and say they wanted to show that, by analysing the connection between the claim to objectivity that knowledge involves and the mechanism through which this knowledge arises (and this was also David Hume's principal intention), this claim to objectivity is unjustified. To show, in other words, that this claim is conventional in character and is not grounded in the nature of things themselves. To this extent, therefore, we can say that the traditional idealist philosophies were animated by an interest in objectivity. Now in Heidegger – for whom every objective interest is tacitly synonymous with an ontological interest, that is to say, with an interest in being – this comes to mean that this interest in objectivity, in a philosophy such as Kant's, is already precisely an interest in being rather than an interest in knowledge. And here he can certainly appeal to certain formulations on the part of Kant himself, where Kant explicitly talks about his objective interest, emphasizes that he is actually interested only in the question concerning objectivity, that the subjective perspective adopted by the *Critique of Pure Reason* is only a vehicle for bringing out the objectivity in question. And Heidegger has certainly performed a very considerable service in having emphasized this moment so strongly – although it is hardly that new or strange to anyone who has seriously engaged with the *Critique of Pure Reason*. This work does claim to show the possibility of objectively valid knowledge – that is, of truly necessary and universal knowledge – and thus to ground 'experience'. And in this very claim the interest in objectivity certainly prevails over any interest in the merely subjective mechanisms that may be involved. And this is naturally also closely connected with the anti-psychologistic approach that Kant emphasized in his revision of the first edition of the *Critique*, and which formed the basis for the second edition. The necessary priority of this objective interest springs from the central intention of the *Critique of Pure Reason*, which is precisely to justify – rather than, with Hume, to put in question – the objectivity of that knowledge which he thinks has actually been demonstrated *ad oculos* by the sciences. But Kant's ruse, as it were – or, since I have spoken of Heidegger's trick, we might also say Kant's trick – in his attempt to provide a stringent justification of this objectivity is to use the same analytical means which Hume himself, the man who crucially roused him from his slumbers, had expressly used to do the opposite, namely to dissolve this objectivity. Behind all this, of course, we can basically recognize a moment that goes further than this, and which can be formulated in general terms: if the interest of philosophy in this borderland between metaphysics and epistemology, where all of the questions we are talking about actually reside, were indeed merely an interest in subjectivity, then epistemology would simply amount to the tautology that the subjectively constituted aspect of our knowledge is, precisely, subjective. But it is just here, I believe, that we find the source of what I would call a misinterpretation of Kant. We must certainly concede Heidegger's claim that Kant's perspective is ontological and, indeed, in a certain sense metaphysical. The *Critique of Pure Reason*, to the central problem of which Heidegger actually dedicated a substantial book,[1] and which is in fact undeniably relevant to all of the questions that we are discussing here, is ultimately a work of *vindication*. And it is actually very hard for us today to grasp how this work originally produced the very opposite impression on so many readers beyond the narrowest sphere of so-called professional philosophers. For they specifically enrolled Kant under the name of the 'All-Destroying One',[2] as those of you who are pursuing German Studies or are particularly interested in literature will immediately be able to understand from the fate of Heinrich von Kleist.[3] Now the situation which confronted Kant was one of radical nominalism, for which the claim that concepts can articulate intrinsic reality had disintegrated, while this nominalism also sees that, once this claim is completely abandoned, something such as knowledge and truth, and all of that, could no longer really exist, even though the latter nonetheless appeared in its eyes – and this is the relevant thing here – to be vouchsafed by the rigour of mathematics and the natural sciences and also of logic (even if this was known only in its imperfect older form). And this is why Kant attempts – and this is a problematic which indeed returns throughout the subsequent history of German Idealism – to rescue or vindicate the moment of realism (in the sense of conceptual realism) or the moment of the objectivity of knowledge precisely by recourse to subjectivity. What Kant envisages here is indeed something like a kind of ontology – I have to concede this to Heidegger – albeit one that is subjectively mediated, precisely because the subjective critique of ontology, or in other words the entire prehistory of Western nominalism since William of Ockham, cannot simply be erased at the stroke of a pen. But this interest in vindication, or what could also be described to some extent, namely from a theological point of view, as an apologetic interest, that we find in Kant is still an interest that is mediated with the critical or subjective element that is characteristic of nominalism. And this is precisely the problematic that governs the entire history of German Idealism which takes Kant as its point of departure, and which you may even take as the formula that opens up a way for you into these thinkers, and especially into Schelling and Hegel. For while they all seek a certain absolute, a certain objectivity, namely the absolute as spirit, they discover this objectivity within themselves, so to speak; they encounter it within the realm of subjectivity upon which the increasingly subjective and self-reflective thought of the modern age has been thrown back. I should also point out, incidentally, that this conception of the subjectively mediated character of objectivity can indeed still be traced, albeit in an extremely attenuated form (as I would put it) in *Being and Time*, for here too it is the analysis and understanding of *Dasein* – in a certain sense a subjectively oriented analysis – which is supposed to provide the categories that then prove decisive for the analysis of being. It is this very moment that Heidegger later abandoned, even though it cannot be banished or thought away from the genesis and thus also from the inner structure of his philosophy all the same.

Now the ψεῦδος [pseudos] or mistake in his ontological interpretation of Kant, it seems to me, and the thing which also reveals the
problematic character of his own way of doing philosophy, is precisely
the moment that I would describe in Hegelian terms as the subjective
mediation of objectivity. And this is why at this point I wish to say
something further about such interpretations of the history of philosophy. What we find in Heidegger (as I believe I have already indicated) is that subjectivity has become the scene or arena, as it were,
of ontology. And this kind of thinking, for which being appears or
manifests itself only in *Dasein*, naturally still harbours something of
that earlier subjective moment. At the same time it loses what was
so decisive for this earlier form of thought – that is, for this earlier
form of modern subjectively directed thought. In other words, it loses
that moment of subjectivity which appears in Kantian philosophy
under the name of *spontaneity* and in Hegelian philosophy under the
name of *labour*. For now – and this is the phenomenological legacy
of the doctrine that Husserl had already developed, namely the idea
of the pure intuiting of the thing in question – subjectivity is actually
introduced as a kind of pure receptivity. And that is what I meant
here when I spoke of a 'scene'. Subjectivity becomes that to which
being manifests itself, yet without that moment of activity, or that
'function', as Kant also occasionally puts it, properly being acknowledged at all. Now of course this remarkable reduction or denigration
of the concept of subjectivity, which incidentally has unfolded rather
gradually and step by step, is by no means merely contingent or just
the expression of a passing mood, something that might simply be
traced back to an exaggerated claim to objectivity on the part of
ontology. On the contrary, this reflects something more – and this
should reveal the full gravity of these things to you, should reveal to
you how the mistakes involved in a significant contribution are also
themselves deeply motivated – and goes back to the way in which,
historically speaking, the subject, the human person, has already lost
to an enormous extent that spontaneity and freedom that actually
characterized the age in which the bourgeois assumed a position of
power, which was that of the French Revolution,[4] the age to which
Kant the Enlightenment thinker indeed belongs and to which he
expressly committed himself. Now the age in which Heidegger's philosophy is conceived is one marked less by the power than by the
powerlessness of the subject. And one of the functions served by this
philosophy, and not indeed the least, is to transfigure this powerlessness, as it were, inasmuch as the latter here appears as the reflection
of something higher and better. For this is the objective truth which
appears to the subject, and is none other than this: the now powerless

subject, which has long since forfeited its capacity to determine itself by appeal to its own reason, has been brought down in the most literal sense, has been reduced simply to a site of reception or registration which duplicates what has objectively come to pass. Karl Löwith has said that Heidegger's thought is in thrall to history in a peculiarly abstract way and in an extremely formal sense bows to its verdict.[5] And, to that extent, this thinking is in fact appropriate to history and in a certain sense capitulates before it. Yet once again it is utterly characteristic of the internal character of this thinking that here too – and this is the underlying structure I am trying to bring out for you – we see how this defect, namely the way the subject renounces the task of thinking itself through and thus also the task of thinking through what confronts it, is chalked up as a credit, and a dearth is made to yield to a metaphysical profit (if you will allow me such a common mode of expression). In other words, this dearth – the fact that the subject really no longer has the strength to think through the world and its contradictions and to think through itself – is turned to advantage through a kind of fraudulent bookkeeping. The subject is thereby vouchsafed a higher truth which can only be distorted and obscured by thinking, but which 'gives itself' purely and immediately as such. I believe that you must bear this dimension in mind all the time if you are really to understand the way that ontology occupies this peculiar intermediate position between subjectivity and objectivity. For 'being', since it already involves *Dasein*, is also characterized – if we may employ an expression such as 'characterize' here, which I emphatically doubt – by the fact that it is ἀδιάφορον [adiaphoron] – in other words, 'being' is indifferent to the distinction between subject and object, and these two moments cannot really be distinguished within it. And this inseparability, if you want to put it like that, this indifference of subject and object within 'being', is indeed specifically claimed by this philosophy, like every other lack or στέρησις [sterēsis], as its unique prerogative.

I believe that this more or less effectively concludes the preliminary observations which I wanted to make in advance regarding the philosophy of being, even if this has taken me rather longer than I had originally intended, which is certainly the fate of a lecture series, if not exactly the fate of being. Now my intention here – as I said at the beginning of these lectures and might also repeat at this crucial 'turning' on our path – is not simply to try and convert you, as it were, by indulging in polemics against ontology or lining up arguments to counter it. For there is something precarious about the process of argumentation itself in this sphere, as the phenomenologists and ontologists have in part quite rightly seen. And in fact people generally proceed according to the rules of a logic which itself stands above everything, although it needs to be justified in the first place[6] – not indeed in relation to 'being', but certainly in relation to the whole field of considerations in which this philosophy – and what I think as well – is rooted. My intention, therefore, is to lend greater weight to this engagement with Heidegger, to save it from what we might describe, with an expression of Kafka's, as an 'empty happy journey',[7] precisely by addressing a range of problems connected with the so-called *ontological need*. In other words, I shall try and bring you closer to the questions under discussion here by exploring the needs which have inspired them. I may thus be able to free you, at a rather deeper level, from the suggestive power that emanates from these things by prompting a certain self-reflection on your part with regard to these needs. This seems better than just presenting you, within the sphere of these already constituted needs, with various counter-arguments which a dialectically accomplished opponent might then simply meet in turn with new counter-arguments. But I would not wish you to misunderstand me here. I believe I certainly owe it to you to present fully developed analyses of the decisive concepts which are involved, and thus above all of the concept of being itself. I have already thought about these analyses and can only hope we shall get to the point in the semester where I can present them properly for you in detail. But I feel it is preferable here, in order for you to understand the functional role of these analyses, if I begin by exploring the entire complex of this 'ontological need' – or, if you are uncomfortable with this expression, of those specific needs which have inspired the effect that has been produced by these philosophies, and thus also in a certain sense these philosophies themselves.

There can be no doubt that such a need does exist, and also exists specifically amongst young intellectuals, and indeed re-emerges with every new generation which has grown up over the last forty years or even longer – since the time of Scheler's book on formalism,[8] let us say. Now it is quite evident, if you will allow me a sociological interjection here, that this need is by no means a pure and spontaneous one, for what sociology today so variously describes with the expression 'compulsion to consume' also extends to the concept of being. And the fact is, to tarry in this domain a little longer, that in the German universities at least we are faced with a kind of exclusive offer, for in Germany there are now hardly any responsible academic positions or professorial chairs in philosophy that do not feel obliged at least to show that they are somehow worthy of what has been achieved by Heidegger and Jaspers. And even those thinkers who for political and other reasons are extremely critical of both philosophers, but especially of Heidegger, still appear to be captivated – in a way I find really hard to understand since I have never experienced this spell myself – by this kind of thinking and seem unable to sever the umbilical cord entirely in this regard. This became especially clear to me in relation to a work by Löwith, which I have already mentioned, and which is actually very rich in particular critical insights, namely his book *Heidegger: Denker in dürftiger Zeit* [Thinker in a Barren Age].[9] The question is whether it is really the time or the thinker that is so barren. Here I am simply anticipating these critical issues in order to go on and discuss the question of this need with you in all its significance. Now the need in question also certainly involves a certain degree of imitation. And this charge of imitation is indeed raised in relation to every new current of thought. One always speaks of fellow travellers in this regard, and through my own experience in matters of art I am all too familiar with the way in which people who dislike new and radical art on the basis of traditionalism and academicism attempt to discredit such art by claiming that all those involved with it are duped by those in charge,[10] or by describing them as nothing but fellow travellers who fall in with the ruling fashion – as if the poetical products of a Carossa or a Weinheber by contrast were actually above fashion rather than beneath it. We should thus be rather sceptical about such suspicions towards alleged fellow travellers and generally be very careful about entertaining them. Yet I believe in the case of the philosophy we are talking about here that these suspicions mean something rather different. Thus a young sociologist[11] may deck out some otherwise quite primitive and indeed trivial and innocuous reflections on the housing situation and the position of the family in this regard with a whole battery of categories from Jaspers – such as the concern for human existence and similar things – and we find that all of this, along with the simplest questions, such as the way that landlords try and charge the highest possible rent to ensure that they themselves do not go without, gets sanctified under an ontological halo as a concern for existence. Then I believe that the notion of the fellow traveller assumes a very different meaning than it does when a writer[12] – who receives far less recognition in this regard – attempts to learn from Joyce and perhaps even surpass him in terms of artistic technique. The formal similarity in the role of fellow traveller here should not simply lead us to overlook the significant differences of achievement and other substantive differences that come into play in such a case. For it is a very popular trick in contemporary cultural life to try and defame intellectual and cultural attitudes that we find uncomfortable by characterizing them formally in the same terms as the position they wish to contest. And this effectively serves to devalue them, so that anyone who criticizes the concept of *Bindung* – of a certain 'commitment' or 'attachment' – for example, is immediately accused of speaking from an 'engaged' position too, and thus of being equally 'committed' in turn. Yet the crucial difference in this regard is silently ignored: namely whether this engagement is an engagement on behalf of autonomy, or whether – as the concept of *Bindung* already implies – it is the moment of heteronomy that essentially predominates. Now I would like to immunize you against such insinuations, and against the analogous ones which suggest that the non-conformism of today is simply another kind of conformism,[13] and against this whole style of argument by which obscurantists of every description attempt to present themselves as modern and progressive too. As I say, I would like to try and immunize you against this whole approach, and thus encourage you to be rather careful when you come across such things, even in your own student newspapers, and not to give immediate credence to narratives of this kind.

But now I come to the 'need' which I have mentioned. But when we think about this need, and especially about the negative side of which I have just spoken, I believe you must also recognize a specifically German aspect that is relevant here, and particularly important for those who have blindly submitted to a certain fascination with language in particular. And this is the fact that Germany never really arrived at Enlightenment and that, even when it finally began to approach it, this Enlightenment was immediately commandeered by a movement that describes itself as counter-Enlightenment – and indeed it also makes sense to ascribe existential ontology to this movement. What I mean by this can be explained as follows. Even in a historical situation where theological ideas are no longer really experienced as authoritative, but where people still see themselves as belonging to a particular positive religion, it is impossible to say anything or talk about anything unless it is dressed up and sanctified as something more than it simply is. This hallowed thinking par excellence, this thinking that promises at every moment to be more than it is, although it requires no more actual content from anyone than could be required of any lively young man in enlightened times, furnishes as I believe one of the essential moments which many people find so alluring about this philosophy. And if we wish to talk of fellow travellers or imitators in this connection, this has a quite specific meaning which goes beyond the very general and questionable one which I talked about before. For here, with very little effort, we can invest ourselves with the semblance of something higher, of something metaphysical, without really needing to transcend the merely factical conditions to which we are bound by the nature of our own work. Thus we might well come to think that the influence exerted by the new ontology, and the ontological need in the somewhat primitive form in which I am introducing it here, is the perfect complement to positivism. In other words, we can see on one side how people are compelled through the reification and objectification of the world to deal with nothing but facts, while separately and independently of this they nonetheless possess what we could call, in a rather crude way, a sense for 'higher things'. And the most felicitous way of combining this sense for something higher with the fetters of facticity, with a sober reality devoid of imagination, is for mere facticity, without intrinsically changing at all, to be presented in a manner which creates the semblance that it is more than it is, that it is already 'possessed of meaning'. Now I believe – and you will allow me to speak quite openly to you here – that if you examine this need, which is so deeply rooted in all our German culture and education, you will probably find one of the reasons why you, or at least quite a few of you, feel so 'addressed' by this philosophy, if I may use its characteristic language here. Indeed I can say – for I by no means exclude myself in this regard, even if I never fell under Heidegger's spell – that in my own book on Kierkegaard, written over thirty years ago, I find there are certain aspects of the language employed which certainly belong to this same dimension. And I would also like to add that we should not make things too easy for ourselves here. When Heidegger resisted the appalling pedantry and pseudo-scientific thoroughness of the philosophies which flourished in the neo-Kantian atmosphere of Marburg and Heidelberg, but also amongst those influenced by Dilthey, and reminded us that what Kierkegaard called the 'how' of communication[14] is itself essential to its truth, and when he thereby emphasized the crucial significance of language for philosophy, this certainly performed a major service, at least for those who were still quite unaware of these things. And the fact that other people, such as Karl Kraus, actually did this better and more radically cannot be held against Heidegger. It is also quite clear that it is undeniably essential to philosophy that it can never be exhausted by confining its attention to the merely factical. For everything merely factical and particular is always more than merely itself precisely because it is also a moment or aspect of some further context that extends beyond it – and it is certainly the task of philosophy to remind us of this moment, as Heidegger rightly recognizes. But the mistake, if I may use this rather pedantic expression once again, lies as it seems to me in the following. What I have just described as a 'moment', as this philosophical moment of transcending the particular, consists for philosophical reflection in the way the merely factual is

never merely itself, is also always more than it merely factually is –
but this is now immediately conferred upon the factual particular
itself, and its own merely factual character is expressed in a way that
makes it appear as if it were already more than it is. In this connection it is entirely characteristic that words which in the first instance
point towards the sphere of mere factuality – such as the substantivized form of the copula 'is' or the expression *Dasein* – come to play
such a distinctive role in this philosophy, and indeed make it possible
in the first place. Now I have to say that this always reminds me (if
I may be so frivolous in this last lecture before we break for the vaca-
tion) of something I experienced as a child with regard to a very old
great-uncle of mine, who was as rich as he was mean. When he wanted
to present my grandfather, his brother-in-law, with a gift, he would
take out a single orange wrapped in fancy paper and, holding it
between his fingertips, would offer it with an elegant gesture and
simply say: 'Valencia!' And I always sense something of this gesture
'Valencia' when I hear this philosophy dispensing its primal Orphic
words.[15] And I think you should be on your guard in this respect. It
is a crying shame that the completely disordered chronology of philosophy has ensured that Nietzsche rightly broke off all communication with this world as early as he did and never had the opportunity
to read *Being and Time* or even *The Essence of Ground*. For he alone
would have known how to call these things by their proper name. I
believe that if you look at the writings expressly directed against
Wagner, and especially *The Case of Wagner*, you could readily extrapo-
late what he would have said against Heidegger. And I think that if
you could actually perform this feat of imagination that I am proposing to you, and envisage such a Nietzschean critique of Heidegger,
then for penetrating insight it would surpass anything which I can
offer you with my modest powers in these lectures. Yet it must also
be added that the ontological need is an index of a lack. And it would
be a shameful forgetting of what we have learnt from Hegel if we
simply tried to dismiss all this in ways that might amuse and gratify
me, and perhaps you as well, but without recognizing that moment
of objectivity and that element of necessity which is involved in it.
One can and must say that philosophy – at least here in Germany,
and I harbour the persistent suspicion that this holds for other countries too – or at least that academic philosophy after the time of Hegel,
has failed to offer what those who engage with philosophy actually
expect of it. And within the academic sphere it was indeed fundamental
ontology which first began to speak of such things once again, and
that is surely the legitimate and entirely understandable reason for
the influence which this philosophy has exercised. For philosophy

that was simply pursued as a special branch of study has in fact hardly been able to touch anyone seriously any more. And in many respects such philosophy lagged behind the current state of society, and behind its current level of consciousness. And I believe that what proved so fascinating and alluring about this whole new philosophy for those who had not become intellectually dulled is precisely that it appeared at least to have overcome this lack of contemporaneity, this seeming indifference and irrelevance, through the dignity of the matters which it undertook to address.

LECTURE 11

5 January 1961

I think we should try and pick up the thread just where we left off last time. You will recall that we had moved on to some rather more general reflections regarding the problem of the ontological need. Perhaps it would be better to speak of the need which has led to the philosophies which are still current under the names of ontology, philosophy of being, existential ontology, and so on. It is indeed rather difficult to bring any of these things under a unified name, for it is one of the controlling techniques (if I may put it this way) of these philosophies that, whenever we try and grasp one of them under some such collective name, it immediately protests and declares: Well, what we do is not the same thing at all, but something quite different. This is one of the most popular defensive strategies adopted in the cultural and intellectual field, for it helps us to escape criticism by insisting on the nuances of the definitions under which things are subsumed precisely in order to avoid the material and substantive considerations by concentrating on these formal considerations which pertain to definition. But I mention this point only in passing. I have already said to you – and this is something we need to say much more about – that the far-reaching effect (and I emphasize *far-reaching* in this context) of this movement of thought, as represented in Germany above all by the name of Heidegger and also that of Jaspers, would be quite inconceivable if a relevant need had not actually existed. The success of these ontological movements is itself an index of something felt to be lacking. As I mentioned last time, philosophy since Hegel has left us wanting, has actually failed to provide what is expected of it by those who come to it untrained and unprepared as it were. In this respect all of us have also been somewhat damaged by our philosophical education. This is a strange situation, for without any background knowledge in philosophy – if we are unfamiliar with the basic concepts or the relevant literature and have not yet been initiated into the tradition, so to speak – there can be no real understanding of philosophical questions. At the same time, this initiation also has a certain tendency to wean us off the very things that led us to seek initiation in the first place. Sometimes I can never entirely shake off the suspicion that the much prized maturity we claim for human beings and which is supposed to be such a positive achievement – though I certainly have no wish to deny its genuinely positive features – also smacks of the way some things are discouraged and drummed out of people precisely because they do not readily fit in with the ruling mechanisms of power. And this recognition of maturity always involves a kind of commendation: Now, you are a real fellow, properly house-trained, one who knows how to behave, and there is nothing to fear from you. And all our education certainly also has something of this fateful house-training about it. I am not trying to encourage you to violate it; rather, I would like you to reflect upon it, and not to take this condition to which our education has brought us in a simple and naive way as some higher condition. I would just encourage you to think seriously about how far our education brings us to sacrifice and renounce what makes us desire education in the first place. If we choose a particular field of study in the human sciences, and actually pursue it, we will probably feel some such sense of disappointment very keenly; we will realize that where we had perhaps hoped to be introduced to great works of art or to the world of language – all this is actually missing, and that such hopes are rather looked down upon as insufficiently rigorous or scientific. But then once we have been immersed in the subject for a few years, and still have so much to study and to learn, we no longer look beyond this. And then we act like the carpenter Valentin in Raimund, and 'find it's just like home'.[1] Finally, when we are let out into the world as people who have now completed their studies, that is all we have become. Now I believe it is not the least task that falls to those who genuinely study that they cease to be infantile while still preserving that aspect of childhood that refuses to be cheated.[2] This has certainly not been accomplished by philosophy in the post-Hegelian period, which has left us wanting in this respect. And when we read the great critics of Hegel, such as Kierkegaard or Schopenhauer, we soon have the sense, remarkably enough, that our own philosophy is like this too, and experience the similar feeling that the best has been denied to us here. It is all too easy to imagine that the responsibility for this lies solely with a philosophy that has really become one academic branch of study amongst others. Now there is no doubt about what critics such as Kierkegaard and Schopenhauer in particular have so insistently and emphatically pointed out – that the loss of interest on the part of philosophy in regard to what ultimately interests or concerns me, of what is actually at stake for me here, is indeed bound up with the departmentalization of philosophy, and thus with the fact that the very form of thought which really needs to think expressly about and reflect critically upon the division of labour as such has been integrated into that very process and become a specific profession in its own right. We see here how a specific sociological moment actually enters into the innermost core of the history of philosophy. And it may be interesting to note that these are not simply the reflections of certain ill-willed modern sociologists who wish to contest the ground of philosophy in a merely external way (as Heidegger seems to think that we do).[3] For it was precisely thinkers such as Schopenhauer and Kierkegaard, about whose purely philosophical credentials there could be no doubt whatsoever, who specifically drew attention to this social moment of philosophy, who emphasized, in other words, that philosophy has forgotten about the best it had to offer once it had to integrate itself and earn a professional living, once it had to find secure employment in an academic business effectively sworn to defend the forms of society as they actually are.

Now I would just like to indicate at least a few of the aspects through which philosophy in the period in question – namely the period between Hegel and the revived forms of contemporary metaphysics – forfeited the best it was able to offer. I have just talked about a certain social motivation behind this development. Now I believe that it is characteristic, at least for the German philosophy of the period after Hegel, that the specific relation to the social world which was formerly constitutive for philosophy was effectively abandoned. I am assuming, ladies and gentlemen, that your own education, whether it is specifically philosophical or pre-philosophical in character, has already predisposed you to regard this aspect I am talking to you about as something that is almost self-evident – in other words, to believe that philosophy, of course, is the systematic study of ultimate things and is thus too good, as it were, to concern itself with social questions at all. Now here I should like to remind you of something quite elementary from the perspective of the history of philosophy, and that is that this conception – which has become so widespread precisely in the wake of the ontological school of philosophy – was entirely alien to the history of philosophy until more recent times.

If one had expected ontological philosophers of the past, such as Plato or indeed Aristotle, to concern themselves essentially with the being of beings without regard to the society in which they themselves were living, this demand would have appeared quite unintelligible to them, and they would have despised the very thought of separating these concerns. And it is surely remarkable that Heidegger in particular, who would otherwise gladly revoke the tendency to dichotomize or separate reflection in the history of Western philosophy, in this particular context is quite prepared to abandon himself entirely to such a form of reflection. In other words, he is ready to banish any consideration of social circumstances and attitudes from the threshold of philosophy itself – whereas, to mention only the most obvious example, in Plato the highest metaphysical idea of all, namely the idea of justice, cannot simply be separated in terms of content from the kind of community or society, marked as it was by a specific division of labour, within which it is actually developed. And if we then attempted to say that the doctrine of Ideas was merely demonstrated by reference to the *polis*, we would surely fall victim precisely to a kind of idealistic stylization that is entirely inappropriate to the atmosphere of Plato's thought, where the life of this *polis* itself is indeed experienced so strongly as the life of truth that any such distinction between eternal truth and social substance is quite inconceivable. Yet in the history of modern philosophy in Germany there eventually came a point – and Hegel's *Philosophy of Right*, already highly retrospective in character as you know, stands at the threshold in this regard – after which philosophy revealed little but a kind of almost embittered disinterest in social questions. I cannot go into the reasons for this development here since that would immediately involve us in some very specific sociological questions, whereas I wish to stay with our principal philosophical thematic for now. But I can at least point out that one essential aspect in this regard is certainly the fact that, for the first half of the nineteenth century, Germany remained so backward in terms of social development that the enormous power of social dynamics did not extend its influence into the very heart of thought. And thought was therefore able to flourish in the rather private and limited sphere which corresponded to the German social and cultural climate in the period around 1800. There is also of course another phenomenon in play here, the full cultural and intellectual significance of which has not yet perhaps been considered as closely as it should have been. I am talking about the emergence of Marxian materialism, and especially of the claim which this philosophy has sometimes raised in an admittedly crass form, namely its claim to liquidate philosophy as such and replace it with *praxis*. I do not wish to say much more at the moment about the whole set of problems involved in this extremely questionable claim.[4] But I certainly believe that in Germany, and in the general consciousness of the German middle classes, which have effectively monopolized the realm of philosophy, the fact of Marxism itself has acted as an enormously powerful means of diverting philosophical attention from such questions. In other words, almost everything of philosophical relevance that was advanced during this period was itself, whether openly or covertly, already apologetically directed in one way or another against this materialist claim. And part of this apologetic trend is precisely the idea that the truth of philosophy should be distanced as far as possible from existing society and its various arrangements and institutions. And if you glance at any of the textbooks on ethics produced in the heyday of neo-Kantianism and the entire world associated with it, you will soon discover how astonishingly remote such ethics is from what is ultimately, for God's sake, the most relevant ethical question there is, namely the question concerning the state of society and its rational structure and character. Now this is not merely a matter that springs from the distance involved in any division of labour but something which also possesses the most far-reaching consequences for the shape of philosophy itself, for its loss of interest in these matters. I shall simply offer one example in this regard and point out one or two particular problems that arise here, although it would be quite possible to identify countless other problems in this connection. Thus in the wake of Kantian philosophy we see how the concept of autonomy, the idea of the self-determining individual, which has no meaning without the establishment of a free society and which was still conceived by Kant and also Hegel in the context of human beings acquiring their freedom as citizens within a free society – how this concept of autonomy was indeed retained, but now without the remotest connection with a society of free individuals, and thus a free society itself, without that implication which it still enjoyed in Kant and the German Idealist thinkers, and in Fichte the younger, to such a pre-eminent degree. But this also means that a concept such as that of 'personality' in the now quite traditional and epigonal philosophy that succeeded them has survived in a highly spiritualized form and led to a certain revival of metaphysics, even though there was no longer really any corresponding substance to the concept in question. In other words, people still continue to talk about an assumed autonomy on the part of self-determining beings in a world where nothing of the kind exists any longer as a social reality. Thus when Heidegger or Jaspers, or, as I would say, when any human being who thinks with nervous sensibility, as it were, and not just with a more or less formal or undeveloped faculty of intelligence, actually avoid the concept of personality[6] – and it is to Heidegger's credit that he does not I believe employ this concept at all – then this reflects the very inadequacy I have been talking about. In other words, we find that a category still appears as central to philosophy when our experience no longer even approaches it, or is exposed to ridicule, if we do ever encounter it, like those fully bearded plaster busts which adorn many a hall of fame but which we expect to be hidden away in some corner the next time they get knocked over.[7]

Another problem of a similar kind concerns the increasing divorce between philosophy and the natural sciences. For this means that, specifically for those who have been engaged where the pulse of society beats most strongly today – namely for those engaged in developing the productive forces of technology – philosophy has also come to appear strangely obsolete. In other words, philosophy, where it has not simply transformed itself into the logic of the natural sciences, has largely lost touch with the results of natural science and now hardly finds it possible to do so at all. And here I am merely raising the point that it would be of tremendous importance both for the history of the natural sciences and for the history of philosophy itself, it seems to me, if proper consideration could be given to the process through which this seemingly irrevocable breach between philosophy and the natural sciences has actually been produced. It is possible to date it with some precision: the connection between them survived to some extent until Kant, but from the time of Schelling's philosophy of nature onwards the breach had already become established. And that part of Hegel's system which was concerned with the philosophy of nature has indeed never really been taken up or examined by the natural sciences themselves in the form in which he presented it. From this point of view we could say that the neo-Kantianism of the Marburg School represents a kind of defensive or retreat manoeuvre, which was basically an attempt to reunite a further development of Kantian philosophy with an increasingly functional conception of natural science – that is, one in which the concepts of substance were essentially replaced by concepts of function. But here too we can see the crisis which afflicted the involved and, I am tempted to say, even desperate attempt on the part of Ernst Cassirer to incorporate even the theory of relativity within the framework of such Kantianism[8] – a conception which is already controversial within the natural sciences since so many scientists now regard even the theory of relativity as something that belongs more to classical than to really modern physics. But again it is not possible to explore this here. The new ontologies also react emphatically to this situation (rather like the way philosophy reacted to Marxism, as I mentioned earlier) insofar as they no longer claim – and this is extremely important, I believe, for understanding the entire ontological approach – that they themselves can resolve the so-called constitutive problems of the natural sciences, or that they can still demonstrate, as Kant tried to do, how natural science is possible in the first place. For the conclusion they now draw from this situation is that they do not need to concern themselves with the natural sciences at all, that they can relegate the natural sciences, in both logical and substantive terms, to the realm of mere beings, and that they can place properly philosophical thought in a sphere which is then vaguely alleged to precede the natural sciences, although it does not itself establish any relation to the latter. And let me just say here that the attempts on the part of certain scientists to establish some such connection from the point of view of natural science by appropriating aspects of ontology for themselves seem to me to be just as questionable and unreliable as the efforts of certain superficial would-be philosophers of culture who help themselves to misunderstood theorems from the natural sciences in order to produce an unappetizing soup of modern painting, quantum physics, Heidegger, and whatever else.[9] These are all tendencies about which you cannot really be warned too often. Both in philosophy – and we must indeed recognize it as a merit of Heidegger's philosophy that he has never attempted to conceal this – and in the natural sciences we now find ourselves in a situation where no such direct transition from one to the other has as yet proved possible. And I believe it is much more important, and much more appropriate and intellectually honest, to acknowledge this state of affairs for what it is, and attempt to comprehend it, than it is to appeal to incantatory words such as 'being' in pursuit of those hasty restitutions of unity which are generally sure to follow. But at least we can say that this complete retreat in the face of the natural sciences on the part of philosophy – of a philosophy which cannot even summon the civil courage to admit that it doesn't really understand them but continues to act as if, like the Kantian philosophy, it constituted the foundation of science itself and thus of the natural science as well – has further contributed to that discredit into which philosophy has fallen, and indeed upon which this whole reorientation of metaphysics rested. And it is then also clear – if I may just mention another aspect of this process through which philosophy forfeited its own relevance in advance of the new ontological movement – indeed flagrantly evident, that philosophy had become entirely alienated from the most advanced art that related to its own period. The relationship between art and philosophy was still more or less intact in Hegel and Schelling, whose contributions to philosophical aesthetics correspond to the most advanced stage of the consciousness of the time, and which for that reason can still prove as extraordinarily productive as they once were even in the context of the most advanced artistic production of today. Everything that was subsequently written in the way of aesthetics – whether we are talking about the work of Carrière[10] or Volkelt[11] or almost anyone else (although I make exception for the phenomenon of Benedetto Croce, who still basically belongs within a broadly Hegelian context)[12] – remains hopelessly provincial and outmoded with respect to the art actually being produced at the time. And if those who enjoyed any living connection with the artistic movement of their own time did turn to the aesthetics which philosophy had to offer them, they would only be utterly disappointed and would inevitably have the feeling that it was just provincial philistines without any real legitimacy who were the ones now talking about art. Thus one of the most essential dimensions of the Kantian system, treated at length in the *Critique of Judgement*, had simply fallen out the world of philosophy.

But now, lastly – and this is the really decisive thing I believe – we must recognize how philosophy has principally failed to provide what it ultimately promises. In other words, the questions which led us to philosophy in the first place have fallen by the wayside. And it was precisely after the great speculative systems, including that of Hegel, had effectively disintegrated, after their claim to construe the universe out of their own resources could no longer be sustained, that philosophy now hopelessly abandoned the task of answering why we should genuinely engage with philosophy at all. I believe that, if we really want to understand why the ontological movements of philosophy have exercised the enormous attraction that they have, we must take very seriously this fact, which is not just accidental but springs from a fatal necessity of its own. For at this point anyway something crucial appears to have changed in those earlier philosophies. We should not make things too easy for ourselves in this regard. And indeed you should not believe that what we are dealing with here is something that can simply be accounted for in terms of the cultural-historical schema of epigonism. For it is not as if the great and really productive philosophies once engaged with the essential questions, whereas the little thinkers who came afterwards simply forgot what had interested the former and now concerned themselves solely with what is directly or indirectly given in experience. Now I do not deny that this was the case, that these thinkers did indeed largely occupy themselves with elaborate details, namely with epistemological questions of supposedly enormous relevance which failed to demonstrate their worth and actually proved irrelevant as far as genuine knowledge is concerned. But I think you must really understand – if we are to get beyond a purely general cultural-historical perspective and consider these things with the seriousness that they deserve – that what I have just described as the necessity of this process is also somehow implicit in the Kantian philosophy itself. So I shall try and show you, at least in a very summary way, how far Kant's philosophy already represents a kind of concentrated disappointment in philosophy that has been inflated and transformed into a mighty system, as it were, and why that abdication of philosophy has already assumed an objective form in the Kantian system, and one which eventually led to a reawakening of a tenacious claim on the part of philosophy. In the first place of course we have the essentially negative result of the *Critique of Pure Reason* – which was indeed a critique: a critique of the capacity of reason to acquire any genuine knowledge of its own truly crucial objects – namely the result that it is impossible for us to make any claims about what is of most importance to us, claims in other words about the existence of God, about our own freedom, and above all about the question of immortality. And in the course of this great cleansing process the concept of being itself also fell away, along with many other concepts, because it now represents simply a synthesis which consciousness performs on what is immediately given, rather than something absolute as such. And on account of our respect for Kant's enormous achievement, and for what is generally called the Copernican Turn[13] – namely the turn to the subject, to the knowing subject itself, on the part of philosophy – I believe that it is very easy for us to miss just what is lost through this turn[14] as far as the need of philosophy is concerned. For we are not even told that there is no God, that there is no freedom, that there is no immortality – even this negative sustenance is withheld from us in our philosophical need. Instead we find a threatening armed guard posted at the gate who tells us: You are not even permitted to ask about this. Now it is very difficult for consciousness to bear this prohibition, and I should point out right away that there is also a question regarding the rightful authority which allows such a prohibition to be announced in the first place. For we may well ask why and in what way reason, if it is no more than reason, feels empowered to decide this. Whence does it derive the power to prescribe this to itself as reason: So far and so far only you may extend your reach. And is the very act of assuming this standpoint not the same as assuming a standpoint that is already beyond reason itself? Would this not already refute the standpoint that reason *alone* and nothing else is at work here? Now I do not wish to present a list of theses, and this is not the place to unfold the dialectic which is involved. And the argument which I have just expressed is not actually my own but derives from Hegel's critique of Kant which is developed in his own *System of Philosophy*.[15]

But I would merely like to draw your attention to something very remarkable about this Kantian commandment which forbids us even to ask after these things, something so problematic that it is entirely understandable that consciousness cannot rest content with a resigned decision of this kind. For it still betrays something of the oppressively bourgeois and provincial mentality which insists: Just stay in the country where you belong and earn an honest living there, and be sure to avoid all foolish and useless thoughts about things that do not really concern a small and insignificant person like you. And what is objectively implicit in Kant, framed in truly impressive form with such tremendous gravity, eventually gave rise in the history of philosophy to that intellectual indifference towards those very questions that thought is ultimately called upon to address. And when we later heard talk about a certain 'resurrection of metaphysics' – as we did in a rather dull and superficial book by Peter Wust that still proved extremely successful at the time[16] – this at least gave expression to the feeling that, in this respect, philosophy was once more at last selling the kind of things which had once provided its sole *raison d'être*.

But there is another disappointing aspect here which can also be traced back to Kant's philosophy, and which has proved equally, or perhaps even more, fateful than this. And this is the aspect – if I may put this rather crudely – through which philosophy in its Kantian form, namely in the form of a scientifically motivated critique of the possibility of knowledge, actually helps to leave our image of the world untouched. You will all be familiar with Kant's celebrated claim that his philosophy is at once a transcendental idealism and an empirical realism.[17] This means that naive realism is indeed excluded in specifically epistemological terms, so that the whole of reality now appears as something which is composed of the chaotic givens of sensory experience together with the categories and the subjective forms of intuition. At the same time, however, once this process of constitution has been accomplished, the world as we have it, or our normal, empirical and everyday world, remains exactly the same as it was before. Now this very aspect, namely the impotence of philosophy before the totality of the *mundus sensibilis*, which simply remains exactly as it presents itself, has persisted throughout the history of philosophy, right up to an immediate forerunner of existential ontology such as Husserl. For once he has performed what he calls the phenomenological reduction, Husserl receives back the whole world as it is, albeit reduced in the sense that we no longer affirm its spatio-temporal existence, its individual facticity. Yet surely one of

the most essential demands of philosophy, to put it simply, is precisely
not to remain with appearance but to discover the essence. In a world
where there is such a difference between the essence, between the
regularity which in truth prevails within it, and the appearance, or
the façade which it presents to us, we may surely legitimately speak
of a need to discover the essence – the need to discover what is genuinely *essential*: to uncover the essence in the sense of what is concealed
behind this façade, rather than in the sense of the purely general
concept that subsumes what it grasps.

Philosophy has promised, as it were, to pronounce the magic word,
or at least, once it became less naive, to provide the language, and
the insights, which might dissolve the semblance that the world is
indeed what it presents itself to be. It is this claim, or this hope, to
discover the essence which philosophy has still failed to fulfil. We
could say that philosophy has turned itself into a merely methodological arrangement that enables the reflective and informed consciousness
simply to reproduce what the scientifically educated person, or I would
say even the ordinary person with a modicum of common sense,
already knows. But since we actually have every reason to have our
doubts about this normal consciousness of the world and its reliability,
then at this crucial point the result of the Kantian philosophy, which
subsequently unfolded in the philosophies of the late nineteenth and
the early twentieth century, has proved problematic and unsatisfactory. And this unsatisfactory state of affairs, for which I have mentioned a number of reasons, and in particular some specifically
philosophical reasons which are rooted in the form that thought has
come to assume, has effectively led, if not exactly to the new ontologies themselves, then at least to the *need* with which you are now
familiar. But I would not want you to imagine that the dissatisfaction
with these things that I have been talking about is something completely new that has simply fallen straight from the sky. For you will
already discover such dissatisfaction at the time when philosophy
itself had reached its peak. Thus you could take a look at Schelling's
Lectures on the Method of Academic Study, which I had intended to
discuss in a seminar during this semester – although I did not actually
get round to it this time for a variety of reasons, it is something to
which I hope to return. If you read this text of Schelling's, which I
can warmly recommend that you do, you will basically find the very
same dissatisfaction with the prevailing business of academic life which
eventually led to the ontological need.[18] Again, when you read what
Schopenhauer wrote on the subject of 'university philosophy',[19] you
will find the same thing, albeit expressed in a particularly crude form.
And here I hardly need to mention Nietzsche, who renounced the

official world of established philosophy and chose a kind of voluntary emigration instead – though I would almost say that he seems too important to me simply to be introduced directly in this connection. In the next session I shall try above all to show you what has basically changed in comparison with the state of critical consciousness that was still characteristic of the leading representatives of philosophy and science in the earlier part of the nineteenth century, and thus bring out for you what is historically and qualitatively new about the modern ontological movements in philosophy.

LECTURE 12

10 January 1961

Last time, as you will recall, I attempted to explain how the indifference on the part of thought towards those questions which motivate us to pursue philosophy in the first place – in a history which basically goes back to Kant's 'Copernican Turn' – was present at least as early as the time of German Idealism.[1] And it is perhaps no accident that amongst the German Idealists it was actually Schelling – the thinker who has most in common with existential philosophy – who reacted most forcefully to this aspect of his time. Yet it would be quite wrong if we simply responded by saying, *plus ça change, plus c'est la même chose.*[2] It is perfectly true that these problems also existed at the end of the nineteenth century, and they were certainly connected with the way that all of the intellectual professions had become competitors in the bourgeois market and were thus caught up in a particular mechanism of accommodation which deprived them of their ultimate vocation. Yet there was something else which had changed quite decisively, and that in several respects. In the first place, a form of positivism had come to prevail within the special sciences in a way that was quite inconceivable in the earlier period I was discussing. Thus I have recently chanced upon a reference to a particular work of Schelling – an early piece of his which I had quite forgotten about – which originally appeared in something which I believe was called the *Journal for Speculative Physics.*[3] Now I imagine you have only to hear a title like this, which was certainly by no means particularly unusual in the years between 1794 and 1800, or again you have only to think of the writings of Ritter[4] or of innumerable fragments of Novalis, to realize right away what has basically changed here. For today, of course, the kind of affinity between philosophy and the natural sciences which still existed at that time is entirely inconceivable. And a journal of that sort, whatever its specific character may have been, would simply be exposed to ridicule within the field of natural science today. We must also recognize that the movement of German Idealism, which so vigorously attacked the reified and pedestrian character which was attached to the business of science, still nonetheless exerted a certain influence upon the whole realm of the special sciences and upon the actual conduct of scientific life itself which we can hardly begin to imagine today. In short, the kind of oppositions which had already begun to emerge at that time, such as that between a genuinely philosophical interest and the conversion of this interest into a particular branch of knowledge, or the increasing separation between philosophy as such and the business of science, have only radically intensified since, so that we can really speak of a transformation of quantity into quality in this connection. But this has a remarkable consequence, and one which I believe has still not been fully appreciated whenever the attempt has been made (though never really accomplished) to grasp the philosophical movements with which we are concerned here in terms of the need involved and the origin of these movements in the cultural and intellectual situation of the times. For the reaction to these aspects of positivism, reification and enervation on the part of both philosophy and the special sciences themselves eventually became so widespread that this counter-movement has also succeeded in fully establishing itself. We could almost say that the protest against the academic character of intellectual life, which is merely supposed to cheat us of what the spirit actually needs, has itself become academic and thus just another approved branch of the sciences. In the context of church history it has often been pointed out that the various orders are actually nothing but heresies which have come to be accepted. Now it seems to me, from the perspective of the sociology of knowledge, that this observation also holds far beyond the field of church history. In other words, the denser the web of existing societies becomes, the more their power extends and the more this power reaches into the life of individual subjects, all the greater is the tendency on the part of such societies not so much to challenge the schools and movements that oppose them as to absorb them. And the various movements of existential philosophy, along with their seemingly radical questions about what philosophy ultimately promises to deliver, lend themselves all too easily, as it has proved, to this kind of reception.

On the other hand, of course, this reception, which the world spirit has accomplished in a compulsive and unconscious rather than a conscious and deliberate fashion, as befits the world spirit, has the tremendous advantage in terms of existing intellectual, academic and other relations that the heresies in question are thereby completely robbed of their real force. What we are dealing with today in all of these movements is an anti-academic pathos that has become an academic branch of its own. It certainly *appears* to be anti-academic when we say: Well, this whole business of science is completely alienating, it just plays out in its own particular sphere of objectivity. But what is that to me, and where am I in all of this? Simmel's famous address on the crisis of culture expresses something of this kind.[5] And it *also* appears very anti-academic when we say: Well, everything depends on whether thinking concerns itself essentially with me and my interests, with all the things which the critical philosophy and positivism in the broadest sense have effectively excluded. Yet the peculiar thing is that precisely what has been excluded, and what indeed to a considerable degree consisted in traditional cultural and intellectual, albeit more or less secularized, contents, now proves ready once again to be administered as a special academic field of its own. It was in this sense that Ernst Bloch once rightly said (at a time when he still opposed ontology, for in the meantime he seems to have become much more sympathetic to it than I actually am) that Heidegger is the Professor of Anxiety, Care and Death.[6] And this perfectly captures the paradox which I am trying to bring out for you here, for what we are clearly witnessing is the transformation of the most urgent and pressing things that there are into little more than problematic titles – in other words, into questions posed by objectifying thought. And the connecting link here is of course the expression 'concern' [*Anliegen*],[7] all of which gives rise to a pervasive but agreeable sense of the uncanny. I have already suggested to you that this supposedly radical questioning, which reaches out beyond all beings, beyond everything that actually is, thereby no longer catches hold of anything. We can indeed question in such a radical way, and immerse ourselves so deeply in the origins, that any conceivable answer to such a radical question is utterly indifferent or irrelevant in relation to the reality in which we exist. And then indeed it is naturally better to say that everything depends upon the question rather than upon the answers, or that it already demeans the question even to hope for an answer – an intellectual gesture which is in fact entirely characteristic of existential ontology.

It seems only right to me that I should at least draw your attention to a certain analogy here. I do not wish to claim that this is more than an analogy which relates in this regard to a number of political tendencies from our own epoch. I am talking about a pseudo-revolutionary form of thought which behaves as if it wanted to over-throw everything, which even appropriates concepts that would usually be repudiated by a reactionary mentality, such as the concept of 'destruction', and expressly describes itself as a kind of destruction.[8] Yet this proves to be nothing but a destruction of Enlightenment in the broadest sense, in other words, a destruction of rational thought, so that what is left at the end of this process lends itself all too readily to irrationalism and counter-Enlightenment. And here we might also think of expressions such as the 'conservative revolution',[9] or the kind of thinking which acts as if it would involve an absolutely new begin-ning, although this new beginning turns out to mean the revival of things that are already caught up in a process of historical decay or have long since been consigned to the past by history itself. But we could just as well speak of the phenomenon of pseudo-conservatism in this regard, something which I have also come across before in a quite different and specifically sociological connection.[10] Here we are talking about the way this kind of thinking presents itself: as if in commemorating a truth that has fallen into oblivion – namely 'being' – it reveals itself as a form of thought which conserves or preserves. And Heidegger has expressly and repeatedly characterized his thought in just these terms, as a thinking that preserves 'being'. Yet in reality this preserving thought, this conservatism, tends to end up, I have to say, in a kind of barbarism precisely because the tradition of European rationality has simply been cast overboard. In other words, this pres-ervation proves extremely intolerant towards everything that really needed to be preserved in our epoch: towards reason, towards auton-omy, towards the thought that human beings might be able to deter-mine their fate on their own behalf. Instead of all this, they must 'hearken' obediently to 'being'. And indeed, in the famous *Letter on 'Humanism'* addressed to Jean Beaufret, we find that Heidegger brings being itself into a direct relationship with 'fate'. The mythic concept of fate is explicitly cited in connection with what must allegedly be preserved.[11] We actually feel that we are more or less on firm ground here since the analyses in question also possess a certain philological character, and in a somewhat opaque way Heidegger almost appears to denigrate philosophizing itself in favour of a particular relationship to language. Thus when we immerse ourselves in the very words of whatever texts are involved, it is as if this were already enough to reveal something of the truth, although the question of whether the texts themselves are actually true or not is hardly raised at all. For everything depends upon our patient service to the word itself – which in accordance with Heidegger's philosophy of language (which I have already introduced to you)[12] is hypostasized in its wholly transient historical form and turned into an absolute. So it comes about that young people in particular, who devote themselves body and soul to such things, feel the full audacity of this, yet also feel in spite of everything that they are still standing on firm scholarly ground, even though the difference between philological interpretation and the truth content of what is being interpreted has not really been considered at all. And here I cannot avoid mentioning my own much appreciated teacher Reinhardt,[13] now deceased, with whom I once raised the question of Heidegger's philological reflections, and specifically the alleged connection between the concepts of ἀλήθεια [alētheia], which means 'truth', and the verb λανθάνω [lanthanō], which means 'to conceal'; as is well known, Heidegger says that ἀλήθεια [alētheia] is that which 'unconceals itself', in other words, is self-unconcealing being. Reinhardt himself regarded this derivation as complete nonsense. And I think it is regrettable that philology, through its own impoverished positivism, now clutches at the straws of this philosophy and evidently forgets the clear-sighted critique of such philological claims which earlier philologists such as Reinhardt were still capable of providing. I want to bring this gesture to your attention and would encourage you to reflect personally upon it whenever you seriously encounter these things, for it is a characteristic gesture of approved audacity. On the one hand, and this is what I would call the 'youth movement' element of this philosophy,[14] it speaks to the youthful prerogative of audacity, to the desire for a bold new beginning, for something beyond the prosaic routine, and to a reluctance to accept the business of life as usual, and so on. Yet, at the same time, we have the feeling that, for all this audacity, we are still covered by the big battalions – namely by the thought that the power of being is behind us, which is all we need to rely on, and moreover that the power of language and the philological disciplines are also behind us here. I believe that this gesture of approved audacity, of a certain licensed excess as I would call it, is itself responsible to a considerable degree for the fate of German cultural and intellectual life between the wars. And I hope you will not take exception if I speak to you today so directly in relation to your own situation and your own intellectual interests, for I believe it is extremely important to recognize what is actually involved here. Whatever the precise character or number of the more or less fascistic revolutionaries amongst the young in the period between 1918 and 1933, they too wanted to overturn everything, to demolish or dismantle the cultural superstructure – in a certain analogy with the Marxian theory of ideology, incidentally

– and adopted the most absurd poses in the process. Yet they intuitively recognized the wisdom of those words in the second part of *Faust* which tell us that the must may foam absurdly in the barrel but in the end still turns to wine.[15] For they were sure from the first that 'the powers that be' were behind them – just as Hitler spoke about himself and his six comrades in the beer cellars as if they had to shoulder the task entirely on their own, while from the very beginning they already enjoyed connections with the 'black' elements in the army – and the black army itself, as is well known, was only a particular branch of the 'white' one.[16] In other words, the risks were never really as huge as all that. And something about this gesture of audacity – which shakes everything that is established but somehow already senses that nothing can actually happen, or that 'being' will simply be confirmed in the end – also clings to this whole philosophical movement. It is no accident that Heidegger once brought himself to write that the darkness of *Dasein* inevitably encounters its limits in 'being'[17] – in other words, that there we are somehow already covered.

This functional change, in which the thinking which assails the merely academic eventually becomes part of the academy, can be traced in terms of numerous categories. But you can see this particularly clearly in terms of the relation to Kierkegaard, who in a sense can be seen as the godfather to this whole philosophical movement, although it has to be said that in the course of his reception the meaning of his texts was turned into the very opposite of what was originally implied. I think at this stage of the lecture course that I really ought to say something more about the connection between Kierkegaard and the philosophies we are discussing. For, if I am not mistaken, it seems to me that Kierkegaard is much less widely read today than he was about thirty years ago. And yet the development which has led to this kind of philosophy and the structural change it has undergone once it became established can only properly be grasped when you have really understood its relationship to Kierkegaard. For the connection between this philosophy and Kierkegaard actually seems to be extremely remote. We can formulate this in an admittedly very crude form as follows – for I do not want to get involved in a lecture on Kierkegaard himself today and am drawing on him here only to help us clarify the specific problems we are discussing. Kierkegaard essentially wanted to be a Protestant theologian, as we can clearly see from his directly Christian writings rather than his pseudonymous ones. And his central concern is the Protestant concept of faith, which essentially makes the salvation of the believer a matter of faith, that is, a question of the subjectivity of the believer rather than of the

objectivity of dogma. While this represents an extraordinary radicalization of the theological claim directed at the individual, it also
involves a critique of dogmatics and the philosophy of religion which
eventually led Kierkegaard at the end of his relatively short life into
a violent controversy with the established Lutheran Church of Denmark,
his own country. And indeed it was precisely during this final struggle
with the Church, when he was publishing the journal *The Moment*,
that he suddenly died. We may well ask what this extreme form of
theological subjectivism, with its central religio-philosophical claim
that subjectivity is truth, can possibly have to do with the mythological objectivism that is defended at least by Heidegger's philosophy
– if I may ignore Jaspers for the moment, who is actually more overtly
Kierkegaardian. For the two approaches do not appear to have the
slightest thing in common. Yet if you look at *Being and Time* you
will find not only that Kierkegaard is repeatedly mentioned but that
the very parts of the work which originally exercised the greatest
influence, and on which to some extent Heidegger's authority in German
philosophical life still rests – I am taking about the theory of so-called
existentials – are actually inspired in all essential respects by Kierkegaard. For what Kierkegaard is fundamentally concerned with is the
character of 'existence'. Now you have already seen from our attempt
to clarify certain points in Heidegger that, for him, the concept of
existence is not really the central issue, even though the initial influence of Heidegger's thought owed much more to the concept of existence than it did to that of being. Now in Kierkegaard the concept
of existence does occupy centre stage. His basic thesis is that Hegel's
doctrine is essentially a doctrine of essence, of 'the Idea' which unfolds
objectively on its own, as it were, behind the backs of human beings,
in a process which neglects the human individual as a finite, sensuous
and mortal being, and in which man cannot possibly see an expression of himself. In one journal entry, directed expressly against Hegel,
Kierkegaard claims that many philosophers construct an enormous
palace for their thoughts while they themselves live in a doghouse
outside.[18] This is the original pathos of the concept of existence inasmuch as it is directed against the concept of metaphysics or that of
speculative philosophy. Now Kierkegaard attempts to 'construct' existence itself, as we might put it in Schelling's language. In other words,
he tries to unfold the fundamental determinations which actually
characterize existence as existence, namely the categories of existence
which specifically resist the claims of system. Now these categories
closely resemble what is presented in *Being and Time* as the 'attunements', or *Befindlichkeiten*, of *Dasein*, such as the concept of dread
or anxiety, to which Kierkegaard dedicated an entire book and which

appears in Heidegger as the fundamental attunement; the concept of decision which sounds extraordinarily like Heidegger's notion of 'resoluteness'; and the concept of despair which is evidently closely connected with 'being-towards-death' in Heidegger. Now, although Kierkegaard himself was hardly sparing in his use of the word 'psychology', and indeed in contrast to his modern post-Husserlian successors often talked about it, you must be quite clear that all these categories appear in his work as categories or fundamental constitutive concepts of existence rather than as psychological structures which can be observed in terms of individual human beings. This is connected with the fact that, for Kierkegaard as the theologian that he was, none of these concepts were regarded simply as properties, structures or dynamic determinations of the finite human being but were all led back to the issue that essentially interests the theologian, and particularly the Lutheran theologian. And this is the relationship between man as a finite being to the infinite, to God, and in particular man's relationship to himself as a being that is at once finite and infinite in a specific metaphysical sense. At this point Kierkegaard is simply continuing the German Idealist approach that he otherwise violently condemns. For there, too, subjectivity involves both of these poles: it is at once a finite sensuous being and an intelligible character. This idea is already very clearly expressed in the *Critique of Practical Reason* and subsequently constitutes the thematic of Fichte's entire philosophy. Indeed, there is a sense in which we can say that Kierkegaard represents at once a nominalistic or psychological *and* a theological transformation and reformulation of Fichtean philosophy. Since these determinations of existence, while they appear immersed in the concrete life of human beings, are really determinations which belong to the *essence* of the human being as at once finite and infinite, and since the relationship between these dialectical moments is conceived in *absolute* terms, we can in a sense already describe the basic intention of this philosophy as objective, or, if you like, as ontological in character. And in my old book on Kierkegaard (which I hope will reappear shortly)[19] I already made an attempt – which even thirty years on does not strike me as so obtuse – to show that this extremely anti-ontological philosophy does implicitly contain an ontology.[20]

Now the ontological movement certainly sensed as much, and undertook to read this ontological interest in subjectivity, this transition from the subject to the domain of objectivity, out of Kierkegaard's work. But the analysis of existence itself, the determination of existence as a relationship between the finite and the infinite – in Heidegger's terms a relationship between being and beings – now becomes an ontological interpretation of existence. In other words, the thesis that

Dasein is that particular being which also possesses the distinctive quality of being ontological, this fundamental thesis of Heideggerean philosophy, is already precisely prefigured in the definition of the human being as an existing finite being which intrinsically relates itself to the infinite. Thus, in spite of the subjectivism involved here, the principal thesis or point of departure for ontological objectivism is already implicitly present. But that has another extremely important consequence which was then also immediately read out of Kierkegaard by Heidegger and, in a somewhat different way, by Jaspers. I am talking about a transformation of the concept of truth. Kierkegaard was really the first person to shift the concept of truth in a genuinely radical way from its old definition as *adequatio rei atque cogitationes*, namely from the conception of truth as the agreement of thought with its object. For Kierkegaard directly challenged this idea – although one might try and argue that Hegel, the thinker so bitterly castigated by Kierkegaard, should also be seen as a decisive critic of this traditional doctrine of truth. But Hegel's relationship to the thesis in question is actually very complex, and I cannot really go into all of this now. For Kierkegaard, at any rate, it is clear that truth can no longer be regarded as something lying out there over against the subject. Truth in his sense is no longer understood as the truth which belongs to the scientific judgement or proposition, for it is essentially nothing other than the relationship of the finite being to itself as subject, insofar as this relationship implies the infinite dimension of the subject. And I should perhaps just remark in passing that this concept of truth ultimately amounts to a tautology, to a mere doubling of the subject itself. Yet I would like to point out that this remarkable double character on the part of truth and *Dasein* or existence also recurs in both Heidegger and Jaspers, and that we can find some quite astonishing formulations in Heidegger regarding *Dasein* as the 'same' as being itself which repeat this very tautology in Kierkegaard. Thus, to the extent that the subject in Kierkegaard is defined as at once finite and infinite, we can say that it is supposed to be both ontic and ontological. And the claim that subjectivity is truth – Kierkegaard's famous principle as expressed in the *Concluding Unscientific Postscript* to the *Philosophical Fragments*[21] – is not to be understood (as I believe should now be obvious from what we have already discussed) as any kind of psychological relativism, as if it somehow implied that there is simply no truth other than subjectivity. In other words, this is not some feeble revival of the kind of subjectivism associated with the ancient Greek sophists. On the contrary, it basically implies the Heideggerean thought that *Dasein*, namely the existence of the human being, by virtue of its own awareness, already transcends itself and

points beyond itself, and thereby participates in a truth which cannot
be sought or discovered outside of ourselves, a truth which is harboured within man himself understood in terms of this very process
and relationship. And Heidegger's thesis – to clarify this for you a
little – that in philosophy everything depends on the *question* rather
than the answer[22] is itself a relatively precise reproduction of what
Kierkegaard means with his thesis that subjectivity is truth. And there
is a common source for both of them here, namely the celebrated
dictum of Lessing[23] that, if he were made to choose between truth
and the striving for truth, he would unfailingly prefer the latter. Thus
here too – and this seems an immutable German characteristic – you
find a privileging of the question over the answer. And in the work I
have just mentioned, namely the *Concluding Unscientific Postscript*,
Kierkegaard dedicated an entire chapter to this saying of Lessing's in
what also amounted to an apostrophe of his predecessor.[24] In Kierkegaard, however, all these moments that I have described for you go
hand in hand with emphatically nominalist, enlightened and anti-
metaphysical elements. Thus in a certain sense Kierkegaard is one
with the young Hegelian, left Hegelian and materialist critics of Hegel
insofar as he emphatically denies that spirit is capable of defining the
Absolute, although he does so in the name of theology, which rejects
the possibility that by means of its own resources the human spirit
can ever know the Absolute. And this distinctive tendency to energize
the concept of truth, this idea that truth lies in the question rather
than the answer or that truth is subjectivity – all of this is intrinsically
bound up with the thought that reason is ultimately powerless to
grasp the Absolute, that the truth can be found only in a particular
mode of comportment on the part of subjectivity – a subjectivity
which cannot of itself furnish the objective measure of truth and is
modelled on the theological concept of faith. And the affinity between
God and the knowing subject here is ultimately grounded in the
paradoxical contact between time and eternity that is vouchsafed by
Christology. What I wanted to bring out is that this theological moment
in Kierkegaard brings him into remarkable proximity with the Hegelian left, namely through a shared opposition to *metaphysics*. Kierkegaard stands to the right of metaphysics, as it were, or perhaps *before*
metaphysics, insofar as he denies that spirit is able to know the Absolute. And the left Hegelians of course believe that, precisely in place
of the Absolute or the Idea in Hegel, we must simply find something
finite, such as nature or whatever else it may be. And from this perspective there are several points of connection and intersection between
both parties. There are certainly many observations in Kierkegaard
where – in express opposition to German Idealism, but especially to

Hegel and indeed to Schelling – he clearly makes common cause with the left critics of Hegel, in particular with Feuerbach, but also with more the positivistic critique of idealist philosophy mounted by Schopenhauer.

Now all this on the one side, and the subjectivism of Kierkegaard on the other, has disappeared, remarkably enough, in the philosophy of Heidegger. And when I spoke before about the functional change which this entire philosophy has undergone, you can recognize this change in the clearest possible way right here. It would certainly furnish an excellent subject for a doctoral dissertation (and maybe one of you would actually consider pursuing this idea) to write a history of the concept, or the word, 'ontology' from Kant or Hegel, say, up until our own time. For in Hegel, as already in Kant as it happens, ontology is basically a negative concept that is identified simply with metaphysics. Now Kierkegaard denies the possibility of providing such a rational account or projection of 'being' in any way that is commensurable with reason.[25] But his own approach is contradictory, for the doctrine of existence which he himself presents – precisely because it attempts to interpret this existence in terms of fundamental determinations such as anxiety or despair, or decision and 'the leap', as I have already pointed out – is itself a covert ontology which is not aware of itself as such. And the philosophers soon latched on to this, for they are always extraordinarily sensitive to such things, and wherever a specific thinker is vulnerable they immediately seize on it and develop this particular moment as such – and there you have the history of philosophy. Thus the philosophers drew out this very point and turned what was a derogatory term in Kierkegaard, namely 'ontology', into the problematic title, as people love to say, for precisely what they want to pursue themselves. For a while indeed the term ontology was the key word here, even if it subsequently faded into the background somewhat. Since Heidegger began by tracing back all the individual ontologies – namely the doctrines of the constitutive dimensions of the various domains of being – to the single question of a fundamental ontology or doctrine of being, he eventually came to the conclusion that something such as ontology, namely a rational articulation of being, was no longer possible at all. And in the end what Heidegger himself (and not merely his imitators) called the question concerning being had completely replaced ontology. Now I would just like to say that the aspect of academicization, the process in which the anti-academic itself becomes established, can be observed here with particular clarity. For in Kierkegaard the counter-concept to 'ontology' is precisely 'existence'. And it is the very concept of existence – which Kierkegaard often presents in the most tangible manner with reference to entirely real and material relations, such as the fact that a young minister finds himself forced to teach doctrines in which he does not truly believe – it is this concept of existence which retreats more and more in Heidegger, which withdraws more and more into the background. And the concept of being itself increasingly assumes the function of a fundamental doctrine, an object of the kind of erudite discussion which this philosophy was originally intended to transcend. And to that extent the reorientation which I have outlined here is the decisive confirmation of that change in function which has occurred in the reception of this philosophy. But this change in function – and this is something we would perhaps do well to bear in mind when we are thinking about this particular process of intellectual and cultural history – was only possible because it actually connected with those features and aspects of the thought we have been discussing here.

LECTURE 13

12 January 1961

In our last session I said something about the relationship between Kierkegaard and existential ontology, or the ontological movements in philosophy generally, and outlined the way in which I think the function of philosophy has changed in the reception of these ideas. I attempted to clarify my general thesis in terms of a concrete example – as I like to do when I reveal the overall approach I am pursuing – by looking specifically at Kierkegaard's concept of existence. For I am trying to show that existential ontology or the things which came out of it actually have a tendency to neutralize their own original intentions. And if you reflect more closely upon this process of neutralization, as I have described it in relation to Kierkegaard (in whose work, as I would remind you once again, all of these moments are already harboured as possibilities), you will see that it ends up in a very marked form of anti-subjectivism. This anti-subjectivism is precisely what has emerged from a philosophy with a radically subjective orientation – and you will recall how I have already referred to Fichte in connection with Kierkegaard[1] – and indeed you could also say that this is something which is highly characteristic of Husserl. In Husserl this is still related to strong elements which derive from transcendental idealism, but in the work of Scheler we can already see how this anti-subjectivist aspect, to Husserl's consternation, had become entirely independent in its own right. I want to say something more about the anti-subjectivism of all these movements because, as yet, we have hardly spoken about this complex of issues in its proper context, and because this is indeed one of the most central aspects in our investigation of the needs which have led to these philosophies. I am talking about the anti-relativistic aspect or moment that we have already touched on in various contexts. Here I would simply ask you to recall Kierkegaard's assertion that subjectivity is truth. This very nominalistic claim in Kierkegaard is connected, like the doctrine of faith in Luther, with a theological motif which doesn't expressly appear in the pseudonymous and apparently more secular philosophical writings that he dedicated to these ideas, but which of course ultimately stands behind everything that he composed. I should say, incidentally, that you will only really understand Kierkegaard in his extremely complex and elusive body of work if you take the explicitly theological rather than the pseudonymous writings – namely the religious discourses and also his very last publications[2] – as the key to his entire authorship. For at the same time that he wrote *Either/Or*, the book which is supposed to present the aesthetic standpoint of life, he also composed, and published under his own name, the first of these religious discourses in order to show that the book in question merely represented a certain 'stage' of development. As far as Kierkegaard is concerned, the problem of relativism only arises when the claim that subjectivity is truth is read without recognizing how this subjectivity is intrinsically related to the Absolute, or, as Kierkegaard would have no scruples in saying, to God – in other words, when we ignore that the subject's relationship to itself as something that is also infinite is synonymous with the paradoxical relationship of faith itself. For then, of course, there is no question of relativism in this philosophy at all. Now in point of fact all kinds of free-thinking and relativistic movements, whether critical or downright hostile in relation to the Church, have appealed to the work of Kierkegaard. And since the philosophy we are concerned with here – as I have pointed out several times, and this is something that must constantly be remembered – no longer either presupposes an explicit theological position or believes it is capable in its own right of affirming one, it is naturally extremely sensitive to this relativistic element in Kierkegaard and subjectivism in general. And it is interesting to note that, at the point where the modern ontological movement really began in earnest, namely in the work of Scheler, we are expressly presented with an objectively binding hierarchy of values which has allegedly been directly intuited as such.

Now I do not actually believe that this question of relativism is nearly as important for the complex issue of anti-subjectivism as you might initially imagine. And there is something strange about the whole problem of relativism. It is indeed a characteristic feature of philosophical consciousness generally – and we shall return to this in another context when we come to examine the concept of a 'question' – that the questions which philosophy throws up cannot be resolved in the same way as the questions which arise in the particular positive sciences or also in the context of ordinary life, where we ask about something specific and then receive a more or less satisfactory answer. Now as far as the history of philosophy is concerned, by contrast, we find that questions actually disappear or get forgotten in a kind of dynamic process which, as far as I can see, has never been properly grasped in the historiography of the subject. Thus let us consider certain philosophies of the earlier modern period and think, for example, about the problem which preoccupied thinkers throughout the seventeenth century, namely the problem of relating the internal world to the external world, of explaining how two distinct substances can actually come together. Now I would say that this question, which was explicitly thrown up by Cartesian philosophy, was not exactly resolved by the ultimately rather artificial and elaborate constructions offered by Spinoza, or by Occasionalism, or by Leibniz, for each of their own proposed solutions attracted intense criticism of one kind or another. And what happened was that this particular question, for reasons that we cannot go into here, was more or less forgotten. It seems to me that the situation is very similar with regard to the problem of relativism. I almost have the feeling that the question of relativism, like so many things that once occupied the attention of the great minds, as people like to say, has fallen to the level of classroom debate, where these days, as we all know, *Hamlet* is reading material too. The young adolescent, or at least the immature student, who responds whenever you express a thought by immediately asking: Well, where's your proof for that? Isn't that just your own opinion? – these are the sort of people who still get excited about the question regarding the relativity of knowledge, but otherwise the question has effectively disappeared from the horizon. And this is surely due in part to the success of Husserl's critique of relativism as expressed in his first famous book, namely the first volume of the *Logical Investigations*.[3] It is not that this work was particularly widely read, for it was hardly known at all outside the scholarly circles of philosophy. Yet the view he expounded probably found considerable resonance nonetheless. Still, I do not believe that this was actually the decisive thing, and I am trying to get at something else here. For the thesis that all knowledge is relative to the subject is what Hegel would have called an extraordinarily abstract one. And as soon as we engage with any particular discipline, and its particular subject matter, and work in detail on some specific problem, we actually find that this question of subjective relativity disappears. It exists only when we remain 'outside', but otherwise it's more like Goethe's chapel:[4] once we get inside a question, it generally exerts such force in terms of the alternatives that the simple assurance that all knowledge is merely relative no longer looks very persuasive.

But I believe there is also something else involved here. The whole idea of relativism, which still enjoys considerable pathos and élan in Nietzsche for example, should not be taken as a purely intellectual thesis, for regarded as a purely theoretical doctrine it is extremely thin. And the criticisms which Plato already directed at the sophists have never really been refuted. But the interest which the relativist thesis provoked was always essentially practical, namely an interest in the greatest possible freedom of the individual subject as far as the pursuit of its own claims and interests was concerned. And it was this aspect which already inspired the Greek sophists, who were concerned far more with applying a practical philosophy which occasionally appealed to relativistic arguments than they were with developing a theory of relativism as such. For, as has often rightly been pointed out, it is actually impossible to develop relativism as a theoretical position precisely because it would be self-refuting if it were presented as a unified and consistent theory. And the fact that this interest in liberated subjectivity has effectively evaporated is connected in turn with Voltaire's observation 'Où il n'y a pas le vrai besoin il n'y a pas le vrai plaisir.'[5] In other words, the weaker the individual subject becomes – as it proves less and less capable of spontaneously pursuing its own ends – the more the subject also loses interest in justifying these ends. And when people speak today of the so-called sceptical generation – although, as you probably know, Schelsky has now disowned or at least significantly qualified this particular expression[6] – it is not intended to imply that the young people in question refuse to conform to objective norms by virtue of their own unrestrained individuality, but almost the reverse – namely that they are so harnessed to the existing social order, and their entire consciousness is so channelled by it, that they have now become sceptical about any ideas that question the pre-established structures of their own life and the paths which that life is expected to follow. What is described as scepticism in this context is the very opposite of that earlier form of scepticism. And if we ventured to suggest that these young people are relativistic in outlook, this would certainly be quite wrong. I do believe that it is true to say that the so-called problem of relativism has – for good reason – largely disappeared from the general consciousness, from the realm of objective spirit, as it were. It is necessary to understand the peculiar power of that anti-subjectivism which has certainly left its mark upon philosophy, and indeed in all its nuances – for I believe there is

hardly any form of thought which has not shared at least something
of this anti-subjectivism. And here I do not exclude myself either, to
quote *Rosenkavalier*.[7] Yet the power which is exercised by this anti-
subjectivism has to be traced back to something more than a simple
expression of anti-relativism. And although I cannot explore this in
detail here, I would just like to mention a further aspect which plays
a significant role, and that is what I once described as the desire to
'break out'.[8] In other words, the concept of the subject itself – to which
indeed all knowledge had been traced back – came to be perceived
more and more as a kind of imprisonment, as a mere fabrication, as
the product of mere culture, we might say, and there was a desire to
break out of this constrictive domain and immediately confront the
things themselves, as they say in Husserlian phenomenology. And this
need to engage with the things themselves is a very strong element
in the philosophy we are discussing. The whole fascination which
emanates from the concept of being is indeed the fascination with the
Sache, the thing par excellence, the matter itself, which is supposed
to precede all and any conceivable subjectivity.

But these remarks are still all too general in character. And in order
to be quite clear about the problem of anti-subjectivism we need to
look rather more closely at certain specific problems within the history
of philosophy. For we shall find that the category of subjectivity – or
not so much the *category* of subjectivity as subjectivity *itself*, since
in all idealist thought subjectivity is the unity of the categories rather
than one category amongst others – that this concept of subjectivity
has actually been profoundly broken or even shattered. And this entire
problematic can be traced back to Kant himself. For in the eyes of
Kant (as I hope you all know) knowledge or cognition is divided in
terms of form and content, of form and matter. And the form is
ultimately nothing but the pure activity which connects the intellectual
operations of my mind, or, as Kant expresses it, is simply 'the "I
think" which accompanies all my representations' – in other words,
is simply the fact that all the particular aspects or moments of my
consciousness precisely qua thought are connected with one another
in *my* individual consciousness. In this sense the concept of subjectivity in Kant is already so abstract, so emptied of all particular content,
that it is very difficult to relate with the concept of the 'I' at all, for
it lacks what, in later terminology, would be called 'egohood'.[9] But
as soon as we consider this 'egohood' or 'I-ness', this feeling of 'I',
of 'my consciousness', then we immediately move beyond mere 'thinking' and encounter something that actually exists, a moment of facticity, namely the individual consciousness which is here and now in
space and time. On the other hand, in Kant, you also find what he

describes as material, or the chaotic manifold of sense impressions. Now this chaos of sense impressions is supposed to be utterly and completely indeterminate. Any specific determinations that it comes to acquire, it acquires solely through the subject. This all seems rather comical. For it is actually as if, in Kant – to put this in a somewhat crude and pointed manner – zero times zero is supposed to produce *something*. This is a consequence which, even as I have just bluntly expressed it, has never really been sufficiently considered. For when something so indeterminate that ultimately nothing at all can be said about it is organized and worked over by something equally abstract and insubstantial, namely thought as such, we suddenly get the world. This is a remarkable and ultimately highly paradoxical construction which rather disappears behind the careful, reasonable and apparently commonsensical way in which the *Critique of Pure Reason* is presented in a series of steps. But I believe that if you really focus on these two poles of the work, and ignore everything in the material or the form which ultimately already goes beyond the pure concept of either, then you are actually left with something utterly indeterminate on both sides. In other words, Kant's transcendental subjectivity is afflicted from the beginning by what can be described with Kierkegaard – since we have already mentioned him – as a certain 'acosmism', namely as a loss or absence of the world.[10]

This is a remarkable state of affairs. For if you think about what German Idealism – the post-Kantian movement of which Fichte, Schelling and Hegel are the principal representatives – attempted to accomplish in relation to Kant, you will probably say (if you are answering questions in an examination) that all these philosophers extended and expanded subjectivity immeasurably beyond anything that Kant had in mind. For the material, which always comes from the outside in Kant, is now itself turned into a determination of the subject. Thus it is now 'posited' in a comprehensive sense by the subject, as Fichte himself put it. And this interpretation is indeed correct. But I believe that this standard account furnished by the history of philosophy is too superficial. For in reality the entire movement of German Idealism, precisely insofar as it appeared to expand the range of subjectivity to an immeasurable extent – to a truly immeasurable extent: namely to the infinite itself, beyond anything that Kant dared to claim – was actually attempting to resolve this problem of acosmism. Thus insofar as the world itself is posited by the subject, it now manifests itself far more clearly in the subject than it ever had in Kant. In Fichte this is because both the I and the non-I appear as something posited. And Schelling developed this further, in a thoroughly consistent way, when he argued that the entirety of nature as something self-determined, since it is equally constituted by the subject, must also be incorporated as a positive content within the determinations of philosophy. And this incorporation within subjectivity is likewise demanded by Hegel's speculative concept, which attempted to encompass the realm of objectivity. This claim culminates in Hegel's dialectic, which actually did undertake to bring the whole substantive character of the world – which Kant had excluded as merely empirical content from philosophy proper – together with Kant's conception of subjectivity by asserting the absolute identity of both. Now this was supposed to be a mediated rather than an immediate identity, one that is only achieved through the process that we have commonly come to describe as dialectical. The Hegelian philosophy is the attempt to overcome acosmism in this very sense, to return the world to consciousness, as it were, the world which consciousness had relinquished precisely by reducing itself to pure consciousness. And it returned the world to itself by showing how consciousness and the world are identical specifically as an infinitely complex and mediated system. But this identity inevitably implies the claim that subject and object are also identical insofar as the world, the object, is recognized as being the same in kind as the subject – namely as being one with the subjective reason which indeed originally produced it. In other words, this conception of objectivity, which is encompassed by universal subjectivity, also involves the claim that the world is essentially rational. But this claim has been fundamentally challenged. This is what has to be grasped if you are to understand the deepest root of the anti-subjectivism under whose sign every conceivable consciousness now stands, and with regard to which even the extreme alternatives to Heidegger, such as the position I defend, would nonetheless agree with his own, for we should not actually deny such points of agreement. For in the last instance this anti-subjectivism can be traced back to this: the thesis that the world as rational belongs to the subject, or the attempt to secure the meaning of the world by recourse to subjectivity, has ended in failure. In other words, this world is *not* rational, and our faith in the central place of subjectivity has thereby been shattered too. Now if you look at Heidegger's earlier work – since the later Heidegger no longer really engages with these questions – you will find clear evidence of all this in the concept of 'thrownness' and all those negative determinations to which the subject is exposed in his thought. For here you will see how the 'situation' of man in the world (as they used to say) is essentially ratified as one that is not indeed meaningful, and that the idea of any such reconciliation between reason and objectivity has now come to seem obsolete.

Now I have to say, ladies and gentlemen, that this has a much broader consequence. Or perhaps it is misleading to speak of a much broader consequence here, for the experience in question is not one that just happens to fall into a social context but one which *naturally* falls into a specific social context. It is a social context in which Hegel's claim that the civil society in which we live is an essentially rational society has been drastically undermined by history. And this process, we must concede in honour to philosophy, has actually been recognized by philosophy since Nietzsche, and long before we came to the great European catastrophes of more recent times. But we are talking about an even more far-reaching state of affairs here, one that I would at least like to mention, even if it takes us into a rather painful area, an area in which the gossipy talk of world-views and particular intellectual fashions – what we like to call fashions – can sometimes capture more and tell us more about what was actually happening than cultivated and refined thoughts and ideas are capable of doing. You will forgive me, therefore, if I express myself for a moment in the rather debased language of the salon, for it is very difficult to say what I want to say in terms that have not already been appropriated in some way or other by this sphere. Thus I believe that the changed situation, which reveals a crisis of the subjectivity which once thought it could render the world rational by concretely deriving the world from itself, has a lot to do with the disillusionment we have experienced regarding the place of man in the cosmos.[11] Thus I would simply like to say that, for a whole number of interconnected reasons, the thought that man somehow determines the world – and this quite apart from the purely philosophical problematic I expounded before when I showed how the world is by no means humanly rational in the Hegelian sense – or the thought that man stands at the centre of everything, has already suffered the sorest challenges. One of the obvious reasons for this is the progressive secularization of theology, so that the notion of man's likeness to God, the idea of man as the image of God, the idea of the earth as a privileged site for the exercise of divine grace, and everything else connected with such ideas, all of this has suffered irreparable damage. Another element at work here – if you will forgive the crudity of these observations – must surely have been the development of modern cosmology, which finally dispelled every trace of the geocentric and indeed heliocentric conception of the world. Of course we can say that the Copernican revolution in science was not really decisive for the experiential horizon of human beings, since our everyday empirical consciousness hardly changes whether we assume that the earth revolves around the sun or assume the opposite. In other words, for us, if we ignore the mathematical-astronomical devices at our disposal today, the appearance that the sun moves around the earth remains the same as it was in pre-Copernican times. But if, in addition to this original Copernican turn, we consider the astronomical discoveries which have consigned the little terrestrial space in which we find ourselves to utter insignificance, and if we also consider the whole complex of reactions which these changes have provoked, then I do not think it is too much to say that the cumulative effect of all these developments has also weakened the concept of subjectivity to an extraordinary degree. Now I realize that a fully fledged idealist – as sublimely aloof to these things as a Heideggerean – would respond to this by saying: Of course, but the transcendental subject we are talking about has really hardly anything to do with the wretched empirical subject of the individual, or the wretched empirical subject of humanity as a whole. Yet anyone who sits on such a high horse as this could easily be unseated by Kant himself, for the universal idea of subjectivity, as defined at the end of the *Critique of Practical Reason*, is precisely that humanity which is here dismissed as a merely empirical quantity.[12] Kant is not nearly so fastidious in this regard. But apart from that there is something even deeper here. For we cannot actually separate or think away the concept of subjectivity, however hard we try, from the concept of ego-hood, as I put it before, namely from the concept of a concrete individual human subject. The fact that the universal subject, the transcendental subject, is an abstraction from individual human subjects should not tempt us to imagine, as Fichte was the first to claim, that this subject enjoys some intrinsic validity of its own, quite independently of individual human subjects. For, irrespective of how we conceive of subjectivity, we cannot avoid this very aspect or moment: we can never completely free ourselves from the thought of the concrete individual human being, and this not for reasons of merely empirical weakness but for precisely structural reasons. And this means that all the other moments which have caused difficulties regarding the central place of man as an anthropological being are also directly relevant to the so-called philosophical questions regarding 'constitution'. And this explains why we are no longer satisfied with the thought of constitutive subjectivity – not to mention all the philosophical questions connected with mediation which do not even allow us to think such a pure subjectivity without also thinking of 'something' else which is not itself subjectivity.

Now there is a double aspect to this whole question of anti-subjectivism which is remarkable and complex in itself. And I believe that the intellectual orientation that we require today really depends on whether we grasp the complexity of the question involved. On the one hand, this anti-subjectivism actually embodies an anti-ideological moment. For in one sense it implies – and here the philosophical critique reveals a remarkable coincidence with that advanced by theology – simply that the individual human subject is called upon to renounce its hubristic arrogance, to abandon the idea that it is the lord and master or the centre of the world. And here philosophy also critically reflects on the concept of the domination of nature which has been sacrosanct throughout the entire history of philosophy from the earliest times until the present day. In Heidegger too we find some very strong aspects and elements of this critique of the mentality which is preoccupied with the domination of nature. When he says that man is in thrall to being, and must yield to being, these formulations cannot merely be dismissed however comical they seem, for they also imply that we must relinquish the illusion that what confronts us, what presents itself to us, whatever it may be – I avoid using any more specific expressions because there is no really appropriate expression here – is something that is actually controlled by us, that is subjected to us, even in our capacity as mind or spirit. This anti-ideological moment also has a social dimension since the claim that this world is already our world, that this world is already rational, has thereby been challenged. I would almost say that there is something extraordinarily materialist in the way that we are recalled to our own fragility as *physis*, to our mortality, in contrast to the ideological transfiguration that insists on treating us as pure mind or spirit. And if so many people are attracted by the so-called radicalism of this philosophy of being, this particular moment is surely an essential element in this. It is also rather remarkable, and this certainly merits further reflection, that the thesis of the preponderance of being over consciousness – even if 'being' signifies something quite different here – is something which is shared by fundamental ontology and by Heideggerean philosophy with its extreme counter-position, namely dialectical materialism. And this is surely no accident, for here too, as in many other things, we see how a basically critical motif – namely the preponderance of the non-subjective over the subject – is absorbed and thereby neutralized. It would certainly be worth exploring this process of neutralization even further. On the other hand, this anti-subjectivism also has something extremely authoritarian about it. For it always harbours the possibility that the subject, since it is not treated as the master of all reality, since it is not in command of the whole, is also regarded as essentially insufficient. And this too has its truth moment, for a concept of reason which already acknowledges its own limitations thereby forfeits the claim to absolute logical purity which appears constitutive of the concept of reason itself. Thus a reason which limits itself as something finite and provisional thereby ceases to some extent to be rational. And this change in the concept of reason is reproduced here too. This leads in turn to the tendency to relinquish reason as if it were so much redundant effort – not unlike the case with those universal rationalizing mechanisms, we might even say, which ultimately replace thinking itself, as the cybernetic robots of today actually promise to do. This is a situation which I leave you to imagine for yourselves, where the 'hearkening' to being effectively seems to converge with cybernetics. At any rate, this now suggests that reason, once it becomes aware of its own limits, merely relinquishes itself, turns into the enemy, or simply abandons itself – as something 'thrown' or 'thrust out into the Nothing' – to what is Other in a purely attentive and listening posture. And this is more or less the situation with anti-subjectivism. I have attempted, as best I can, to show you the truth moments involved here but also to indicate those of illusion and untruth. The untruth lies in a turn of thought which is crucial in every regard and can be put like this: the negativity which the subject encounters in its relation to others and to the world is here transformed, as if by magic, into the positive. In other words, we find that the subject, rather than trying to engage in some way with the condition under which it suffers, only enhances this condition of its own meaninglessness, and even declares it meaningful by saying: the meaning of being is just this thrown and meaningless existence that is thrust out into the Nothing. And the subreption or ideological dimension with which I have charged fundamental ontology ultimately lies precisely here, in this hypostasis of subjectivity which transforms something negative into the positive and meaningful experience of being.

LECTURE 14

17 January 1961

In the last session I tried to unfold something of the dialectic which is implicit in this anti-subjectivist turn of philosophy in general. But I think we should now relate this rather more directly to Heidegger. For we will see there is something specific about this anti-subjectivist turn in Heidegger when considered in the context of his own philosophical development – if we can really speak in this way, since the concept of development becomes increasingly problematic the more we approach the thing that is supposed to have developed here. But if we do want to speak in this way, it turns out that the subjectivist moment which was certainly present in the earlier stages of Heidegger's thought, in his theory of 'existentials' and in all of those ways in which he strove to express something essential about human existence, becomes weaker and weaker as time goes on.[1] In other words, in terms of Heidegger's own central interest, we find that the concept of 'existence' retreats further and further into the background. I think it is certainly worth noting that the influence of this philosophy sprang originally from the way its analysis of the essential character of human existence promised to provide an answer to those questions which, as I pointed out, inspire the ontological interest in the first place. In other words, questions about man's place in the world; about how man relates to the Absolute; about those aspects of experience which go beyond any merely psychological features, namely the *Befindlichkeiten*, or 'attunements', as they were called, which arise out of man's fundamental relationship to reality. This appeared to offer the possibility of developing a concrete concept of man and defining the a

priori forms of human existence. Now one might almost say that this
entire interest has been thrown overboard in *everything* that Heidegger
has published since *Being and Time* and the book on Kant. And he
has effectively disqualified this interest by claiming (with a certain
justice, as I already pointed out) that the whole existential analysis
– namely everything that promised to respond to those questions
about human existence – was only ever undertaken with a view to
elucidating 'being' itself. Now both these things are true. I believe I
have already substantiated this point with a number of quotations,
but you need only to look at the first thirty pages of *Being and Time*
to confirm it; and if you want to follow these lectures properly I
encourage you to maintain close contact with the texts throughout.
Thus, on the one hand, you will find several formulations in which
the analysis of *Dasein*, the existential analysis itself, is described simply
as a stage on the way to the ontological analysis in the most emphatic
and fundamental sense, namely the analysis of what 'being' really is.
On the other hand, you also find in *Being and Time* that a crucial
position is specifically ascribed to the subject, to *Dasein*, precisely as
an ontological mode of being itself, as something that is at once ontic
and ontological. For existence is something transparent to itself, as
Kierkegaard puts it,[2] and is thus itself ontological in character. A
particular kind of privileged status is therefore accorded to the subject
after all. And in this sense Heidegger, like his teacher Husserl, stands
in the idealist tradition. Thus the idealist form assumed by the concept
of being itself, as I already indicated in the earlier lectures, is bound
up with the way in which this philosophy starts out from the crucial
character of subjectivity. But I believe that it has not yet been sufficiently understood how this extreme objectivism, which effectively
neutralizes the subject and transforms it into 'the questioner', or ultimately into the instrument (to put this in a deliberately exaggerated
way) by which being questions itself, has led to a situation in which
all of those aspects which originally provoked such interest in this
philosophy have now completely retreated into the background. Hence
this thinking profits to this day from a certain interest, namely the
interest in responding to essential questions, when it has actually long
since ceased to respond to them. There is something very peculiar
here which reveals a strange cultural and historical parallel with another
figure who is radically opposed to Heidegger and yet in several respects
not entirely unlike him. I am talking about Lukács, who in all his
work from around 1925 onwards, if not slightly earlier, has completely
retracted and repudiated all the things to which he owes his intellectual reputation.[3] Yet this turn has done nothing to damage this
reputation. On the contrary, the reputation has now been transferred

to products which no longer justify anything of the kind. I believe it would be a most interesting exercise to pursue this structure in more detail. What this reveals, of course, is the tremendous need for authority which also prevails amongst intellectuals in our own time. Once they have found something which speaks to them and strikes them as significant, they cling to this phenomenon in an almost sectarian fashion, even when its original quality has long since vanished and been converted to the opposite. One cannot really say that the later writings of Heidegger – which are now simply dedicated to interpreting the concept of being – have anything whatsoever to do with that earlier interest, with that element of personal involvement and urgent concern which I tried to illustrate for you by reference to Kierkegaard. But this brings us back once again to the concept of the philosophical need. And I would just like to say a few more words about this question today.

The fact that an intellectual and cultural need exists does not guarantee the possibility of its fulfilment. Let me try and explain this more precisely. It certainly means that there is a particular interest in certain areas, that this interest rightly expects to be pursued and explored, that we respond to the questions that it throws up or that it specifically articulates as questions. But the fact that we are interested in some specific cultural and intellectual content, that we are interested in finding some purchase and meaning, in finding something reliable which we can really trust or affirm – in short, as they say, the kind of thing that would bring soldiers under a hail of fire suddenly feel the need for God – none of this guarantees that the interest in question would actually reveal itself as something real and true and present in the light of the careful analysis whch consciousness demands. Now if we consider the way that Heidegger's philosophy has turned distinctively against the kind of need which originally inspired it and to which it also owes its sectarian appeal, I believe we may clearly recognize the consequences of a thinking which is increasingly beholden to this concept of being. But we can thereby also recognize that such thinking – and I have already indicated that it is essentially a kind of strategic thinking, one that wishes to occupy a certain cultural and intellectual position of power – has proved unable to satisfy the need in the particular form in which it undertook to address it. And that is why this thinking, in accordance with its very structure, has had to perform a kind of volte face. In other words, it renounces the satisfaction of the need, since that cannot actually be satisfied, yet continues to act as if the satisfaction in question had already been effected. In one of his later writings – I am not quite sure whether it is in *The Genealogy of Morals* or in *Beyond Good and Evil* – Nietzsche

pointed out how often theological apologists have argued for the
existence of God on the grounds that human beings have such a great
need for it. And he claims in response that the fact that a certain
thought or proof springs from a need is itself almost an argument for
its falsehood.[4] In other words, to put this very simply, we think what
we want to think, or just indulge in 'wishful thinking', as they say in
English. Thus we are hardly capable of free thought, hardly capable
of judging a phenomenon unless it somehow already answers to our
own emotional and instinctual needs. Now I would not like to try
and decide here how far this rather plausible and 'enlightened' analysis
on Nietzsche's part holds in absolutely every case. For without some
need or other we cannot think at all. A thought which is not somehow
really concerned about the object which it intends will never reach
its object. I believe that the relationship between need or instinct and
the object itself is rather more complex than it is presented here.
Nonetheless, I think that what Nietzsche brings against theology here,
in a style of argument already familiar to the Enlightenment, holds
just as much for metaphysics in its secular rather than its theological
form. In other words, the so-called metaphysical need, of itself, says
nothing about the genuinely substantive character of what it asks
about or is directed towards. Now this is directly related to what I
described earlier as the volte face or the leap performed by this philosophy. And it has to be seen as a stroke of genius, if I may use the
expression in a less exalted sense here, that this philosophy has chosen
this path. For the fundamental structure of Heidegger's philosophy
dictates that the impossibility of answering metaphysical questions
– and Kant indeed had already recognized this impossibility – is itself
substituted for the answer that it fails to provide. Thus Kant says:
You cannot ask about God, freedom and immortality, or, rather: You
can certainly ask about them, but if you try to think about these
things, or make cognitive judgements regarding them, you are instantly
entangled in contradictions, and these contradictions prove that your
question, however unavoidable it may otherwise be, is actually an
illegitimate question. Now Heidegger would respond, if I may extend
this line of thought in a very crude way, and say: Yes, indeed, and
that I cannot give this answer is actually the answer itself. In other
words, the human being as such, in accordance with its own metaphysical constitution, is characterized by all those features of finitude
that Kant ascribes to it, and which specifically make it impossible for
us to answer the so-called fundamental questions of metaphysics. And
this is related to a structural characteristic of the entire philosophy
of being, one which becomes particularly evident at this point and
which I have mentioned on various occasions already. This is the

priority of the question over the answer. And there is something analogous at work in the philosophy of Jaspers, incidentally, even if this philosophy, in its fundamental structure, would wish to distance itself from the somewhat earlier existential ontology developed by Heidegger. Philosophy of this kind expressly turns the impossibility of answering the genuinely metaphysical questions into its own content, or into the content of metaphysics, and transforms this very impossibility into some sort of positive interpretation of human existence. Thus it cannot help ascribing a much higher dignity to the questions themselves, once the answers to its questions have been excised, than we find in philosophies which are undisturbed by these hovering doubts, such as that of Plato, which in its earlier Socratic form amply recognized the dignity and priority of questioning, even if questions were subsequently reduced to a kind of technique once Plato had developed a positive, transcendent and metaphysical doctrine, namely the theory of Ideas. This was a technique for articulating natural concepts that were also clearly differentiated from one another. The process of questioning thereby becomes a technique of thinking rather than a substantial metaphysical quantity in its own right. Yet it appears precisely as the latter in all ontology in its current phase.

Now it is relatively easy here to draw the conclusion – which is surely already implicit in what I have said so far – that this is a kind of 'sour grapes' metaphysics. In other words, a metaphysics which inevitably realizes it is unable to answer its own questions, yet still insists on being metaphysics. Thus it simply glorifies questioning as such and makes that into a kind of metaphysics, turning itself into something that is already supposed to be meaningful and indeed supposed to be more than a mere question. This is how the question comes to assume a certain aura in Heidegger and Jaspers, as is evident from the way both thinkers address this entire problematic of 'the question'. But here, once again, I want to try and make my criticisms of these particular approaches sharper and more convincing than they might otherwise be by going beyond the argumentation which I have just exemplified and suggested to you. In other words, I would like to show you that here too, as in almost all aspects of this philosophy, there is a truth content to be uncovered – or at least some relation to a truth content. For in philosophy the concept of the question has a different meaning and structure than it possesses in the context of the special sciences. When a mathematician talks about a certain problem, for example, this is something for which in fact he currently has no solution, and he will undertake to discover one by means of mathematical methods. And it is similar in physics, where the physicist may certainly have his hypotheses – or, to put this in a rather freer and more relaxed fashion, may have his 'hunches', as scientists say in America. In other words, he may suspect that this is how things will probably turn out to be. But these hypotheses or suspicions have no constitutive significance for the thing itself; they possess a merely instrumental function and disappear once the particular scientific question has been solved. If we really wanted to, we could almost distinguish the practice of philosophy and that of the special sciences, including logic and mathematics, specifically by reference to the way that questions are raised and addressed in each case. For what we find in philosophy – and I am well aware that you will probably laugh, or, if you wish to be a little more polite, at least smile at this – is that the questions raised here are not really answered at all. And of course I realize that you might then simply say to yourselves, Well, why on earth are we bothering with this stuff? But that the fact that you continue to do so seems to me to show that philosophy is still relevant, and that it involves a different understanding of what a question is. In the first place, philosophical questions are never neatly tied up or resolved, although they often reveal a tendency to be overtaken by subsequent developments and then forgotten.[5] Thus in philosophy these questions never just remain what they were, and they are not always constantly being raised in the way that the textbooks of philosophy sometimes imply, when you read for example that every philosophical system has tried in its own way to answer certain fundamental questions of being. For that is just a fancy phrase. If you consider the specific form of individual philosophical systems, you will find that, while there is some kind of contextual relation between them, some categories effectively disappear and get replaced by new ones, even though such categories are not expressly thematized as such and theoretically evaluated in a positive or negative way. The whole structure of philosophical questioning is completely different. I should add that not enough thought has really been given to this distinctive structure of questioning in the history of philosophy, and I think it is high time that someone attempted such a thing – though certainly not under the spell of the prevailing Heideggereanism, for then every question would simply turn into the one and only question of being – as long as this was pursued in the differentiated way that I have just tried to suggest. On the other hand, in spite of the unresolved character of so many central controversies – and let me just say that the theses which the *Critique of Pure Reason* declares with such tremendous confidence to have been definitively established still keep returning as problems, so that the word 'definitive' is certainly out of place here – we can say that philosophical questions in a very peculiar way imply their own answers. When we really think – and philosophical thinking is indeed very rare – we find that the rhythm of such thinking is quite distinctive. It is not as if there is something we don't know, and we just sit down at the desk, with our head in our hands, and think about the question until we arrive at the answer. If you took this as your model of genuine untrammelled thinking, I believe it would utterly misrepresent what actually transpires in thinking. For surely what generally happens is that thought grasps something in a rather immediate way – we will go into this in more detail next time – or that something strikes us, or that we clearly 'behold' something, as they liked to say thirty years ago, and only then, I would suggest, do we actually look for the questions which help to bring what we have just realized into the continuity of our conscious life. We might also express this by saying that, in philosophy, the relevant answers are implicitly contained in the shape of the question in a manner that is very different from the case of the special sciences. Now these structures, which I have suggested here only in a very general and provisional way, and which I must leave you to explore in more detail for yourselves, are certainly also part of Heidegger's own experience. And he has certainly recognized that the shape of an intrinsically philosophical question is quite different than it appears to be for those philosophically naive approaches which simply attempt to transfer what currently counts as the logic of science to the practice of philosophy. And that is the truth moment to the priority which philosophy accords to the question. Yet it seems to me that the ψεῦδος [pseudos] here – if I may avoid the cruder word 'mistake' – lies in the way that Heidegger is misled by the distinctive shape of the philosophical question into devaluing the theoretical answer which is its correlate. Since the question in philosophy addresses itself to experience, and since the question therefore already implies its answer in a way that is quite different from the special sciences, he ends up by immediately ascribing something like the dignity of truth to the question itself. But he fails to make it clear that the distinctive questioning character of philosophical thinking is substantiated only when we relate what has been disclosed to us, and which we go on to explore in our questions in a way that brings it into some rational continuity, into some context of justification, into some self-transparent and clearly motivated relationship. And Heidegger one-sidedly ignores these achievements of conscious reflection and rationality in the context of philosophical experience precisely by hypostasizing the question. But this means that the question is effectively turned into an absolute, and thereby becomes just as abstract and independent as that which supposedly corresponds with this wholly abstract and general question devoid of all determination – namely 'being' itself.

Ladies and gentlemen, you should be quite clear what the structure of the question implies for the problem we were discussing earlier, namely for the fact that this philosophy, for reasons that are grounded in the philosophy of history, for all its positivity, cannot actually fulfil what is expected of it. And here, I believe, you stumble upon something that is really quite simple and primitive. I do not hesitate to put it this way, although I realize it impugns the hallowed nimbus of this philosophy. I have always tried, and will never stop trying, to account for this nimbus and explain it to you – namely as a kind of absolutized aura. But I am not remotely tempted to bow down to it in a ritualistic way. For it seems to me – and here again I speak *ad homines* and appeal directly to your own philosophical concerns – that, if you think about the crucial strategic aspect of this philosophy which I have emphasized throughout, you will see that the fact that certain questions are constantly talked about or 'thematized', as Husserl or the earlier Heidegger used to say, already becomes a splendid substitute for the fact that these questions are never actually answered. Human beings may really ask such questions as: What we are here for? Can we believe in a Beyond? If we can find no meaning in this life, if we feel confronted by Nothing, if we feel we are nothing, then what can philosophy offer us? What consolations can philosophy provide for us? Now I do not wish to ask here whether philosophy can actually provide such consolations, although I do not believe it can. In fact I would almost like to say – and would here agree with Heidegger – that it belongs to the very essence of philosophy to deny mere consolation. Yet it turns out in Heidegger, so it seems to me, that this nuance, even if it is only a nuance, constitutes the entire difference between truth and lie. Thus when we talk about all these categories, about the finitude of man, about the 'thrownness' of *Dasein*, about the blind contingency and arbitrary character of *Dasein*, about the ineluctable and unconditional character of death – even when we repeat the sort of trivialities we find in *Being and Time*[6] where Heidegger declares in vatic tones that the only thing left when we die is a corpse – it appears as if the problems were already solved just by talking about them. It is rather like the situation where people throng to public lectures in learned institutions because they imagine that, when certain more or less prominent individuals hold forth about the crisis of culture, something has thereby already been done to resolve this crisis. The crucial mechanism here is that, if people only talk long enough about the fact they have to die and that life has no meaning, they would not actually need to die and life would indeed possess a meaning. I believe that the secret fascination of this philosophy lies in this very mechanism, which Kant would have called a mechanism of subreption, a secret fascination which is intimately bound up with the phenomenon that I spoke about in the last lecture when I pointed out how the anti-institutional impulse, the revolt against the academic professionalization of philosophy, eventually became an academic profession in its own right. For this thematization of something that is not just a theme for discussion but something profoundly serious only robs it of this seriousness and integrates it within the existing order of business, an existing order which, we know all too well, effectively sets up these questions in such a way that we cannot actually address them. And now at last you will understand why I said that the questions which are raised by fundamental ontology and related movements of philosophy are all indices of a certain lack. I believe it is important that you grasp this state of affairs really clearly if you are to have any real chance of guarding against this wretched mechanism. For when people are so entangled in the completely prosaic and more or less mechanized business of life – in the domain of science, in administrative fields such as pedagogy and social work, or whatever it may be – it is all too easy for ontological philosophy to transfigure the prose of life with the products it has to offer the consumer. Thus a self-respecting person who is supposed to write a book on the state of rented housing in the countryside will at least provide an introduction in which 'solicitude for human existence' and other similar categories are sure to play a certain role. Both things belong together perfectly: the completely unimaginative administrative mentality with all its facts and metrics – to which the mind has now predominantly been reduced – and the sauce which is poured on everything, a sauce knocked from pre-packaged cubes I might add, that lends a certain aroma to the whole business. And the meaning that has vanished from this facticity is conjured back into it through a philosophical decree which has nothing but contempt for that factical realm.

I would just like to consider a couple of the most important of these ontological categories to show in brief how far they are indeed indices of a lack. First there is the category of man, the category of *Dasein*, which is of course usually the preferred term here. If we were to take a general vote today with regard to the most important philosophical categories available, then surely 'man' would be mentioned first of all. And the idea that it all comes down to man is constantly regurgitated everywhere, on business trips or in academic lectures, as if such repetition were not already a cause for profound suspicion. I might just point out that this intolerable emphasis on the word 'man' was quite alien to the classical age of humanism in the time of Wilhelm von Humboldt, for example. You will certainly not find Humboldt, or Fichte, or Hegel using this word with anything like the same emphasis or quivering emotion. For what is taken to be truly substantial here is 'spirit' or 'the Idea', and man therefore simply appears as what he is, namely as a biological species. The concept of man was only hallowed when nothing else meaningful was left and the profane world had to become a sacred double of itself. I would say that all this talk of man in the *singular* already expresses illusion and ideology in a world of essentially conflicting interests where there is no longer any such thing as a collective subject – that we harp on about man and *Dasein* all the time, and keep saying that *everything* comes down to man, precisely because in the world in which we live this is very far from the case. And every single one of us in this room understands, in terms of our own experience, the enormous degree to which we have become little more than functions of an overpowering apparatus, and we realize that perhaps the best we can hope for is to snatch just something of what we think of as our genuine human vocation from this apparatus. For I hardly have to spell out for you how things now stand with a vocation of which human beings have effectively been robbed. In other words, the entire pathos that is bound up with words such as 'man' and *Dasein* and the rest is ultimately a *lucus a non lucendo* in the most literal sense imaginable.[7] It is proof that *man* himself does not truly exist, that man is only marketed by philosophy, as it were, so that *human beings* can all the more easily be deceived about their own loss of humanity. The meaning of their own existence as subjects is transfigured the way it is only because they are in truth no longer subjects, because they are aspects of the apparatus. In this particular context I always like to refer to expressionism, where of course the word 'man' also plays a significant role, even though it had very different undertones and expressed a protest against reified conditions. Thus I remember a book by Ludwig Rubiner, a kind of manifesto, with the title *Man in the Centre*.[8] There may perhaps have been something rather superficial and ideological about such talk, but it certainly signified a protest against the reality of mechanized warfare. Now a few years ago a book appeared under the title *Man at the Centre of Business*.[9] This is what has become of man in the centre! I fear that the entire ideology of man at the present time, now we are all subjected to business, consists simply in persuading us that man is the real centre of concern. We are no such thing, but simply, as Karl Kraus put it,[10] either producers or consumers.

LECTURE 15

19 January 1961

In the last session I offered an example of how modish concepts are often indices for the absence of the things they are supposed to concern and suggested that all this talk of 'man' and the 'centre' that he allegedly occupies is an indication that man certainly no longer stands in this position today.[1] I am not claiming of course that every concept that arises in philosophy and is expressly thematized as such is invariably an index of absence in this sense, although I believe that this thesis has a greater validity, and is capable of far broader application, than we would commonly imagine. Thus one might plausibly argue, for example, that the thematic which was so important in seventeenth-century philosophy – namely the problem of the relation between the inner world and external world and how they influence or interact with each other – is directly connected with the demise of the medieval cosmos in which inner and outer experience were still articulated in terms of a single principle. Or again we might claim – and this is by no means an original idea, but one that has cropped up quite frequently in modern discussions of the history of philosophy – that the Platonic theory of Ideas itself and the hierarchical social structures connected with it were conceived in a spirit of restoration. In other words, they are an attempt to re-create the feudal order of social classes that had existed in Greece before the advent of democracy and the rise of the Greek enlightenment, now that enlightened Greece had become entangled in the Peloponnesian War and all those difficulties which are so clearly reflected in the philosophy that subsequently emerged. Indeed there is something to be said in general for the idea that the owl of Minerva not only begins its flight with the falling of dusk[2] but still hovers over history, as it were, seizing upon precisely what falls from the chariot of world history (if you will permit me the rather involved metaphor). Nonetheless, I believe that we are talking about something more specific in this case. For here we find that a series of concepts which possess a certain aura, to use this word once again, and seem to cast a very particular metaphysical glow, like the concept of 'man' which we talked about last time, are emphatically treated *in abstracto* precisely when these same concepts *realiter* have suffered considerable disenchantment already. I believe that the phenomenon I have in mind, and which is nonetheless quite specific, as I say, is perhaps easiest to grasp when you think about the rather striking fact that people always talk about tradition, always appeal to tradition or invoke the concept of tradition itself, when the tradition can longer be presupposed, once it has become weaker or problematic in some way or other. It is really only after the advent of revolutions, and especially in the wake of the French Revolution, that we witness the emergence of a philosophy which undertakes to justify the monarchy and the old order of 'estates', as in thinkers such as de Bonald and de Maistre.[3] When the feudal order is still unbroken, for example, the sheer presence of tradition suffices to make the idea of challenging such a system seem impossible. Such things are not done, we simply say, and the idea is effectively eliminated if it even emerges. But once the living power of tradition is no longer present, people begin to call upon it explicitly, to transfigure the tradition itself into a kind of substantial essence. And then they say: Yet tradition tells us that we have to behave this way rather than that. At that point we may even develop a metaphysics or doctrine of tradition precisely to try and find some justification for what cannot otherwise be justified. I have already tried to explain why the concept of man has moved into the very centre of philosophy in the way that it has. Now what is called the 'philosophy of life', which is usually traced back to Nietzsche and would later find its most famous representatives in Dilthey, Simmel and Bergson, also reveals something similar, for the concept of life was only transformed into a metaphysical entity when life in its immediate character was no longer self-evidently accessible to us through the ever-increasing impact of technological rationalization. In the great periods of metaphysical speculation, on the other hand, life itself is never glorified – for the very simple reason that life in itself belongs in the realm of what just is, or represents the dynamic context of beings, while philosophy was then specifically attempting to explain the dynamic context of beings as *more* than what *merely* is in this context. It is only once something like immediate life had become a problem in an increasingly technical world that people began to consider that life has a 'value', as they loved to say, and to create a whole philosophy out of this idea. Although it has to be said that Simmel's thesis that life is more than life essentially revives the classic idealist thesis that the complete context of things in immanence transcends this immanence itself. In this regard, Simmel's philosophy belongs to a traditional form of thought.[4]

In touching on this here I am perhaps just reminding you of something that may have occurred to you at various points already and that has actually often been pointed out before. And this is that existential ontology, the philosophy of existence as a whole, is to a certain extent the successor and inheritor of the philosophy of life – although it regards itself as higher or perhaps deeper because the underlying substance of the philosophy of life, namely the idea of life itself, remains bound up in the context of beings, whereas the philosophy of existence claims to uncover the constitutive factors behind the context of beings themselves. Yet many of the characteristic motifs of the philosophy of life can be found in Scheler in particular, but also in Heidegger and in existential ontology. And in a certain sense the entire philosophy we are talking about here – above all in its irrationalism, which we have touched upon on several occasions already – is a kind of attempt to continue the philosophy of life by stripping it of its positivist element – the element that identifies life with the context of mere beings – and turning it into something which its arbitrary hypostatization of the biological principle of life had prevented it from becoming. But existential philosophy is by no means as radically new or as radically different in relation to the philosophy of life as it likes to present itself. In material terms the categories it employs go back to the philosophy of life, and precisely in the distinctive complementary fashion we have indicated. For philosophy, which has relinquished more and more of the areas and regions for which it was once responsible to the realm of the special sciences, nonetheless believes it can find a little garden for itself as long as it discovers some interest which can no longer be accommodated within an entirely technologized and standardized world. And this little garden takes on different names in accordance with the specific situation in which it finds itself – in the times of great industrial expansion and economic growth it will assume the accents of the philosophy of life, whereas in dark times, in times of war, in times when it is obvious that our actual lives hardly correspond with the promise of life itself, it will assume the gloomier accents of the philosophy of existence, for which death is ultimately more significant than life. Yet the horizon within which the respective questions are raised remains the same in both cases. You can also see this very clearly when you consider the importance of the concept of *time* in Heidegger, for precisely through its intimate relationship to *Dasein* time becomes the category in which *Dasein*, and thus beings in general, are constitutively related to being, and vice versa. And this relationship between beings and the metaphysical principle, a relationship which is here grounded in time, is connected extraordinarily closely with that immanent transcendence – if I can put it in this way – which belongs to life. Now I believe that my view of this *lucus a non lucendo*, my view that these concepts emerge specifically when their own substrate is no longer available to experience, applies with particular force to the concept of time. Now of course you may immediately object that all of us exist in time, and that without some awareness of time something like the unity of consciousness and thinking itself could never arise in the first place. And that was indeed Kant's view, and Heidegger's defence of the centrality of time, as specifically expressed in his book on Kant,[5] is based on the idea that the ontological substrate in Kant's philosophy of knowledge, the dimension relevant to being, is to be found in the priority which is here ascribed to time. For it is time, as the medium of all the relations of consciousness, that makes knowledge possible in the first place. (This is the basic idea, expressed my own terms, behind Heidegger's book on Kant.)

Now it is of course perfectly true that we cannot deny the continuing significance of time or the actual existence of our consciousness of time. But I believe it is essential, if we are to understand what we mean by the inner life, and if we are to grasp the inner form or connection of philosophical categories, that we do more than simply indicate these constituent elements *in abstracto* and point out that they cannot be thought away. For they assume the distinctive character and quality that they do only in the broader context of the life in which they present themselves. It may well be that no human experience can even be envisaged without reference to the horizon of time. In fact I would not dream of denying this. But what time actually means, precisely how time is experienced, and above all the mode in which we specifically reflect upon how we come to experience time – this is something entirely different. And I would think that these historical variations in the actual experience of categories such as 'time', or indeed 'the individual', are so central that you can no longer really isolate or extract the seemingly immutable substrate that appears to be involved here, namely time as such or the individual qua singular biological entity. For these things can only be experienced insofar as they are configured in specific social and historical contexts. And, in this rather more subtle and more sublimated sense, I believe that something has decisively

changed in our consciousness of time, even if the formal character of
this consciousness remains the same. This is in part connected with
the structure of labour, and especially industrial labour, the technically
rationalized character of which basically consists in the repetition of
ideally identical processes and operations on the part of the labouring
individuals and the machines which are involved, a development to
which human beings are simply supposed to adapt. And I specifically
want to draw your attention to the distinctive sociological fact that
these changes which occur in the form of labour itself – in the actual
state of the productive forces, as we say in the social sciences – also
reach far beyond this particular sphere. In other words, the fact that
something like experience, in the sense of genuine temporal continuity, is no longer needed at the heart of our telling concepts of labour
now extends its influence upon every conceivable area of life, albeit
in ways that are still largely unrecognized, which admittedly makes
this claim sound in turn rather mystical and dogmatic. So let me try
and demonstrate what I mean here, since it may be far from obvious
to you precisely what I am driving at, with a very simple example.
Thus I believe that, if someone were to describe an older person to
you these days as *wise*, you would either have no idea of what that
was supposed to mean, or you would just smile and imagine they were
talking about a poseur (perhaps rightly) who has managed to live for
so long, far longer than the statistical average at least, that he is now
also privileged to enjoy much greater insight or whatever than anyone
else. But the concept of wisdom itself has become an anachronism.
It has become anachronistic because what we properly understand
by wisdom – if we still possess an ear for such things and we really
wish for a moment to do phenomenology in the good old sense of the
word – is not merely intelligence in the sense of cognitive capacity, or
even in relation to particular objects of one kind or another, and not
merely experience as such. Rather, it is the capacity to appropriate
experience, the capacity to realize the continuity of an entire life in
terms of the actual consciousness that an individual has attained over
time. I am talking here about the achieved unity between experience
itself and the mental and spiritual capacities that develop and unfold
in response to this experience. And that is what is no longer available
today. For mental and spiritual capacity today consists more in the
ability of human beings to adapt to constantly changing situations, to
be flexible, to earn a living in different ways, to exploit the opportuni-
ties that present themselves, than it does, for example, in the ability
to acquire knowledge and experience of some particular discipline
over a period of many years, in such a way that their life continues to
reveal the structure of this knowledge and experience. The fact that

today the type of well-educated worker or craftsman has largely given
way in social terms to the uneducated or merely trained worker also
belongs in this context, from which you can infer that something has
also changed with respect to the experience of time, that something
specific has happened here. And this is particularly evident, in a very
blunt way, when we consider something that has often been analysed
(especially by Heimpel). I am talking about the peculiar loss of any
sense of historical continuity which emerged in Germany after the end
of the Second World War, and the impact of which can be traced in
terms of specific research methods. Thus we find that young people
today, unless they have an academic background of some kind or other,
hardly have any awareness of who Bismarck or Wilhelm I was,[6] whereas
in my youth, for example, the awareness of this whole era in which
the German Empire was founded, and everything connected with it,
was probably still very much alive to everyone. It also has to be said,
incidentally, that these German phenomena, which have so often been
pointed out and are indeed constantly encountered here, are hardly
unique when we consider how in America, which in capitalist terms
is the most advanced country in every respect, this loss of a sense of
historical continuity has long been evident. For in America, at least
outside the specifically academic context, there is a prevailing suspicion, indeed almost an aversion, with regard to history in general as
a sphere of traditionalism[7] which expressly contradicts the dominant
principle of exchange rationality. And Henry Ford's famous remark
that 'history is bunk' seems a perfect expression of this.[8] There is a
very widely shared general feeling in America that, if all something
can say for itself is that it has arisen historically, and that is 'there',
then it really belongs in the rubbish bin. And the American passion for
antiques and similar things that can be snapped up in Europe is merely
the other side of this general sentiment. Thus these processes that we
observe here in Germany are little more than than a confirmation to
this global tendency.

Now I just mentioned the antiques business and, when we read
the effusions of fundamental ontology on the subject of time, it is
indeed sometimes hard to avoid the impression that we are dealing
with a kind of sublimated antiques business. In other words, it is
precisely when the consciousness of time, understood as the consciousness of the continuity of life, has faded away that we are consoled,
as it were, with the idea that something like time, something like
continuous life, still exists. You need only to consider how utterly
remote it seems when the Bible tells us that Abraham died in good
old age, an old man, and full of years,[9] to appreciate something of
the nostalgia that clings to this experience of time as a fundamental,

and I am almost tempted to say rural, dimension of life. And this yearning for time itself, once our consciousness of time has been shattered or destroyed, is exploited by the philosophy of being which confidently assures us that time is irredeemably essential to us even when we no longer have any genuine experience of time. It then goes on to present the entirely abstract consciousness of time that is naturally all that is left to us as an attribute of being itself that is manifest to us in *Dasein* as if it were the *ens realissimum*. And I believe we also find a similar complementary relationship at work when we consider the highest concept in Heidegger, namely the concept of being itself. Just consider for a moment all of the associations which arise for you when you hear the word 'being'. And this suggestion is quite legitimate, for we are assured, after all, that 'being' is not a concept but is being itself. And in order to apprehend such trans-conceptual being we must obviously appeal to something more than a set of simply authoritative definitions. Now I believe that there is very little to object to in this method once the concept of being has been interpreted in this way. Thus if you explore what happens when you hear a word such as 'being', and simply consider the gratifying effect which is produced by such talk, then you will surely feel a certain sense of security, of reliability, of dependability in this regard – and you must forgive me if I express myself in such vague terms, but this vagueness is appropriate to the stratum of experience we are dealing with here. Thus when people say, 'That is someone who speaks to me in his very being', we have a sense of what was once described by words such as 'character' – in other words, the impression of something solid, reliable and substantial. I think the slightly elevated term 'substantial' perhaps captures this best. And it is perhaps particularly characteristic of the highly conservative climate of this philosophy that, whereas Kantian thought essentially dissolved the concept of substance in the ontological sense and transformed substantiality into a category, into something first constituted through subjectivity,[10] this concept of substance is hypostasized in our contemporary ontological forms of thought. In other words, it is expressly turned into something over which the process of subjective constitution exercises no power whatsoever. I believe there is a peculiar need which finds expression here too, for it belongs to the essence of our contemporary society – and I think this goes beyond relatively external aspects such as the increasingly technological character of life and touches on the very principle of society itself – that it no longer contains anything which really exists in its own right, that exists for its own sake. Kant already alluded to this in the *Critique of Practical Reason* when he claimed that everything has either price or intrinsic worth,[11] where 'worth' belongs to what exists for its own sake, whereas 'price' is what exists only in relation to something else, or something that is valued only insofar as one gets something else for it – in other words, something subjected to the principle of exchange. In this sense, we could describe the concept of being as the attempt to restore the idea of worth or dignity. At the same time it actually ignores the worth or dignity of humanity, even though the idea of worth or dignity is itself bound up with that of humanity. For if anyone now tried to ascribe worth or dignity to us as the constantly buffeted and increasingly powerless individuals that we have become, this would surely be met with the kind of derision that I mentioned at the beginning of this lecture, and to which Heidegger himself, I would suggest, was particularly sensitive. I would almost say that the attempt to avoid such derision, while developing concepts which would instantly provoke this reaction if they were nakedly presented as such, is an art which this philosophy understands perfectly.

In other words, we live in a state of society which can be described as one of universal fungibility, where the prevailing principle of exchange ensures that nothing exists for itself, for its own sake, but exists only insofar as it possesses exchange value, and we are elevated and consoled in such a world by this concept of being. For it would like to convince us that there is something else beyond this principle of fungibility, something more weighty and reliable – and interestingly enough it seems we need rather old-fashioned words to capture this: something 'sterling', as they say in English, or *pfundig* as they say in South German dialect. And it is precisely this aura of reliability which lends the concept of being its incomparable and anachronistic contemporaneity. The very way it eludes direct confrontation makes us feel that this sterling quality, this well-crafted durability and reliability, will never be lost but can somehow survive in a realm beyond all criticism. For this philosophy avoids all contact or confrontation with the current state of experience. If I may just recall the thought I adumbrated a few moments ago: if we were actually to replace 'being' with the concept of worth or dignity – the particular attributes of which correspond perfectly to that aura which I have suggested attaches to 'being' – then the intimate connection between the concept of worth or dignity and the experience of real human beings would itself reveal the anachronistic and misleading character of this thinking. For instead it confers worth or dignity upon something entirely abstract, which certainly possesses all the power of this solidity, of this impenetrability, of this 'thereness', but is also supposed to be something more than mere existence, namely something higher which is thereby protected from the disenchantment of mere existence. In this way we somehow manage to preserve all these things while simultaneously protecting them from any kind of controversy, from any kind of possible criticism. If you wish to maintain an autonomous consciousness of your own – and this is what I am trying to encourage in these lectures – if you want to develop the power to resist the very powerful temptations which clearly spring from this philosophy, then I believe it would almost be better for you to think through these connections, and thus explore the dispositions within yourselves to which such thinking responds, than simply to content yourselves with a merely intellectual analysis of the implications of these concepts. That is precisely why I have tried to bring out these particular aspects of the concept of time and the concept of being. And I should just say here that there is another concept which plays a significant and ambiguous role in Heidegger, namely the concept of *meaning*, which derives from the specifically phenomenological approach to the analysis of meaning. For this concept also plays a similar complementary role in relation to the phenomenon that Max Weber famously described in terms of the 'disenchantment of the world'.[12] The more disenchanted the world becomes, the more philosophy reacts by presenting you with meaning precisely as a complementary ideology. Yet since philosophy is incapable of furnishing such substantial meaning on its own, here too it performs what I call a volte face. In other words, it behaves as if the analysis of meaning, the analysis of concepts – that is, of words such as the word 'being', the word '*Dasein*', the word 'existence' – as if the analysis which furnishes the meaning of these *words* were the same as *that* meaning, whatever it may be, which has fallen victim to the disenchantment of the world. Whereas the simplest human understanding would object that, while we may very well grasp the meaning of concepts such as being, *Dasein*, existence, time, that we may perfectly understand what they signify, our insight into this meaning still has no power over the process of disenchantment itself. Yet Heidegger's entire philosophy characteristically suggests that, if we only attend to these concepts carefully enough, if we 'behold' them in a spirit of veneration, this suffices to reverse the disenchantment of the world. In other words, to repeat what I argued earlier, the thematization of these categories is already taken as a kind of fulfilment, and this makes it appear as if the real need in the face of the disenchantment of the world, a need which is generated by suffering under this disenchantment, had already been dispelled – as if the thing in question were ultimately guaranteed by appealing to the concepts which generally conceal it.

Ladies and gentlemen, I believe that you will have derived something from these analyses. For when we are talking about this philosophy in its most recent form, or perhaps in the light of our analysis today, let me say, when we are talking about this ideology in its most recent form, you should be very clear that this ideology is also extraordinarily clever. Thus we are not invited to contemplate some divine meaning; we are not regaled with stories about the eternity or immutability of being; we are not reassured in concrete terms that something of our actual life in time will never utterly be lost. Rather, the power of this philosophy lies in the way it actually manages to fulfil all the functions that I have analysed for you, even though it accomplishes all these things – and the concept of being is eminently well suited to ensure this, as I shall presently show – by exploiting invariant elements which enjoy the cachet of such invariance without ever really being tied down as such. Yet we have to say that these invariants, that the archaism and the relationship to certain obsolescent phases of social development which have already been condemned to the past, are nonetheless much stronger and more evident in this philosophy than it is itself prepared to concede. You are all well aware that Heidegger's philosophy likes to claim two things in particular. In the first place, it regards language itself as the organ of 'being' rather than simply, with nominalism, as a system of signs that lets us bring humanly defined and determined things to light θέσει [thesei] or 'in accordance with convention'. This is one particularly emphatic claim on Heidegger's part. And the other equally emphatic claim is that the thinking of being is really at home in an area that we might describe as prior to or indifferent to the distinction between poetry and philosophy as it has come to be established. And Heidegger certainly drew the ultimate conclusion from this idea once in his life, when he published a little volume containing what I am not exactly sure we should call poems or maxims and aphorisms. He would almost certainly reject such descriptions and prefer instead to speak of manifestations of being or something of the kind. Now in view of the extraordinary significance which falls to language and the poetic word, and in view of my own claim about the concealed but powerful historical archaism and anachronism of this style of thinking, I think it would be worth looking at this particular text a little more closely. The book in question, *From the Experience of Thinking*, was written in 1947 and published by Pfullingen about six years ago now, in 1954. I imagine that a few of you at least will have seen the text already. Now I cannot resist reading some of it out to you here in order to give you some sense of the specific place this philosophy occupies. Thus we find things like 'When the early morning light quietly / grows above the mountains', or again, 'The darkening of the world never reaches / to the light of beyng.' Here I would just remind you of my remarks about the affirmative character of this philosophy: thus the darkening of the world – here it is just immediately blurted out – is supposed to be weaker than 'the light of beyng'. Or here is another motto from the book: 'When under a torn rain-clouded / sky a ray of sunlight glides suddenly / across the darkling meadows' – we are immediately offered the image of a mountain landscape, and then we are told: 'We never come to thoughts. They come / to us. / That is the fitting hour of dialogue.' Or we even hear: 'When at summer's threshold solitary narcissi / bloom secretly in the meadow and the / rock rose gleams beneath the maple.' And the motto that immediately follows is simply: 'The splendour of the simple'. Or just listen to this: 'When the mountain brook in night's / stillness tells of its plunging / over the boulders' or 'when the cowbells tinkle from / the slopes of the mountain valley / where herds slowly wend their way.' Or the final poem of the collection: 'Forests spread / Streams plunge / Rocks endure / Rain runs / Meadows tarry / Springs well / Winds dwell / Blessing muses.'[13] Now you all laughed, ladies and gentlemen, and I take this laughter extremely seriously. For it actually shows, it seems to me, how you reacted to the massive contradiction between the emotional claim of such lines and the language in which it finds expression. And this contradiction springs from its appeal to a particular stock of images, to a particular linguistic and imaginative world, which has long since been overtaken both by the development of language as a poetic medium and by the development of the world itself. Hence you simply have the feeling here that one is trying to speak about the gravest and most profoundly touching things, although the effect is rather like asking Max Jungnickel or Cäsar Flaischlen to act as authorities on the most difficult philosophical questions.[14] Now you may say it is unfair of me to insist on these things in the way I have. And I almost expect the objection on the part of common sense, which is always ready to defend things that are bad, and in this case would probably say, Well, he is a philosopher after all, and you cannot really hold it against him if he writes bad poetry. But my reply would be this. Since as a philosopher he expressly claims to be at home in a sphere beyond conceptuality, a sphere of 'saying' which is ἀδιάφορον [adiaphoron] or indifferent to the distinction between poetry and philosophy, he must submit to the criteria which the poetry and language which he loves also set for him. Otherwise the whole thing appears as arbitrary as I actually suspect that it is, although I am slightly wary of putting this quite so bluntly. In other words, if it turns out that our specific linguistic formulation, if the specific relation between language and what it is we have to say, is indistinguishable from stale provincial kitsch, then I would think that this tells us something decisive about the truth content of this philosophy itself.

LECTURE 16

24 January 1961

I would just like to come back for a moment to the poems, if that is what we should call them, which we talked about last time. Now I believe you will not imagine that I am simply making jokes at Heidegger's expense here, for that is far from my intention. Nor will you charge me with the base ambition of proving once again that some professor of philosophy writes really bad poems. That has certainly been demonstrated often enough in the course of intellectual history. I can remember a contributor to the old series *Philosophie der Gegenwart in Selbstdarstellungen* who chose to present his philosophy as a travesty of Goethe's lines 'Once in a wood I strolled content',[1] although he wasn't immediately struck down by lightning as we should rightly expect – nothing happened at all. Without wishing to explore the metaphysical implications of all this here, I would still like to say a few more words about Heidegger's poems for substantive reasons. And this is because the inferior character, the very wretchedness, of these poems is not just accidental, nor is it something that is simply to be ascribed to the author as a particular individual. On the contrary, it is objectively grounded in a philosophy which presumes in expressions of this kind, in this specific form of language, to become nothing less than a 'Saying'. In the first place, what Heidegger intends to bring out, namely 'being' – even though, according to its own concept as something distinguished from beings of any kind, it has nothing whatsoever to do with anything temporal – can manifestly be characterized only in archaizing language. And this holds not only for these particular sayings of Heidegger but also for a host of expressions in *Being and*

Time and in his most recent publications, in which he has attempted to describe what 'being' ultimately is. In this respect the sayings in question are no different from the propositions we encounter in his philosophy more generally. This already shows that what is intended here cannot be expressed in anything but archaic language. In other words, it cannot be expressed at all in a language that is appropriate to our own current level of consciousness. But that indicates we are talking about something which, by virtue of the historical process itself, has become impossible for us to say at all, if indeed there is anything intelligible to be said here in the first place. And, finally, it shows that something which is allegedly timeless and supra-temporal can itself only be expressed in temporal terms, as something which has been. And the impossibility of atemporal expression here gives the lie to Heidegger's own claim that such 'being' assumes priority over against what concretely exists, for that which concretely exists, with respect to which 'being' is supposedly prior, is precisely temporal in character. The necessity of employing temporal expressions points to the way that time cannot be anticipated by 'being' in this manner in advance of any actual concrete existence, which is what is claimed here. That this archaic dimension eludes adequate expression is evident from the way in which the expressly chosen old-fashioned expressions fail to reveal the genuine power of the archaic and merely exhibit what I have called an artificially confected or fictive moment.[2] For while these words attempt to suggest or conjure up the archaic, they cannot really capture it. What I have described as artificially confected is something which is not simply a matter of taste. It lies in the fact that the chosen mode of expression claims to express something essential even as it inescapably reveals its own incapacity to do so. And this is connected with the way that the archaizing language which is employed here is not a language that belongs to the origin at all – any more than the 'originary' thinking espoused by Heidegger is a thinking which belongs to the origin. For this is a language which feigns an essential origin, which insinuates an origin with forms of language that clearly belong to the most recent past. On the one hand, what is allegedly original or primordial is purloined from particular phases of an essentially agrarian economy, especially from the world of the shepherd or of cattle-rearing, which here becomes the key to being itself. On the other hand, the particular figures of language which are deployed here certainly lack the power of any ancient or original world. For considered in aesthetic terms they simply point us to what we find in the poems that we have discussed, the sort of things which are simply accepted as they are by the local editor of the Sunday supplement of the local newspaper – probably with gritted teeth – once they have been sent in by the usual circle of readers. This peculiarly archaic feel which presents itself as if it were somehow beyond society by using the kind of expressions you have just been listening to – the cow bells that tinkle, the blessing that muses, and so on and so forth – actually occupies a particular historical place which these expressions specifically negate, namely that of the petit bourgeois world. Just as the historical narrowness and characteristic limitations of petit bourgeois existence finds expression in the way that petit bourgeois ideology readily avails itself of supposedly eternal values in an extremely unreflective and unhesitating fashion and imagines that it has already grasped something of eternity by simply announcing that snow falls or that the mighty mountains tower up eternally. The impotence of this approach is evident in countless terrible poems which prate about the eternal mountains even though the writer who talks like this is utterly incapable of expressing such eternity. But with this philosophy we discover that, for all the highfalutin talk surrounding it, for all the claims to authenticity it likes to raise, it is rather reminiscent of the Andersen story of the emperor's new clothes, where no one sees what really lies beneath. And I wanted to show you this right here, so you can see that, if eternity is hardly present in those arbour verses or poems from the local paper which speak of forest snow and the eternal azure of the skies, the presence of being is hardly vouchsafed in a philosophy that believes it has purchase on 'being' precisely because it thematizes it and talks about it all the time. That was my intention in showing you these poems, and I hope you have properly understood this intention, which in one sense is far less malicious than some of you may have thought, though in another sense it is far more so. For it touches on the entire issue, and not simply on the question of Professor Heidegger's literary talent.

But here I would like to pursue the particular thought to which I have brought you at this point, namely the question as to why this ontology is not in fact possible. I would express this as the thesis that it is the irreversible character of historical processes which has brought about the dissolution of traditional ontology. This holds not only for the substantive point here, namely the impossibility of any ontology conceived as a positive task, but also – and this is what I wanted at least to bring out for you by looking specifically at the poems – for the impossibility of the chosen form; in other words, the impossibility of even projecting, as Heidegger would say, something such as ontology, of even supposing that a project of this kind could be remotely genuine. And I believe it is good for you to realize quite clearly here that philosophies cannot somehow be thought up out of the blue, that they cannot be thought independently of social relations and conditions, of the social structure, in which they arise, any more than it would now be possible for us, just to make this point clearer, to write a courtly romance or a chivalric epic in the grand style, even if we took a work of considerable quality such as Wolfram's *Parzival* as our model. Thus, even if we concede a certain dignity to these forms of ontology, it would still be quite impossible to project and develop anything similar today. The substance of intellectual and cultural forms – and philosophy itself is just such a form, something mediated and created by human beings rather than some immediate manifestation of truth – is inevitably indexed historically, and inevitably reveals a certain historical meaning. And whatever may be eternal or of enduring significance about such forms can only be preserved insofar as it changes in the course of history, insofar as it is penetrated by history. It cannot be preserved under entirely different social circumstances by developing philosophies which originally arose under completely different conditions. The social conditions of the great medieval ontologies – and I would prefer to leave aside the question of Platonic and Aristotelian philosophy in this regard, since this involves some rather difficult and complex sociological problems which I cannot explore here – are those of an essentially static and hierarchically organized society which is not exposed to constant change. The articulated character of this society finds clear expression in the objective and hierarchical structure of the basic categories which have no need to be justified before the bar of reason. And the really static nature of this world reflects the fact that feudal society itself was not essentially dynamic but fundamentally traditionalist in orientation. If we were to put this more precisely and more concretely, it would of course be necessary to present a rather more differentiated analysis. Although I do not want to get lost in deeper and more detailed sociological considerations of philosophy here, when we specifically think about the great ontologies and recall how nominalism emerged in a particularly close connection with the school of one of the greatest of these ontological systems (if I may put it like this), namely that of Duns Scotus,[3] we may say that, as long as the medieval hierarchy was still intact and continued to seem unproblematic, it remained free of such self-reflection. For the ontologies generally belong to a point of time when the static character of a society is already beginning to dissolve, when thought is starting to assume a more bourgeois aspect and an urbanized market society is increasingly emerging. And it is widely accepted today that something like a proto-Renaissance was already making itself felt in the thirteenth century during the High Gothic period before unfolding as the Renaissance in the full sense.[4]

And if this interpretation is valid, we can see that these great ontological philosophies invariably arose at a moment when static and
hierarchical societies were effectively threatened and already beginning
to dissolve, even though they still enjoyed a substantial presence in
the general consciousness. These societies thus found themselves reflected
in philosophies which attempted to hold onto them at the very moment
of their demise.

Now I am offering you this interpretation less as a definitive account
of the issue than as a way of encouraging you to think about these
things for yourselves. But what speaks in favour of such an interpretation is the way that it would also shed light on the emergence of
the two great ontologies that have come down to us from antiquity
in the philosophies of Plato and Aristotle. In both of these philosophies
(although of course far more strongly in the case of Plato) we see the
attempt to legitimate a more or less static-aristocratic or elite-based
society at a moment when its social structure is still visible yet is
already threatened by the bourgeois principle represented by the nominalism of the time – i.e. by the sophistic movement. But since these
particular social relations no longer obtain today, and since the possibility of experiencing the world as a closed, unchangeable and objectively structured one which is independent of subjective labour and
subjective value no longer exists, and since the static character which
actually reveals itself in our society today[5] is essentially different from
the static character of the Thomist conception of things, the very
attempt to philosophize in an ontological fashion today is a fundamentally anachronistic one. And indeed this was drastically revealed
right at the start of these recent ontological movements (as I think I
have already mentioned)[6] when Paul Ludwig Landsberg published his
little book *Die Welt des Mittelalters und wir*,[7] in which he specifically
recommended medieval ontology as a philosophical model for us
without realizing that the anachronism involved in such a programme
already contests the possibility of what was being proposed. And,
indeed, in all of this philosophy we are dealing with a movement that
is also intimately connected with the archaizing tendencies of the art
of our time. We could almost say we are talking about a kind of
philosophical neo-classicism here. In other words, we find the attempt
to construct an objectively binding order of being since the subject
feels such an order to be valuable,[8] even though the order in question
is intrinsically marked by arbitrariness. Perhaps it is not immodest if
I now point out that the things I analysed in the context of the philosophy of music are intimately related to the philosophical critique
I am developing here. In other words, I must confess that this insight
into the inner structural impossibility of such regressions first became

clear to me through the aesthetic impossibility of anachronism, the aesthetic impossibility of restoring an order of art simply through the *will* to do so, even though this order is no longer truly actual or substantially present in the world in which we live. But the way things stand is quite different in the case of philosophy, for the philosophical concept of truth involves a different dimension as compared with the aesthetic concept of truth. Here we are talking not just about the degree to which philosophy lives up to a certain level of consciousness but, rather, in a much more tangible sense, about the truth of philosophy in terms of its own coherent judgements. Whereas art is distinguished from philosophy in being an articulated expression of truth that dispenses in principle with judgements, that makes no use in principle of the form of the judgement. Now you might be tempted to object that I am rather arbitrarily transferring a certain impossibility that I have experienced in the field of art and simply applying it to the field of thought where it does not belong. But I would not really accept this objection. For I believe, on the contrary, that this impossibility can actually be shown with greater rigour in the field of philosophy than in that of art. In other words, in philosophy we do not have to rest content with abstract assurances about whether a certain philosophy is adequate to the current historical situation. For the fact that in philosophy things have led to something like the disappearance of ontologies, and to the continual rejection of every new attempt to revive ontological philosophy – the rationalist philosophy of the late seventeenth and early eighteenth century was the last such attempt – already shows that thought itself was no longer able to endorse the relevance of such ontologies.

If what has actually survived of the ontological philosophies is the thought that we must not be hindered from pursuing that which ultimately matters, that we should penetrate beyond the façade, that we should not yield to the merely apparent and superficial, that we should attempt to grasp the principles which govern the organization of the whole – if this claim still survives, then it can genuinely do so only in the form of *critique*, which has taught us that the attempt to grasp 'being' immediately is impossible. And in this sense I would say that the entire critique of ontology, which was pursued in an extremely trenchant way by Kant and Hegel in particular, is not something that can simply be banished from the world by reference to the alleged subjectivism or idealism of these two thinkers. The significance of philosophical thoughts cannot merely be measured in terms of the system within which these thoughts stand, for these systems themselves arise essentially from a range of arguments and considerations with a certain logical compulsion. And it is very often the case – and especially in Hegel, as I tried to show in some detail in my essay on 'The Experiential Content of Hegel's Philosophy'[9] – that the inner argumentative force of certain particular reflections, and even of the critical considerations which a specific philosophy involves, reach far beyond the general premises which the philosophy in question actually defends. Thus the arguments that Hegel in his own time raised in a splendid passage against the concept of being in Jacobi[10] – whom he compared to the Tibetans who simply contemplate their own navels while reciting Om, om, om – also apply to the structure evinced by the tautological and insistent repetition of the word 'being'. I gladly confess to a certain lack of modernity in that I certainly do not believe that recourse to the pluperfect, the most distant past, is *eo ipso* to be considered more modern than what has more recently come down to us in the perfect tense. On the contrary, I believe that the pluperfect must really be confronted with what has *subsequently* been thought in a binding and convincing way. I believe this is simply a matter of intellectual integrity, and something we should not be encouraged to relinquish on account of the need for meaning – unless we really are prepared to become defeatists of reason. But I would just like to say – if I may offer a solid piece of advice here – that, if you really wish to form a considered judgement on this question, then you should pay very close attention to the critique of ontology in Kant (which is partly to be found in the chapter on amphibolies and partly in the 'Transcendental Dialectic')[11] and also the critique of ontology which is expressed in many different places in Hegel. For the thought that 'We are surely far beyond that today!' may often replace genuine *inner* intellectual progress with a merely abstract temporality, namely with the fact that we now enjoy the questionable fortune of writing in 1960 rather than in 1786 or 1820. In other words, this attitude falls back behind the inner consistency or inconsistency of what has been thought before. Thus I believe that the critique to which ontology was once subjected by the great German thinkers has by no means lost its force, despite all assurances that we have long since emphatically moved on.

Heidegger is, of course, far too clever – and here again I would say far too strategic – to employ the crude device of simply appealing to older forms of ontology. And if you look at his later writings in particular, you will find that he repudiates the idea of such a recourse as far too external and superficial, as a complete misunderstanding of his intentions. The strategy of this philosophy – if I may deploy this concept once again – is a different one. For he attempts to evade the controversy between the ontologies which have been historically handed down to us and the critique to which they have been subjected by recourse to a kind of thinking which could be described as pre-ontological. In other words, this thinking contains none of the tangible and specific theses which philosophy has already criticized as ontology, such as the thesis regarding the eternal and immutable character of being or of whatever being was supposed to signify. His approach is so archaic, as I would put it, that he attempts – and here I am speaking of him as a philosopher rather than as the author of poetic sayings – to reach back beyond the archaism of the Middle Ages, for example, and tries to avoid the charge of anachronism by claiming that the origins which he is talking about have nothing whatever to do with what is *historically* more ancient, that he is talking about origins in an essential rather than a temporal sense. As far as the atemporal character of this mythological recourse is concerned, I think I have already clearly shown what this amounts to with reference to his poetic verses. But I would just like to add this: I do not want you to think that I have been 'unfair' here by singling out the poems in question. For if you look at Heidegger's prose works – such as the famous essay on 'Plato's Theory of Truth' – you will find that they teem with precisely the same archaisms that I pointed out to you in the poetic verses. It turns out that this form of thinking – which is allegedly not archaizing at all, which is so original or primordial that it does not even want to have anything to do with the origins of philosophy – cannot possibly express itself in anything but this archaic way. The attempt to avoid the controversy regarding ontology means that Heidegger also tries to evade the controversy between the intrinsic being of essence and the question of its mediation in and through the thinking subject (which is what the entire controversy is ultimately about). And he evades it by claiming that the theses of philosophy, which can only be formulated in conceptual terms and indeed in Heidegger himself are conceptual in character, are themselves ultimately *non-conceptual*. And this leads him to that cult of the origin, or of renewal, which is by no means accidentally related or simply external to that sympathy with barbarism which appears in the history of his political engagement.[12] I believe that in a certain sense we do Heidegger an injustice if we simply try to class him, as he seems to have done himself, as a fellow traveller of National Socialism and regard the fact that he was so quick to follow Hitler as an unfortunate case of the profoundly naive Sage. Yet in that cult of the origin, in that belief in renewal, in that belief that the power of being would now triumph over the power of darkness – in this entire nexus of elements we actually find the very real nexus of National Socialist ideology – so that we might in a certain sense read Rosenberg,[13] *cum grano salis*, as a key to *Being and Time*. Be that as it may, there is a moment of ultimate and arbitrary decree here, something peculiar to charisma in our times, to the claim of the Leader, the One who becomes the *Führer* precisely by declaring himself to *be* the *Führer*. And we can grasp this moment of arbitrariness very precisely in Heidegger by reference to the concept of *Entwurf*, or projection. I would just like to say a few words about this here.

In substantive terms this concept of projection derives from Husserl, even if the word itself does not feature in his work. And this is very interesting in itself. If you look at Kant's *Critique of Pure Reason* or Hegel's *Logic*, or the transcendental philosophy of Schelling,[14] or any of the relevant major texts that have come down to us, you will find that the specific character of the philosophy in question is not defined simply by some kind of arbitrary act or choice on the part of the reflecting philosopher. For all these philosophies attempt to provide some rational grounding or justification for the approach adopted in each case, for the specific way in which they begin – and of course everyone has to begin somewhere, and there is no philosophy without a deliberate beginning. Now if you read Husserl's *Ideas*[15] – and I believe this is at once one of the greatest difficulties of the book and to a certain extent the key to all of the new ontologies – you will find the situation is very different. For it just suddenly starts. And I believe this is connected with the fact that Husserl was a mathematician, and that it is quite possible for mathematics to posit and generate manifold forms freely out of itself precisely because such forms need to measure up to any substantive content. In this regard mathematics has played a highly paradoxical role, and if you like even an irrational or anti-rational role, in the history of philosophy. Thus if you look at Husserl's *Ideas* you will find that he really wants to get 'to the things themselves'. In order to do so we have to proceed as follows: we suspend or bracket the whole of the natural world, we bracket ourselves as natural persons, we also bracket God and a range of other things, and finally we bracket all individual factical being over against the realm of essence. And what we then have left is the 'things themselves', the field in which phenomenological philosophy is now free to roam around at will. But *why* I should bracket all this, what justifies me, if I wish to express truth, in abstracting from that facticity whose confrontation with truth is demanded by the concept of truth itself – of this Husserl's *Ideas* at least tells us nothing. In his later writings, in his theory of judgement for example,[16] Husserl attempted to fill this gap as best he could through an extremely complicated detour of material fulfilment in the context of experience. But initially everything simply depends on the 'phenomenological attitude'. Thus you get to the doctrine of essences simply by adopting a specific attitude to the world and omitting certain aspects or given features as you choose. And, once you have performed this arbitrary act, what remains is the truth – even though this attitude itself – and this is the decisive thing – has not specifically been justified and has not been rendered intelligible as such on the basis of this philosophy. Now of course you may say that the idealist philosophy of the past also performs similar forms of reduction, by claiming for example that the legitimate ground of truth is to be found in the internal connection of the given, that I cannot speak of transcendent things at all but must trace things back to the sensuous data that I receive and the categorical apparatus that I possess, as empiricists and rationalists have argued in their different ways. But in these cases the particular orientation which they adopted was a specifically motivated one. Thus it was claimed, for example, that apparent objectivity might turn out to be a dream or a delusion unless I could somehow reduce it to the sphere of the subject. You have only to think of the First Meditation of Descartes, where he says that the entire external world is not something that is absolutely indubitable, that it could all be a dream,[17] and that the only thing which is absolutely indubitable is then at least that I am dreaming. Or again you might say that the experience that is given to me through the senses is deceptive and cannot therefore claim an a priori character, whereas our concept of truth requires something that is utterly necessary. Whenever we encounter such reductions in the history of philosophy, they are themselves grounded in the necessity of acquiring genuine truth. Husserl took over this technique of reduction from the tradition – namely the idea that the object of philosophy is what is left, as it were, after the initial costs have been deducted, and that this is what truth is – but he no longer grounds or justifies it. For, if he did try to ground it, he would already be revealed as an idealist, and that is precisely what he wanted to avoid. Instead he says: I take up the phenomenological attitude or position – rather like the way in which we choose a specific position from which to take a photograph. It is not possible here to go into the rather interesting history of this word *Einstellung* – an expressly adopted attitude or position – which is certainly connected with photography but also indeed with the age of *Jugendstil*. Nowadays the word has fallen almost entirely out of use. It is of course still found when we say things like: 'My position forbids me to share views of that kind.' Here I just wish to point out that, right at the beginning of the new ontological philosophy, we can already see how the seemingly heightened demand for 'objectivity' announced by the turn to 'things themselves' is simultaneously paid for by the arbitrary character of the attitude or position we are supposed to adopt.

And we find this faithfully repeated in Heidegger with the concept of *Entwurf*, or 'projection'. For his philosophy attempts to 'project' being, or the structure of being, specifically through the analysis of *Dasein*, though it fails to ask how the possibility of such projection itself is to be justified. The apparently direct and utterly spontaneous character of this approach, the lack of concern for any accompanying epistemological reflection here, is doubtless extremely appealing to many but is actually nothing but an arbitrary act which exempts the philosopher's activity from reflective scrutiny and effectively avoids any engagement with critical reason. But here again you can see how, in Heidegger, all these things are taken to an extreme. He is far too intelligent not to recognize this moment that is bound up with the concept of projection and helps himself by performing a turn which any circus artist would envy. For the most arbitrary aspect of his philosophy – the idea that I set forth, that I project, that I sketch out in the broadest strokes, without concern for what has been already been thought, that which inwardly holds the world together[18] – now seems very different: it is not I or we that is responsible for all this, and if we ask who it is that does the projecting, the answer is simply 'being'! And in case you think that I am exaggerating or caricaturing Heidegger here, I would like to substantiate this with some particularly striking quotations. Thus in the *Letter on 'Humanism'* you will find the following: 'the projection is essentially a thrown projection. What throws in such projection is not the human being but being itself, which sends the human being into the ek-sistence of *Da-sein* that is his essence. This destiny [*Geschick*] comes to pass [*ereignet sich*] as the clearing of being – which it is. The clearing grants nearness to being. In this nearness, in the clearing of the "There" [*Da*]' – this is a secularization of the old concept of revelation, even though it shuns that venerable name – 'the human being dwells as the ek-sisting one without yet being able properly to experience and take over this dwelling today' – once again the image of dwelling which is drawn from the concrete realm of the world and also sounds both archaic and homely. 'In the lecture on Hölderlin's elegy "Homecoming" (1948) this nearness "of" being, which the "There" of *Dasein* is, is thought on the basis of *Being and Time*' – Heidegger actually says so himself – 'it is perceived as spoken from the minstrel's poem; from the experience of the oblivion of being ... it is called the "homeland" [*Heimat*].' And Heidegger continues: 'This word is thought here in an essential sense, not patriotically or nationalistically, but in terms of the history of being. The essence of the homeland, however, is also mentioned with the intention of thinking the homelessness of contemporary human beings from the essence of being's history.'[19] Here you really have everything together: the contamination of the archaic with the pure structure of being, the arbitrary positing and, finally, the justification of this arbitrariness as a structure of being itself, or as some kind of 'destiny' – in short the mythologization of philosophy. Thus we actually find that *Being and Time* already contains at least something, on an incomparably higher level and with incomparably greater sophistication, of what another book on a far lower level once claimed to provide, namely the fiction of a myth for the twentieth century.[20] But I shall say a little bit more about that next time.

LECTURE 17

26 January 1961

At the end of the last session I tried in some haste, as tends to happen in the final minutes of a lecture, to show you how Heidegger's philosophy has a tendency to pass over into or revert to mythology. Now mythology is a very easy word to invoke here, and it is of course a typical expression of the philistine consciousness to denounce comprehensive philosophical reflections which stray too far from the standard or familiar interpretation of reality as nothing but 'conceptual poetry', if I may use that fine phrase here. It is not much of a step from talk of conceptual poetry to that of mythology – and there are many who have spoken of the thought of Nietzsche, Hegel, Schelling, and God knows who else, as nothing but mythology. Now if I have described Heidegger's thought as a kind of mythology, I was employing the term 'mythology' in a much more precise sense than this. For I mean something much more specific than is conveyed by this general and usually rather subaltern way of speaking, which is adopted by a mentality that is alien or hostile to philosophy itself precisely in order to conceal its own ignorance and unfamiliarity. I believe that it is necessary to distinguish two aspects or moments here. In the first place we have the moment that I have tried to suggest with expressions such as the myth of the nineteenth[1] or the twentieth centuries. This is the moment that essentially feigns the idea of breaking out of a rational level of consciousness in order to attain a supposedly immediate consciousness of the Absolute or of Nature as a whole. But then we also have the untruth and questionable character that belong to myth itself precisely where it is genuine, as they say. Now I believe we would be making things too easy for ourselves if all that we had to say against such approaches today is that they are false mythologies; and if we were simply to respond, as it is very easy to do in the German context, by trying to hold on to genuine and authentic myth and glorifying the latter. For the real task is to glimpse the genuine myth itself at the heart of the false one, if there is indeed such a thing as genuine myth. The task is to recognize how the untruth of these mythical formations actually reproduces the old untruth which comes in a very distinctive way to permeate the new one, namely the fiction of a new mythological consciousness that no longer exists. Let me try and show you more precisely why this whole form of thought is to be seen as mythological in a questionable sense. And let me add right away that the criterion here is certainly not the fact that the concepts employed are remote from the immediate appearance of factical life as the latter is generally registered by everyday consciousness. For that is not what is essential here. What is essential is the *content* of the doctrine itself. When I speak of a reversion to mythology, I am specifically referring to the revocation of freedom, the cancellation of that aspect of freedom through which the subject has wrested itself from the blind, opaque, immediate context of nature, from the sway of fate or destiny. The great religions, and what can be called the general process of European enlightenment in the broadest sense, which ultimately reaches from the pre-Socratics through to the modern age, have striven to bring consciousness to bear on blind compulsion, to save consciousness from the dread which lies in this blindness by showing how the blindness is only produced by the consciousness which experiences the dread. In other words, the context of nature itself, which confronts us as hostile or demonic, is actually an anthropomorphic projection. While the theory of Epicurus was careful not to deny the reality of the Gods, it presented them as utterly indifferent to and entirely unconcerned with human life, as mere spectators of this sorry spectacle. Since the Gods refused to intervene in the world, there is nothing we have to hope for from them, but equally nothing we have to fear from them,[2] and in this sense the theory may be regarded as the first self-conscious expression of demythologization in the history of humanity. I do not recall whether Heidegger, who is certainly well versed in classical philology, has ever really talked about Epicurus, but it seems unlikely.[3] In this respect, too, the great 'destroyer' is of one mind with the official history of philosophy, for the thinkers who have received a bad press in the mainstream tradition (if I may put it that way) either fail to appear in his work at all or are merely treated dismissively. I say this simply in passing to indicate the image of the history of philosophy which you will basically find here.

You may recall the passage that I read out for you last time, and which prompted me to speak of myth in this connection. That which 'projects', we were told, is not the human being but 'being' itself, and it is 'being' which 'sends [*schickt*] man into the ek-sistence of Dasein as his essence'. Of course Heidegger intends us to hear the concordance of *schickt*, 'sends', with *Schicksal*, 'fate' or 'destiny', for he constantly operates in a mechanical sort of way with pseudo-etymological connections of this kind. The point here is fundamentally to ascribe the same quality to 'being' that is usually ascribed to 'fate'. And we can say that the concept of being which Heidegger develops here – precisely on account of its abstractness, its indeterminacy, its vague self-identity – bears all the features of that concept of fate from which humanity has struggled with such tremendous effort to raise itself. The greatest monument to this process of human emancipation from the blind compulsion of fate is surely Attic tragedy. Here I would just like to draw your attention to certain aspects of this kind in Heidegger's concept of being. In the first place this concept of being involves the concept of hubris, the idea that man fails to know his limits. In this connection this implies that man as a pre-eminent and sovereign being already rises up above this immediate context of nature as in himself a kind of spontaneous natural power. But he thereby actually falls victim to this natural context itself, thus becoming caught up in the guilt context of the living, as Benjamin once aptly and insightfully defined the concept of fate.[4] And I would specifically like to point out here that you find this very concept of hubris in the doctrine that what ultimately 'throws' or 'casts' in the process of 'projection' is not man but 'being' itself. For you should just reflect for a moment, ladies and gentlemen, about what this really means. For it signifies that thoughts and conceptual constructions like that of philosophical 'projection' – for we are certainly talking of a philosophical projection here, namely that of being itself – are immediately treated as if they were direct manifestations of 'being'. In other words, it is as if the activity of human beings, involved as it is in such 'projection', were immediately transformed – without any further reflection or justification – into the objective voice of being itself. The mediating processes of subjectivity which can never be eliminated from the activity of thought are here simply deleted. This is the ultimate consequence of the basic contention of the entire phenomenological school that things present themselves to consciousness purely and simply as what they are – thus forgetting the subject to whom they present themselves, and forgetting the fact that they must presuppose a consciousness in order to present themselves at all. You may recall that early on in these lectures[5] I showed how this very concept of being, which is so suspicious of the subject and so ready to relinquish all subjective determinations, actually reveals itself to be an unwittingly self-imposed form of idealism or subjectivism that is blind to its own character. And you can take the passage that I have just discussed as a direct confirmation of this claim. For that which can be conceived only as spontaneity, subjectivity and thought is here relegated at a stroke to the side of being itself simply by appeal to language and the talk of thrown 'projection'. The subject which is at work here is silenced but is immeasurably intensified in the process, presenting its own work as if it had now escaped the limits of subjectivity, as if it were now immediately the object itself. Thus it is the very anti-subjectivism of this theory, the very claim that it is not some subjective expression of thinking, which inwardly reveals, as I would say, the heinous arrogance of the subject which imagines its own thinking to be entirely free of subjective limitations and acts as if the Absolute itself were speaking through it.

But then I would say that the concept of fate or destiny here ascribed to 'being' is that of a blindly entangled will – for what is ascribed to 'being' in this context bears all the marks of irrationality. In other words, 'being' is characterized as something utterly obscure that may somehow be intimated and venerated, but about which nothing substantive can ever be said. In the first place, you should clearly observe how this very passage moves directly to the concept of *Schicksal* or fate, and how this concept of fate, even if it is indeed indexed historically, is furnished with that blind and ineluctable character which belongs to the ancient or traditional notion of fate. Heidegger writes: 'This destiny [*Geschick*: or that which sends what is the essence, namely 'being itself which sends the human being into the ek-sistence of Da-sein'] comes to pass as the clearing of being – which it is.' That this comes to pass as the clearing of being already implies the subordinate clause which follows – which is thus entirely superfluous and tautological, simply a kind of ἐν διὰ δυοῖν [hen dia duoin],[6] which mimics a mythological way of speaking. 'The clearing grants nearness to being.' But note the aspect of blindness here: 'In this nearness, in the clearing of the There, the human being dwells as the ek-sisting one without yet being able properly to experience and take over this dwelling today.' Yet if the possibility of experiencing this is in principle cut off from us, if this is something which is utterly blind, we have to ask how thinking can possibly be justified in talking about it in the first place. In view of the blindness which is ascribed to being, and which requires nothing but what Heidegger elsewhere describes as *Hörigkeit*, or 'obedient hearkening', a hearkening to being which sounds like blind submission, it is not hard to understand why the concept of *anxiety* becomes such a decisive 'existential' in Heidegger. But we must be quite clear that this existential is not actually a fundamental dimension of being itself which is revealed in *Dasein*, as Heidegger maintains. On the contrary, this anxiety is itself mediated in the sense that it prevails and dominates in an absolute way only when thinking is unable to recognize any authority other than that of blind fate – although in terms of the philosophy of history it must certainly be admitted that the current state of the world and the undeniably increasing impotence of the individual subject actually furnish abundant grounds for such anxiety. And it would actually be commendable if this philosophy were at least courageous enough to express its own anxiety instead of constantly striking a heroic posture, except that the general Heideggerean trick characteristically ensures that this expression of anxiety itself is counted as the truly heroic achievement, specifically in relation to death as the ultimately unconditioned. Yet it was just such anxiety which philosophy and the great religions formerly undertook to dispel. And I am quite unable to understand – though I am hardly qualified to speak for theologians or to talk about theological matters – how modern theology itself, in what can only be seen as a symptom of its current insecurity, has completely failed to recognize this frankly pagan moment of Heideggerean philosophy, which is so fundamentally at odds with its own essential concerns. What we constantly find instead, on the Protestant and Catholic side alike, is a touching and deeply disturbing eagerness to assimilate and respond to this philosophy, without suspecting that such attempts to demonstrate its own contemporary philosophical credentials actually encourage the dissolution of everything that religion once effectively stood for.[7]

When I speak of mythology and describe it as a reversion to a religion of nature, to a cult of nature, the notion of homeland [*Heimat*] also naturally crops up in this connection – and indeed duly makes an appearance in the passage which I have just been reading and interpreting for you. For it is an essential characteristic of the religions of nature that the natural divinities are bound up with particular places, and that the sacredness of place, and indeed the narrowly defined place to which the individual is bound by birth and family, appears as a numinous power that is to be venerated. And here again you see how this reversion to the mythical notion that the Absolute is essentially bound up with a natural category such as place is directly connected to a politically regressive mentality, namely to the glorification of our own tribe, of our own lineage, of our own land, where we just happen to find ourselves, as the ultimate and essential thing. Now when Heidegger says at this point that the word *Heimat* is thought here in an 'essential' sense – not in patriotic or nationalistic terms but in terms of the history of being – this is nothing but a *captatio benevolentiae*, an attempt to win us over. If everything that he here abjures were not really the case, this thinking would surely have the strength to find any other word but *Heimat*. But that it cannot do so, that it remains so beholden to the characteristic mentality of homely art, reveals only how essentially and intrinsically such mythic notions also involve the regressive dimension of contemporary nationalism, so that these things cannot simply be regarded as external or accidental. In the case of Heidegger's philosophy – and something similar is also true of Hegel – I believe it is impossible to write off what are often described as political eccentricities and aberrations simply as missteps of a thinker who has gone rogue, as it were, and imagine that we can then hold on to the unadulterated wisdom or the purified doctrine that remains. For the very aspects or moments of his thinking which allowed him to identify the *Führer* with 'being'[8] are already harboured in this concept of being itself, are necessarily involved in the constitution of his thought. You can readily see from this that the whole separation between social-historical categories and philosophical ones, whether these belong to the history of being or represent the kind of epistemological categories which people are once again so keen to instil in us today, is ultimately quite arbitrary and serves merely to reserve a little grove for philosophy, which has nothing to do with the world, on one side, while preserving the social-political sphere from critical philosophical reflection, on the other. Wherever there has been any philosophy which really deserved the name it has never recognized this division between 'proper' philosophy on one side and 'mere' social philosophy on the other. And we fall below philosophy not when we engage with social thought but when we try and enforce a rigid and mechanical separation of both these two moments. The actual social consequence, as I already pointed out, of this mythological aspect, of this understanding of being, which basically stands in for the *kosmos* as conceived by the philosophy of nature, is that all we can ultimately do is blindly subject ourselves to something precisely because it is intrinsically irrational and impenetrable. In other words, it effectively demands that we submit to the blind course of history as the unfolding of the history of being. The relationship to history in Heidegger is a complex one. On the one hand – as I think I have already suggested in passing – the concept of history itself is all too quickly sublimated in the sense that real history is replaced by historicity – that is, by history as a structure which arises from *Dasein*. This is an 'existential' which allegedly belongs to *Dasein* itself and, on account of its essentially ontological character, is not meant to have anything to do with real history in the ontic sense. On the other hand, the way this philosophy constantly changes back and forth between the ontic and the ontological – we could speak of changing outfits here, though I would prefer to describe this as a sort of shimmering alternation – is precisely what lends it the semblance of life. Thus, wherever history proves to be the strongest power in reality, it is easy to interpret this as the power of being and thereby encourage subordination to the course of history. And if you take a look today at the writings which Herr Professor Heidegger published during the early years of National Socialism,[9] you will actually find this very argument that the power of being itself is manifest in the historical events of the time and that we are to submit to this power of being in the form of these historical events. We see here how history is ontologized or emptied of substance on the one hand yet also deified as if it were the blind course of nature on the other. There is no longer any question of asking about the rational justification or rational meaning of history, for all we have to do is catch the voice of being at work there and do what it requires of us. Now this very thought (as I am particularly gratified to point out here) has also been very clearly and candidly expressed by a critical and thoughtful former student of Heidegger's, my Heidelberg colleague Karl Löwith, in his essay on this *Denker in dürftiger Zeit*.[10] And I would specifically recommend this piece by Löwith in connection with the critical reflections I have been pursuing. His discussion is particularly instructive because it shows how the independent exercise of thought, even when it originally springs from this quarter, is effectively compelled to draw conclusions which are hardly remote from those I have unfolded here. He also reveals how the generally mythologizing tendency in Heidegger leads to a specific mythology of history.

I have spoken of myth as such and indicated that there is always a certain unrestricted aspect about it. Myth is a world in which anything can also mean anything else, in which there is no absolutely univocal meaning. You have only to take a look at a book such as Zimmer's *Maya*,[11] or at Ovid's *Metamorphoses*, which basically develops variations of the the inherited myths in a playful Hellenistic way, to see how indeterminacy itself, how the fluid interplay of every conceivable form and shape, how the constant intermingling of everything, plays a central role in all these myths. And this corresponds precisely to the intermingling, wavering and shimmering concept of being as that which is allegedly ἀδιάφορον [adiaphoron], or indistinguishable, with respect to beings and being – and with respect to the conceptual itself, as I should prefer to say. In other words, this mythologizing philosophy – and this is surely part of its suggestive power, part of its theological seductiveness, if I may put it like that – essentially involves a kind of vagueness and indeterminacy which is rooted in its own irrational character, but which it actually ascribes to itself as if it were some special higher quality. Yet this philosophy is essentially abstract. And here you stumble upon something really quite remarkable in the history of this whole cultural and intellectual movement, if that it is indeed what it is, that we have been talking about. If you recall what I was trying to explain to you before about the origins of all those philosophies where you encounter the word 'existence' or 'existential' in the wake of Kierkegaard, you will also remember that one of the most essential and original motivations at work here was to escape the formalism of Kantian and of all post-Kantian theory. In other words, all of these philosophies can be interpreted in terms of a longing for *concreteness*. And, if you read Heidegger himself, you will constantly encounter in the language which is deployed here – like that of the short passage which I read out for you earlier – innumerable expressions which certainly aspire to concreteness. Now in Kant and Hegel you will look in vain for expressions such as 'the clearing of the "There"' or the 'sending' of being or 'the homeland', or any concepts of that kind. Yet at the same time, and this is very telling, it must always be added right away – as with the aforementioned passage, which is indeed quite exemplary for this whole philosophy – that it is indeed concrete, but that this concreteness is not concrete at all. In other words, the concrete here is not actually what you conceive it to be but is something 'wholly other', and ultimately something abstract. It skims the cream off the concrete and gives us the feeling that we have something really tangible to hold onto and are not just being fobbed off. At the same time, however, it skims the cream off philosophy and tells us that it is not of course talking about that lowly concreteness you had in mind; rather, it is talking about something much higher and more essential, something that is bound up with eternal and immutable being. It thereby perpetuates the gesture of killing two birds with one stone. I pointed out before that this whole movement of philosophy was originally anti-formalistic in character. That is the point where Kierkegaard's critique of Hegel (though he was significantly misunderstood in this regard) essentially converged with Scheler's critique of the formalism of Kantian ethics in his famous early book on the subject.[12] For both thinkers claimed that these earlier philosophers remained caught up in the domain of purely abstract concepts without being able to reveal what mattered as far as the real relations and essential interests of the actual human being were concerned. And Scheler sought to counter such abstractness with the idea of a material ethics of value, with a hierarchy of values, which no longer undertook to identify the universal principle of legislation in terms of the categorical imperative for example. His material ethics attempted instead to articulate and systematize, in an extremely precise and almost casuistical fashion, the various values that actually exist, from the very lowest to the highest, so that philosophy might then in a certain sense concretely tell us what is good and what is bad. And the influence specifically exerted by Scheler at the time was due to this admittedly rather dubious claim on the part of his philosophy. Now you should not imagine that this element has simply disappeared from Heidegger. Think of the concrete turns of phrase which I have already pointed out: 'the clearing' – who would not love to come upon a clearing in the woods? – or 'the homeland' – who would not love to come back home, especially those of us who have actually experienced emigration? Such concrete elements are constantly introduced into philosophy here. Yet in being turned into philosophical elements they forfeit the very concreteness they claim to possess. I believe it is no exaggeration to say that this philosophy, which begins with such a claim to concreteness, ultimately surpasses in abstractness – i.e. in formalism – anything that Kant himself ever accomplished. In Kant's philosophy the highest place is occupied by the Ideas, the most universal concepts of all, and then those synthetic a priori judgements which are actually nothing but propositions under which possible experience is subsumed but which themselves possess no experiential content at all. Now the concept of being you find in Heidegger is just as empty, indeed I would say even emptier, so that at the end of this whole movement of thought we find we are cheated of what we were authentically promised in the first place. This notion of the genuine or the 'authentic', of what is truly at stake, of that which previous philosophy failed to give but is now provided for us – this is here accomplished by concepts which are defined or determined no longer in relation to other concepts but simply through themselves, and which finally become little more than constantly invoked and endlessly repeated formulae.

In support of this thesis I think it might be a good idea if I just read out a passage from the essay *On 'Humanism'* and undertook to interpret it for you. But since I want you to understand the method I am actually pursuing and would not wish you to be misled in this connection, I would point out that here too I am not concerned simply with criticizing the formalism or abstractness of the philosophy of being. The real task, as I see it, is precisely to *explain* the distinctive fact that a philosophy which began expressly as a doctrine of what is most concrete ends up as the most abstract kind of thinking. You can only move *beyond* these things once you have been *inside* them, that is, once you have comprehended them. It is not enough for you just to say: I really wanted something concrete, but it turns out that it is not concrete at all. You must understand precisely why this cannot be concrete, for only then is the power of critical thinking which is meant to take you beyond these things truly effective. Now the passage I shall read to you, which incidentally is rather famous, comes from the *Letter on 'Humanism'*, a text which, apart from *Being and Time*, is probably the most fruitful source if we wish to capture the distinctive physiognomy of this thinking. Thus on page 76 of the 1954 edition of this essay we read the following: 'Yet being – what is being? It "is" It itself. The thinking that is to come must learn to experience that and to say it.' Now we would think the claim that being is itself, and therefore pure identity, is not so terribly difficult, and may well feel that we are just struggling to lift a feather here. '"Being" – that is not God and not a cosmic ground.' Here I can only say that Heidegger is quite right, for 'being' here is nothing but the utterly blind and indeterminate context of nature as such. 'Being is essentially farther than all beings' – now we can certainly say that too, for it is precisely a concept rather than a being or entity – 'and is yet nearer to the human being than every being ...' There you have the claim to the immediate givenness that belongs to 'being' itself: on the one hand it is supposedly pure, universal, free of anything factical, while on the other it is supposedly nearer, more immediately evident to us, than any particular being or entity can be. And now beings or entities are introduced: 'being' is nearer

> than every being, be it a rock, a beast, a work of art, a machine, be it an angel or God. Being is the nearest. Yet the near remains farthest from the human being. Human beings at first cling always and only to beings. But when thinking represents beings as beings it no doubt relates itself to being. In truth, however, it always thinks only of beings as such; precisely not, and never, being as such.

Here one would surely like to say that it is hardly possible to think being as such without thinking beings at the same time, precisely because 'being' for Heidegger is expressly supposed to be distinct from any pure concept, because it is supposed to involve both conceptuality and beings, and because being as such cannot be thought at all without reference to some determinate filling or content. You cannot possibly think being without beings, any more than you can conceive of time without anything that is temporal or of space without anything that is spatial. And when Heidegger charges thought with a 'forgetfulness of being' insofar as it is incapable of thinking in this way, he really goes beyond the limit of possibility for all thought, as Kantian philosophy has so impressively shown.[13] 'In truth, however, it always thinks only of beings as such; precisely not, and never, being as such.' Now if you take really seriously this expression 'being as such', and specifically the 'as such' here, then of course it means 'being' in opposition to or with the exclusion of 'beings'. But Heidegger in turn is unfaithful to the claim involved in this 'as such', inasmuch as all of the attributes, whatever they may be, which he bestows on 'being' are themselves derived from the domain of 'beings'. He continues:

> The 'question of being' always remains a question about beings. It is still not at all what its elusive name indicates: the question in the direction of being. Philosophy, even when it becomes 'critical' through Descartes or Kant, always follows the course of metaphysical representation. It thinks from beings back to beings with a glance in passing toward being. For every departure from beings and every return to them stands already in the light of being.

Now if we accept that no particular being or entity is exhausted simply in terms of itself, and that every being, as a moment or aspect of a whole, is more than what it merely is as a particular being *hic et nunc*, then I would agree with Heidegger. But you cannot conceive this 'Otherness', this 'More' or, as I would put it, this process of transcendence – in which all beings are involved – without reference to beings or entities themselves, any more than you can regard particular beings or entities themselves as something absolute. And in this sense he does indeed appear to take something abstract, namely the concept of being – for this is something abstract – as if it were that which is immediate and the nearest to us. You will recall that he actually explicitly says here that 'being' – something mediated, something produced through abstraction – is indeed distinct or separate from all particular content and from all beings but is still what is nearest and most immediate to us. Yet it is not possible for thought to recuperate this thesis of the nearness and immediacy of being in any way. Every attempt to define or determine 'being' more closely must inevitably fail, since any conceptuality would either necessarily turn it into something abstract and remote or, if we took the claim to concreteness seriously, simply turn it into a mere being or entity.

And this is precisely the reason why all that can ultimately be said about 'being' is the tautology that 'it is itself'. This tautology is not an intellectual mistake, nor is it some vatic palaver without the accompanying religion. It is simply that nothing now remains for thought but the incomprehensible repetition of the same concept, for any attempt to fulfil it would immediately conflict with the concept itself. But this is precisely what we shall explore next time.

LECTURE 18

31 January 1961

You will recall how in our last session I drew attention to the tautological characterization of 'being' in the *Letter on 'Humanism'* where we learn that 'it is itself', and how I pointed out that it was not enough simply to identify this tautology, since the real task – which I have already started to undertake – is precisely to explain the tautology in question. Not exactly of course to deduce the tautology, for any attempt to deduce tautologies would instantly lead to considerable logical difficulties, but rather to explain for you exactly why we end up with this tautology. And let me just say in advance that the peculiarly elusive character of the philosophy of being is not the least source of its attractiveness, for it is extraordinarily difficult to argue with this philosophy without immediately encountering the charge that this or that is not actually what was meant at all. Now this is intimately connected with the tautological character we have been talking about. But in order to get at the root of this tautological character it might be a good idea if I do not focus simply on Heidegger's own words, which of course already exhibit that elusive quality of which I have spoken several times already. Rather, I shall try and trace this tautological character back to two principal theses already advanced by his teacher Husserl. As I believe I have shown in detail in my book *Metakritik der Erkenntnistheorie*,[1] Heidegger was far more deeply indebted to Husserl, and had far more in common with him, than he felt it wise to admit either in the immediately prefascist period or especially at the height of the fascist era. I am speaking here of the mature and extremely influential philosophy of Husserl's middle period, when he published the discussion of 'categorial intuition' from the second volume of the *Logical Investigations* and in particular the first book of his *Ideas for a Pure Phenomenology and Phenomeno-logical Philosophy*, the text which has remained the most decisively influential part of his work. For in Husserl's philosophy here you will come across two claims which are ultimately incompatible with each other, although this was not clearly realized at the time. One of these claims is evident from the very title of Husserl's principal work, namely *Ideas for a Pure Phenomenology*. To put it rather crudely, the concept of purity is to be understood here in a Kantian sense. Now I do not wish to go into the nuanced point that this doesn't entirely cohere with the Kantian approach, because Husserl upholds the idea of a *material* a priori in addition to the formal a priori which is acknowl-edged by Kant[2] – although this too is echoed in what I described as the wavering character of Heidegger's concept of being. Thus the 'purity' of which Husserl speaks is supposed to be the same as that ascribed by Kant to 'the pure concepts of the understanding' or to 'the pure a priori synthetic judgements'. Now from what are all these supposed to be free exactly? They are supposed to be free from any-thing empirical or transitory that might destroy the pure a priori character of these determinations by sharing it in any way with beings that merely exist. But the path which Husserl takes to attain this purity is completely different, methodologically speaking, from the Kantian one. And I would argue that this specific modification remained binding for Heidegger as well. In terms of the history of philosophy I should point out that Husserl was a student of Franz Brentano, and Brentano's philosophy represented a very distinctive synthesis of fea-tures of the scholastic tradition – he was originally a Catholic priest, although he later abandoned the calling – with elements of empiricism, and especially with psychological and other empirical findings. And, if you wish, you could even trace the whole aporetic structure of Heidegger's philosophy of being back to this remarkable constellation of scholastic ontology and empiricism. It would be an extremely rewarding task for anyone attempting to write a rational history of philosophy to explore these connections in detail. Husserl certainly conceived the concept of purity in the scholastic sense insofar as he understood this purity in terms of the priority of the concept over the real phenomena which it comprehends. In this respect he reinvented the approach of medieval realism and indeed – as is often the case with reactive movements (and that of Brentano and Husserl was certainly a reaction against the nominalism which it nonetheless also acknowledges) – he emphatically affirms the priority of the *universalia* over the *res*. In this respect we can see how the mediating position of Aristotle, and to a certain extent that of Aquinas as well – both of whom claimed that the essences of things are present within the actual beings or things themselves – was effectively marginalized here.[3]

Now you must clearly recognize that Husserl's method consisted in intuiting the concept on the basis of the given being or entity, on the basis of the particular instance which we behold, and which is perceptibly 'given' to us in the usual epistemological sense – for in this respect Heidegger never really ceased to consider himself a follower of Husserl. The specific point here is that one was not supposed to derive the relevant concept by a process of comparative abstraction – that is, by taking a range of objects, abstracting from all the respects in which they differ, retaining everything they have in common, and identifying the latter as the general or universal concept. On the contrary, all we allegedly have to do is to attend to any particular being or entity in its givenness in order to apprehend its essence in each case. But in Husserl this apparent immediacy, which is already implied in the concept of categorial intuition or *the intuition of essences*, has a moment or aspect which does not deny, and to Husserl's credit does not wish to deny, the activity or subjectivity which is involved in conceptuality. According to Husserl, all you have to do, if you wish to intuit the essence of a particular object or comprehend its essential character, is something quite simple which amounts to a kind of abstraction, namely to bracket or ignore its facticity. Thus if some object or other is 'given' before your very eyes, you simply need to cancel the thesis of its actuality, its individuated reality in space and time, and attend to the object precisely as it is given to you as the object of your thought, as the specific object of an 'intentional act', without undertaking to affirm anything at all regarding its spatio-temporal existence. What remains after this simple process of subtraction, in other words, what remains of this blackboard if you completely ignore its particular spatio-temporal character at this point in time in this particular lecture room – that is supposed to be simply identical with the essence of this blackboard. And this essence is supposed to be pure, to be binding and independent of all actual experience. Yet at the same time this essence – which is the whole point of this philosophy, which has derived the essence from just such a particular being or entity – is supposed to retain this very quality of givenness and perceptibility. And this brings me to the second desideratum of this philosophy, which we could describe as an empirical one or, if you prefer, as an empirical desideratum at the second level. For these pure essences, these a priori features, which are supposedly independent of space and time and resemble Platonic Ideas in being uniform, immutable and without beginning or end – these essences are also

taken to be immediately accessible, to be immediate objects of primordial experience or, as Husserl himself usually puts it (although he
also employs the expression 'primordial experience'),[4] to be 'given in
originary intuition'.

This is the constellation of elements which characterizes this entire
school. And I would really emphasize that this specific character actually provides the key for understanding what Heidegger means by the
concept of being as such, and how these mutually exclusive predicates
of immediate givenness and intuitive immediacy on the one hand and
purity and a priority on the other are both fulfilled at once. It also
helps us to understand how we are supposed to reach this pure and
a priori level through a relatively simple act, namely by setting aside
the spatial and temporal determinations of whatever is intuited in
any given case. In order to be precise, I should also add that this
theory of subtraction, this process of abstracting from concrete individuation, is not the only interpretation which Husserl provides in
this regard. For in an earlier and perhaps even more important text
for the reception of these things – the sixth investigation in the second
volume of the *Logical Investigations* – he adopted a rather different
approach. Here he develops a theory of categorial intuition according
to which we can become directly aware of categorial matters or intellectual states of affairs just as we can directly intuit perceptible phenomena. Husserl never came to a clear decision between these two
not entirely concordant theories because it is clear from his later
writings – although this can already be traced back to the writings
of his middle period – that the entire construction did not really satisfy
him, and because he believed that he would have to ground insights
into intellectual states of affairs through a theory of transcendental
subjectivity, in other words, in a traditional Kantian epistemological
sense after all. But we can leave this particular question aside for
now.[5] You will easily discover that this distinctive and, as I am tempted
to put it, antinomic structure which attaches to the givenness of intellectual states of affairs in Husserl – which appears antinomic because
that which is essentially mediated, that which is thought and conceived
as such, is also supposed to be independent in its own right. And I
claim that this same antinomic structure recurs in Heidegger's philosophy, and indeed especially in his doctrine of being. What appears
in Husserl under the name of purity, under the name of the intuited
essence, or εἶδος [eidos] (which is just the old Platonic name for
essence), is reproduced in Heidegger's concept of being, in the notion
of the separation of being from the entire realm of beings. I would
just point out in passing that the ambiguity we find in Husserl is
simply perpetuated in Heidegger's philosophy, for, while 'being' is

supposedly contrasted with and expressly distinguished from 'beings', it is not supposed to be a pure concept, or something else again. On the contrary, it is supposedly something which precedes all this, which ultimately cannot be expressed at all, which is itself indifferent to the distinction between being and beings.

Here I would just like to say a word about Heidegger's concept of ontological difference, which I have already mentioned in various contexts. For you might object here – and many formulations in Heidegger would certainly encourage you to do so – that the charge I have repeatedly levelled against Heidegger, namely that of ontologizing the ontic, is baseless precisely because he himself already expressly emphasizes the distinction between being and beings in his own doctrine of ontological difference. But this is merely an illusory claim. For it turns out – as I could easily show you in relation to numerous formulations on the part of the later Heidegger, and perhaps we shall get to discuss this – that he sets up the concept of ontological difference only in order to do away with it. And he does so with a relatively simple argument that is also relatively easy to see through, for he claims that the ontological difference itself, namely the difference of being and beings, can only be understood by analysing the meaning of being. In other words, this difference lies in the character of being itself; it belongs to being to reveal itself or to appear in the context of beings. Thus the ontological difference which is announced with such a fanfare is simply reabsorbed by the indifferent concept of being. I would ask you to believe what I am saying here, since at this particular point I do not really wish to pursue what you could call philological proof for the correctness of this thesis. But I can promise you that I will not fail to provide such detailed proof in due course, if only in the form of future publications.[6]

Then again we see as well how the concept of immediacy or primordial experience which Husserl ascribed to the intuition of essences also returns in Heidegger when he explicitly and indeed emphatically says that 'being' is not a universal concept, not even the most universal concept of all. I can substantiate this directly with a quotation that I have to hand, although it would not be difficult to find many others of the same tenor. Heidegger writes:

> But now the question is whether the assessment of being as the most universal concept reaches the essence of being, or whether it so misinterprets being from the start that questioning becomes hopeless. The question is whether being can count only as the most universal concept that is unavoidably involved in all particular concepts, or whether being has a completely different essence, and thus is anything but the object of an 'ontology', if one takes this word in its established meaning.[7]

This formulation reveals something that we find in several other writers, including Sigmund Freud, where certain theses or distinctions are introduced in an apparently tentative and problematic form even when a very specific thesis is actually intended. Thus it is quite clear from other passages in Heidegger that he emphatically denies the conceptual character of what he calls 'being'. On the one hand you have the claim that being is non-conceptual, the demand to acknowledge its immediacy, and thus the demand for a primordial experience of being in this regard. We are repeatedly assured that everything depends on some such primordial experience – although Heidegger gives a characteristically objectivist twist to this idea by insisting that this experience is not ultimately down to us at all. The process is mythologized when we are told that whether we come to experience being lies at the disposal of being itself, that being reveals or unveils itself, that being lights up for us, and indeed only for us; and, furthermore, that its hiddenness – in other words, the impossibility of immediately perceiving it – already belongs to its ontological character. On the other hand, being is supposed to be pure, or entirely independent of any individual or determinate being or entity. In other words, being is supposed to enjoy every advantage of the conceptual in comparison with the content of experience, and every advantage of immediate experience in comparison with the conceptual. The only difference from Husserl – and there is a certain objective irony here – lies in this: what was still intended by Husserl in an essentially epistemological sense as an explanation of specific states of affairs, of our capacities for specific types of insight, is now withdrawn, with a distinctive Heideggerean twist, from the subject altogether. It is thus interpreted objectively, if you will allow me to put it like that, in terms of 'being', which is now completely emancipated from the subject. What I would really like you to think about, now that I have recited these fundamental determinations or enactments of Heidegger's for you – and enactments seems the right word here, since they actually read like decrees – is precisely that being is not supposed to be a concept, not something that has been brought about in any way. For those of you who are following these things with direct reference to Heidegger's texts, I would like to point out that what I describe as a concept, or in Hegelian terms as something posited by the subject, is described by Heidegger in terms of teutonic neologisms or archaisms (whatever you prefer): as a realm of fabrication or 'machination', of that which is made merely by the subject. This kind of expression can be traced in many of Heidegger's later writings.[8] In this regard the moment of subjective mediation, to which I have repeatedly drawn your attention, is already downgraded – as if it simply belonged to the superstructure of consciousness, as if it were something which a busily interfering and superfluous consciousness externally introduces and imposes, thus sacrilegiously disturbing or contaminating the purity or givenness of being itself. And Heidegger even responds to this sense of sacrilege in an objectivistic way by expressly locating this very sacrilege within the history of being. In other words, he defends the claim that being itself hardly permits any other historical relationship to it than this sacrilegious approach and the forgetfulness of being which accompanies it. We are thus eventually driven to downright Gnostic speculations about the character of being itself, as if it were a sort of Evil Demon that has already destined human beings to mistake their own relationship to it.

I think I have now shown you how these determinations of purity and immediacy really constitute the fundamental constellation of Heidegger's thought. And I believe it is not very difficult to realize the incompatibility of these two basic determinations, since the history of this incompatibility is, to put it bluntly, identical with the history of philosophy itself. For that which is pure and free from all contamination by experience cannot actually be regarded as something immediate precisely because immediacy is experience itself, something which involves a kind of primary evidence. But that which is immediately present to us is not itself pure, is not something a priori – unless the subject, the moment of reflection, also comes into it, yet this further moment of subjective reflection is precisely what is repudiated by Heidegger and fundamental ontology. In short, the construction of the concept of being, which is meant to meet these contradictory demands, cannot be redeemed if we apply a two-valued logic,[9] which seems right only for a two-valued philosophy such as Heidegger's. When I claimed that it was impossible to think anything whatsoever under the term 'being', that this concept is entirely empty, that it eludes any further determination, this is a consequence of the aporetic reasoning which I have presented for you. In other words, I have shown, or I hope I have shown, that nothing determinate can possibly be thought here precisely on account of the contradictory character of the construction in question. For every determinate thought of what being could mean would inevitably compromise one or other of these demands – either the purity of being as distinct from beings or the primary experience or self-manifestation of being. Thus the emptiness or inconceivability of the concept of being, what I have called the elusiveness of this concept, is not merely an intellectual error but something grounded in the very structure and approach of this kind of thinking. These two contradictory demands can only be brought together in the *word* being – for I do not believe that we should employ the *concept* of being here – once every determinate distinction within being has been ruled out. And it is only by means of such determinate distinctions that we can really secure any meaning for this concept at all. Heidegger's own procedure – and once again this belongs in the realm I have rather disrespectfully described as strategic – is precisely to elevate the inconceivability or incompatibility of the moments that essentially constitute his concept of being into a distinctive advantage and particular merit on the part of this concept. Now this is connected with a rather ancient theme in the history of philosophy, which we also find in Hegel and indeed in almost all philosophies in one form or another. I am talking about the idea of a kind of original 'Fall' occasioned by the emergence of thought itself. This is the idea that we can no longer immediately share in some full and undivided unity on the part of being or beings, a unity which has effectively been ruptured by thought. Thus the emergence of 'reflection' intellectually mirrors the original Fall in the most literal sense, the process through which we have learnt to distinguish good and evil, the punishment for eating of the Tree of Knowledge, as we read in the Old Testament.[10] And this philosophy interprets the punishment for eating of the Tree of Knowledge as something that essentially afflicts the process of knowing itself. In other words, the knowledge that we have subsequently acquired is inevitably forgetful of being precisely because it is a dividing, separating and distinguishing form of cognition associated with the reflective understanding. In other words, this is supposed to be an emphatically false kind of knowing. Now although this particular construction cannot be found in Heidegger in so many words, I nonetheless believe that it captures the atmosphere of his entire oeuvre. This is directly connected with the characteristically aporetic construction of the concept of being in the sense that this very lack of determinate distinction, the lack involved in our inability to think being *at all*, is expressly claimed by Heidegger as the privilege of such being, as the privilege which belongs to this thinking of being over and beyond all our usual and merely reflective knowledge. He acts therefore as if the practice of evocation could overcome the original Fall of reflection. Once he has ascribed this Fall itself to the history of being in a rather Gnostic way, as I pointed out before, he does not ask precisely how, if all of us, including him, are caught in a stage of mere reflection, we can possibly find the strength to revoke this approach, to share once again, at a stroke, in the undivided truth of being that, according to him, we have already forfeited for essential reasons. Instead he presents all this as a message which he allows his exegete Beaufret[11] to proclaim to all the world: this turn to being, in direct contrast to all merely reflective thought, involves a 'turning' – not a turning simply in philosophy or the realm of knowledge but one in being itself. This looks like the crudest act of hubris which philosophy has allowed itself since time immemorial and far surpasses anything that once offended theology – which seems so well disposed to Heidegger – in the later writings of Nietzsche, such as *Ecce homo*.

You may now be in a rather better position to understand the peculiar cachet of Heidegger's philosophy than you could before I offered the analysis that I have developed for you today. If the words of this philosophy sound so tangible – whether in a kind of artisanal or agrarian way, as I pointed out – such language reflects an immediate claim to tangible sensuous presence, such words draw on the conception of primordial experience, on the idea of the immediacy and incomprehensibility of being. At the same time, the distinctive ontological resonance of all these words – precisely what I called their metaphysical aura – draws on the idea of purity. On the one hand, such words relate to the immediacy of the empirical world, and without this relation they could not possess the immediacy they do. On the other hand, given their pure and a priori character, they are supposedly relieved of any confrontation with the material domain. Indeed the very idea of such a confrontation would be regarded as the crudest misunderstanding, and anyone who attempted such a sacrilegious thing could expect to be charged with forgetfulness of being, if not accused of something even worse – of being an 'inauthentic' human being consumed by chatter or 'idle talk'. Now this notion of idle talk has something of 'Stop thief!' about it. It seems rather characteristic of this philosophy – which is not so far from the traditional idea of idle talk in the sense that it also uses concepts which are not really intellectually redeemed – that it looks down on the very *thinking* which insists that our talk should be redeemed in terms of determinate thought, and associates it with chatter, vulgarity, everydayness and 'the They'. I do not actually wish to be unjust to Heidegger in this regard, for I believe this is the most serious point we have come to in our reflections so far. I do not even wish to deny that there is the kind of experience that he talks so much about in terms of the word 'being', although every attempt to pin down this experience or express it in so many words runs the risk of succumbing to the kitsch which I surely brought out for you, even if I did not exactly demonstrate it, in reciting Heidegger's poems. Now I believe there are very few people (you must forgive the somewhat questionable example here) who, in the right state of mind at least, would fail to feel, on hearing the rustling of leaves, that the leaves are speaking to us, that there is something like a language of nature, that we are the only ones who cannot understand it, although it is a very distinctive language. The experience of music involves something of what I am intimating here: something quite particular and distinctive is communicated to us, but it somehow eludes our concepts. It is entirely legitimate that thinking should also address such phenomena, that we should try and think about what is happening here, though far too little has actually been done in this direction. This would be a fitting task for a genuine aesthetics, and a central theme for aesthetics as such.[12] Yet here I believe Heidegger is guilty of arresting and reifying a kind of experience which is graced and distinguished by its intrinsically fugitive character and can never become merely thing-like. He zealously protests, of course, that 'being' is anything but a thing – it cannot possibly resemble a thing or manifest thing-like features for there is not supposed to be anything remotely determinate about it – yet he turns the truth we sense in the rustling of leaves or the flow of music, which lies precisely in its fugitive and perishable character, into something merely positive in the concept of 'being itself' – into something that we can have and hold, into something which is, after all, essentially an object of thought. And it is in this move to positivity, where the content is thereby instantly converted to untruth, that the πρῶτον ψεῦδος [prōton pseudos] of this philosophy consists. For the truth of such experience is inseparable from its fugitive character. As soon as it is seized and arrested, as soon as it is transformed into a general structure, which is what Heidegger invariably does, it already becomes delusory, already becomes reified. And it is precisely here that we find a spurious aesthetizing of thought where forms of experience that are possible only in art, and then only by virtue of that semblance which belongs to art, are treated as if this semblance were immediately available to us in the realm of knowledge. And this parody of art in a false claim to knowledge is also the origin of false art.

LECTURE 19

2 *February 1961*

Ladies and gentlemen, since the semester is really getting on and I have the laudable intention of not falling too far behind the stated programme of these lectures and stopping when we are only half-way through, I have decided to do something that I have avoided up to this point. In other words, I shall now increasingly draw upon or simply read from texts which I have already prepared, even if they have not yet been published as such. I am not generally very keen on this approach, and you will have noticed that I like to speak as freely and spontaneously as possible. And there is a good reason for this. For I realize that, on account of the way I usually write, things can become so involved, *tant mieux que mal*, that they are not always particularly easy to follow. That is why I prefer to reproduce the processes, or in certain circumstances to produce the lines of argument, which originally lead to such formulations, rather than simply to confront you with the final sedimented literary product. But since I am mindful of what you all require here, I shall improvise freely when I come to passages that also strike me as particularly difficult and, though I apologize for this, try and become the commentator of my own formulations.[1]

Heidegger's philosophy, as you know, at least in the famous period of *Being and Time*, reveals an extraordinary antipathy to what he there describes as *das Man*, or 'the They', an expression designed to denounce the anthropology of the sphere of circulation. Subsequently, however, Heidegger revoked this aversion, which clearly betrayed certain proto-fascistic accents, insofar as he attempted to interpret the sphere of 'the inauthentic', of 'the They', of 'idle talk', and all the categories which appear at this point, in expressly ontological terms, namely in terms of the 'forgetfulness of being'. In other words, these categories are now ascribed to the mythic and enigmatic fate or 'sending' which belongs to being itself. But this strikes me as another expression of Heidegger's strategy for avoiding any genuine determinacy rather than as something that would change anything in the basic structure of his thought. And when he finally starts talking about the homelessness of thinking, and about a kind of thinking that might indeed find its way home, this is only an extension of the same old structure. That is why I feel I should draw your attention to something which perhaps emerges from the context of the deduction which I presented last time: the deduction of the empty and tautological essence of the central Heideggerean category of being, an essence that can never indeed be fulfilled by thought. In other words, Heidegger's philosophy resembles a highly developed system of credit in which one concept constantly borrows from another. The wavering condition that ensues throws ironic light on the bearing of a philosophy which feels so rooted in native soil that it prefers the 'German thinking' to a foreign word such as 'philosophy'. The old joke tells us the debtor enjoys an advantage over the creditor since the latter actually depends on whether the former pays up or not; in the same way blessings flow to Heidegger from everything he owes. That 'being' is neither fact nor concept exempts it from critique. Every kind of objection is branded as misunderstanding. The concept borrows its air of concretion from the factical, from the plenitude of all that is not the product of thought, in short, from the 'in itself'. But the realm of beings borrows from the synthesizing mind that aura of being more than it actually is, that sense of hallowed transcendence – and indeed at one point Heidegger specifically describes being as 'the *transcendens* par excellence'.[2] But this quid pro quo is itself hypostasized as a kind of higher 'third' in contrast to the reflective understanding which divides conceptuality and actual things with a knife. And if I even speak of such a 'third', then Heidegger (or one of his trusty disciples) would instantly point to his own words to show that he has expressly warned against regarding being as a third and would claim that the very idea of a third with respect to being and beings is already a reified form of thinking. For then 'being' would be turned into a principle, and such a principle is precisely what it is not – although we never actually learn what it is supposed to be, if it is neither a concept, nor a being, nor some kind of differently constituted third with respect to both. The only possible determination that remains for it is precisely its indeterminacy.

The first thing we have to do is to discover exactly how we get to this claim that being transcends subjectivity – and I have just drawn your attention to Heidegger's characterization of being as the *transcendens* par excellence.[3] He is weary of the subjective prison-house of knowledge into which we have been driven through merely epistemological reflection, and which only obstructs our access to things. This was already implied by Husserl's watchword 'to the things themselves' – something which of course becomes even more obvious and emphatic in Heidegger's concept of being. There is no intention that the latter should be regarded as anything like an objective thing, for a thing suggests something fixed and solid, something specific and clearly defined. 'Being' has the distinctive merit of not being thing-like at all, of not possessing any such substantive or objective determinacy. It is this weariness with the subjective limitations of knowledge, with its mediated character, which leads Heidegger to assure us that what transcends subjectivity is something immediate for subjectivity, something that is not contaminated by conceptuality, by anything that is arbitrarily produced or fabricated by subjectivity, as I pointed out last time.[4] Along with romantic trends such as the Youth Movement,[5] fundamental ontology actually feels itself to be anti-romantic. In protest against the limiting and disturbing moment of subjectivity it believes it can 'overcome' all this – to use a fatal word expressly deployed by Heidegger himself in his *Introduction to Metaphysics* (see page 155 of that work).[6] This hideous talk of 'overcoming' imagines that the whole cultural and intellectual world consists solely of enemies who somehow have to be confronted directly or indirectly before finally being overcome; that every dark and negative aspect of consciousness, like the so-called phenomenon of nihilism, must be overcome; that the experienced negativity of a thing is already proof that it has no right to exist and must therefore be thought away. It is quite true that this climate of thought is only occasionally betrayed or named as such by Heidegger through this kind of *lapsus linguae*, but it effectively pervades his entire philosophy. But since subjectivity cannot just think its mediations out of the world, it wishes back levels of consciousness which precede all reflection on subjectivity and mediation. This miscarries. Where Heidegger's thought turns its back on subjectivity, as it were, hoping to cling directly to things as they show themselves to be, attempting to do material justice to things themselves in a way that seems at once archaic and soberly objective, he removes and withdraws every determination from what is thought – just as Kant once proceeded with the transcendent dimension of his philosophy, namely the thing in itself as the unknown cause of its own appearances. Such determinations would prove equally offensive either as a work of merely subjective reason or as a derivative effect of merely particular entities. That is what I meant in the previous lecture when I claimed that Heidegger effectively tries to unify contradictory demands. These demands suppress one another precisely through the relationship in which they are placed, leaving nothing behind. While there is no speculative exploration of what thought can accomplish here, it is equally impossible for anything actual to impinge on thought, for such a piece of the world could only compromise the priority of 'being'. Thought no longer trusts itself to think anything but what is wholly empty and abstract – far more of an unknown X than the old transcendental subject which, qua unity of consciousness, at least still bore a trace of an actually existing consciousness. Heidegger turns this X, this absolutely inexpressible moment beyond all predicates, into an *ens realissimum* under the name of 'being'. But Hegel's judgement upon pure being is verified – against the will of this philosophy of being – in the resulting conceptual aporia:[7] it is indistinguishable from nothing, and Heidegger himself is the one who is deceived here. We should not actually reproach existential ontology, as he rightly insists himself,[8] with that nihilism in terms of which, to his horror, the leftist existentialists in Paris interpreted this ontology. It is to be reproached instead for proclaiming the nothingness of its highest word as something essentially positive.

And the word 'being' lends itself perfectly to this. That which belongs to mind or spirit is now translated into a given that is *sui generis*. In this connection I would like to quote from an extraordinarily important book by Karl Heinz Haag. I would highly recommend his *Critique of Recent Ontology* to all of you who have been following these lectures. For, in a completely independent spirit, he has developed ideas which emerge from the line of thought I have been pursuing here and has expressly drawn the most positive consequences from these reflections. Haag puts it as follows: 'Ontology ends up by arbitrarily proposing "being" as the utterly immediate, although in its very purity it is precisely the opposite of pure immediacy, is mediated through and through, and is meaningful only in terms of mediations.'[9] The Kantian question of constitution which would inevitably destroy the ontological thesis of the priority of 'being' is swept aside. The core of rationality, the domain of the concept, is reinterpreted in terms of that which simply 'shows itself' and converted into the utterly irrational, which eludes all judgement on the part of reason – something that was certainly still retained in Husserl. This is the crucial difference between Heidegger's philosophy and Husserl's doctrine of essence. That which is actually mediated is elevated to the matter itself, the thing κὰτ'ἐξοχήν [kat'exochēn], to something that, as I said, is no longer a thing or matter at all. Mind becomes simply receptive and spared all rational critique. But it is also spiritualized and elevated as 'being', accessible only to the pure gaze of thought, far beyond the multivarious ὄντα [onta] for which 'being' serves as a *prius* only through a kind of pre-established harmony. While such ambiguity demands constant wariness in both directions, and 'being' inevitably shrinks to a dimensionless point, this procedure certainly possesses its own *fundamentum in re*.[10] Categorial intuition, the realization of the concept, tells us that a 'something' must always correspond, over and beyond the sensuous matter, or ὕλη [hulē], to the categorially constituted states of affairs which traditional epistemologies know only as products of synthesis. Just as a simple mathematical proposition has no validity without the numerical synthesis which establishes the equation, it is equally true – though Kant in fact neglects this – that no synthesis is possible unless the relationship of the relevant elements corresponds to the synthesis in question. Otherwise – to put this drastically and thus perhaps misleadingly – the two sides of the equation would simply be identical. Just as we cannot meaningfully speak of this mutual correspondence, of this reciprocal objective parity – if I may put this once again in a slightly misleading way – without any reference to conceptual synthesis, it also true that no rational synthesis is conceivable without that correspondence with the relevant state of affairs. This reciprocal dependency – which means that you cannot even express the aspect of synthesis or the aspect of correspondence independently of each other – is the very paradigm or classic case of what is meant by the concept of *mediation*. And perhaps this is the best context for bringing out for you the strict meaning of this concept. Indeed, when we reflect upon these things, the fact we are never really sure whether to regard thinking simply as an activity or as an effort to respond and measure up to something is already an indication of this. Whatever we spontaneously think about is inseparable from the way it reveals itself. Now Heidegger's emphasis upon this aspect, upon the way in which things actually appear or show themselves, his resistance to any reduction of this process of appearing to mere thought about things, would be a very welcome corrective to the standard philosophy of mind. Yet he then isolates this moment of givenness, of the *Sachverhalt*, or 'state of affairs', and treats it just as abstractly – to use Hegel's terminology – as idealism does, in the opposite direction, when it isolates the moment of synthesis and treats that abstractly by separating it from that which is synthesized. Once it is hypostasized, this aspect or moment of correspondence *in re* ceases precisely to be an aspect or moment and is reified as a result – which is the very last thing that ontology intended in its protest against the division between conceptuality on the one hand and beings or entities on the other. The synthesizing consciousness really does have something receptive about it, and this moment was certainly acknowledged in the detailed descriptions which Husserl provided in his phenomenology of mental acts. And in the later phase of his thought Husserl spoke explicitly of receptive spontaneity.[11] What belongs together in a judgement reveals itself in an exemplary rather than a merely comparative fashion. There is a sense in which you should regard a judgement not merely as something abstracted in comparison with other states of affairs but as something with an immediacy of its own where a specific state of affairs is 'evident' in this individual determinate judgement. There is no need to dispute the immediacy of insight in this sense, to challenge the idea that there is such a thing as immediate insight. But we do need to challenge the tendency to isolate and hypostasize, or to bestow absolute significance, upon such insight. When we become directly aware of something in the specific object which is not universal, which does not belong to the 'species', this casts a very sharp light on the latter. It is this aspect or moment alone which leads beyond the tautology which tells us only how the species is already defined through the common feature which encompasses all its instances. Without this moment of immediate insight, Hegel's claim that the particular is the universal would be pointless. Phenomenology after Husserl has preserved this, though also at the cost of the complementary element. But the phenomenological intuition of essences involves contradictions which cannot simply be resolved on the side either of nominalism or of realism. On the one hand, the intuition of essences is ideation, with its elective affinity to ideology, to the fraudulent importation of immediacy through something that is mediated, which it clothes in the authority of an absolute being-in-itself that is incontestably evident to the subject. On the other hand, the intuition of essences captures something that is right and true, namely a physiognomic insight into states of affairs. It is legitimated by the fact that the mental or spiritual is not constituted by the consciousness which is directed towards it in the act of knowing but is objectively grounded in itself, far beyond the individual agent, in the collective life of spirit. The aspect or moment of immediate insight is adequate to that objectivity of spirit. As something already pre-formed in itself, it can also be intuited or perceived, as ordinary sensuous things can be perceived. It is just that this intuition is not absolute and irrefutable, any more than the things of sense perception are absolute and irrefutable. Husserl rightly insisted on the intuitable character of perceptible things, but he then proceeded to identify what this physiognomic insight disclosed with universal scientific concepts based upon a method of abstraction distinguished from the intuition of essences. Thus he wavers between scientism as a philosophical model and philosophy as the self-reflection of science. And the resulting confusion is responsible for the ideological misuse of categorial intuition. As in the case of Kant's synthetic a priori judgements, necessity and universality are ascribed directly to what springs from sudden physiognomic illumination. Yet what categorial intuition, fallible though it is, might help us to achieve would be comprehension of the matter itself rather than its reduction to a defensive classificatory system. The ψεῦδος [pseudos], or original deception, here is not the unscientific character of categorial intuition but a dogmatic scientistic appropriation of it which expects it to provide what it is unable to provide. The ideating gaze rouses the moment of mediation which was ossified in the apparent immediacy of spirit as given. You could even say that the intuition of essences is very close to the allegorical consciousness which awakens in images and objects what they used to be, awakens the intentions which formerly gave them life but now lie petrified within them. As the experience of what has already come to pass with things that are supposed to be no more than what they are, such ideation, such intuition of essences, would almost be the very opposite of what it is taken for: not the obedient acceptance 'being' but a critique of being as the merely apparent, not the consciousness of the identity of thing and concept but rather a consciousness of the breach between them. What the philosophy of being insists on, as if it were the organ of something which is actually spurious, finds its truth in negativity.

Heidegger's emphasis on 'being', which is meant to be more than any mere concept, might appeal to the way that the content of judgements cannot simply be dissolved in judgements themselves, just as Husserl once appealed to the ideal unity of the 'species'. And the functional role of such exemplifying consciousness may well increase historically. The more completely socialized the world becomes, the more densely its objects are enveloped in universal determinations,[12] the more the individual phenomenon or state of affairs can distinctly manifest its universal character, and the more can be exposed through micrological immersion in the phenomenon. All this, indeed, is sharply opposed to the intentions of ontology, although it may well have prompted the doctrine of the intuition of essences in a way unknown to ontology itself. I am talking about the sheer sameness of the standardized and administered world[13] – where we have only to scrutinize a particular aspect to discover what is effectively the principle of the whole – even if the philosophy of being has not really thought about this at all. Categorial intuition, the procedure central to the intuition of essences, is particularly instructive in contrast to those classificatory tendencies now so evident in the social and cultural sciences and which ultimately rob them of their own reason to exist. But if the procedure of categorial intuition is repeatedly charged by the particular sciences, by a long since automatized reason, of indulging in spurious or at least over-hasty generalizations, that is not simply the product of an intellectual outlook which has long misused its rationalized scientific ethos – the supposedly modest one of organizing the facts it has recorded in an external fashion – in such a way that it can no longer recognize itself in facts which it doesn't actually understand any more. On the contrary, where empirical investigations are able, in a genuinely concrete way, to demonstrate in relation to the anticipations of thought, to the medium of exemplifying thought, that the categorial character quasi-immediately intuited in the particular does not possess universality attributed to it, then they already reveal the mistake of a method adopted by Husserl and Heidegger alike.

The claim that 'being', prior to all abstraction, is not really a concept, or is at least a qualitatively unique one, fails to recognize that the moment of immediacy – which, as Hegel's *Phenomenology* already teaches, is constantly reproduced at every level of consciousness and in every process of mediation – is an aspect or moment rather than the whole of cognition.[14] But no ontological project ever gets by without bestowing absolute significance on some particular aspect or moment that is singled out. If cognition is the interplay of conceptual synthesis and that which is to be synthesized, where neither process is independent of the other, one cannot appeal to the kind of immediate commemoration that Heidegger stipulates as the only ultimate justification worthy of a philosophy of being – unless the activity or spontaneity of thought that he despises were directly involved. If reflection would lack content without the moment of immediacy, the latter would lack any binding force, would remain entirely arbitrary, without reflection, without the thoughtful discriminating exploration of what self-showing 'being' allegedly means for a purely passive thinking that does not think. And this is what gives rise to the artisanal tone of the *pronunciamenti* that 'being' illuminates or unveils. If the thoughtful exploration, determination and fulfilment of the primordial word, if the critical confrontation of this word with what is ultimately at stake, proves impossible, then all this talk of 'being' is fruitless. It has not properly been thought because it cannot be thought at all in the indeterminacy which it demands. And when this unthinkability is turned into a fitting expression of thoughtful reverence, this reverence resembles the attitude of the fox who claimed to find the grapes too sour. As I said, it has not been thought because it cannot be thought at all in the indeterminacy which it demands. But the way in which the philosophy of being turns this inconceivability into unassailability, this exemption from rational examination into a form of transcendence beyond the reflective understanding, is a violent act that is as clever as it is desperate. Heidegger wants to break out of the immanent sphere of consciousness more decisively than the phenomenology of Husserl, which stopped only half-way there. Yet he breaks out only into a mirror, as it were, being blind to the moment of synthesis in the substrate. He ignores the way that mind, which confessed itself identical to 'being' in this apostrophized philosophy of being, is already implied in what he presents as the pure 'Itself' which mind would allegedly have before it, namely as 'being'. Heidegger's critique of the philosophical tradition objectively becomes the opposite of what it promises. In underestimating the moment of subjective mind or spirit, and thus also inevitably underestimating the task of exploring its counterpart, namely the material, the facticity, on which synthesis operates, in pretending to offer what is articulated in accordance with these moments as if it were somehow unitary or absolute, this philosophy fails the challenge of breaking the spell that human beings have made of their concepts; it ends up, to use Heidegger's own language, chasing something actually made or 'fabricated'. Instead of diagnosing human relations in the process, it conflates them with the *mundus intelligibilis*. It repeats and preserves precisely what it rails against, the intellectual constructions which, according to its own jargon, were the targets of 'destruction' – although they emerge rather well from this destructive impulse. Under the pretext of helping to reveal what they allegedly conceal, these constructions are once again unwittingly turned into the kind of reality 'in itself' which they have anyway already become for reified consciousness. What acts as if it were destroying the fetishes serves only to destroy the conditions which would allow one to see them as festishes. The apparent breakout terminates in the very thing that it would flee. The 'being' in which it issues is θέσει [thesei] rather than φύσει [phusei]. Heidegger's understanding with fascism and the ideology of the conservative revolution – the more elegant version of fascist ideology[15] – was not a reckless act of thoughtlessness but lay in the content of his doctrine.[16] In ceding 'being', which is mediated by mind, to a kind of purely receptive vision, philosophy converges with the irrationalist vision espoused by the life philosophy which fundamental ontology treats with such disdain. Recognition of irrationality would not itself already be the same as philosophical irrationalism. Irrationality is the mark which the ineliminable non-identity of subject and object leaves behind in the knowledge that postulates identity through the mere form of predicative judgement. Irrationality here also represents the hope that the merely subjective concept might not be irresistible, the pledge that not everything which exists can be exhausted by conceptuality. But, in turn, irrationality itself remains a function of *ratio*, specifiable in relation to the self-determination of the latter: what slips through the net is still filtered by it. The philosophies of irrationalism themselves cannot do without concepts and thereby involve a rational moment that gives the lie to their general thesis. Heidegger evades the aporia which it was one of the intentions of dialectical thought to resolve in that he feigns a standpoint beyond – you could also say prior to – the distinction of subject and object, one where the inadequacy of *ratio* to what needs to be thought is clearly revealed. Yet this leap miscarries with the means of reason. Thought is incapable of occupying any position in which the separation of subject and object that is involved in every thought, in thinking as such, could simply vanish. And that is why the truth moment in Heidegger's philosophy is corrupted into an irrationalist world-view. Philosophy today, as in Kant's time, would be a critique of reason conducted by reason itself rather than the banishment or dissolution of reason.

By prohibiting thought, thinking sanctions what simply exists.[17] The genuinely critical need for thought – namely to rouse us from the phantasmagoria of culture – is here arrested, channelled and redirected towards false consciousness. Imbued with the culture that surrounds it, thought is discouraged from asking what all this is really for or, to put it loosely, from raising the question about the *meaning* of all this. The question vanishes behind the 'This is how it is and must be' of everything that claims, as culture, to evince real meaning. Beneath the burden of existing culture, it is not asked whether the meaning which culture claims to have is actually realized, or whether the meaning that it claims even has any truth of its own. And fundamental ontology now steps forward as the advocate of this interest in meaning. And this is not the least reason why it directs its polemic specifically at epistemology or the theory of knowledge which deems such interest prejudicial. Nonetheless, fundamental ontology cannot simply annul the theory of knowledge. In the doctrine of *Dasein*, of subjectivity, as the royal road to ontology, we see how the old *intentio obliqua*,[18] the reference back to the subject, though humbled by ontological pathos, is still secretly at work. The invocation of the phenomenological method at least on the part of the early Heidegger shows how deeply this thinking is rooted in the tradition of Western philosophy even as it undertakes to disempower that tradition. The primordial impression which such thinking makes springs from the

increasing loss of intellectual culture amongst those who are so enthused
by this philosophy. The fascination exuded by the question concerning
the meaning of being or its traditional variant: 'Why is there anything
at all, rather than simply nothing?'[19] – a question originally formulated
by Leibniz, I believe[20] – is ceded phenomenologically to the analysis
of the signification of the word 'being'. What the word 'being' or
'*Dasein*' supposedly signifies is declared identical with the meaning
of being or *Dasein*. Something which is itself already immanent in
culture, such as the significations which semantic analysis reveals to
be at work in particular languages, is presented as if it had escaped
the finitude of all that is made or produced, of all that belongs to the
domain of mere beings. Heidegger's interpretation of the priority of
language is based upon this approach. The claim that the meaning
of the word 'being' is immediately the same as the meaning of being
is a spurious equivocation according to the generally accepted rules
of logic, and also according to the distinctions developed in the second
volume of Husserl's *Logical Investigations*. Now equivocal expressions
are not simply a matter of the imprecise use of language.[21] And the
parity of words does indeed point to something truly identical. Both
significations of 'meaning' are entwined here. Concepts, the instruments of human thought, can possess no meaning if meaning itself is
negated, if all memory of some objective meaning beyond the mechanisms of concept formation is merely expelled from these concepts.
Positivism, for which concepts are simply arbitrary and exchangeable
counters, has drawn the relevant conclusions from this, has extirpated
truth in the name of truth, and the philosophy of being has pointed
out the absurdity of this undertaking. Yet the unity of the equivocal
is revealed only in an implicit process of difference, not in some
ominous night of indifference.[22] This difference – involved in all talk
of meaning – is what falls away in Heidegger. Here too he follows a
characteristic tendency to hypostasis: by the very mode in which they
are expressed, findings from the domain of the conditioned are magically invested with the spurious appearance of the unconditioned.
What makes this all possible is the scintillating character of the word
'being', the scintillating character of the word 'is'. And Heidegger
himself is perceptive and reflective enough even to speak on certain
occasions of these equivocations, although he then attempts to eliminate them by recourse to more or less sophistical forms of argument.
I cannot stop to analyse these here since I now wish to move on
directly to the crucial considerations that need to be addressed.

LECTURE 20

7 February 1961

Ladies and gentlemen, you will remember that in the previous session I began by telling you something about the problems which are bound up with the concept of the meaning of being in fundamental ontology.[1] In Heidegger's work, as I explained to you, being is, in phenomenological terms, essence in something like Husserl's sense – that is to say, it is unconnected with the *facta* individuated in time and space, with the ὄντα [onta].[2] If true being is presented as radically separate from beings, as radically separate as it is presented in the programme of *Being and Time*, then 'being' is actually identical with its merely semantic, grammatical meaning. When being is so completely separated from any real or factical content, one has only, therefore, to give it the meaning of the *essential* in order to reach the meaning of being itself. Thus according to this schema in Heidegger's work – I hope you have all understood this – we find that being is a pure essence which does not relate to anything factical at all, but (if you will allow me to put it this way) is simply exhausted in its intellectual content. But then, in order to secure being itself, I no longer need to appeal to any *facta* which might be involved in 'being'; all I need instead is the meaning of this *expression*, of what is meant by it, and then I know what being itself is. For being itself is a pure essence; in other words, it is nothing but a pure *meaning*, without reference to any actual beings. But, with this schema, the attempt to break out of idealism which, as I said, all ontological philosophy once undertook is already revoked. The theory of being regresses into a theory of thinking, that is, of pure meaning, and being is deprived of everything

which would be more than mere thought. This manoeuvre obeys a
need. In order to find some meaning for being, of whatever kind –
although it has already been decided negatively by the question of
the meaning of being as precisely that which is absent – what is sum-
moned up is something constituted in advance as the domain of
meaning, that is to say, the theory of signification. The fact that
concepts have to mean something in order to be concepts at all becomes
a vehicle for suggesting that what lies behind them, namely being
itself, has meaning, because being is not given in any other way than
as concept, as linguistic signification. But Heidegger assures us that
this concept for its part is not a concept at all but is supposed to be
something immediate, something which appears or manifests itself,
and this confers ontological dignity on the semantic meaning – that
is, on the object of an analysis of signification – as if we were talking
about meaning here in the same way as we do when we ask, pre-
philosophically for example, whether life has a meaning or not. And
that now redounds as a consolation to the philosophy orientated in
this way. Consolation is actually the magnet of fundamental ontology,
going far beyond the latter's theoretical content. But, in this, fundamental ontology, with its delicate sensorium for intellectual power-
relationships, adapts itself to the situation and protects itself from
the kind of all-too-blank affirmativeness which hardly anyone would
be able to believe in such dark times. On the contrary, its metaphysical instrumentarium resembles the political appeal to the necessity of
'blood, sweat and tears', which, even fifteen years after the war, and
long after Churchill spoke these famous words, still serves a propa-
gandistic purpose in enlisting the masochistic potential of the popula-
tion at large.[3] The 'authentic' realities are transposed into a tragic
minor key, which encourages us to make sacrifices, even though we
do not really know what they are made *for* – this is how it was, at
least, at the stage of *Being and Time*; in the meantime, however,
fundamental ontology itself has become much more cautious in this
regard. That 'nothing' into which the aporetic concept of being readily
changes at times also permits a gesture of brow-furrowing hopeless
earnestness which no longer allows any suspicion of the official opti-
mism to surface.

Despite this, ontology wishes to restore, by means of spirit, the
order which was shattered by spirit, along with the authority that
order once enjoyed.[4] The expression *project* betrays the tendency of
this philosophy to negate freedom by means of freedom: what is
trans-subjective binding is handed over to an act of positing subjectivity. But the arrogance of the claim to posit order in this way, which
I demonstrated by showing you how Heidegger attempts to turn his

conception of project into that of being itself, is forced upon him by the very structure of his thinking, for the loss which resonates, in a rather kitschy way, in the word *Seinsvergessenheit* [forgetfulness of being], has reasons behind it. That which is mourned here, namely the legacy of the early ἀρχαί [archai], has with good reason melted away from that consciousness which has wrested itself away from nature – it has not, for instance, slipped from its grasp because of some original sin of inauthenticity, nor has it withdrawn (on account of our exclusive concern with beings) into the seventh heaven of pure being. Myth dissolved because it was a deception; only a deception can revive it and commend it. The self-stylization of being as something beyond the critical concept is supposed to establish myth's legal title; the heteronomy of that title is required as a refuge for as long as anything at all of enlightenment still survives in the world. Suffering at the hands of what Heidegger's philosophy registers as the loss of being is not only untruth; otherwise he would find it difficult to seek support precisely in Hölderlin. The very concept of society requires the relations between human beings to be grounded in freedom, even though such freedom has not been realized to this day, which implies that this society, for all its rigidity and predominance, is a kind of deformation. The production and reproduction of life, and everything which is covered by the name 'superstructure', are not transparent to that *ratio* whose own inner coherence and reconciled realization would alone constitute true order, an order without violence. The old, endogenous orders, however, have either vanished or have outlived their own legitimacy; they still vegetate, as they say, and they are crumbling. Society, indeed, nowhere assumes the kind of chaotic course that appears in the irrational contingency of the fate of individuals. The claim that we are living in chaos belongs to the favourite stock-in-trade of those who would subject us to their order against our own will and own better insight; and I think you should equip yourselves with a modicum of scepticism whenever anyone drivels on at you about the chaotic present and how it has abandoned the world of values, or, again, about how the world has lost its 'centre', which comes to much the same thing. What the subject experiences as chaotic in the world is not too much freedom, but too little: that is the point which the various projects of ontology either misunderstand or – and I consider this to be the more pressing motive – actually frantically deny. This is precisely why order, in itself, becomes a fetish for the ontological projects, right through to the 'structure of being'. And even if Heidegger takes great care not to say anything of the kind, detailed linguistic analysis would be able to reveal this archaic faith in the 'most blessed Daughter of Heaven'[5] in every sentence. At the same time, however, the world everywhere seems more prepared to embrace the horrors of 'order' than to accept that anarchy which, openly or secretly, is lamented by apologetic philosophy. We need to be saved not from anarchy but from the order which the apologists wish on us, and which they would like to be permitted to provide for us. The fact that freedom has, largely, remained an ideology, that human beings are impotent before the predominant power of institutions,[6] and that they are not able to determine their life or the life of the whole in accordance with their own reason – indeed, that they are no longer even capable of thinking such a thought without incurring further suffering: all this puts a spell on their rebellion, so that it takes an upside-down form. They would rather have what is openly worse than the illusion of the good, and the up-to-date philosophies fall into line with this. They sound a false note, however, since they already feel that this order is right behind them and that they can rely on its power, even while they, like Hitler, put on an act of lonely daring. That they behave as though they were metaphysically homeless and 'held out into the nothing'[7] serves order as a self-legitimating ideology which allows people to despair and threatens them with physical annihilation. The resonance which these ideas find anticipates their implicit understanding with that repression which still has the potential to triumph even in the West and has long since proved victorious in the East, where the thought of realized freedom has been warped into the reality of unfreedom. Heidegger encourages an obedient thinking and repudiates the use of the word 'humanism' with a standard gesture directed against the market of public opinion. In this he makes shameful common cause with those who rail against the so-called Isms.[8] It may well be asked whether he wishes to do away with all facile talk of humanism – which is certainly repulsive enough – only because he wants to put the thing itself, namely humanism, in fear of its life.

Ontology, despite its authoritarian *parti pris*, has learnt at least something from experience and rarely praises hierarchy[9] openly any more, as it did in the times when Landsberg, a pupil of Max Scheler's, published a monograph on *The Middle Ages and Ourselves*.[10] The tactic of self-protection all round harmonizes with a social phase which no longer grounds its relations of domination in a past stage of society. The seizure of power calculates on the ultimately structured nature of society, and depends upon it. Just as the leader elevates himself above the atomized people, rails against snobbery and, in order to perpetuate himself, changes the guard occasionally, so the qualitatively hierarchical moments from the early stages of the ontological renaissance disappear into the omnipotence and all-encompassing unity of being. Even this, ladies and gentlemen, is not *only* ideology. The anti-relativism which dates back to Husserl's early attempt to ground so-called logical absolutism, the *Prolegomena to a Pure Logic*,[11] blends with an aversion to static or reified thinking, an aversion which was also expressed in German Idealism and in Marx's work but was initially neglected in Scheler and in the earliest attempt to provide a new ontology. The contemporary significance of relativism has in any case diminished. The state of the world no longer leaves any room for that arbitrariness of individual action with which relativism has been concerned since the time of the Athenian sophists. What has come to light is the weakness of the relativistic approach itself, which can only be sustained in abstraction from the matter at hand, but which dissolves irresistibly whenever thought comes into contact with a specific discipline and its particular field. If you make the experiment, in the course of your own specialized studies, of developing, maintaining and securing some particular cognition, you will see, in such cases, that the notions associated with so-called universal relativism are actually as remote as the peoples in Turkey who contend with one another in *Faust*,[12] while the possibility that individual cognitions might prove to be relative does not itself prevent us from achieving knowledge. And this indifference of any particular cognition towards the possible blanket clause of relativity as such reduces the thought of this relativity to a conversation topic for candidates for confirmation who do not really know whether they should permit themselves to be confirmed or not. Now the philosophical need has almost imperceptibly changed from a need for reliable and substantive content – which is what it was when the movement we are talking about here actually began – into a need to evade, in thought at least, the reification which has been brought about by society and is emphatically dictated to the members of society. It would evade it by recourse to a metaphysics, or a kind of successor to metaphysics, which denounces such reification, which assigns its limits by appeal to some inalienable origin, and which thereby creates as little difficulty for the prevailing course of the world of things as ontology does for the prevailing course of the scientific and academic world – which last, indeed, instead of being rendered nugatory by ontology, constantly permits itself to be 'stimulated' by it. In the later phase of Heidegger's philosophy, nothing remains of the embarrassing eternal values but the confidence in the sacredness of being as an essence which is elevated beyond all that is thing-like. The reified world, on account of its contemptible inauthenticity in the face of being, is regarded as somehow not worth changing; the depreciation of relativism is ramped up into a depreciation of the progressive rationality of Western thought, of subjective reason as such. The long-standing and still lurking animus against the dissecting intellect is here combined with the hatred, the justified hatred, for what is thing-like and alienated: for a very long time, at least since Rousseau and Herder, and certainly since the German student movement of the early nineteenth century, both attitudes have reinforced each other. Heidegger is hostile to things and anti-functional at the same time. Being must not, at any cost, be a thing, yet, as his metaphors indicate over and over again, it is supposed to be the 'ground', to be something firm – this is precisely how it is formulated in the text *On the Essence of Ground*, which particularly emphasizes this aspect of the concept of being.[13] In reality, subjectivization and reification do not simply diverge from each other but are also correlated. The more that which is known is functionalized, and the more it becomes a product of cognition, all the more completely is the dynamic aspect in what is known turned into an activity of the subject, and all the more completely does the object, the result of the labour congealed in it, become something dead. For the reduction of the object to mere material, a reduction which precedes any subjective synthesis, as a necessary condition of that synthesis, sucks all of the object's own dynamism out of it; deprived of qualities, the object is closed down, robbed of anything of which movement as such might be predicated. Not for nothing does Kant call one class of categories 'dynamic':[14] dynamism is shunted off in advance, therefore, into the transcendental subject. The stuff that remains, however, when bereft of dynamism, is not something utterly immediate but, rather, for all its illusion of solid givenness, something mediated by abstraction; it is something cooked up in advance, as it were. Life is polarized into the wholly abstract and the wholly concrete – I almost wanted to say, the *concretistic* – whereas, really, it would exist only in the tension between the two. Both poles, the pole of pure synthesis, of the pure concept, and the pole of pure quality-less givenness, are equally reified. And even what remains of the spontaneous subject, the unity of apperception, ceases to be a subject when it is detached from any living 'I' to become the anti-psychologistic Kantian 'I think' which accompanies all of my representations. Even this pure apperception, even this innermost centre of subjectivity as pure essence, is, in its self-sufficient purely logical character, affected by the all-prevailing rigidity. But Heidegger's critique of reification, without further ado, blames the reflecting and comprehending intellect, which comes upon such determinations, for something that originates in a reality which reifies the intellect itself along with the experience that belongs to it – a reality in relation to which even the speculations of epistemology actually represent no more than a kind of reflex response. Indeed, in a certain sense, epistemology is the most delicate and most sublime reflex action through which we respond to reality, where we try and abandon thought to reality completely and attempt to reproduce what is actually determined as a reflex as though it existed purely and simply in its own right. Thus that which self-reflection might, perhaps, be able to change, only finds itself pushed back, untruthfully, into being or, more recently, into the 'history of being', and thereby mourned and consecrated as fate. The doctrine of being does indeed continue – and against the prevailing positivism this is entirely legitimate – something grounded in the whole history of philosophy otherwise defamed by the philosophy of being, and especially in Kant and Hegel: the thought that the dualisms of inside and outside, of essence and appearance, of concept and fact, are not absolute. But now the reconciliation of these dualisms is projected back into the irrecoverable origin, and thus dualism itself, against which all this was first conceived, is falsified into a second eternity. The funeral song over the forgetting of being sabotages reconciliation; the history of being, to which hope clings, destroys this hope through its very blindness,[15] through those very features which I have tried to bring out for you as the mythical features of this philosophy.

At the beginning of this lecture, in analysing this talk about the meaning of being, I drew your attention to the fact that the schema (to speak amicably), the trick or the ψεῦδος [pseudos] (to speak less amicably) of this whole philosophical approach consists in a kind of hypostasis, in taking a kind of indistinct equivocation as a starting point. And indeed this goes very well with what I explained earlier when I showed you how this mythological thinking allows itself to invoke the sort of fusion or indistinctness against which the whole history of enlightenment, in the broadest sense, was directed; and how, in a certain sense, it allows itself to invoke something like the primordial shudder of mana.[16] Now it is time, I think, that we should consider how this quid pro quo extends right into the centre of Heidegger's philosophy – that is, into the theory of the '*is*' and, thereby, into the innermost cell of what Heidegger calls 'being'. And I would like now to turn to the considerations – to the decisive arguments, I would say – which are to demonstrate this.

I told you[17] that 'beings' and 'being' refer back to a grammatical unity; that the one is a participle, the other an infinitive of the same lexical stem – and this, indeed, not only in an etymological but also in a semantic sense. In other words, they are syntactic or grammatical forms of exactly the same meaning-bearing word. Now the word 'is', the copula, belongs to a similar context; and I believe that the really central considerations which should be addressed, in a critical sense,

to Heidegger's philosophy must engage with the concept of the copula.[18]
The 'is' allows an existential judgement which connects the grammatical subject with the predicate (you just have to think of ordinary
grammatical sentences here): A is B. This 'is' thereby expresses something ontic, this A = B = 'is' – that is, a state of affairs which applies
to that which is, which through this very 'is' becomes a being that
is. At the same time, however, this 'is', taken purely for itself (that is,
as a copula) signifies the universal categorial state of affairs of this
synthesis and does not, therefore, to this extent, represent something
ontic. Let me try and elucidate this: just put yourself, not in the position of someone who is examining what is accomplished in some
particular proposition 'A is B', but in the position of a linguistician
who has to define what 'is' means – then you will probably reply that
this 'is' represents a synthesis between two given moments which we
usually designate, grammatically, as subject and object; but that this
synthesis as such is nevertheless something accomplished by thinking,
is a joining together of such moments; and that this synthesis, in
contrast to the sense of the 'is' in the proposition itself, cannot really
be considered as anything ontic. You will say, instead, that it is something *ontological* because this 'is', taken in isolation, cannot be relegated to the ontic, because this 'is' has no meaning *in abstracto* as
a being, as a particular being, although this 'is' does also have a
meaning. (For, if it had no meaning, it would then, of course, be
unable to keep serving as the bearer of meaning in every predicative
judgement.) Thus from the logical character of the copula – that is,
from the general function which it serves – Heidegger draws an ontological purity which accords with that allergy towards anything factical
that I have so often described for you. From the existential judgement,
however, he draws that reminiscence of the ontic which then allows
him to hypostasize the categorial performance of synthesis as a given.
Thus he draws from this tangible 'That is that and nothing else',
which is also contained in the 'is', the possibility of interpreting it
ontically and not merely ontologically. Certainly the 'is', as I have
already said, corresponds to a state of affairs: to the simple fact that
in any predicative judgement this 'is' has a meaning, just as do A and
B, subject and predicate. But this meaning – and that is the decisive
point here – is, as Kraus (I mean Oskar Kraus) puts it, not autosemantic, but synsemantic.[19] For it consists merely in the relationship
between subject and object and is not something independent. Yet,
insofar as Heidegger mistakes this meaning for something beyond
this interdependence, in which alone it finds its meaning, the thing-
like thinking of the old pre-critical logic, against which Heidegger
otherwise protests, wins out in his work. If Heidegger fixes the 'is'

as an absolute, ideal state of affairs – and the state of affairs that is supposed to correspond ontologically with this 'is' for Heidegger is precisely what is celebrated as 'being' – then what is intended by subject and predicate in a judgement would, once separated from the copula, also have the same rights. Then the synthesis of subject and predicate through the copula would be a merely external arrangement, would be exactly what the concept of being was thought up for in order to counteract. Then 'being' would actually be just such a bringing together of subject and object through an isolated third term – while being, of course, is precisely what is supposed to outrank, to be prior to and superior to (however you wish to put it) any such arrangement, any such merely externally provided unifying factor. Subject, copula and predicate would then be independent and self-enclosed affairs, just as they are treated in ancient logic. But the copula 'is' in its entirely general meaning – as the constant grammatical form for the synthesis involved in judgement – is by no means identical to the specific meaning which the 'is' acquires concretely in any individual judgement. To this extent, the 'is' is to be compared to what are known as occasional expressions.[20] On the one hand, in general terms, the 'is' has the meaning of a placeholder, of a mere function; but in the specific context in which it stands it is filled with particular content – namely as the mediation of this very thought that A is the same as B. And this divergence in the meaning of 'is' is suppressed by Heidegger. And that is the decisive point at which his concept of being allows him to exploit equivocation and, in a sense, to pocket a profit from this equivocation. The universality of occasional expressions, like the universality of 'is', is something that *points us towards* particularization; it is the universal form for the actualization of particular judgements. Language recognizes this insofar as it keeps the term 'copula' for this universality and keeps the 'is', precisely, for the particular actualization which is required. Heidegger mixes the two up. And we will look into this in the next lecture.

LECTURE 21

9 February 1961

Last time we began to unfold what is really, in my unauthoritative view, the central analysis of Heidegger's concept of being through a critique of the hypostasis of the copula.[1] You will perhaps recall how I said that there is a state of affairs – a categorial state of affairs – which also corresponds to the 'is' in the simple predicative proposition; that in every judgement the 'is' has its meaning, just as subject and predicate do. This 'is' is just as much a bearer of meaning as the A and B in the predicative judgement – otherwise we could simply leave the 'is' out. Its meaning is just that the relation between the concept of the predicate and the concept of the subject is established precisely through this 'is'. But – and this is what you must really hold on to here – this meaning is properly realized only in the relation between the subject and the predicate. It is not independent but is, as we say in the language of formal logic, synsemantic rather than autosemantic. Heidegger mistakes the meaning of the copula for something beyond that by virtue of which alone it comes to have meaning. That is why the reification against which he protests wins out in him, even though he strives against any reification of being. If he now turns this 'is' into an absolutely ideal state of affairs – in other words, if he turns this 'is' into the expression of the state of affairs which stands behind it, namely 'being' – then what is meant by subject and predicate, once separated from the copula, would naturally have the same right. Synthesis by means of the copula would then be a merely external arrangement – which is precisely what the concept of being was really thought up to counteract. Subject, copula and predicate would then be complete and self-contained things, just as they were in the old-fashioned mechanical-formal conception of logic. But – and here we come to the distinction which I think is essential, so I would ask you to follow these rather abstract matters really closely; I cannot avoid this abstractness, which has something false about it, because Heidegger's elucidations themselves, with which we are concerned here, are of exactly the same degree of abstractness, and one must always address and confront a thought that one is criticizing in the form in which it actually presents itself. But, as I was about to say, the copula 'is' – in its general meaning as the constant grammatical form for synthesis in any judgement, in other words, for the interconnection of A and B – is by no means identical with the specific meaning which the 'is' acquires in any given judgement – that is, in the judgement that this particular A is this particular B. And the meaning which the 'is' acquires in a concrete judgement is, indeed, precisely this: that this A is this B; and that is something quite different from the general and syntactical function which merely implies that a synthesis of some kind is in question. To this extent, this 'is' can be compared with those 'occasional expressions' which are only fulfilled in the context in which they appear, and which only really acquire their meaning in that context. Thus we are talking, as it were, of two meanings: on the one hand, the universal syntactical feature, or formal feature, that this copula brings about a synthesis; and then, on the other hand, the specific meaning through which the copula is realized by affirming in a particular proposition that this A is precisely this B. The universality of the copula points in the direction of particularization; it is the universal form for the realization of particular judgements. The language we use recognizes this insofar as it reserves the logical-epistemological term 'copula' for this universality and reserves the concrete expression 'is', as it actually appears in a proposition, for the particular achievement which the judgement is to accomplish. Now Heidegger mixes the two up – and, by saying that he 'mixes them up', I do not of course mean (lest you misunderstand me) to reproach Heidegger with some primitive confusion here. Rather, the point is that he effectively turns this ambiguity – which is involved in the expression 'is' and can be clarified semantically in the way I have suggested – into an absolute, and believes that this very ambiguity, which reveals itself to critical linguistic reflection, harbours something through which language announces something absolute, something true in itself, which lies beyond the reach of such linguistic criticism. Because he mixes these two things up with each other, the particular work or achievement of the 'is' – this concrete 'is' whose content is precisely the relation of A to B – turns into something like a mere mode of appearance of that universal truth. The distinction between the category of the copula and the specific content of the existential judgement disappears. The substitution of the universal grammatical form for the content of the judgement transforms the ontic achievement of the 'is' – where the 'is' says of a particular being A that it falls under a concept B – into an ontological one, into a mode of being of being itself. But if we neglect what is postulated in the sense of the 'is', if we neglect the mediated and mediating achievement involved in any specific context, then no substrate of this 'is', of whatever kind, is left behind. All that is left is the abstract form of mediation as such, and that, as Hegel says about 'pure becoming',[2] is no more capable of constituting a fundamental principle than any other, unless we wish to drive out the Devil with Beelzebub – in other words, drive out Parmenides with Heraclitus.

The word 'being' has a certain overtone which any merely arbitrary definition of it might miss; this overtone lends Heidegger's philosophy its distinctive tone colour. Any given being is more than it merely is, and 'being', in contrast to 'beings', reminds us of this. There is no being which, in being determined in some way or other or in determining itself in some way or other, does not stand in need of some other being which is not itself – since it could never be defined or determined in terms of itself alone. It would be, as Plato already knew, nugatory – and that is why the individual being points beyond itself. What Hegel calls mediation is only another word for this way in which the determinate particular points beyond itself, just in being specific or determined in some way. Heidegger, however, attempts to keep this dimension of pointing beyond itself, while somehow discarding that which points beyond itself as rubbish on the heap of what is eliminated in the process of philosophical production. Entanglement turns, in Heidegger, into its absolute opposite, into a kind of graspable, static, thing-like essence, into the πρώτη οὐσία [prōtē ousia], precisely into a kind of primary being as 'being'. Even mediation is mediated, namely through what is mediated. You can no more hypostatize the category of mediation and turn it into an absolute than you can do the same with the mediating moments, for of course mediation as such possesses meaning only as the mediation of the mediated components. Heidegger's concept of being, however, is really nothing other than the absolutization of mediation, without regard to what it mediates. As a reaction to what Benjamin described in the philosophic-historical context as the loss of aura – you can read about this in his essay on 'The Work of Art in the Age of its Technical Reproducibility' and also in the essay 'On some Motifs in Baudelaire', which have appeared in the first volume of his selected *Writings*[3] – as a reaction

to the historical loss of aura, Heidegger conserves aura, precisely as
that aspect of things which points beyond themselves, that aspect of
things which is more than merely themselves. It is made into a substrate, and thereby is itself made the same as the things. Heidegger
ordains a repristination of the shudder once provoked by the inter-
connectedness of things long before the formation of the mythical,
polytheistic religions of nature: under the German name of *Sein*, or
being, mana is dragged back up again, as if the dawning powerlessness of today were the same as that once felt by primitive pre-animistic
man at the roar of thunder. Just this immemorial thing, however, is
not absolute truth but absolute illusion, a torpid captivation in a
nature whose inscrutability is merely parodied by what would be
more than nature. I merely point out in passing that there is much
in Heidegger's philosophy that suggests a rebirth of pantheism, albeit
an unconscious rebirth which would therefore certainly be denied.
Heidegger's transcendence is an absolutized immanence which is obdu-
rately set against its own immanent character. The illusion involved
here requires explanation: of how that which is derived and mediated
as such, namely 'being', can wrest the insignia of the *ens concretis-
simum* to itself. This illusion is based on the fact that the poles of
traditional epistemology and metaphysics – that is, the pure 'this-here'
and pure thinking – are equally abstract. All determinacy has been
removed from both poles, has been withdrawn, so that nothing more
can be said of the poles as such, if judgement still wants to know
what it is judging about. The two poles – the pure 'this-here', the
τόδε τι [tode ti], on the one side and the pure 'I think', the abstract
function of thinking on the other – have thus become mutually indistinguishable, and this permits the one to be treated, imperceptibly, in
place of the other, according to what the *thema probandum* requires.
That which exists absolutely, beyond any category, which is nothing
but that which merely is, does not need, in its utter lack of qualities,
to be identified with any specific being, and, just because it cannot
be reduced to any being in particular, it can, with an illusion of pro-
priety, be named 'being'. Yet 'being', conversely, as an absolute concept,
does not itself need to be legitimated as a concept. For if any specific
range were assigned to this concept – and every concept is defined
by its specific range – then 'being' would be a limited concept and
would thereby violate its own meaning as the highest concept of all,
namely its completely unrestricted meaning. That is why 'being' can
be invested with the dignity of the immediate just as easily as the τόδε
τι [tode ti] can be invested with that of the essential. The quid pro
quo, the wavering or hovering between two mutually indifferent
extremes, provides the leeway, the space in which Heidegger's entire

philosophy is played out. Yet, against Heidegger's will, it is the domain of beings that wins out in 'being'. For 'being' receives its life from forbidden fruit, from the domain of beings, as if they were indeed the apples of Freia.[4] While 'being', for the sake of its auratic absoluteness, would never wish to be contaminated by anything from the domain of beings, it only acquires that immediacy which furnishes its legal title to absoluteness, because it also just means: beings as such.

The moments which belong together in the logical state of affairs with which we began today – in other words, the moments which belong to the simple predicative judgement, which make the synthesis involved in that judgement possible and which cannot be separated from that judgement – are linguistically expressed by the 'is'. What the 'is' says must always already be contained in the concept of the subject – and here, of course, I mean the grammatical subject rather than the subject in an epistemological sense – if the predicate is to be predicated of the subject. Predication is not externally added here, but, rather, in coupling subject and predicate together, it is what both would already be in their relationship to each other, if this 'would be' could somehow be imagined without the synthesis of the 'is'. This prohibits any extrapolation from the copula to 'being' as something which is allegedly prior, as much as it prohibits any extrapolation to a 'pure becoming' – in other words, to any absolutized synthesis that is somehow hanging in the air. The illusion of the ontological transition which is involved in this hypostasis of being is, however, strengthened by the fact that any analysis of judgements leads to two moments, neither of which can be reduced to the other. Any thought which is enthralled by the chimera of an absolute First, as it is in traditional philosophy, will ultimately tend to take this very irreducibility as what is Last. A reduction to such irreducibility also resonates in Heidegger's concept of being. But it is a formalization which does not chime with what is formalized. Taken on its own, it implies only the negative point that the moments of a judgement, whenever a judgement is made, do not imply that they disappear into each other on one side or the other – in other words, that they are not identical. Apart from this negative point, this relation between the moments of a judgement, irreducibility is a nothing, and there is nothing to be thought here. It cannot therefore be accorded any ontological priority over the moments involved in judgement. The fallacy, the paralogism here, lies in the conversion of this negative point – that neither of these moments can be derived from the other – into something positive and into a state of affairs *sui generis*, into a state of affairs independent of its own moments. Heidegger approaches the verge of dialectical insight into

THE COPULA AND THE QUESTION OF BEING

the non-identity involved in identity but, undaunted, still applies the traditional logic of non-contradiction to the pre-logical or meta-logical realm of his philosophy. The contradiction in the concept of being is not confronted but suppressed. Whatever can be thought under the concept of 'being' mocks the identity of the concept with what it would refer to. Yet Heidegger mistreats this as identity, as 'being' which is purely and simply itself, bereft of its own otherness. The non-identity within absolute identity is hushed up like a family scandal. Since the 'is' is neither a merely subjective function nor any thing-like being, since it has no objectivity in the traditional sense, it becomes, for Heidegger, a third, namely 'being'. But the logical step which leads to this conclusion changes the intention of the expression 'is' or that of the expression 'being'. The recognition that the 'is' is neither merely a thought nor merely a being does not permit us to resettle the 'is' in some third region, transcendent with respect to both of those determinations. Every attempt to think the 'is' at all, even in the palest universality, leads back to beings and to concepts. The constellation of these moments cannot be grasped in terms of some singular essence, because this constellation involves something which is not itself an essence. The unity promised by the word 'being' lasts only as long as it is not truly thought, only as long as its meaning is not subjected to analysis, as Heidegger's own method would require. Any such analysis would reveal precisely what disappears where the ontologists hold forth so readily on the abyss of being. But if the analysis of being is tabooed as a result, if we are not permitted on account of this difficulty to think any further about what 'being' means, then the substantive aporia which is involved here turns into the trick of prohibiting thinking from thinking about the very thing this thinking claims to be thinking about. The absolute is supposed to be thought in terms of 'being', but it is the absolute only because – according to Heidegger's argument – it cannot really be thought at all. Only because the magical lustre of 'being' dazzles recognition of the moments involved does it appear beyond such moments. Because reason is unable to think at its best, reason becomes something bad in its own eyes.

The child – as fundamental ontology might argue on its own behalf, if this were not far too ontic or psychological for it – already asks about being.[5] Reflection drives out such questioning in later life, and reflection on reflection – in other words, philosophy – would like to bring it back, as idealism also always wished. But double reflection of this kind hardly asks in the same way as the child actually does. Philosophy – from the anthropomorphic perspective of the adult, as it were – imagines the child's behaviour as the childhood of the entire species, as something pre-temporal or supra-temporal. What the child

is wrestling with is its relationship with words, which the child makes
its own with an effort which is hardly conceivable in later years,
rather than with the world – with which the child in the early phases
of life is to some extent familiar, as a world of used or handled objects.
The child wants to make sure of the meaning of words, and its preoc-
cupation with this, as well as a carping obduracy on which psychoanalysis might be able to shed some light, brings it to the relationship
between word and thing. A child is capable of pestering its mother
with the irritating question as to why a bench is called a bench. The
child's naivety is non-naive. Culture has, as language, already penetrated
the earliest stirrings of the child's consciousness, which should caution
us here about any talk of primordiality. The meanings of words and
their truth content, their 'position towards objectivity',[6] have not yet
become sharply distinguished from each other. Knowing what the
word 'bench' means and knowing what a bench actually is – including a judgement about its existence – are not strictly differentiated
for this consciousness. After all, in countless cases, the question of
the meaning of a word and the question of what the relevant object
really is can be separated from each other only with a considerable
effort. But, in the domain of 'being' which is in question here, this
distinction is actually central, for the pure meaning of a word, exactly
as with the essences of phenomenology, does not yet imply anything
about actual existence. But the word 'being' already involves some
claim to existence – so that to infer something about the truth content
of an expression simply from the meaning of a word amounts to a
μετάβασις εἰς ἄλλο γένος [metabasis eis allo genos], to an illegitimate
transition from one sphere to an entirely different one. In being orientated through the stock of words the child has learnt, its immediacy
is already mediated in itself, and the persistent search for the why,
for what is primary, is pre-formed. Language is experienced by the
child as φύσει [phusei] rather than as θέσει [thesei], or, as they say in
English, 'language is taken for granted'. At the beginning there is
fetishism, and the hunt for the beginning is always subject to fetishism. It is hardly possible, admittedly, to render that fetishism intelligible, for whatever has been thought at all is already linguistic.
Unreflective nominalism is just as false as the realism which bestows
on fallible language the attributes of the revealed word. It speaks for
Heidegger that there is no In-itself bereft of language, that language
is part of truth rather than truth being part of language, as if it were
something merely designated by language. But that language constitutively shares in truth does not mean that language and truth are
identical. The force of language is demonstrated by the way that
expression and the matter expressed come apart in the context of

reflection – Dr Schweppenhäuser has expounded these things very thoroughly in his dissertation, and here I would refer you to this important text on the critique of Heidegger's philosophy of language.[7] Language becomes an authority over truth only when we realize that expression is not identical with what is meant. Heidegger refuses this reflection, and he comes to a halt after the first step of the dialectic of the philosophy of language. I used the term 'repristination' earlier on in relation to Heidegger. His thinking is also repristination – namely the restoration of something older and past – in that it wishes, through a ritual of naming, to restore the power of the name. But this power is not present in secularized language in such a way that it could simply be purloined by the subject. Through secularization, subjects have deprived language of the name, and the objective claim of language now demands intransigent exertion on the part of the subject rather than some philosophical faith in God. This objective claim becomes what it is only through the persistent confrontation between expression and the matter expressed. The ideal that subjective intention should meet its demise in linguistic truth requires not less subjectivity, but more. Karl Kraus, who was himself inclined to an ontological view of language, was essentially concerned with this. But Heidegger's procedure[8] amounts to hyper-Germanizing cabbalism. He behaves towards historical languages as if they were the languages of 'being', and in this he proves as romantic as violent anti-Romanticism invariably is. His version of 'destruction' falls silent in the face of a culture readily taken at its face value. Such an unreflective, and by no means radical, consciousness finds it has an understanding with, or at least accommodates itself to, what actually surrounds it. Genuine philosophical radicalism, whenever it has appeared historically, is a product of doubt.[9] The radical questioning which destroys nothing but doubt is itself illusory.

The emphatic expression of the word 'being' is shored up by Heidegger's old category of *authenticity*, which I have discussed with you on several occasions already. The term 'authenticity', it is true, hardly crops up in his later work, for subsequently, when he regarded himself exclusively as a philosopher of 'being', he clearly preferred to suppress the historico-philosophical connotations of this expression, with all those aspects of the analysis of *Dasein* in *Being and Time* which seemed to privilege inwardness and reveal a certain hostility to civilization.[10] Nonetheless, the transcendence of 'being' with regard to beings and the domain of conceptuality would gladly redeem the canon of authenticity as something beyond illusion, something which would be neither contingent nor simply instituted by the subject. Heidegger protests, with good reason, against the way the historical

development of philosophy, not excluding Hegel, has tended to efface
the distinction between essence and appearance – in this respect Heidegger captures an inherent impulse of philosophy as θαυμάζειν[11]
[thaumasdein], as wonder or astonishment, as dissatisfaction with the
mere façade of things. Unreflective enlightenment negated the metaphysical thesis that essence was the true world behind appearances,
with the equally abstract counter-thesis that essence, as the epitome
of metaphysics, was merely illusion – or, in Nietzsche's words, was
simply a *Hinterwelt*, a world behind the world,[12] as though appearance itself were thus the essence. Thanks to the bifurcation of the
world, the actual law of this bifurcation is concealed. Indeed, if it
were not concealed, human beings would hardly tolerate the world
as it is. Positivism – which concurs with this by deleting whatever is
not a *datum*, whatever is hidden, as myth and subjective projection
– reinforces what is illusory through this denial of essence just as
much as any of those theories which once offered consolation for
suffering in the *mundus sensibilis* by affirming an essential world
beyond. Something of this mechanism has acquired new life in Heidegger. But what he presents as authentic immediately reverts to positivity, becomes a procedure of consciousness which, being exiled from
profanity, adroitly but nonetheless impotently imitates the theological
bearing of the old doctrine of essence. The hidden essence is shielded
from the suspicion that it might prove essentially monstrous. No one
dares to consider that the categories of massification which are developed in *Being and Time*, no less than in Jaspers's famous volume on
Man in the Modern Age,[13] might themselves already be that hidden
monstrosity which makes human beings into what they are. For then
they would also have to put up with being abused by philosophy
because they have forgotten what is of the essence. The resistance to
reified consciousness, a resistance which stirs in the pathos of authenticity, is thus castrated. The remnant of critique is unleashed upon
appearance – that is, upon the realm of subjects rather than upon
that of essence – the guilt of which is simply reflected and reproduced
in that of the subjects, so that essence, thanks to this exoneration,
now shines spotlessly white. Now, all the same, I must qualify this
somewhat, or at least make it more precise. For there is some glimmer
of this in Heidegger himself when, in his later work, he takes 'inauthenticity' and 'forgetfulness of being' – all the categories which, in
Being and Time and in all his most influential writings, were castigated
as part of a theory of the decay of European civilization – and tries
to push them back onto 'being'. Those categories are thereby removed
from that subjectivism which I was just talking to you about. On the
other hand, insofar as they are now simply transposed into the

absolute, they are also removed from that criticism of their decisive objectivity which is still possible as long as they are understood as merely subjective categories. Quite apart from the fact that ascribing something like the 'forgetfulness of being' to being itself is a sort of demonology, which is really very reminiscent of doctrines like that of Ludwig Klages,[14] Heidegger insists that, objectively speaking – at a particular point in time which he is even prepared to date as the year when Nietzsche succumbed to madness – these categories lost their aura. Here there actually is a connection between the cloudiest and most obscure speculations of Klages, the ultra-Romantic, and the philosophy of Heidegger. Such a connection would certainly prove very embarrassing to the Heideggerean school, but it is very illuminating precisely because it is undeniable. For this forgetfulness of being, as the destiny of being, can only really be imagined as an intrinsic demonization of 'being' itself as something which eludes human beings altogether. And, with that, the regression into pure natural religion, into a religion of demons, appears complete.

But I want to come back to the way we described Heidegger's philosophy before and to its specific relation to θαυμάζειν [thaumasdein]. If the welcome thing about fundamental ontology is the tenacity with which it clings to this θαυμάζειν and claims to experience astonishment over everything and anything (including, admittedly, things which can hardly astonish anyone), it nonetheless prevents itself from answering the question of what truly and genuinely is precisely by the way it frames the question. It is not for nothing that it arms itself here with the distasteful term *Seinsfrage*, or the 'question of being', a term which Heidegger's epigones were not the first or the only ones to use. This expression, *Seinsfrage*, which finds an echo in the alleys, or rather the motorways, of Germany, is as mendacious as it is because it appeals to the most direct personal interest of every individual – the naked interest of Hamlet's soliloquy before the question of whether the individual is completely annihilated by death or may entertain the hope of a Christian *non confundar*.[15] Yet it replaces what Hamlet means by 'to be or not to be' with a pure essence which swallows up existence. Existential ontology deals with 'existence' in the same way as it deals with 'anxiety'. By treating matters thematically in a phenomenological manner, by summoning up a range of distinctions and descriptions, it appeases this direct interest while simultaneously deflecting us from it. 'The question of being', to quote Heidegger word for word,

thus aims not only at an a priori condition of the possibility of the sciences, which investigate beings as this or that kind of being and

which thus always already move within an understanding of being, but
also at the condition of the possibility of the ontologies which precede
the ontic sciences and found them. All ontology, no matter how rich
and tightly knit a system of categories it has at its disposal, remains
fundamentally blind and perverts its innermost intent if it has not
previously clarified the meaning of being sufficiently and grasped this
clarification as its fundamental task.[16]

What this over-strained and elaborate phenomenological approach
manages in such sentences to extract as 'the question of being', the
latter forfeits whatever the word *Seinsfrage* might actually be imagined
to mean, while that imagined meaning is even dismissed as a bustling
lack of vision. The impossibility of answering the question is thus
impressed on us as the higher truth, as the authentic answer to the
evaded question. In order to be authentic enough, the so-called question of being shrinks to the dimensionless point which alone is now
permitted to count as the genuine meaning of 'being'. The question
of being ends up as one with the prohibition on going any further,
ultimately on going beyond that tautology which is manifest in Heidegger's claim that self-unconcealing being never means anything other
than being. Being is just – itself.

LECTURE 22

16 February 1961

Today I should like to conclude my treatment of the relationship[1] between the concepts of being and existence, as well as the analysis of the concept of being which we discussed last time, in accordance with my existing text.[2] Then I would like to use what remains of this lecture and the next – which will unfortunately be the last one – in order to offer you a few thoughts about the concept of *negative dialectic* and about the sort of things which a concept of dialectic might be able to address. The dialectic of being and beings means that being, thanks to its conceptual aspect, cannot be thought without beings, and that beings cannot be thought without mediation through the concept – and all this appears in Heidegger's work under the name of 'being'. But this dialectic becomes essentially undialectical in Heidegger: the moments here, which cannot exist unless each is mediated through the other, constitute an immediate unity for him, and he sees this unity as being in a positive sense. But the sums don't add up. The debt incurred by the categories has to be called in. The beings which have been turfed out with a pitchfork come back all the same, for 'being', once purified of 'beings', remains a primordial phenomenon only insofar as it inwardly preserves those very beings which it initially excluded. The way in which Heidegger manages this is his strategic masterstroke and the matrix of his philosophy itself. With the term 'ontological difference', this philosophy lays hold on the irreducible aspect of being. Yet, at the magic touch of this term, this difference turns into an ontological fact, a hidden and hypostasized expression of the fact that being can no more be thought without beings than beings, according to Heidegger's fundamental insight, can be thought without being. This is how it executes its sleight of hand. For ontology thereby incorporates its own predicament: that it cannot dispense with what stands opposed to it, that it cannot dispense with the ontic. It absorbs the ineliminable scandal of ontology itself, namely the entanglement of the ontological principle with its own counterpart. Heidegger's triumph over the other, strategically far less canny ontologies lies in the ontologization of the ontic. The truth that there is no being without beings is expressed in the form that the being of beings belongs to the essence of being, which turns this truth into an untruth, or, in other words, confers a kind of essential being on beings themselves. Being thus takes possession of precisely what, considered in itself, it would never wish to be: it takes possession of beings, whose conceptual unity is nonetheless what is captured by the meaning of the word 'being'. The whole edifice of ontological difference is only erected so that doubts about 'being' may be all the more elegantly dispelled, thanks to the thesis that beings are a mode of being of being itself.[3] Insofar as every particular being is brought to its concept, the concept of the ontic, everything which makes it a particular being, when confronted with the concept, disappears. The formal, universal and conceptual structure of this talk of the ontic and all its equivalents usurps the place of the content of this concept, a content which is heterogeneous to the conceptual. This is the reward for the fact that the concept of a being – hardly less exceptional in this regard than the concept of 'being' so celebrated by Heidegger – is a concept which includes the non-conceptual as such, which includes that which is not exhausted in the concept, without this concept itself ever expressing its difference from what it includes. Because 'beings' is the general concept for everything that is, beings themselves become a concept for Heidegger, the concept of an ontological structure which seamlessly becomes the ontological structure of being. Now I would not want you to think, ladies and gentlemen, that this is all a case of interpretative ingenuity on the critic's part! For this ontologization of beings is succinctly formulated in *Being and Time* itself where we read (I quote from page 42): 'The "essence" of *Dasein* lies in its existence.' It is necessary for you to understand this correctly: from the fact that something which is there, which exists as such, is defined by the concepts of *Dasein* and 'existence', it is meant to follow that whatever about *Dasein* is precisely *not* essential, *not* ontological, *is* ontological. The ontological difference is eliminated precisely by conceptualizing the non-conceptual as non-conceptuality. This ontologization of the ontic, however, proves useful not only for the ontic but also for the centre-piece of Heidegger's theory, the hypostasized word 'being'.

For ontology can only avoid the burden of the ontic if the ontic is the same as ontology itself. It is this subreption, this act of smuggling, which grounds the priority of ontology over the ontological difference (I quote from the later text *On 'Humanism'*): 'However, here the opposition between *existentia* and *essentia* is not what is at issue, because neither of these metaphysical determinations of being, let alone their relationship, is yet in question.'[4] What is allegedly prior to the ontological difference, that is, prior to the opposition between *existentia* and *essentia*, nonetheless falls in truth, in Heidegger's work, on the side of essence. Since the distinction which is expressed by the concept of a being is denied, the concept is elevated through the non-conceptual which is meant to be below it. This can, perhaps, be grasped even more clearly from another passage of the *Letter on 'Humanism'*. The passage turns the question of existence away from this world and transforms it directly into a question of essence (I quote again): 'The sentence the human being "ek-sists" is not an answer to the question of whether the human being actually is or not; rather, it responds to the question concerning the "essence" of the human being.'[5] The talk of the not-yet, just where the antithesis between existence and essence is dismissed,[6] is, not accidentally, a temporal metaphor for something atemporal. For this really is archaic thinking, more like that of the Ionian hylozoists than that of the Eleatics, where essence and existence are obscurely mingled in the sparse philosophemes which have come down to us. From the Eleatics, who first had to separate thought and being in order then to identify them, through to Aristotle, the task and effort of ancient metaphysics lay in enforcing the separation between being and beings. Demythologization is separation; myth is the deceptive unity which belongs to what has not yet been separated. But since the primordial principles which were invoked to explain the world before us proved insufficient, these principles came to be differentiated and subjected to analysis, so that the magical extra-territoriality of being, wavering as it did between the realm of essence and the realm of fact, now found itself caught in the meshes of the concept. In order to uphold the privilege of 'being', therefore, Heidegger is obliged to turn the tables here and to condemn the critical labour of the concept as a process of degeneration. He annuls this critical labour, as if philosophy could assume a historical standpoint beyond history, although philosophy is also enjoined to obey history, which is then, like existence, itself ontologized. Heidegger is anti-intellectual for systematic reasons and anti-philosophical for philosophical reasons, just as the contemporary renaissances of religion are inspired not by the truth of their doctrines but by the philosophy that it would be good to have religion.

But since the history of thinking, as far as we can trace it back, is a dialectic of enlightenment, Heidegger does not linger, as he might have been tempted to do in his youth, at any one of its stages but, rather, resolutely enough, plunges back with a Wellsian time-machine[7] into the abyss of archaism, where everything can be anything and everything can mean anything. Like the National Socialists, he reaches for myth; like theirs, his myth remains that of the twentieth century – the illusion which history has unmasked it to be, striking only for the utter irreconcilability of myth with the rationalized form of reality in which consciousness is equally entangled. Consciousness presumes to claim the status of mythology, as if this were possible without being the same as myth, without being mythical consciousness itself. Thus Heidegger's concept of being also duly brings in the mythical concept of fate [*Schicksal*]. I quote: 'The advent of beings lies in the destiny [*Geschick*] of being.'[8] The much extolled inseparability of essence and existence in 'being' is thereby named for what it is: the blind context of nature, the fateful interconnection of things, the absolute negation of that transcendence which quivers in the talk of being. The illusory aspect in the concept of being is precisely this transcendence; but it springs from the way that Heidegger's characteristic descriptions, which are abstracted from *Dasein*, and thus from the distress of real human history to this day, have forfeited their memory of this. They become moments of being itself, and thus of something which assumes precedence over existence. Their astral power and glory is cold before the disgrace and fallibility of historical reality, even as this historical reality itself is sanctioned as inalterable. What is mythical here is the celebration of what is meaningless precisely as meaning, the ritual repetition of natural relations in a symbolic particular, as if this elevated them beyond the realm of nature.

The emphasis on being is taken to be characteristic of the later Heidegger, and the mythologization which this has spawned is frowned upon by the more moderately inclined who nonetheless admire *Being and Time* as a great work of philosophy. Now we should defend Heidegger here, for his claim that *Being and Time* was already concerned principally with 'being' rather than with 'existence' is not some retrospective projection on his part but can be verified in the earlier work. Here already, as in Jaspers, the ontic is ontologized. This is what the theory of existence is primarily concerned with.[9] Following Kierkegaard's example, 'existence' is honoured, while at the same time, against Kierkegaard, it is neutralized. Existence, as a mode of being which belongs to being, is no longer antithetically opposed to the concept. It receives the dignity of a Platonic Idea, but also the bullet-proof quality of that which cannot be thought otherwise, since there is no thinking which does not concern existence as it is. Jaspers innocently recounts this neutralization of existence against Kierkegaard: 'I ... sensed in his negative resolutions ... the opposite of everything which I loved and wished for, and which I was and was not ready to do.'[10] Even Jaspers's existentialism, which did not allow itself to be infected, in constructing its own concept of being, by the *pater subtilis*,[11] understood itself from the start as a 'question concerning being' – as you can read for yourself right at the beginning of Jaspers's *Philosophie*, on page 4. Both dignitaries were able, without being dishonest, to cross themselves before what, in Paris, under the sign of 'existence', led all too quickly, for their taste, from the lecture hall to the café.[12]

Despite this, the ontologization of the ontic finds its model in Kierkegaard's theory of existence.[13] While Kierkegaard plays off existence against essence in nominalistic fashion, as a theological weapon against metaphysics, we find that existence, namely the individual, is immediately endowed with meaning in accordance with the dogma that the human person is made in the image of God. Kierkegaard polemicizes against ontology, but an actual existing being, 'the singular individual', absorbs the attributes of ontology into itself. Existence is marked out for special attention in *Being and Time* too, in a way that is reminiscent of the opening reflections of *The Sickness unto Death*.[14] Kierkegaard's idea of the 'transparency' of the subject, of consciousness, provides the warrant for ontologization. Thus Heidegger says: 'We shall call the very being to which *Dasein* can relate in one way or another, and somehow always does relate, existence.'[15] Or, as Heidegger then literally puts it: 'On the basis of its determination as existence *Dasein* is in itself "ontological".'[16] The concept of subjectivity shimmers no less than that of 'being' and, for that reason, can arbitrarily be made to accord with the latter. On the one hand – despite all the efforts made to accomplish this since Fichte – subjectivity cannot be detached entirely from the individual and its consciousness, if what Schelling called 'egoity',[17] without which subjectivity would be inconceivable, is not to dissolve. On the other hand, consciousness as the universality of thought is constitutive for subjectivity. This ambivalence permits *Dasein* to be equated with a mode of being itself and allows the ontological difference to be analysed away. *Dasein* is ontic, thanks to its spatio-temporal individualization; as logos, it is ontological. What is false in Heidegger's inference from *Dasein* to being is that 'at the same time', which is implied by Heidegger's talk of the 'manifold priority' that '*Dasein*' enjoys 'over all other beings'. The fact that consciousness is what makes the subject a subject does not mean that everything in the subject to which consciousness clings is also nothing but consciousness, is completely transparent, is 'onto-logical'. The individual endowed with consciousness, whose conscious-ness would not exist without this individual, remains something spatio-temporal, something factical – remains a being rather than 'being'. That this actual being is capable of thinking does not suffice to strip it of its character of being a being, as if it immediately belonged to the realm of essence. It is precisely not 'in itself ontological', since this selfhood postulates just that ontic character which the doctrine of ontological priority expels from itself.

The concept of 'the existentiell', which Heidegger prefers to sub-ordinate to the already ontologized 'existential' of *Dasein* qua 'being', suggests the idea that the measure of truth is not its objectivity, however constituted, but existence, the way the thinker purely and simply is, purely and simply acts.[18] Jaspers, in this regard, unhesitatingly follows Kierkegaard; Heidegger's objectivism, however, would hardly allow him to subscribe to the proposition that subjectivity is truth. This proposition, nevertheless, still resonates throughout the analysis of the existentials in *Being and Time*. The popularity of this proposition in Germany was enhanced by the fact that its radical gesture and devout tone sit well with an ideology of the earthy and authentic to which anti-Semitic instincts readily respond. It is the ideology of the hard-working settled resident, who feels cheated of the fruits of his labour by the suspiciously mobile. It would be far better if the long-established natives could see through this ideology as the context of guilt in which both parties, the mobile and the settled, are equally entangled. If subjectivity dissolves the solid substantial realities that confront it, by virtue of the essentially functional character which Kant ascribes to it, the ontological affirmation of subjectivity represses the anxiety in the face of these realities and does so, to use the relevant term 'psychoanalysis', which Jaspers hated, by identifying with the enemy, by going over to the other side. Subjectivity, the principle of mobility itself, becomes something absolutely solid, as is already implicit in Kant's theory of transcendental unity, which is ultimately nothing but what we might call the objectified lawfulness of the pure concep-tual determinations of logic. But truth, the constellation of subject and object where both interpenetrate each other, can no more be reduced to subjectivity than, conversely, it can be reduced to 'being', whose boundary with subjectivity Heidegger endeavours to blur. What is true in the subject is unfolded in its relationship to what it is not itself, not through the production of a blank identity with itself. Hegel knew this, and said so repeatedly, as did Goethe; but the schools of repristination find this uncomfortable. If truth were really subjectivity, if thought were nothing but a repetition of the subject, thought would be nugatory. The existential elevation of the subject eliminates, for the sake of the subject, everything which might concern the subject. It thus delivers itself over to that relativism which it imagines far beneath it and debases the subject into the opaque contingency of its just being as it is. I would substantiate this with a quotation from Jaspers, from his book *Philosophie*:

> The philosopher, however, risks talk where there is no separation between genuine speech with a philosophical source and empty intellectuality. Whilst a human being, as a researcher, always possesses relevant universal criteria for his results, and is satisfied with their unassailable validity, as a philosopher all he can appeal to, in order to distinguish empty talk from the speech which awakens existence, is the always subjective criterion of his own being. Thus the ethos of theoretical conduct is at root quite different in the sciences and in philosophy.[19]

Existence, which thereby declares itself to be the criterion of thinking, is already the lie of a self-appointed elite. Lacking anything beyond itself, anything to which it might open itself, it confers validity on its own decrees in an authoritarian way, just as, in political practice, the dictator confers validity on his own world-view. Through this reduction of thought to the thinker, the flow of thinking, through which alone it can become thinking at all, and in which alone subjectivity can live, is arrested. Subjectivity, precisely as the heavily trodden ground of truth, is objectified. All this can already be overheard in the word 'personality'. Thinking thereby becomes whatever the thinker already is, a tautology, a form of regressive consciousness. The utopian potential of thinking, however, would be for thought, mediated through that universal reason which is embodied in individual subjects, to break through the limitations of thinking individuals. The strength of thinking would be to surpass the work of weak and fallible thinkers. Thinking has been paralysed by the existential concept of truth, ever since Kierkegaard developed this idea for obscurantist ends, and has served to propagate narrow-mindedness as if it were the strength for truth; this is why the cult of existence, in all countries, flourishes so well in the provinces.

Ontology has long since toned down the opposition to idealism present in the concept of existence.[20] The realm of actual 'beings', once invoked to counter the consecration of a humanly constructed ideal realm, has now been invested with the far more ambitious consecration of 'being' itself. The ether of being serves to ennoble beings in advance, over against the conditions of material existence – although that is what the Kierkegaard of *The Moment*[21] had in mind when he confronted the idea with existence. Once the concept of existence has

been absorbed into 'being', and once it has been worked up philosophically as a universal concept for general discussion, we find that
history has been chased away again, whereas, in Kierkegaard, who
thought a lot about the left Hegelians, history had erupted into to
the field of speculation, under the theological sign of the paradoxical
contact of time and eternity. The ambivalence of the doctrine of being
is the way that it addresses beings while simultaneously ontologizing
them – in other words, the way that it robs them of what is non-
conceptual by recourse to their *characteristica formalis* – and this
also determines its relationship to history. On the one hand, the thorn
of the historical is removed by transposing it into historicity as an
'existential', and the claim of all *prima philosophia* to furnish a theory
of invariance is now extended to that which varies: historicity freezes
history into something unhistorical, with no concern for the historical
conditions to which the inner composition and the constellation of
subject and object are exposed.[22] Then the verdict on sociology is
spun out of this too. Sociology is distorted, as psychology was by
Husserl, as a merely relative reflection external to the real issue, and
is claimed to damage the solid work of thinking, as though real history
were not accumulated in the core of everything which can be known;
as though it were not the case that all cognition which resists reification in earnest brings the petrified things into flux and thereby becomes
aware of the history inside them. On the other hand, in turn, the
ontologization of history allows the power of being to be awarded
to unexamined historical power, and thus justifies our subordination
to peremptory historical situations, as though such subordination
were demanded by being itself.[23] That history can always be deified
or conjured away, as required, is a useful political consequence of the
philosophy of being: its apolitical aspect is itself, like so much that
is apolitical today, a political factor. Time itself and, with it, transience,
when made eternal by these existential-ontological projects, are just
as much absolutized as they are transfigured. They have come to an
understanding with death and thereby, inexorably, with all that is
bad. The concept of existence, as the essential character of transience
itself, as the temporality of the temporal, holds existence at a distance
by naming it. As soon as it is treated in terms of a phenomenological
problem, it has already been integrated. These are the latest consolations of philosophy, of mythically euphemistic stamp, the falsely revived
belief that the spell of the natural could be broken by appeasing it
through imitation. Existential thinking creeps away into the cave of
long-lost mimesis. In this, however, it obeys the most fateful prejudice
from the history of philosophy (which it has dismantled or dismissed,
like an employee surplus to requirements), namely the Platonic

prejudice that the unchanging must be the good, which is as much as to say that whoever happens to be stronger is, in a permanent war, always in the right. If Plato's pedagogy cultivated the martial virtues, these virtues, according to the *Gorgias*, still had to answer to the idea of justice, the highest idea.[24] Existential theory, however, adapts itself to a state of consciousness whose darkened heavens no longer reveal any criterion for the idea. Existence is consecrated without anything that would consecrate it; it is secularized, but what is the secularized is not recognized for what it is. Nothing remains of the eternal idea in which existence was supposed to participate, or by which it was supposed to be conditioned, but the pure principle of power, which was once attributed to the unity of the idea against the dispersal of the many.

Ladies and gentlemen, I announced this lecture under the title 'Ontology and Dialectics'; I believe you will concede that this announcement should not really have led you to expect that I would discuss ontology in the first part and then, as a counter-pole, dialectic in the second; I believe that I have done what I promised you – that is, to practise immanent critique. In other words, I have treated the ontological problematic in itself in such a way that the motifs of dialectical thinking have emerged from this very problematic and from the questions that arise with regard to its own truth. I have, then, tried to extract the dialectic which is implicit in ontological philosophy, if I may put it that way. I should like to spend the time remaining to us today, and in the final lecture, which will take place on Thursday, in sharing at least a few thoughts with you concerning the *concept of dialectic* which I have in mind. And I would like you to allow me, so that we can get a little bit further in developing this concept of dialectic, to begin with this right away. The critique of ontology, as I have set it out to you, does not aim to arrive at a different ontology, not even at an ontology of the non-ontological: it does not aim to arrive at any fixed foundational position.[25] For, if it did, it would posit something else as the immediately First; not absolute identity, being, the concept, but the non-identical, beings, facticity. But then it would just hypostasize the concept of the non-conceptual and would treat it in a way that contradicts its own meaning. Foundational philosophy, πρώτη φιλοσοφία [prōtē philosophia], necessarily involves the primacy of the concept; an approach which resists this primacy of the concept must also relinquish the form of philosophizing which appeals to foundations. Philosophy could come to rest in the thought of transcendental apperception, or the thought of 'being', because these concepts were identical to the thinking which thinks them. But if the general thesis of this identity is revoked, then its collapse takes the repose of the concept as a last principle with it. Philosophy must expose itself without reservation to the movement which is motivated by the concept of the concept itself. If the universal concept of some being or entity wished, in the end, to argue that being or entity away, then its own fundamental character would dissolve in the face of a particular being or entity. Philosophy has the latter, along with all its mediations, for its object, however little philosophy may hope to attain totality in this regard.

The concept of objectivity recalls an object, something ontic which cannot simply be resolved into its concept.[26] If thought ever collides with its other – as ontology imagines it does with 'being' – then it is just this unruly element which thought would like to dispel. This element does not fit with the domination of the concept or, thereby, with the idea of something immutable and self-identical that could be derived simply from the character of the concept itself, which had to be constant with respect to its contents. Thus history, not historicity, becomes the medium of philosophy. The transition of philosophy into history, the movement of something individualized in spatio-temporal terms, cannot be prevented by invoking the supposedly authentic essence of philosophy. Apologetics of this kind only betrays the increasingly bad conscience of philosophy. Whenever philosophy has been in command of itself, it has got involved with the realm of beings, not only in Schelling and Hegel but even, against his will, in Plato, who christened beings as the domain of 'non-being' but nonetheless presented a theory of the state in which the Ideas become entangled with empirical determinations such as exchange value and the division of labour. The distinction, academically established today, between, on one hand, a regular philosophy, which is concerned with being, or with something like an ontology of cognition, after the individual sciences have torn from it what once alone furnished its *raison d'être* – namely the interpretation and establishment of what is genuinely real – and, on the other hand, a merely genetic and extra-philosophical relation to society, which would fall to the sociology of knowledge and the critique of ideology, is as dubious as the need for 'regular' philosophy itself. It is not just that philosophy, worrying belatedly about its purity, now turns away from everything in which it once found its substance. But philosophical analysis too, in the interior of its allegedly pure concepts, without μετάβασις [metabasis] to the origin and function of these concepts, collides with that ontic element before which the claim to purity shudders and which it cedes, through the division of labour, to the individual sciences. The smallest stain of the ontic in these concepts, rubbed at in vain by pure philosophy, suffices, thanks to its connection with the existing world, to compel thought to reflect upon that which exists itself instead of settling down cosily into the mere concept of the latter. What even Hegel's dialectic still maligns as 'lazy existence'[27] would be the starting point of a truer dialectic; it could find its theme, first of all, in those individualized qualities which traditional philosophy excludes as contingent dross. Once the superstitious belief in a last or ultimate thing, whatever it is called, and which comes down every time to the identity thesis, and thus to the superiority of the subject, once this belief is broken, the contrary approach will no longer be able to parade its concepts as the ultimate truth. The contents of philosophical thought are neither remnants left over once divested of space and time, nor general discoveries about the spatio-temporal as such, but constellations of the particulars determined in time and space. The concept of beings or entities as such is only the shadow of the false conception of being, and is not superior to the latter.

Dialectic could unfold by following closely the alteration of every category, including those of subject and object.[28] The abstract polarity between subject and object is to be given content by confronting them with the play of forces latent in the concept, the interplay of concepts and things: by means of critique. That subject and object are not last or ultimate things, that they are not rigidly antithetical entities, did not escape fundamental ontology. Hegel had essentially criticized the dichotomous thinking which he saw at work in the so-called philosophy of reflection, but fundamental ontology dams up this critique, in an anti-critical way, by appealing to another 'First' – which has allegedly been forgotten or deformed by dichotomous thinking – instead of driving this dichotomy even further and differentiating it, so that the mediating moments in both poles, and the relationship between mediation and what is mediated, could then emerge. Once fundamental ontology has recognized the untruth in subject–object metaphysics, it allows itself to be led astray by the same directive tendency in thinking which brought about the rigid antithesis between subject and object in the first place. For this reason it merely blurs the divergence between what the philosophy of reflection deemed to be last or ultimate entities. The abstract opposition between subject and object as an irreducible one is then itself located in the realm of ontological illusion. But the unity of subject and object does not license us to raise the question about what would precede this unity. We see instead how the dichotomous structure disintegrates into concrete determinations which demonstrate the presence, in each of the poles, of the opposed moment. Thus the dualism here is not the proper framework for philosophical thought but – please understand this correctly – false. Mediation is only the most general and still very approximate expression for it. The very meaning of the subject conceived of as intrinsically mediated drives it to consider those moments which ontology deems to be merely derivative, namely the history of the species which determines its essence. When the claim to the priority of the subject falls away, so too does the disparagement of what is allegedly secondary, which was the strategic goal of traditional philosophy. At the same time, the thought that the subject is constitutively mediated by the objective resists the vulgar idea that everything is seen simply through the spectacles of the beholder, coloured simply by his or her group or kind, while the subjective mediation of the objective implies a critique of metaphysics as a view of a pure reality in itself.

LECTURE 23

23 February 1961

Ladies and gentlemen, I welcome you to what, with reference to the democratic legislature, is usually called a rump parliament; and I will try to bring to a conclusion those hints towards the concept of a negative dialectic which it is possible for me to provide in the last two lectures. I told you, in the first place, that the thought of the mediated character of the subject prevents us, as always, from falling into the vulgar subjectivism which would have us believe that everything depends, as people like to say, on the standpoint of the beholder; but that, at the same time, the subjective mediatedness of the objective implies a critique of the type of metaphysics which acts as though metaphysics were a view upon a pure 'in-itself'. Using a dramaturgical analogy, I have called this type of metaphysics 'peephole metaphysics'. One looks out of the window and sees outside the stars in the black sky – a rather primitive and impossible conception, the critique of which, however, I must leave aside for today.[1] In any case, the situation presented here, with both of those moments which I have described for you, gives rise at least to the appearance of paradox.[2] Subjectivity is not to be explained simply from itself, but from factical society, which as an interconnected context, as a totality, is itself admittedly much more than a tangible factical given. But the objectivity of knowledge, in turn, is not to be explained simply from this dependence and is, above all, not relativized by this dependence. This paradox originates in the Cartesian norm, long established as supposedly self-evident, that explanation must ground what is later, or at least what is logically posterior, in that which is earlier and prior. The dialectical state of affairs which the subject–object relation has revealed itself to be in accordance with our earlier reflections does not answer to this norm – simply because, by virtue of the reciprocal relationship between subject and object, the distinction between a ὕστερον [husteron] and a πρότερον [proteron] in the usual sense does not apply here. In terms of that distinction, the relationship, as I have explained it, would involve a simple logical contradiction. Dialectical thought by contrast – as a philosophical approach, now, and not as an objective state of affairs – is the attempt, by means of cunning, the oldest medium of enlightenment, to unravel the knot of the paradox here, the inner bond between the mythical context of nature and the freedom which is wrested from that context. It is no accident that paradox is always the decayed form of dialectic, and this is especially the case in Kierkegaard's work. Here you will therefore be able to grasp at its root what many of you, I am sure, will experience as the most disconcerting aspect of dialectic – namely that the principle of contradiction, in its usual form, does not apply. This springs from the fact that dialectical reason longs to transcend the blind immediate context of nature without imposing in turn its own domination, the domination of reason, on this context; in other words, it attempts to transcend nature without incurring that sacrifice and rage which would merely perpetuate the same context of nature. Dialectic does not try to establish some middle ground between relativism and absolutism. It seeks the objectivity of the concept nowhere else than through the nominalism which the situation of the epoch now dictates. Dialectic strives to think conceptually the qualitative element which eludes the concept; it attempts to break through to the particular precisely as the universal, by persisting with the particular rather than subsuming it beneath the universal. The essence of dialectic is also something which has come to be, something mutable, like antagonistic society itself. It may not be falsified into some dialectic of being in itself. The extrapolation from a suffering which could be brought to an end, from an avoidable suffering which is not rooted in being itself, to a fundamental principle, would, as an abstract negation of the positive thesis of the meaning of existence, be equivalent to such a thesis. Such an extrapolation would be similar to a mythology of natural demons, would be secretly affirmative, since, as in Schopenhauer, that suffering which could be brought to an end would be confirmed as incurable, or, as in Hegel, the epitome of transience would be celebrated in its totality as its own opposite, as a kind of reconciliation. Admittedly, antagonism is no more limited to society than suffering is. If it is true that dialectic should not to be extended to nature, in the manner of a *prima philosophia*, it would nonetheless be equally wrong to set up two kinds of truth against each other – a dialectical one, concerned with what goes on inside society, and another kind, outside of that. The absolute division between social and extra-social being is too innocent: it fails to reveal that blind nature continues to thrive in heteronomous history. Nothing leads beyond the dialectical context of immanence but this context itself. Dialectic thinks critically about that context and registers its own movement; otherwise Kant's rightful claim against Hegel would never expire. I describe this dialectic as 'negative'. The idea of such a dialectic marks its difference from Hegel. Even if Hegel saw determinate negation as the *movens* of the speculative concept, the τέλος [telos] here, the totality of all reciprocally mediated individual determinations, remained a positive one as the absolute. Identity and positivity were the same; the inclusion of everything non-identical and objective in a subjectivity expanded and elevated to the level of spirit was presented as achieved reconciliation. In contrast to this, negative dialectic thinks the power of the whole which is at work in every individual determination not merely as a negation of that individual determination but also as itself the negative – in other words, as the untrue, as that which thwarts reconciliation. The surplus, in the material parts of Hegel's later philosophy, of what is external to the subject, of heteronomous institutional power, a surplus which qualified him for the role of state ideologist in the period before the revolution of 1848, is not some mere accident or distortion of the philosophy of the absolute subject. For the principles of identity and constitutive subjectivity themselves remain particular. The total deduction of everything that exists from spirit brings all these things under the yoke of the merely existent; otherwise the two sides would never cohere. It is precisely the radical principle of identity which eternalizes the antagonism, by dint of reason's suppression, in its domination of nature, of what is antagonistic. Whatever cannot tolerate anything that is not identical with itself makes itself the adversary of that very reconciliation for which it mistakes itself. The coercive act of levelling reproduces the contradiction it would eradicate.

This is why the attempt to develop a negative dialectic is not a nuance of neo-Hegelianism or the historically superseded left-Hegelian approach, which is an accusation sometimes raised in this connection.[3] The fear of being derivative, of musty academicism, which clings to every reprise of motifs that have already been codified in the history of philosophy, has long tempted precisely the most academic tendencies into advertising themselves as something which has never been seen before, as something absolutely new. This is just what reinforces the fatal continuity of that which has always been before, of what is allegedly 'First'. However questionable the procedure which declaims all the more loudly about primordial experiences, the more promptly its categories are socially fabricated for it, thoughts are nevertheless not to be subsumed under their genealogy; this habit, too, is a part of the philosophy of origins. If we defend ourselves against forgetting, we are talking about historical forgetting, not, like Heidegger, about pre-historical forgetting – that is, against the sacrifice, enjoined almost everywhere, of that freedom of consciousness which had earlier been achieved – we are not advocating any intellectual-historical restoration. Hegel's trust in totality sought dialectic not merely, in accordance with his programme, in the process of 'simply looking on'[4] but also, with secret inconsequence, in a relatively self-sufficient method. First of all, dialectical method is a *contradictio in adjecto*. The reward for this is that, in the end, dialectical method cannot even posit its own concept. Along with the Cartesian–Kantian separation of form and content, Hegel wanted to do away with the conception of a portable method independent of the matter itself, a conception which corresponded to a separable form; and yet he also inevitably proceeded in a methodical fashion. The critical reconstruction of consequent thought, which would deprive negative dialectic of its potential, remains consequential itself as long as it clings to method. Without this moment of unity, dialectic would disintegrate into paradoxical insights; dialectic is always inclined to this. A liberated consciousness in its freedom would be free even of dialectic. The subjective moment in the way dialectic executes thinking represents something of this. Negative dialectic is neither a strict method nor a supposed mirroring of reality[5] – as Marx, weary of an arid debate, once tried to dispatch the issue. It is not a method, because the unreconciled reality, which, precisely, lacks that identity for which thought offers a surrogate, is full of contradictions, which is revealed by the fact that every attempt to improve circumstances in a piecemeal way proves futile. It is not a mirroring, because thought is not a reproduction of the thing – as it was taken to be by the Epicurean metaphysics which claimed that matter was capable of sending out little pictures of itself[6] – but is concerned with the thing itself, without recourse to images at all. The enlightening intention of thought, the process of demythologization, eliminates precisely the image-character of consciousness. All that cleaves to images remains caught up in myth, remains idolatry, and the totality of images becomes a barrier before reality; dialectic, however, means thinking in contradictions for the sake of the contradiction encountered in experience.

Critique of identity, actually pursued rather than noisily declaimed, feels its way towards the preponderance of the object.[7] Identity thinking, even when it contests this, remains subjective. To turn it around critically, to ascribe untruth to identity, does not establish any equilibrium between subject and object: the restricted subject is, rather, in a certain sense, already disempowered through this very restriction. With good reason it instantly senses an absolute threat in the smallest surplus of the non-identical, for the measure is just its own absoluteness. It will come to grief, as a whole, even on something minimal, since its meaning is to be the whole. The determination of the non-identical permits reflection on the subject as mediation. But the identity principle cannot, in principle, tolerate the non-identical, for the non-identical is something which contradicts the identity principle itself. This is confirmed by the fact that the context in which subjectivity finds its variable place involves more than any context which could be developed out of subjectivity itself. The subject enters into the object in quite a different way from that in which the object enters into the subject. The object can only be thought through the subject but always remains, with respect to the subject, something other; the subject, however, by virtue of its own character, is already also object, although no *aqua regia* of epistemology has ever been able to distil this objective element. The object cannot, even as an idea, be thought away or eliminated from the subject. Actual existence is implied in the very meaning even of the logical 'I think which accompanies all my representations',[8] since it has temporal sequence as a condition of its possibility, and temporal sequence must imply something temporal. The expression *Dasein*, or actual existence, alludes to this. That the subject exists, is derived from objectivity, and lends to the subject itself an element of objectivity; it is not accidental that the term *subjectum*, namely 'that which underlies', reminds us of just that which, in philosophy's terms of art, is now precisely called objective. Subjectivity, however, does not, in the same or in any comparable way, form part of the meaning of objectivity but, on the contrary, is only disclosed through reflection on the possibility of determining the object. It is not that objectivity is something immediate; not that, for example, the critique of naive realism could be revoked. But mediating subject and mediated object are not the same;[9] even in the sphere of the highest abstractions, the concept of mediation would be too abstract. The fact that subject and object reciprocally mediate each other, that they are not ultimate entities in their own right, that we cannot infer some absolute unity behind subject and object – in short, the need to think about non-identity is the need to provide a critique of subject–object dualism. If philosophy simply persisted with this dualism, it would be false; not only as another variant of first philosophy, but because abstract dualism itself, as with Fichte's dualism of the I and not-I, would imply the primacy of the abstracting subject.

To pursue this line of thought further would also mean resolving this irresolvable dualism. The pre-eminence of the object does not signify its priority; rather, it signifies the progressive qualitative differentiation of mediation in itself. Kant still allowed the moment of the pre-eminence of objectivity not to be completely silenced. He guided the subjective analysis of the cognitive faculty by the objective intention of the critique of reason[10] but also stubbornly defended the transcendent thing in itself; the fully developed philosophy of identity chalked this up against him as inconsequence and as a contradiction of the theory of the categories. What Kant had in mind was that the concept of an object as such did not contradict the idea of its existence in itself; that the subjective mediation of the object was to be attributed less to the idea of the object than to the subject which remains caught up or, I could even say, imprisoned within itself. While the subject in Kant does not manage to escape from itself, it does not, despite that, sacrifice the idea of otherness. Without this idea, cognition would shrink to a mere tautology. Completely indeterminate thinking would have to create something out of an equally indeterminate material. This absurdity clearly troubled Kant's meditations more than the theorem that the thing in itself was the unknown cause of appearances, even though the critical approach specifically ascribes the category of causation to the subject. That consciousness does not 'have' the object, as people like to say, but is always implicit in the object does not mean that the subject could in some way be imagined without an object. The subject in both its poles is impossible without an existing being, without that which bears consciousness, or that which is implied even in the most formal conception of 'something'. All exertions of the speculative concept, and not only Kant's, really desire the object, and the construction of transcendental subjectivity is only the magnificently paradoxical and unsuccessful attempt to achieve control of the object. To this extent, negative dialectic would like to complete what the positive, idealist dialectic already aimed at. In this sense negative dialectic also has an ontological moment, since ontology too deprives the subject of its conclusively constitutive role. But negative dialectic does not, like Nicolai Hartmann, replace the subject with the object as its static counterpart. The pre-eminence of the object can only be attained by means of subjectivity – that is, by exploring the divergence between the concept and the thing intended by the concept. One may get a little closer to the issue here – one which can be expressed in current logic only with difficulty, and which, in its abstract form, may strike you as inconsistent – by saying that, while it would be quite possible to write a prehistory of the subject, such as Horkheimer and I attempted to outline in the *Dialectic of*

Enlightenment, there is no prehistory of the object, since that would already be dealing with objects from the start. If it were objected that there cannot be any cognition of an object without a cognizing subject, this would still not permit us to infer the ontological priority of consciousness. That consciousness is able to reflect upon itself as something which has originated, and that its origin can only be thought by the subject, in no way implies that it is itself the absolute origin. Analogous considerations on the genesis of the object would be nugatory. The mediation of objects can be thought in real terms apart from thinking itself; but the possibility of thinking cannot be thought without something objective. That is the qualitative difference between the proposition that everything objective is mediated through the concept and the proposition that there is no subject without an object. Mediation of the object implies that it may not be statically and dogmatically hypostasized but can be grasped only in its entwinement with subjectivity; mediation of the subject implies that, without the moment of objectivity, it is simply nothing. If we identify mediation, identification as such, with domination, this double character testifies to that of domination itself, as both true and illusory. Domination is true since nothing is exempt from domination, since nature itself is negatively determined through its exemption from domination, and thus is still determined in turn by domination. What is illusory, however, is identification and, thereby, domination, since from the beginning domination also has something arbitrary and unnecessary about it which gets passed on to all the necessities which flow from domination. An index of the pre-eminence of the object is the impotence of spirit, in all of its judgements and its attempts to arrange reality. The negative experience that spirit, through its quest for identification, has failed to achieve reconciliation, that its own pre-eminence has therefore miscarried or gone awry, becomes the motor of its own disenchantment in the disenchanted world. Enlightenment thereby transcends its own traditional self-understanding: enlightenment is demythologization not only as *reductio ad hominem* but also as insight into the deception perpetrated by a subjectivity which deems itself absolute. The subject is the belated, and most ancient, shape of myth, which fails to recognize itself as such.

Finally, however, it is precisely those determinations through which the concept of subjectivity, following the tradition of philosophy, distinguishes itself from things and beings that are modelled on those things and beings.[11] Not only is the pure I mediated by the empirical one, not only is the object of possible thought mediated by something which does not belong to the subject, but the transcendental principle itself, in which philosophy believes that it possesses its 'First' with respect to things and beings, is mediated too. The transcendental principle, the universal and necessary activity of spirit, has social labour concealed within it.[12] The aporetic concept of the transcendental subject – of a μὴ ὄν [mē on], a non-being, which is nevertheless supposed to do things, of a universal which is nevertheless supposed to experience something particular – would be chimerical if it were not constructed on the model of something essentially other than the purely immanent context of consciousness. With respect to the former, the concept of the transcendental subject presents itself not only as something more abstract but also, by virtue of the way in which it transcends the latter and by virtue of its formative power, as something more real. Beyond the magic circle of the philosophy of identity, the transcendental subject would be revealed as society, unconscious of itself. This unconsciousness can itself be deduced. Once intellectual labour separated itself from bodily labour, and this separation fused with the dominating power of spirit, with the justification of the primacy of the socially privileged, spirit, already sundered, has to justify that claim to mastery which spirit makes for itself as the alleged origin or first principle and has to forget where the claim comes from if it is not to collapse. In its innermost being, spirit has an intimation that the mastery which it asserts and establishes is not the mastery of spirit at all but possesses its *ultima ratio* in the physical power of which it disposes. It may not, on pain of its own demise, express this thought; negative dialectic reminds it of this. The abstraction, which, even according to the testimony of extreme idealists such as Fichte, first turns the subject into a constitutive power as such, is itself one with this separation from bodily labour, as becomes evident once it is compared with the latter. When Marx, in the *Critique of the Gotha Programme*, argued, against the Lassalleans, that labour was not, as the vulgar socialists constantly proclaimed, the only source of wealth,[13] he expressed nothing less – in a period when he had already turned away from official philosophical questions – than that work is not to be hypostasized in any form, neither in that of industrious manual production nor in that of so-called spiritual production, and that such a hypostasis only perpetuates the illusion of the preponderance of the productive principle. This spiritual principle finds its truth only in relationship to that non-identical for which Marx, who held epistemology in contempt, chose the name 'Nature'. That which, since the *Critique of Pure Reason*, has constituted the essence of the transcendental subject, the functionality, the pure activity which is realized in the specific acts of individual subjects and simultaneously transcends these subjects, is not only analogous to the objective theory of value but, when seen from the outside, coincides with this theory of value, here projected onto the pure subject as an ontological ground. If Kant also limited the functionality of the subject by stipulating that the latter would be nugatory and empty without some material provided for it, he thereby unerringly confirmed the character of social labour, namely that it is work on something, a point which the greater consistency of the succeeding idealists unhesitatingly eliminated. The universality of the transcendental subject is that of the functional context of society as a whole, which connects individual spontaneities and qualities but simultaneously curtails them through the homogenizing principle of exchange, thereby virtually disqualifying these spontaneities and qualities as impotent in themselves and entirely dependent upon the whole. The universal domination of exchange value over human beings, which, a priori, prevents subjects from being subjects, degrades subjectivity itself to a mere object and convicts the universal principle which claims to establish the predominant status of the subject of its untruth.

Yet here, at the most extreme point of ideology, the transcendental subject comes right up against truth.[14] For transcendental universality is no mere fiction of the subject's, no mere hypostasis of imaginary autonomy, but has, in turn, its own *fundamentum in re*. It is as real as the domination which is accomplished through the principle of equivalence. The procedure of abstraction which is absolutized in philosophy is really played out in exchange society. The definition of the transcendental in terms of necessity, which consorts so readily with functionality and universality, betrays the principle of the self-preservation of the species, what Spinoza calls *sese conservare*.[15] This principle provides the justification for the constitutive abstraction without which it cannot work; that abstraction is the element in which self-preserving reason moves. To parody Heidegger, it would hardly strain ingenuity to suggest that the necessity, *die Notwendigkeit*, involved in the philosophical concept of the universal could be interpreted as the imperative to avert need or distress, *die Not*, to supply the lack of goods by means of organized labour. This would, of course, turn Heidegger's mythology of language on its head, since in that mythology, which deifies objective spirit, any reflection on the material process which penetrates objective spirit is defamed in advance as merely ontic. How far that necessity was ideological, from the beginning, is a matter for debate. The unity of consciousness, in the end, bears the particularly visible trace of individual human experience and, thereby, the trace of things and beings. The unity of consciousness remains, as Husserl puts it, a piece of the world,[16] without any priority over external reality. Insofar as the unity of consciousness is constructed upon the model of objectivity, however – in other

words, insofar as it takes its measure from the possibility of constituting objects – it is the conceptual echo of the total and seamless nexus
of those acts of production in society through which the objectivity
of what is produced – in truth, its object-like character or *Gegenstän-
dlichkeit* – is formed in the first place.

Ladies and gentlemen, I am coming to the end of our lectures. In
the eyes of traditional philosophy, whether idealist or ontological, I
realize that something of the μετάβασις εἰς ἄλλο γένος [metabasis eis
allo genos][17] inevitably clings to the kind of speculations I have presented to you. Thus it might be objected, with apparent rigour, that
they presuppose the very process of mediation which they then attempt
to derive as something mediated: namely the subject, the activity of
thought; it might be objected that all the determinations involved
here, insofar as they are determinations at all, are precisely determinations of thought. But negative dialectic contradicts any positive and
unconditionally total dialectic precisely because it doesn't lend itself
to the postulate of some ultimate and immediate principle. It has no
desire to foist upon the object the royal throne now vacated by the
subject, a throne on which the object would be nothing but an idol.
On the contrary, what it wishes to do is to displace hierarchy. It is
quite true that the illusion of the preponderance of the transcendental
subject cannot be broken immanently, by analysing subjectivity purely
in its own terms. For this illusion also contains the truth – even if
this cannot surgically be detached from the mediations of thinking
– that society precedes the individual consciousness and everything
which that consciousness experiences. The insight that thinking is
mediated by objectivity negates neither thinking nor the norms which
make thinking thinking. That we cannot reach beyond these norms
points to our reliance on that which is not itself thinking, that which
thinking would deny and try and establish on its own account. The
reason for the real transcendental illusion, an illusion which goes far
beyond Kant, is, however, transparent, the reason why thinking, in
its *intentio obliqua*, always ends up, ineluctably, in asserting its own
primacy, in hypostasizing the subject. For abstraction, which in the
history of nominalism, ever since Aristotle's critique of Plato, has
been charged to the subject as a mistaken form of objectification, is
itself the principle through which the subject becomes a subject at
all, is the very essence of the subject. Hence any recourse to what is
not itself must always strike the subject as a wilful and extraneous
act. Whatever shows the subject its own arbitrariness, whatever reveals
the priority of the subject to be its own aposteriority, always sounds
to the subject as if it were simply its arbitrary transcendent antithesis.
As ideology, the subject is spellbound by the name of subjectivity, just

as Hauff's dwarf Nase is under the spell of the herb *Nießmitlust*, or 'enjoy-with-pleasure'.[18] This herb was withheld from the dwarf, and he never learnt how to prepare the most delicious pie of all. Self-reflection alone could not reveal the secret either of his own deformed shape or that of his work. For this required a shock or push from outside, the wisdom of the goose Mimi. Such a 'shock', or *Anstoß*, is anathema to philosophy, especially to the highest kind of philosophy, that of Hegel. Immanent critique finds its limit in the fact that, in the end, the law of the context of immanence is one with the delusion that is to be broken through. But this moment, which alone is the truly 'qualitative leap', begins only once the immanent dialectic is completed. The urge to cancel itself is immanent to negative dialectic; if it were totally closed in upon itself, it would already be that totality which goes back to the principle of identity. This interest was grasped by Schelling, against Hegel, and he thereby exposed his thinking to scorn for its inconsistency, for seeking refuge in mysticism. The materialist moment in Schelling, who attributed to matter something like a motive power, may be connected to this aspect of his philosophy.[19] But the leap is also not to be hypostasized, as it is in Kierkegaard. Otherwise it maligns reason. Dialectic must limit itself from within, through its own consciousness of what is. But the disappointment that philosophy cannot awake from its dream simply through its own movement, without any leap at all, the disappointment that, in order to waken, philosophy needs just what its own spell withholds: something new and other – this disappointment is none other than that of the child who cries on reading Hauff's fairy tale because the dwarf, who has escaped his own misshapenness, never gets to enjoy the triumph of serving the duke the most delicious pie of all.

EDITOR'S NOTES

Abbreviations

Adorno's writings are cited from the German editions, *Gesammelte Schriften* (ed. Rolf Tiedemann in collaboration with Gretel Adorno, Susan Buck-Morss and Klaus Schultz, Frankfurt am Main: Suhrkamp, 1970–) and *Nachgelassene Schriften* (ed. Theodor W. Adorno Archiv, Frankfurt am Main, Suhrkamp, 1993–); where available, English translations have also been used, and the corresponding references and publication details are provided in the editor's notes to the lectures. The following abbreviations are employed:

GS 1	*Philosophische Frühschriften*, 3rd edn, 1996
GS 3	Max Horkheimer and Theodor W. Adorno, *Dialektik der Aufklärung: Philosophische Fragmente*, 3rd edn, 1996
GS 4	*Minima Moralia: Reflexionen aus dem beschädigten Leben*, 2nd edn, 1996
GS 5	*Metakritik der Erkenntnistheorie / Drei Studien zu Hegel*, 4th edn, 1996
GS 6	*Negative Dialektik / Jargon der Eigentlichkeit*, 5th edn, 1996
GS 8	*Soziologische Schriften I*, 4th edn, 1996
GS 9.1	*Soziologische Schriften II*, Erste Hälfte, 3rd edn, 1997
GS 10.1	*Kulturkritik und Gesellschaft I: Prismen / Ohne Leitbild*, 2nd edn, 1996
GS 10.2	*Kulturkritik und Gesellschaft II: Eingriffe / Stichworte*, 2nd edn, 1996
GS 11	*Noten zur Literatur*, 4th edn, 1996

GS 14	*Dissonanzen / Einleitung in die Musiksoziologie*, 4th edn, 1996
GS 18	*Musikalische Schriften V*, 1984
GS 20.1	*Vermischte Schriften I*, 1986
GS 20.2	*Vermischte Schriften II*, 1986
NaS I.3	*Currents of Music: Elements of a Radio Theory*, ed. Robert Hullot-Kentor, 2006
NaS IV.3	*Ästhetik* (1958/9), ed. Eberhard Ortland, 2009
NaS IV.12	*Philosophische Elemente einer Theorie der Gesellschaft* (1964), ed. Tobias ten Brink and Marc Phillip Nogueira, 2008
NaS IV.14	*Metaphysik: Begriff und Probleme* (1965), ed. Rolf Tiedemann, 1998
NaS IV. 15	*Einleitung in die Soziologie* (1968), ed. Christoph Gödde, 1993

Lecture 1

1 The transcription of the tape recording of the first lecture expressly indicates that Adorno's opening remarks are missing, and the transcription proper actually begins a few sentences in with the words 'on the one hand'. The preceding section of text has been reconstructed by the editor on the basis of Adorno's own notes and jottings for the lecture, which read as follows: 'Start with the Webern anecdote. It is precisely this "we have Strindberg" that must be avoided. This temptation arises from the need for some initial orientation on the part of those who are not students of philosophy. The task is to move beyond a philosophy of standpoints' (Theodor W. Adorno Archiv, Vo 6258). The Webern anecdote had already been used by Adorno in his monograph on Mahler (GS 13, p. 217; *Mahler*, trans. E. Jephcott, University of Chicago Press, 1992, p. 69).

2 Arthur Moeller van den Bruck (1876–1925), writer and spokesman for neo-conservative causes. His principal work, entitled *Das Dritte Reich* [The Third Reich], was published in 1922 and supplied the Nazis with one of their slogans, although the work itself was 'less a menacing piece of propaganda than a tedious melancholic lament quite remote from all politics' (Carl von Ossietzky). Moeller van den Bruck also edited the first German translation of Dostoyevsky's collected works (*Sämtliche Werke*, trans. E. K. Rahsin, 22 vols, Munich, 1906–19). His own writings on Dostoyevsky were published posthumously by Hans Schwarz in a volume entitled *Rechenschaft über Russland* (Berlin, 1933).

3 To describe something as a 'philosophy of standpoints' was one of Adorno's most damning verdicts. Thus he writes: 'The task of philosophy is not to adopt a standpoint but to destroy them', or again: 'A moment of exclusion inevitably belongs to any philosophy of standpoints' (GS 20.1, p. 325). But Adorno seems to be mistaken in ascribing a comparable attitude to Hegel (GS 5, p. 251; *Hegel: Three Studies*, trans. Shierry Weber Nicholsen, MIT Press, 1993, p. 2 – 'Standpunktphilosophie' is translated in that context as a 'philosophy of perspectives'). Hegel does

not himself use the expression, and he does not appear to show anything
but a neutral or even positive attitude to the idea of 'standpoints'.

4 Gerhard Maletzke (born 1922, from 1952 active with the Hans Bredow
Institute for Radio and Television at the University of Hamburg, and
subsequently with the German Institute for the Politics of Development
in Berlin and the Asian Mass Communication Research and Information
Centre in Singapore; from 1983 honorary professor in Hohenheim.
Adorno corresponded with him in the early 1950s; Maletzke served on
the editorial board of the journal *Rundfunk und Fernsehen* [Radio and
Television], which published two essays by Adorno in 1953.

5 Aristotle defines a *petitio principii* as a logical error which attempts 'to
establish what is prior by means of what is posterior' (*Prior Analytics*,
Bk II, ch. 16, 64b28f; *The Complete Works of Aristotle*, ed. Jonathan
Barnes, Princeton University Press, 1984, vol. I, p. 103).

6 'Immanent critique' is a central concept of Adorno's philosophy and, in
a specific sense, constitutes its methodological centre. Adorno explains
what he understands by immanent critique a little further on in the
lectures:

> Critique is actually nothing but a process of distinguishing, namely a
> process of confronting different aspects or moments in order to see whether
> the conceptual moment is genuinely fulfilled in its respective objects, whether
> it is an empty or a legitimate conceptuality, namely one to which something
> corresponds; and, on the other hand, a confrontation of the realm of
> beings, of what is there, with the concept. In other words, we must ask,
> like Hegel, how far something that exists corresponds or answers to its
> concept, namely whether that which merely exists actually is what it
> purports to be. (Lecture 8, above p. 78).

Adorno's concept of immanent critique is indebted to the definition
developed by Walter Benjamin in his dissertation *On the Concept of
Criticism in German Romanticism*, where he argues that the way in
which Friedrich Schlegel and Novalis use the concept of *Kritik* 'does
not mean a judgement of the [art] work ... Criticism of a work is, rather,
its reflection, which can only, as is self-evident, unfold the germ of the
reflection that is immanent to the work' (Walter Benjamin, *Gesammelte
Schriften*, ed. Rolf Tiedemann and Hermann Schweppenhäuser, Vol. I.1,
Frankfurt am Main, 1990, p. 78; *The Concept of Criticism in German
Romanticism*, in *Selected Writings*, ed. Marcus Bullock and Michael W.
Jennings, Harvard University Press, 1996, vol. I, p. 159). Thus Adorno
argues very much in the spirit of Benjamin when he writes in the *Philosophy of Modern Music*:

> The process is immanent: the internal consistency of the phenomenon – in
> the sense that this is to be developed within the phenomenon itself –
> becomes proof of its truth and the ferment of its untruth. The guiding
> category of contradiction itself is twofold in nature: that the works for-
> mulate the contradiction and, in turn, through such formulation reveal it

in the markings of its imperfections; this category is the measure of its success, while at the same time the force of contradiction mocks the formulation and destroys the works. (GS 12, p. 34; *The Philosophy of Modern Music*, trans. Anne G. Mitchell and Wesley V. Blomster, Seabury Press, 1973, p. 27)

Hegel's concept of determinate negation also provides a model for Adorno in this regard: 'it confronts spirit with its realization and presupposes the distinction between the true and the untrue in our judgements as well as the claim to truth implicit in what is criticized' (*Beitrag zur Ideologienlehre*, GS 8, p. 466). It is in this sense that Adorno brings immanent critique to bear on the philosophy of logical positivism in particular:

> Cognitive criticism, of knowledge and especially of theorems, necessarily also examines whether the objects of knowledge are what they claim to be according to their own concept. Otherwise it would be formalistic. Immanent criticism is never solely purely logical but always concrete as well – the confrontation of concept and reality. It is for criticism to seek out the truth which the concepts, judgments and theorems themselves desire to name and it does not exhaust itself in the hermetic consistency of the forms of thought. (Ibid., pp. 304ff.; *The Positivist Dispute in German Sociology*, trans. Glyn Adey and David Frisby, London, 1969, p. 23)

7 The transcription reads 'dialectical need', which seems to be a mistake even if it is what Adorno actually said.
8 Nicolai Hartmann (1882–1950) had undertaken to develop a 'new ontology' in a thorough and systematic fashion ever since the publication in 1921 of his book *Grundzüge einer Metaphysik der Erkenntnis* [Fundamental Elements of a Metaphysics of Knowledge]. This ontological approach appeared to reverse Kant's Copernican Turn and thus return to a kind of naive realism, a position which could even appeal in certain ways to the later Lukács. Hartmann unfolded his ontology in a succession of works: *Zur Grundlegung der Ontologie* [On the Foundations of Ontology] (Berlin, 1935); *Möglichkeit und Wirklichkeit* [Possibility and Actuality] (Berlin, 1938); *Der Aufbau der realen Welt* [The Construction of the Real World] (Berlin, 1940); and *Neue Wege der Ontologie* [New Paths in Ontology] (2nd edn, Stuttgart, 1947). Compare Adorno's discussion in Lecture 4 below, pp. 34f.
9 Hegel is referring to Friedrich Heinrich Jacobi (1743–1819), German pietist philosopher and defender of "immediate knowledge". In this regard, compare the third remark in the first chapter of the 'Logic of Being' in Hegel's *Science of Logic*:

> With this wholly abstract purity of continuity, that is, indeterminateness and vacuity of conception, it is indifferent whether this abstraction is called space, pure intuiting, or pure thinking; it is altogether the same as

what the Indian calls Brahma, when for years on end, physically motion-
less and equally unmoved in sensation, conception, fantasy, desire and so
on, looking only at the tip of his nose, he says inwardly only *Om, Om,
Om*, or else nothing at all. This dull, empty consciousness, understood
as consciousness, is – *being*. (G. W. F. Hegel, *Werke in zwanzig Bänden*,
Vol. 5: *Wissenschaft der Logik I*, p. 101; *Science of Logic*, trans. A. V.
Miller, Allen & Unwin, 1969, p. 97)

> See also NaS IV.14, p. 148; *Kant's Critique of Pure Reason*, trans.
> Rodney Livingstone, Polity, 2001, pp. 97f.

10 It is not clear what text Adorno means to refer to here. The term *Gerüst*
('framework') does not figure significantly in Heidegger's later writings,
although it sometimes appears in *Being and Time*. Thus Heidegger writes
that 'meaning must be conceived as the formal, existential framework
of the disclosedness belonging to understanding' (*Sein und Zeit*, 7th
edn, Tübingen, 1953, p. 151; *Being and Time*, trans. Joan Stambaugh,
rev. Dennis J. Schmidt, State University of New York Press, 2010, p.
147). However, the meaning of the term in this passage hardly corresponds to Adorno's point here. It may be that Adorno is thinking of
Heidegger's later 'use of the word "enframing" [*Gestell*] as the name
for the essence of modern technology' (see Heidegger, *Vorträge und
Aufsätze*, Pfullingen, 1954, p. 28; *The Question concerning Technology*, trans. William Lovitt, Harper & Row, 1977, pp. 19ff.). But he is
certainly not alluding to the later Heidegger's use of the word *Geviert*, or
'fourfold', for a realm that lies beyond the sway of technological thinking (see Heidegger, ibid., pp. 176ff.; 'The Thing', in *Poetry, Language,
Thought*, trans. Albert Hofstadter, Harper & Row, 1975, pp. 173ff.).

11 See Lecture 2 above, p. 12.

12 Adorno is probably thinking of the following remarks: 'One thrives on
the erroneous opinion that ontology as the question concerning the
being of beings means a "realistic" (naive or critical) "attitude" as
opposed to an "idealistic" one' (Heidegger, *Vom Wesen des Grundes*,
4th edn, Frankfurt am Main, 1955, p. 15 n.; *On the Essence of Ground*,
trans. William McNeill, in *Pathmarks*, ed. McNeill, Cambridge University
Press, 1998 (pp. 97–135, n. 17, p. 368).

13 An allusion to the fact that *Befindlichkeit* (rendered as 'state of mind'
in the Robinson and Macquarrie translation and as 'attunement' in
the Stambaugh translation) is an important category in *Being and
Time*. The concept of 'situation' also plays an important role in the
thought of Jaspers and Hartmann, and particularly in Sartre and French
existentialism.

14 See Lecture 10 below, pp. 96ff.

15 This particular formulation does not occur in Heidegger. It appears that
he only ever refers to 'the meaning of being', as Adorno himself implies
in the discussion in *Negative Dialectics*. Adorno is surely thinking of
Heidegger's 'preliminary characterization of the thematic object' of *Being
and Time* as 'the being of beings, or the meaning of being in general'
(*Sein und Zeit*, [n. 10], p. 27; *Being and Time*, Stambaugh, p. 26).

16 On the phenomenological concept of *Abschattung* ('shading' or 'adumbration'), see NaS IV.13, p. 442, n. 280; *History and Freedom*, trans. Rodney Livingstone, Polity, 2006, n. 2, p. 317.

17 On the phenomenological intuition of 'red', see also *Metakritik der Erkenntnistheorie*, specifically the sections on 'The Origin of Essential Intuition' and 'Ideational Abstraction' (GS 5, pp. 102f.; *Against Epistemology: A Metacritique*, trans. Willis Domingo, Blackwell, 1982, pp. 95–101).

Lecture 2

1 [Translator's note:] When Adorno speaks of one of the 'most famous passages' in Aristotle, he may have been thinking of *Metaphysics* 1003 a 20ff.: 'There is a science which studies being qua being [*to on hēi on*], and the properties inherent to it in virtue of its own nature. This science is not the same as any of the so-called particular sciences, for none of the others contemplates being generally qua being.' Or it is possible he may have been thinking of the famous passage at *Metaphysics* 1028 b 2-4: 'Indeed, the question which was raised long ago, is still, and always will be, and which always baffles us – "What is being?" [*ti to on*].' The discussion later in the lecture suggests he may also have had in mind Aristotle's particular use of the expression *to ti ēn einai*. See Günter Ralfs, 'Was bedeutet die Aristotelische Formel τὸ τί ἦν εἶναι?', in Ralfs, *Lebensformen des Geistes: Vorträge und Abhandlungen*, ed. Hermann Glockner, Cologne, 1964, p. 30:

> Aristotle makes considerable use of the remarkable formula τὸ τί ἦν εἶναι. The expression is encountered not only in the books of the *Metaphysics*, which are specifically concerned with fundamental philosophical principles and with the concept of substance, but also in the *Organon*, in the *Nicomachean Ethics* and in all of the writings on natural science .... The formula is obviously one of his most fundamental concepts, although no completely convincing or generally accepted interpretation of its conceptual content has ever been provided.

Aristotle's expression *to ti ēn einai* is often rendered as 'essence' or 'the what is to be' of a thing (or rendered more literally: 'the what it was to be of a thing', since the *ēn* here is the imperfect tense of the verb 'to be'). See the discussion in W. C. K. Guthrie, *A History of Greek Philosophy*, Vol. VI: *Aristotle: An Encounter*, Cambridge University Press, 1981, p. 147, and J. Owens, *The Doctrine of Being in the Aristotelian 'Metaphysics'*, 2nd edn, Toronto, 1963, pp. 93–6.

2 The concept in question does not seem to be used in or before *Being and Time*, although it appears in many of Heidegger's later writings from *On the Essence of Ground* (1929) onwards. See the dissertation by Kurt Jürgen Huch, a student of Karl-Heinz Haag, which discusses the prehistory of this Heideggerean category in German Idealism. (Kurt

Jörgen Huch, *Philosophiegeschichtliche Voraussetzungen der Heidegger-schen Ontologie*, Frankfurt am Main, 1967, pp. 21ff.)

3   Husserl distinguishes between formal and material ontology and in effect is already concerned with questions of ontology in the *Prolegomena* of 1900, the first volume of his *Logical Investigations*. But he does not explicitly deploy the concept of ontology until his *Ideas* of 1914: 'At the time I did not venture to take over the expression "ontology" which was objectionable on historical grounds; rather I designated this investigation ... as part of an "apriori theory of objects" ... Now that times have changed, however, I consider it more correct to rehabilitate the old expression, "ontology".' (Edmund Husserl, *Gesammelte Schriften*, ed. Elisabeth Ströker, Hamburg, 1992, Vol. 5: *Ideen zu einer reinen und Phänomenologie und phänomenologischen Philosophie*, p. 28; *Ideas Pertaining to a Pure Phenomenology and Phenomenological Philosophy*, trans. F. Kersten, Nijhoff, 1982, p. 22, fn).

4   Martin Heidegger, *Sein und Zeit*, 6th edn, Tübingen, 1949, p. 11; *Being and Time*, Stambaugh, p. 10. The passage in question is also found on p. 11 in the 7th German edition, which is otherwise used throughout the notes to these lectures. The pagination of the latter 'corresponds with very slight variations to that of the earlier editions of the work'.

5   Ibid.

6   Ibid.

7   Ibid.

8   Ibid. The whole passage is emphasized in Heidegger's text.

9   *Petitio principii* – the Latin phrase literally means 'the demand for demonstration'. In traditional logic, it signifies the logical error of 'begging the question'. See Aristotle, *Prior Analytics*, Bk II, ch. 16, 64b 28ff.; *Complete Works of Aristotle*, Barnes, Vol. 1, p. 103 : 'To beg and assume the point at issue is a species of failure to demonstrate the problem proposed; but this happens in many ways. A man may not deduce at all, or he may argue from premises which are more unknown or equally unknown, or he may establish what is prior by means of what is posterior; for demonstration proceeds from what is more convincing and prior.'

10 See Heidegger, *Sein und Zeit*, p. 153; *Being and Time*, Stambaugh, p. 148:

> Rather, the fulfilment of the fundamental conditions of possible interpretation lies in not failing to recognize beforehand the essential conditions of the task. What is decisive is not to get out of the circle, but to get into it in the right way. This circle of understanding is not a circle in which any random kind of knowledge operates, but it is rather the expression of the existential *fore-structure* of Dasein itself. The circle must not be degraded to a *vitiosum*, not even to a tolerated one. A positive possibility of the most primordial knowledge is hidden in it.

11 Compare the quotation from Nietzsche's *Twilight of the Idols* in the Introduction to the *Metakritik der Erkenntnistheorie* in the section entitled

'Persistence as Truth' (GS 5, pp. 25f.; *Against Epistemology*, Domingo, p. 18).

12   Wolfgang von Goethe, *Faust Part One* (lines 534–41): 'What you don't feel, you will not grasp by art, / Unless it wells out of your soul / And with sheer pleasure takes control, / Compelling every listener's heart. / But sit – and sit, and patch, and knead / Cook a ragout, reheat your hashes, / Blow at the sparks and try to breed / A fire out of piles of ashes' (Goethe, *Sämtliche Werke*, ed. Friedmar Apel et al., I. Abt., Vol. 7/1: *Faust: Texte*, ed. Albrecht Schöne, Frankfurt am Main, 1994, pp. 38f.; *Goethe's Faust*, trans. Walter Kaufmann, New York, 1963, pp. 105f.)

13   Translator's note: In the passage which immediately follows there appears to be some confusion in the transcript regarding various Greek expressions used by Aristotle, and specifically between the expression *to on hēi on* ('being qua being') and the formulas *to ti ēn einai* (the essence: the what it is/was to be of something) or *ti to on?* (what is being?). The text has been reconstructed to indicate what Adorno is trying to bring out here. In the formula *to ti ēn einai* the word *ēn* is actually the imperfect tense of the verb *einai* (to be).

14   See the second stanza of Goethe's poem *Vermächtnis* [*Testament*] of 1829: 'The true is found and known forever / And joins all noble minds together, / The ancient truth perceive and hold! / To the sage give thanks now, earthling, / Who ordered round the sun earth's circling / And orbits to the planets told' (Goethe, *Sämtliche Werke*, I. Abt., Vol. 2: *Gedichte 1800–1832*, ed. Karl Eibl, Frankfurt am Main, 1998, p. 685; *Selected Poems*, trans. John Whaley, London, 1998, p. 151).

Lecture 3

1   See Lecture 2, note 10, above.

2   See also NaS IV.4, pp. 20f., and passim; *Kant's Critique of Pure Reason*, Livingstone, pp. 8ff.

3   On Adorno's interpretation of the pre-Socratics, see T. W. Adorno, 'Das Problem des Idealismus: Stichworte zur Vorlesung vom Wintersemester 1953/4', and 'Fragmente einer Nachschrift', in *Frankfurter Adorno Blätter* V, 1998, pp. 105ff.

4   Martin Heidegger, *Was ist Metaphysik?*, 6th edn, Frankfurt am Main, 1951, p. 16; *What is Metaphysics?*, trans. Walter Kaufmann, in *Pathmarks*, McNeill, p. 285. The passage cited by Adorno is found in the 'Introduction' which Heidegger added to the 6th edition.

5   See the famous words of Parmenides: τὸ γὰρ αὐτὸ νοεῖν ἐστίν τε καὶ εἶναι [to gar auto noein esti te kai einai] ('for the same thing can be thought as can be' – see G. S. Kirk and J. E. Raven, *The Presocratic Philosophers*, Cambridge University Press, 1971, p. 269). The phrase has sometimes been translated simply as 'being and thought are one and the same'. See also NaS IV.14, pp. 143f.; *Kant's Critique of Pure Reason*, Livingstone, pp. 93f.

6   Adorno's reference to 'one of his last letters' appears to be mistaken. He was probably thinking of the lines from Goethe's poem *Vermächtnis*, cited in Lecture 2, note 14, above.

7   In this connection Adorno may have been alluding to certain scientists who had expressed sympathy for aspects of Heidegger's thought and had contributed to the Heidegger *Festschrift* of 1959, such as the physicists Werner Heisenberg (1901–1976) and Carl Friedrich von Weizsäcker (1912–2007).

8   See M. Heidegger, *Platons Lehre von der Wahrheit: Mit einem Brief über den 'Humanismus'*, 2nd edn, Bern 1954, p. 119; 'Plato's Concept of Truth' and 'Letter on "Humanism"' are translated in *Pathmarks*, McNeill, pp. 155–82 and 239–76 respectively; see p. 276 for the remarks cited by Adorno.

9   Adorno is probably referring to Walter Bröcker, *Dialektik, Positivismus, Mythologie*, Frankfurt am Main, 1958.

10   Conjectural reading instead of 'thesis' (Vo 5721).

Lecture 4

1   Franz Brentano, *Vom Ursprung der sittlicher Erkenntnis*, Leipzig, 1889.

2   Oskar Kraus (1872–1942), executor of Brentano's literary remains, published the second edition of Brentano's book and provided his own Introduction and accompanying notes (Leipzig, 1921). Kraus specifically discussed the relationship between Husserl and Brentano in his Introduction to the first volume of Brentano's *Psychologie vom empirischen Standpunkt* (Leipzig 1924), especially pp. LXIIIff.; the introduction was also published independently under the title *Franz Brentanos Stellung zur Phänomenologie und Gegenstandstheorie: Zugleich eine Einleitung in die Neuausgabe der Psychologie* (Leipzig, 1924).

3   It was not possible to discover textual evidence for Adorno's claim here.

4   *Critique of Pure Reason*, B 134; see also NaS IV.4, p. 368, n. 18; *Kant's Critique of Pure Reason*, Livingstone, p. 242 (n. 6).

5   Heidegger himself understood his own philosophy as a 'hermeneutics of facticity' and in this sense also drew, however ambiguously, on the thought of Wilhelm Dilthey and Count Paul Yorck von Wartenburg (*Sein und Zeit*, pp. 397ff.; *Being and Time*, Stambaugh, pp. 377ff.). It may be, however, that Adorno is specifically thinking of Hans-Georg Gadamer, who explicitly claimed that his own thought was attempting 'to pursue the intentions of Heidegger's later philosophy' (see H.-G. Gadamer, *Gesammelte Werke*, Tübingen, 1999, Vol. III: *Neuere Philosophie* I, p. 220).

6   On this question, see Adorno's lectures on Kant's first *Critique*: Kant 'is not content simply to liberate these basic concepts from their linguistic forms. Incidentally, as you may be aware, in Aristotle there is often no clear distinction between the intuitive forms and the conceptual ones:

they are all mixed up together in his table of categories like apples and oranges' (NaS IV.4, pp. 36f.; *Kant's Critique of Pure Reason*, Livingstone, p. 20).

7 For Adorno's critique of the concept of 'being' as a hypostatization of the copula, see GS 6, pp. 107ff.; *Negative Dialectics*, trans. E. B. Ashton, London, 1973, pp. 100ff. See also Karl Heinz Haag, *Kritik der neueren Ontologie*, Stuttgart, 1960, pp. 69f.

8 See Lecture 3, p. 28.

9 Adorno referred explicitly to Wittgenstein's philosophy of language in the 'Introduction' to *The Positivist Dispute in German Sociology*:

> The inescapability of paradox, which Wittgenstein frankly expressed, testifies to the fact that generally the lack of contradiction cannot, for consistent thought, have the last word, not even when consistent thought sanctions its norm. Wittgenstein's superiority over the logical positivists of the Vienna Circle is revealed in a striking manner here: the logician perceives the limit of logic. Within its framework, the relationship between language and world, as Wittgenstein presented it, could not be treated unambiguously. For him language forms a closed immanent context through which the non-verbal moments of knowledge, for instance sense data, are mediated. But it is no less the intention of language to refer to what is non-verbal. (*The Positivist Dispute in German Sociology*, Adey and Frisby, p. 20 [translation modified])

10 On the positivist concept of 'protocol sentences', see Adorno GS 8, *Soziologische Schriften I*, pp. 285 and 309.

11 See Nietzsche's essay of 1873, 'On Truth and Lies in a Nonmoral Sense', where he argues that language does not arise from logical considerations and that the language with which the scientists and philosophers work in their pursuit of truth does not reflect the essence of things:

> Let us still give special consideration to the formation of concepts. Every word immediately becomes a concept, inasmuch as it is not intended to serve as a reminder of the unique and wholly individualized original experience to which it owes its birth, but must at the same time fit innumerable, more or less similar cases – which means, strictly speaking, never equal – in other words a lot of unequal cases. Every concept originates through our equating what is unequal. No leaf ever wholly equals another, and the concept 'leaf' is formed through an arbitrary abstraction from these individual differences, through forgetting the distinctions; and now it gives rise to the idea that in nature there might be something besides the leaves which would be 'leaf' – some kind of original form after which all leaves have been woven, marked, copied, coloured, curled, and painted, but by unskilled hands, so that no copy turned out to be a correct, reliable, and faithful image of the original form. (Friedrich Nietzsche, *Sämtliche Werke*, ed. Giorgio Colli and Mazzino Montinari, Vol. 1, Munich, 1988, pp. 879f.; *The Portable Nietzsche*, ed. and trans. Walter Kaufmann, New York, 1968, p. 46)

12 Reading *Bedeuten* here for *Bedeutenden* (Vo 5732).
13 Adorno and Horkheimer first started deploying the concept of 'mimesis'
    in *Dialectic of Enlightenment* (see, for example, GS 3, pp. 27, 30, 42,
    passim; *Dialectic of Enlightenment. Philosophical Fragments*, trans.
    Edmund Jephcott, Stanford University Press, 2002, especially 'The Concept
    of Enlightenment', pp. 1–34). For a detailed analysis of Adorno's concept
    of mimesis, see Joseph Früchtl, *Mimesis: Konstellation eines Zentralbe-
    griffs bei Adorno*, Würzburg, 1986. 'Mimesis' and 'the mimetic' represent
    categories of Adorno's thought which become more and more important
    after *Dialectic of Enlightenment* was completed in 1944. It is not clear
    whether Adorno and Horkheimer were already influenced in this regard
    by Walter Benjamin's essay 'On the Mimetic Faculty', which was written
    in 1933 but only published in 1953. They could have known the text
    of this essay from 1941 onwards (see W. Benjamin, *Selected Writings*,
    Jennings, vol. 2, pp. 720–2). They were certainly familiar with *Le Mythe
    et l'homme* (Paris, 1938), by Roger Caillois, in which he talks about 'le
    mimétisme' (see GS 3, p. 260; *Dialectic of Enlightenment*, p. 189). While
    the philosophical tradition from Plato onwards has been accustomed
    to interpreting art as the *mimesis* or 'imitation' of nature, the authors
    of *Dialectic of Enlightenment* also distance themselves from this tradi-
    tion, even if it is true that the later Adorno takes over the concept in
    the context of his aesthetic theory. He here interprets mimesis principally
    in terms of the 'participation' in nature – indeed the concept becomes
    almost synonymous with this idea. The word mimesis is intended to
    evoke and recall aspects of the experience of prehistoric humanity, as
    this has been emphatically described by ethnology and interpreted as a
    magical stage in the development of the species in which the affinities
    between things were not yet subjected to the instrumental domination
    of nature but were experienced in terms of 'resemblance' and the 'name'
    (GS 3, p. 27; *Dialectic of Enlightenment*, p. 7). Adorno regarded the
    'organic adaptation to otherness' as 'mimetic behaviour proper' (GS 3,
    p. 205; *Dialectic of Enlightenment*, p. 148). In the magical phase of
    development mimesis allowed human beings to resemble their environ-
    ment rather than simply making their environment resemble themselves
    (GS 3, p. 212; *Dialectic of Enlightenment*, p. 154). The perspective on
    the philosophy of history outlined in the *Dialectic of Enlightenment*
    considers the development of humanity all the way from an immediate
    mimetic relationship to nature through a deliberate manipulation of
    mimesis by priests and medicine-men right up to the development of
    ratio or instrumental rationality as a means of dominating nature. In
    other words, this process eventually leads to an organization of labour
    in which mimesis itself is repressed but where mimetic behaviour lives
    on in a mediated form. And finally, with the deliberate imitation of
    magical practices in modern totalitarianism, we end up in a kind of
    return to mimesis, or a 'mimesis of mimesis' (GS 3, p. 209; *Dialectic
    of Enlightenment*, p. 152). We should have to say, in Adorno's terms,
    that mimesis has remained to this day a counterpart to the rationality

that dominates nature, a regression that falls back behind such rationality and a corrective to it at the same time.

The ongoing process of enlightenment has increasingly demythologized mimetic modes of behaviour, and the realm in which mimesis belongs has been largely repressed or marginalized as a result; but the return of this realm does not inevitably or exclusively have to be, as it is in Heidegger's thought, a return to myth as something intrinsically bad or obscurantist (see Lecture 7, pp. 67f). For as 'immemorial mimesis' it also brings to mind that 'reflexive imitation, that impulse however impotent it may seem to be, from which all that transcends the simply existent, namely spirit, once sprang' (GS 16, p. 227). The mimetic dimension, which Adorno's later thought undertook to preserve and which he even recognized in Hegel, constitutes an integral moment of the truth which concerns all philosophy: 'The speculative Hegelian concept rescues mimesis through spirit's self-reflection: truth is not *adaequatio* but affinity, and in the decline of idealism reason's mindfulness of its mimetic nature is revealed by Hegel to be its human right' (GS 5, p. 285; *Hegel: Three Studies*, p. 41). The deepest intention of Adorno's negative dialectics ultimately lies in the reconciliation between *ratio* and its apparent opposite, mimesis: 'The concept has no other way of capturing the import of what it has repressed, namely mimesis, than by taking up something of the latter into its own approach, while not just abandoning itself to it' (GS 6, p. 26; *Negative Dialectics*, Ashton, p. 14). While this thought preserves Adorno from the charge of 'aestheticizing' theoretical reflection, it should not be forgotten that the concept of the mimetic is nowhere more frequently invoked than in *Aesthetic Theory*, his very last work. What he was trying to do was not so much to convert knowledge into art as to recognize works of art as forms of knowledge:

> The sentimentality and debility of almost the whole tradition of aesthetic thought is that it has suppressed the dialectic of rationality and mimesis immanent to art ... The survival of mimesis, the nonconceptual affinity of the subjectively produced with its unposited other, defines art as a form of knowledge and to that extent as 'rational.' For that to which the mimetic comportment responds is the *telos* of knowledge, which art simultaneously blocks with its own categories. Art completes knowledge with what is excluded from knowledge and thereby once again impairs its character as knowledge, its univocity. (GS 7, pp. 86f.; *Aesthetic Theory*, trans. Robert Hullot-Kentor, Continuum, 2004, p. 70)

This epistemic concern to rescue the mimetic content of art corresponds to the actual rescue of the mimetic dimension which he desired to see accomplished in life. Thus in some notes that were jotted down in the final year of his life Adorno observed:

> Yesterday I wrote in *Aesthetic Theory*: nothing transcends without that which it transcends [see GS 7, p. 424; *Aesthetic Theory*, p. 365]. Yet isn't this something that goes far beyond art? Does it not harbour – for *thought*

– the answer to the question regarding the infinite significance of the conditioned for the unconditioned? – the very heart of mystical experience? ... It harbours nothing less than the *communication* between everything that is, or the objectivity of mimesis. Crucial to develop this further. (Ms Notizheft Z, p. 138f.)

The fact that he was not actually granted the opportunity to develop these thoughts as he hoped has only encouraged the charge that his conception of the mimetic was illegitimately borrowed from the field of art, even though this conception already reveals the inadequacies of every existing theory of communication in view of what Adorno had seen here.

Lecture 5

1 See Heinrich Rickert, *Die Grenzen der naturwissenschaftlichen Begriffs-bildung: Eine logische Einleitung in die historischen Wissenschaften*, 3rd and 4th edns, Tübingen, 1921, p. 28:

> What we realize when we think about how knowledge reproduces reality in time and space is that this reality is *different* at any given point from any other point, and that we never therefore know what new and hitherto unknown things this reality will show us in future. That is why we can describe actual reality as a heterogeneous continuum in contrast to the non-actual homogeneous continuum of mathematics. (*The Limits of Concept Formation in Natural Science*, trans. and abridged Guy Oakes, Cambridge University Press, 1986; this specific passage is omitted from the translation of Rickert's book, but the for the context of these remarks see pp. 36–45.)

The present editor cited this passage in NaS IV.4, p. 388, n. 156, although Karel Markus has correctly pointed out Adorno's numerous references to this expression of Rickert's may refer back to Rickert's 'System of Philosophy'. There Rickert writes:

> It can easily be shown that what we immediately 'sense' [*erleben*], to use a fashionable contemporary word, if we *remove* all our forms of apprehension from the process, is simply a disorganized 'welter' of constantly changing impressions, and it is indeed not merely the world as a whole, but also every part of the world, however small it may be, which forms a restless flux with merely gradual transitions in a process of ceaseless change. For the scientifically oriented individual this completely unsystematically conceived world is a *heterogeneous continuum* which he confronts in a theoretically helpless fashion, or which is, to put this more generally, a chaos. (Heinrich Rickert, *System der Philosophie*, Pt I, Tübingen, 1921, p. 6)

2 Adorno is thinking here of a particular passage in Plato's *Phaedrus* (265) (as we can see from GS 6, p. 53). In his edition of Adorno's lectures on

Kant's first *Critique* (NaS IV.14, p. 198), where Adorno also alludes to this passage, the present editor overlooked this parallel and referred the reader to another passage in Plato (ibid., pp. 389f. note 166; *Kant's Critique of Pure Reason*, Livingstone, p. 131 and pp. 261f.). Again I should like to thank Karel Markus for drawing my attention to this.

3 Adorno is referring to one of Spinoza's most famous propositions: 'Ordo, et connexio idearum idem est, ac ordo, et connexio rerum.' See *Ethics*, Book II, prop. 7: 'The order and connection of ideas is the same as the order and connection of things', in *The Collected Works of Spinoza*, ed. and trans. Edwin Curley, Princeton University Press, 1985, Vol. I, p. 451.

4 See NaS I.1, p. 287, n. 35.

5 Adorno alludes to the words of the student in *Faust*, Pt I (lines 1966–7): 'For what we possess black on white / We can take home and keep for good' (Goethe, *Sämtliche Werke*, Vol. 7/1, p. 84; *Goethe's Faust*, Kaufmann, p. 201).

6 'Therefore mind (*nous*) thinks itself, if it is that which is best; and its thinking is a thinking of thinking (noēsis noēseōs)', *Metaphysics*, Bk XII, ch. 9, 1074b 33ff.; trans. Hugh Tredennick, in *Metaphysics, Books X–IV*, Loeb Classical Library 287, Harvard University Press, 1935, p. 165.

7 After the so-called *Kehre* or 'turning' in his thought, which Heidegger himself seems to date back to his lectures on Plato in 1931/32, the philosopher started to write 'Seyn' (beyng) rather than 'Sein' (being) in order to emphasize an immediate access to 'being' in a mythical sense in contrast to the earlier approach on the basis of human existence or *Dasein* as presented in the published portions of *Being and Time*. Heidegger also used the word 'being' in crossed out form (~~Sein~~) in the short text *Zur Seinsfrage* of 1955, addressed in the form of a letter to Ernst Jünger, where this form of the word is expressly discussed. (See M. Heidegger, *Wegmarken*, Frankfurt am Main, 1967, pp. 238ff.; 'On the Question of Being', trans. William McNeill, in *Pathmarks*, McNeill, pp. 291–322.)

8 Hermann Schweppenhäuser (1928–2015) took his doctorate with Adorno and Horkheimer in 1956 with a dissertation entitled 'Studien über die Heideggersche Sprachtheorie'. The work appeared in the journal *Archiv für Philosophie*, 7(3/4) and 8(1/2) (1957–8). The text was also published under the auspices of the Theodor W. Adorno Archive as part of the series *Dialektische Studien* (Munich, 1988).

9 The expression 'old fighter' [*Alter Kämpfer*] was a term used by the Nazis for the 'old guard', namely those who had been members of the National Socialist Party or one its affiliates before 1933. Adorno is alluding to Heidegger's decision in 1933 to endorse Hitler and his atavistic followers, a move that would have prevented Heidegger from recognizing any affinities with the tradition of Jewish mysticism.

10 *Intellectus archetypus*: an original paradigmatic or intuitive understanding. Kant uses the term in the *Critique of Judgement* (§77) for the divine

intuitive form of thinking which could create its objects through thinking alone in contrast to the *intellectus ectypus*, or 'our discursive human understanding which requires the use of images'.

11   Reading *Reimen* here for *Reinen* (Vo 5740).

12   Adorno is alluding to the book which appeared in its original form in 1963 and in its final form in 1964 as *Jargon der Eigentlichkeit* (see GS 6, pp. 413ff.; *The Jargon of Authenticity*, trans. Knut Tarnowski and Frederic Will, London, 1973).

13   Adorno had already used the expression 'jargon of authenticity' on various occasions. See, for example, GS 5, p. 42; *Against Epistemology*, Domingo, p. 34; GS 8, pp. 140 and 454; GS 11, pp. 14 and 221; *Notes to Literature*, 'The Essay as Form', Vol. 1, p. 7, and 'Words from Abroad', p. 190), just to mention texts which were written in or before 1960.

14   Adorno is alluding to the sacred spring of Parnassus, whose waters were used for ritual purification by the priests of Delphi. See the opening choral song in Euripides, *The Phoenician Women*, lines 222–3.

15   See note 8 to Lecture 23.

Lecture 6

1   The sixth lecture is available in two transcriptions which differ only very slightly from each other (see Vo 574ff. and Vo 6977ff.). The first transcription was erroneously classified in the context of Adorno's lectures on aesthetics from the winter semester of 1961/62.

2   Adorno discusses the problem of genesis and validity on various occasions. See, for example, GS 5, pp. 79ff., or his lectures on Kant's *Critique of Pure Reason*, NaS IV.4, pp. 252f. and 396f., n. 210.

3   On Adorno's view of Scheler's metaphysics, see NaS IV.14, pp. 63f.; pp. 249f., n, 82; p. 264, n. 143; *Metaphysics: Concept and Problems*, trans. Edmund Jephcott, Polity, 2000, pp. 39f.; p. 160, n. 13; p. 170, n. 5.

4   It was not possible to identify a relevant passage that would confirm Adorno's point here.

5   Edmund Husserl, *Ideen zu einer reinen Phänomenologie und phänomenologischen Philosophie*, p. 10 n.; *Ideas*, Kersten, p. 5.

6   For Adorno's critique of Dilthey, see NaS IV.13, pp. 385f., n. 29, and p. 399, n. 106; *History and Freedom*, Livingstone, p. 273, n. 11, and p. 283, n. 1.

7   It was not possible to identify a relevant passage to this effect.

8   See M. Heidegger, *Sein und Zeit*, p. 35; *Being and Time*, Stambaugh, p. 33.

9   See T. W. Adorno, *Zur Metakritik der Erkenntnistheorie: Studien über Husserl und die phänomenologischen Antinomien*, Stuttgart, 1956, pp. 196ff.; now in GS 5, pp. 190ff.; *Against Epistemology*, Domingo, pp. 186ff.

10   For Husserl's own example of the eidetic intuition of 'red' and Adorno's critique, see the references in note 17, Lecture 1, above.

11 In his earliest writings Adorno had already criticized Scheler's turn to a material ontology as 'an arbitrary absolutization of immanent historical facts which perhaps for specifically ideological purposes were now supposed to obtain the status of eternal and universally valid values' (GS 1, p. 349). See also NaS IV.14, pp. 249f., n. 82; *Metaphysics: Concept and Problems*, Jephcott, p. 160, n. 13. Scheler himself discussed the concept of ontology in a late text which can also be seen as a critical response to *Being and Time*:

> My own view ... is that we can only develop an ontology of 'man' once we have already clarified the ontic dimension of 'knowing', 'consciousness', the 'mind', the 'person', 'life', the so-called 'subject', the 'thing', the 'body', and so on. Naturally, the validity of each of these concepts must first be demonstrated in its own right – and indeed specifically by the ontology of all these given phenomena. (Max Scheler, *Späte Schriften*, ed. Manfred Frings, 2nd edn, Bonn, 1955, p. 281)

Lecture 7

1 See Lecture 2, pp. 12f. above.
2 See Lecture 2, pp. 19f. above.
3 See GS 5, p. 128; *Against Epistemology*, Domingo, p. 122; also NaS IV.14, pp. 44ff.; *Metaphysics: Concept and Problems*, Jephcott, pp. 26ff.
4 See Edmund Husserl, *Méditations Cartésiennes: introduction à la phénomenologie*, Paris, 1931; *Cartesianische Meditationen und Pariser Vorträge*, ed. Stefan Strasser, Haag, 1950; now in *Gesammelte Schriften*, Vol. 8; *Cartesian Meditations: An Introduction to Phenomenology*, trans. Dorion Cairns, Nijhoff, 1977.
5 Reading *damit* for *darin* (Vo 5758).
6 See René Descartes, *Meditationes de prima philosophia, in qua Dei existentia et animae immortalitas demonstratur*, Paris, 1641; *Meditations on First Philosophy*, trans. E. S. Haldane and G. R. T. Ross, in *The Philosophical Works of Descartes*, New York, 1955, Vol. 1, pp. 131–99.
7 See NaS IV.4, p. 385, n. 143, and NaS IV.13, p. 452, n. 327; *Kant's Critique of Pure Reason*, Livingstone, p. 257, n. 15, and *History and Freedom*, Livingstone, p. 325, n. 5.
8 In the *Cartesian Meditations* Husserl claims that the phenomenological method extends and 'develops' transcendental analysis into eidetic analysis:

> Though each singly selected type is thus elevated from its milieu within the empirically factual ego into the pure eidetic sphere [!], the intentional outer horizons pointing to its uncoverable connexus within the ego do not vanish; only this *nexus-horizon itself becomes eidetic*. In other words: With each eidetically pure type we find ourselves, not indeed inside the de facto ego, but *inside an eidos ego*; and constitution of one actually

pure possibility among others carries with it implicitly, as its outer horizon, a *purely possible ego*, a pure possibility-variant of my *de facto* ego. (E. Husserl, *Gesammelte Schriften*, Vol. 8, p. 73; *Cartesian Meditations*, Cairns, p. 71)

9 See the section 'Essence and Pure Ego' in GS 5, pp. 190ff., and especially pp. 224ff.; *Against Epistemology*, Domingo, pp. 186ff. and 222ff.

10 Reading *von Objekt im Subjekt* for *Objekt am Subjekt* (Vo 5761).

11 It was not possible to find a corresponding passage in Karl Kraus. But it is also possible that Adorno may have been thinking of something that Theodor Haecker once said about Kraus:

> it would be necessary to pursue every step of these people, from the brightest to the dimmest, just as Karl Kraus pursued the masters of the Vienna Press and saw what bugs his sovereign enquiries managed to turn up overnight. It is the ideality of the man and the thinker (as opposed to the youth and the poet) to engage energetically with the everyday world, and to be resolutely prepared to get his hands dirty if necessary, for they can always be washed clean again. (Theodor Haecker, Afterword to *Sören Kierkegaard, Kritik der Gegenwart*, trans. Theodor Haecker, 2nd edn, Innsbruck, 1922, pp. 84f.)

12 On the concept of the mythical in Adorno, see Rolf Tiedemann, '"Gegenwärtige Vorwelt": Zu Adornos Begriff des Mythischen', in *Frankfurter Adorno Blätter* V, 1998, pp. 9ff., and *Frankfurter Adorno Blätter* VIII, 2002.

13 See Brüder Grimm, *Kinder- und Hausmärchen*, ed. Heinz Rölleke, Stuttgart, 1993, Vol. I, pp. 269ff., particularly p. 275:

> The Queen stood secretly before the mirror and spoke, saying: 'Mirror, mirror on the wall, / Who is the fairest one in all the land?' And the mirror answered as before: 'O Queen, thou art the fairest here, / yet Snow White beyond the mountains / amongst the seven dwarves / is a thousand times more fair than thee.' And when she heard the mirror speak, she shook with rage and trembled. 'Snow White must die', she cried, 'though it cost my life!'

14 Hylozoism: the doctrine of the early Ionian philosophers of nature which posits an animated primal stuff as the ultimate substance of the world. See *Dialectic of Enlightenment*: 'Just as the images of generation from water and earth, that had come to the Greeks from the Nile, were converted by these cosmologies into Hylozoic principles and elements, the whole ambiguous profusion of mythical demons was intellectualized to become the pure form of ontological entities' (GS 3, p. 22; *Dialectic of Enlightenment*, Jephcott, p. 3). And again in *Negative Dialectics* Adorno claims: 'The Eleatic move to the concept of "being", which is so glorified today, was already enlightened in relation to hylozoism, though Heidegger is less interested in that' (GS 6, p. 79; *Negative Dialectics*, Ashton, p. 71).

15   See Adorno's essay on 'Kierkegaard's Doctrine of Love':

> While his philosophical writings attempt to present this process of exis-tential appropriation in accordance with its various stages, and through this dialectic to lead the reader towards the theological truth, he felt it necessary to posit the positively Christian dimension that was to be attained over against this as a 'corrective' right from the beginning, even though he did not claim to have attained it himself. The *Religious Discourses* are supposed to furnish this corrective. (GS 2, p. 217)

16   Adorno also discusses the question of reification in Heidegger in the highly critical essay which he wrote in 1949 in response to Lukács's own essay 'Heidegger redivivus' (GS 20.1, pp. 251ff.).

Lecture 8

1   See Rudolf Carnap, 'Überwindung der Metaphysik durch logische Analyse der Sprache', *Erkenntnis* 2 (1931), pp. 219ff.; 'The Overcoming of Metaphysics through Logical Analysis of Language', in *Heidegger and Modern Philosophy*, ed. Michael Murray, Yale University Press, 1978, pp. 23–34; this English version is also available under the title 'The Elimination of Metaphysics through Logical Analysis of Language', trans. Arthur Pap, in *Logical Positivism*, ed. A. J. Ayer, New York, 1959.
2   The word *mana*, which derives from a Melanesian language, is used in ethnology and in Durkheim's sociology of religion to refer to the obscure origins of religious life in that elemental power to which 'primitive' man felt himself to be exposed (see Émile Durkheim, *Les Formes élementaires de la vie religieuse: le système totémique en Australie*, 4th edn, Paris, 1960, pp. 87f., 277f., 378f.; *The Elementary Forms of Religious Life*, trans. J. W. Swain, Allen & Unwin, 1976, pp. 62ff., 188, 194f., 218f.). The authors of *Dialectic of Enlightenment*, who found the word in the writings of Durkheim or his school, employed it to interpret the earliest phase of human history:

> The murky, undivided entity worshipped as the principle of *mana* at the earliest known stages of humanity lived on in the bright world of the Greek religion. Primal and undifferentiated, it is everything unknown and alien; it is that which transcends the bounds of experience, the aspect of things which is more than their immediately perceived existence ... The doubling of nature into appearance and essence, effect and force, made possible by myth no less than by science, springs from human fear, the expression of which becomes its explanation. This does not mean that the soul is transposed into nature, as psychologism would have us believe; *mana*, the moving spirit, is not a projection but the echo of the real preponderance of nature in the weak psyches of primitive people. (GS 3, p. 31; *Dialectic of Enlightenment*, Jephcott, pp. 10–11)

Adorno returned to the concept of *mana* in some notes from 1968 about the way that art preserves a memory of *mana*:

> Music is the process of being touched, the experience of what is immediately other, the shudder as a phenomenon that is just as much within the world, *mana* as something empirical. This is the entire dialectic of music. Once it is in the world, we cannot just stay with its abstractness, it has a law of its own, to be experienced it must determine itself, it must once again – in disguise – become the world (the motivation of this dialectic a crucial task still to be accomplished). In a certain sense this also works against the process of being touched, or – as in Beethoven – it somehow becomes governable, becomes *semblance*. This element becomes weaker in the professional musician, once one is involved in music it loses this dimension of shudder, or rather it is secularized, and persists in the purity of its immanent articulation (caution needed here: this is true, but still not concrete enough. What is now left, and what is not, of this process of being touched? That is what we need to answer). (Ms Notizheft Z, p. 132f.)

And he writes in a similar vein in *Aesthetic Theory*: 'Only through spiritualization, and not through stubborn rank natural growth, do artworks break through the net of the domination of nature and mould themselves to nature; only from within does one issue forth. Otherwise artworks become infantile. Even in spirit something of the mimetic impulse survives, that secularized mana, what moves and touches us' (GS 7, p. 411; *Aesthetic Theory*, Hullot-Kentor, p. 356). See also Lecture 20, p. 213, and Lecture 21, p. 219.

3 The expression 'formal indication' which Adorno used quite frequently in lectures and seminars was, according to Gadamer, specifically formulated by Heidegger in connection with Kierkegaard's idea of 'indirect communication' (see Hans-Georg Gadamer, *Gesammelte Werke*, Vol. 3, p. 389; for an interpretation of what Heidegger precisely intended by this expression, see ibid., p. 429f.).

4 M. Heidegger, *Einführung in die Metaphysik*, Tübingen, 1953, p. 31; *Introduction to Metaphysics*, trans. Gregory Fried and Richard Polt, Yale University Press, 2014, p. 45; in fact the text represents a series of lectures which Heidegger originally delivered in 1935. This is a work that was published relatively late in Heidegger's career but cannot really be regarded as one of his 'later works'.

5 Adorno explained the precise context in which he used the expression 'counter-Enlightenment' in a letter to Franz Böhm, dated 14 January 1957, which referred to his argument with Peter R. Hofstätter regarding a sociological 'group experiment' (GS 9.2, pp. 378ff.):

> Of course, this whole thing with Hofstätter really belongs in a much broader context. And here it is illuminating to look at the controversy between Schelsky and Hochheimer in the journal *Psyche* ... Somebody should really write something about the regressive tendency which is evident in contemporary German social science. For so-called empirical research is tending more and more to become a pretext for not acknowledging and talking about difficult or painful things. A basic consensus

seems to prevail amongst people like Hofstätter, Schelsky, Wurzbacher, and a whole series of others, and attacks like those of Hofstätter are a symptom of a reinvigorated will to rein in the claims of science under pretext of scientific method itself. In the end they don't want to fall behind the gynaecologists who claim they knew nothing about the programmes of sterilization. This is what they now call 'counter-Enlightenment', to use Schelsky's expression.

Sociologists who were prepared to describe themselves as partisans of some sort of 'counter-Enlightenment' were actually rather rare. Yet in 1955 Schelsky had written: 'In many scientific fields we are now rediscovering the functional significance of tradition as a matter of insight. In this process of counter-Enlightenment against the more superficial outlook we find in ages and movements of enlightenment' (Helmut Schelsky, *Soziologie der Sexualität: Über die Beziehungen zwischen Geschlecht, Moral und Gesellschaft*, Hamburg, 1955, p. 8). But Schelsky later complained about the way he was 'condemned as a partisan of "counter-Enlightenment"' (Schelsky, *Die Arbeit tun die anderen: Klassenkampf und Priesterherrschaft der Intellektuellen*, 2nd edn, Opladen, 1975, p. 399). According to Iring Fetscher, the 'only ambitious counter-enlightenment position in the Federal Republic of Germany would be that of Arnold Gehlen and his followers' (Fetscher, 'Aufklärung und Gegenaufklärung in der Bundesrepublik', in *Aufklärung und Gegenaufklärung in der europäischen Literatur, Philosophie und Politik von der Antike bis zur Gegenwart*, ed. Jochen Schmidt, Darmstadt, 1989, p. 538).

6 See Lecture 3, p. 30.

7 These remarks are directed against certain theoretical views of Robert K. Merton. See GS 8, p. 290, or NaS IV.15, p. 39.

8 The typical difference between the present lectures and the text of *Negative Dialectics* is that, while the opening chapter of the latter concentrates on what Adorno calls the 'ontological need', the lectures, up to this point at least, have been concerned essentially with 'preliminary reflections'.

9 See M. Heidegger, *Platons Lehre von der Wahrheit*, p. 84; *Letter on 'Humanism'*, in *Pathmarks*, McNeill, p. 248: 'the human being occurs essentially in such a way that he is the "There", that is, the clearing [*Lichtung*] of being.'

10 *Platons Lehre von der Wahrheit*, p. 84; *Letter on 'Humanism'*, p. 252: 'The human being is the shepherd of being.'

11 See the Preface to the first edition (1818) of Arthur Schopenhauer, *Die Welt als Wille und Vorstellung*; *The World as Will and Representation*, trans. E. F. J. Payne, New York, 1966, Vol. I, pp. xii–xvii.

Lecture 9

1 Richard Wagner, *Tristan und Isolde*, Act I, scene 3, where Brangäne addresses Isolde : 'Kennst du der Mutter / Künste nicht? / ... Für Weh

und Wunden / gab sie Balsam; / für böse Gifte / Gegengift ...' [Know you not your mother's arts? ... For pains and wounds she offered balm; for evil poisons counter-poison ...] (Wagner, *Dichtungen und Schriften*, ed. Dieter Borchmeyer, Vol. 4, Frankfurt am Main, 1983, p. 25).

2 See Hegel, *Werke*, Vol. 6: *Wissenschaft der Logik II*, pp. 119ff., specifically p. 122: 'When all the conditions of a fact are present, it enters into existence ... The whole fact must be present in its conditions, or all the conditions belong to its Existence, for *all* of them constitute the reflection; or, determinate being, because it is condition, is determined by form; consequently its determinations are determinations of reflection and the positing of one essentially involves the positing of the others' (*Science of Logic*, Miller, p. 477).

3 For Adorno's critique of Heidegger's category of historicity, see especially GS 6, pp. 134ff.; *Negative Dialectics*, Ashton, pp. 128f., and NaS IV.13, p. 177ff., and p. 419f., n. 177; *History and Freedom*, Livingstone, pp. 122f., and p. 300, n. 7.

4 Schopenhauer presents his law of motivation, the principle of sufficient reason that accounts for action, in §43 of his dissertation *On the Fourfold Root of the Principle of Sufficient Reason*. On the general relation of will and motive, see §62 of *The World as Will and Representation* and the third part of his work on the freedom of the will (Arthur Schopenhauer, *Sämtliche Werke*, ed. Wolfgang von Löhneysen, Vol. III: *Kleinere Schriften*, Darmstadt, 1962, pp. 172ff. and pp. 562ff.; Vol. I: *Die Welt als Wille und Vorstellung I*, Darmstadt, 1982, pp. 457ff.; *The World as Will and Representation*, trans. E. F. J. Payne, New York, 1969, Vol. I, p. 334ff.).

5 'Jaspers' is a conjectural reading on the editor's part. In the transcription (Vo 3784) the name was omitted, but an unintelligible word was subsequently inserted here by someone else.

6 For the following interpretation, compare *Negative Dialectics*, especially the last part of the section 'Being and Existence' (GS 6, pp. 125ff.; *Negative Dialectics*, Ashton, p. 119ff.), which contains the fully developed version of the ideas Adorno was developing in the lectures here.

7 An allusion to Fichte's essay *Die Bestimmung des Menschen* (Berlin, 1902), which had been aimed at the general educated public; *The Vocation of Man*, ed. R. M. Chisholm, Indianapolis. 1956.

8 Søren Kierkegaard, *The Sickness unto Death*, trans. Howard V. Hong and Edna H. Hong, Princeton University Press, 1980, p. 13:

> A human being is spirit. But what is spirit? Spirit is the self. But what is the self? The self is a relation that relates itself to itself or is the relation's relating itself to itself in the relation. A human being is a synthesis of the infinite and the finite, of the temporal and the eternal, of freedom and necessity, in short a synthesis. A synthesis is a relation between two. Considered in this way, a human being is still not a self.

9 Reading ... *als unendlich voraussetzungsvolle übernommen werden* for ... *nie als unendlich voraussetzungsvolle übernommen werden* (Vo 5788).

10 See above Lecture 2, p. 18; Lecture 5, p. 47; Lecture 7, p. 72, and passim.

11 A common definition of a synthetic judgement and one that Adorno often deploys. See NaS IV.4, pp. 21ff.; *Kant's Critique of Pure Reason*, Livingstone, pp. 9ff.

12 See, for example, GS 1, p. 167; GS 2, pp. 23, 38, passim; *Kierkegaard: Construction of the Aesthetic*, trans. Robert Hullot-Kentor, University of Minnesota Press, 1989, pp. 13, p. 24, passim.

13 Bruno Liebrucks (1911–1985) was appointed as professor of philosophy in Frankfurt in 1960 with considerable support on the part of Hork-heimer and Adorno. His inaugural lecture, delivered on 9 January 1960, was concerned with 'The Dialectic in Kant's Objective Deduction of the Categories'. The text does not appear to have been published. Liebrucks dedicated volume IV of his principal work *Sprache und Bewusstsein* entirely to Kant's *Critique of Pure Reason*.

14 This never came to pass.

Lecture 10

1 See Martin Heidegger, *Kant und das Problem der Metaphysik*, 2nd edition, Frankfurt am Main, 1951; *Kant and the Problem of Metaphysics*, trans. Richard Taft, Indiana University Press, 1997. On Heidegger's interpretation of Kant in this connection, see in particular Karl Heinz Haag, *Der Fortschritt in der Philosophie*, Frankfurt am Main, 1983, pp. 149ff.

2 See NaS IV.4, p. 377, n. 100; *Kant's Critique of Pure Reason*, Living-stone, p. 252, n. 9.

3 NaS IV.4, pp. 132 and 76f., n. 99; *Kant's Critique of Pure Reason*, pp. 85 and 251f., n. 8.

4 The subordinate clause has been supplied by the editor. The transcrip-tion reads simply: *wo ...? in der französischen Revolution* (Vo 3796).

5 See Karl Löwith, *Heidegger: Denker in dürftiger Zeit*, Frankfurt am Main, 1953; now *Sämtliche Schriften*, Vol. 8, Stuttgart, 1984, pp. 124ff. See, for example, p. 185:

> It is no accident if Heidegger's essential-historical thinking can be inter-preted in the opposite way: as an extreme consequence of historicism insofar as it thinks in a boundlessly historical fashion in a historically specific way, and as an unhistorical mode of thinking insofar as it distances itself from all merely historical 'representing' and thinks essential history as a 'sending of being'. If it is not only that the temporal being charac-teristic of finite *Dasein* is historical, but that being itself is being *and* time in a still unclarified sense, since time and history already originally come to presence in the clearing of being, then nothing at all, that is to say, no determinate being, is characterized by historicity, for everything is levelled down to a single way of being that is at once both pseudo-historical and historically indeterminate.

6   Reading *die selber eigentlich noch oberhalb ist, die erst abgeleitet werden muß* for *die selber eigentlich erst oberhalb, die erst abgeleitet ist* which appears in the transcription (Vo 5798).

7   See Franz Kafka, *Nachgelassene Schriften und Fragmente II in der Fassung der Handschriften*, ed. Jost Schillemeit, Fischer, 1992, p. 123.

8   See Max Scheler, *Der Formalismus in der Ethik und die materiale Wertethik: Neuer Versuch der Grundlegung eines ethischen Personalismus*, Halle, 1913–16 (now in *Gesammelte Werke*, Vol. 2, Bern, 1954).

9   See note 5 above.

10   See Adorno's essay 'Vorschlag zur Ungüte', GS 10.1, pp. 330ff.

11   It has not been possible to identify whom Adorno may have in mind here.

12   Adorno was probably thinking of Hans G. Helms in this connection. Adorno had given a lecture on Helms's text 'Fa: M'ahniesgwow' in Cologne at the end of October 1960. See GS 11, pp. 431ff.

13   Adorno also returned to this issue in his lecture series 'Zur Lehre von der Geschichte und von der Freiheit' in the winter semester 1964/65. See NaS IV.13, pp. 82f.; *History and Freedom*, Livingstone, pp. 55ff.

14   On Adorno's interpretation, Kierkegaard's 'doctrine of communication' is essentially antinomic in character. If, on the one hand, 'the "how" of communication remains a subjective surrogate for the compelling appearance that threatens to perish of its own abstractness', it must equally be recognized that 'the "how" – developed by Kierkegaard in opposition to the shallow dualism of form and content – gains its philosophical justification as the expression of objective laws in the manifestation of truth' (GS 2, p. 191; *Kierkegaard: Construction of the Aesthetic*, Hullot-Kentor, pp. 134–5).

15   Adorno is alluding to Goethe's 'Urworte: Orphisch' of 1817, a poem of five eight-line stanzas in which the poet invokes and explores certain 'primal' Greek words such as *daimōn, tychē* and *erōs*. See Goethe, *Selected Poems*, trans. John Whaley, pp. 123–5 ('Primal Words: Orphic').

Lecture 11

1   'Youth with all its might / Seeks happiness in everything / But once we're just a little older / We'll soon fit in alright' (Ferdinand Raimund, *Sämtliche Werke*, ed. Friedrich Schreyvogl, Munich, 1960, p. 383 [from *Der Verschwender*, Act II, scene 6]).

2   See Adorno's remarks on Alban Berg: 'He managed to avoid becoming fully adult without thereby remaining infantile' (GS 13, p. 367).

3   On Heidegger's suspicious attitude to sociology, see NaS IV.4, pp. 252 and 396, n. 208 (*Kant's Critique of Pure Reason*, Livingstone, pp. 166 and 266, n. 9). According to Hermann Mörchen, Adorno's complaint about Heidegger's 'verdict on sociology' (GS 6, p. 135) actually derived from a 'rumour' that he had already encountered in Frankfurt in the pre-fascist period (see H. Mörchen, *Adorno und Heidegger: Untersuchung*

einer philosophischen Kommunikationsverweigerung, Stuttgart, 1981, p. 469).

4   For more on this question, see especially *Zur Lehre von der Geschichte und der Freiheit*, NaS IV.13, pp. 184ff.; *History and Freedom*, Livingstone, pp. 128f.

5   Adorno is referring not of course to Immanuel Hermann Fichte (1796–1879) but to his father Johann Gottlieb Fichte (1762–1814).

6   In this connection, see Adorno's *Glosse über Persönlichkeit* of 1966 (GS 10.2, pp. 639ff.).

7   The same can sometimes be said of modern busts as well, even without the traditional full beard, such as the appalling one of Adorno himself which can be seen at the house where he lived in Frankfurt until the time of his death.

8   See Ernst Cassirer, 'Zur Einsteinschen Relativitätstheorie: Erkenntnistheoretische Betrachtungen', in Cassirer, *Zur modernen Physik*, Darmstadt, 1994, pp. 1f.

9   For the scientists Adorno probably has in mind, see note 7 to Lecture 3 above. Adorno regarded Max Bense (1910–1990) as an exemplary case of those who simply 'prattle about cultural-philosophical questions' and reduce everything to a characterless 'homogeneous brew'.

10 See Moritz Carrière, *Aesthetik: Die Idee des Schönen und ihre Verwirklichung im Leben und der Kunst*, I. Teil: *Die Schönheit: Die Welt. Die Phantasie*; 2. Teil: *Die bildende Kunst: Die Musik, die Poesie*, 2 Vols, 2nd edn, Leipzig, 1873. There is a brief discussion of Carrière's aesthetics in relation to the earlier idealist systems in Bernard Bosanquet, *A History of Aesthetic*, London [1893] 1966, pp. 410–14.

11 See Johannes Vokelt, *System der Ästhetik in zwei Bänden*, Munich, 1905; compare Adorno's *Aufzeichnungen zur Ästhetik-Vorlesung von 1931/32*, where he takes Vokelt's aesthetics as a basis for his own projected discussion (*Frankfurt Adorno Blätter* I, 1992, pp. 35ff.).

12 See Benedetto Croce, *Estetica come scienza dell'espressione e linguistica generale*, Bari, 1901; *The Aesthetic as the Science of Expression and of the Linguistic in General*, trans. Colin Lyas, Cambridge University Press, 1992.

13 For Adorno's understanding of Kant's 'Copernican Turn', see NaS IV.4, pp. 9; 55f.; 358, n. 1; and 367, n. 43; *Kant's Critique of Pure Reason*, Livingstone, pp. 1; 32; 238, n. 1; and 245, n. 13.

14 Reading *Wendung* for *Bewegung* here (Vo 5814).

15 See especially §60 of the *Encyclopaedia Logic* (*Werke*, Vol. 8, pp. 143f.; *Encyclopedia of the Philosophical Sciences in Basic Outline*, Part I: *Science of Logic*, Dahlstrom, pp. 105ff.).

16 See Peter Wust, *Die Auferstehung der Metaphysik* [The Resurrection of Metaphysics], Leipzig, 1920.

17

In order to arrive at the reality of outer objects I have just as little need to resort to inference as I have in regard to the reality of the object of

inner sense, that is, in regard to the reality of my thoughts. For in both
cases alike the objects are nothing but representations, the immediate
perception (consciousness) of which is at the same time a sufficient proof
of their reality. The transcendental idealist is, therefore, an empirical realist
and allows to matter, as appearance, a reality which does not permit of
being inferred, but is immediately perceived. (Kant, *Kritik der reinen
Vernunft*, A 371; *Critique of Pure Reason*, Kemp Smith, p. 347)

See also Adorno's remarks in his lectures on the first *Critique*:

the Kantian formula for this complex of ideas is one that I should certainly
mention to you, and it is undoubtedly one of which you will have already
heard. It is the idea of 'transcendental idealism/empirical realism.' This
means that in transcendental terms, that is, in terms of synthetic a priori
judgements, we are talking about an idealism – that is, something arising
exclusively from the mind; this objectivity is rooted in mind. On the other
hand, it is empirical realism in the sense that the interaction of these transcendental conditions with the data of reality leads to the constitution of
the world which surrounds us as the world of our experience. It would be a
gross misunderstanding of Kantian idealism if we were to conceive of it as
an acosmic philosophy, as a denial of empirical reality; or if we were even
to go so far as to impute to Kant the desire to suggest that the world is no
more than a dream – a suggestion made by Descartes in his Meditations,
as many of you will know. It is this very hypothesis that Kant ridiculed so
scathingly under the title of 'dreamy idealism' in his now famous polemic
against the empirical idealism or spiritualism of Berkeley. (NaS IV.4, pp.
146f.; *Kant's Critique of Pure Reason*, Livingstone, pp. 95–6)

18   See Schelling's lectures *On the Method of Academic Study* (1803):

The impulse and the desire to investigate the essence of things is so deeply
implanted in human beings that they eagerly snatch at the partial and the
false if it has but the appearance of truth and offers any hope of leading
to knowledge. Otherwise it would be incomprehensible that the most
superficial attempts in philosophy should arouse the interest of the most
earnest minds, once such attempts hold out the promise of certainty in
any sphere. The understanding which nonphilosophy calls sound common
sense wants the truth in hard cash, as it were, and tries to get it regardless
of the inadequacy of its resources. When the understanding oversteps its
limits, it produces the monstrosity of a crude dogmatic philosophy, which
seeks to measure the unconditioned by the conditioned and to extend the
finite into the infinite. The kind of logic by means of which the understanding can infer one finite thing from another is supposed to help it
cross the gulf separating the relative from the absolute. As a rule, however,
it does not soar so high, does not go beyond what it calls 'the facts.' The
most modest philosophy of this type proclaims that experience is the only
or primary source of knowledge. It concedes that Ideas may have reality,
but if so, this reality is wholly inaccessible to human knowledge. We may
well say that to study such philosophy is worse than to study none at all.
(F. W. J. Schelling, *Werke*, ed. Manfred Schröter, 3: *Schriften zur Iden-
titätsphilosophie 1801–1806*, Munich, 1927, p. 290; *On University Studies*,
trans. E. S. Morgan, Ohio University Press, 1966, p. 63)

19   See the following passage from Schopenhauer, for example:

> If, therefore, it were now only a question here of encouraging philosophy
> and progressing on the path of truth, the best recommendation I should
> make would be to stop the prevarication and humbug that are carried on
> in its name at the universities. For these are not the place for philosophy
> that is seriously or honestly meant; only too often is its place there occu-
> pied by a puppet dressed up in its clothes which, as *a nervis alienis mobile*
> *lignum* [a wooden doll that is moved by extraneous forces], must gesticulate
> and make a show. Now if such a chair-philosophy still tries to replace
> genuine ideas by incomprehensible, mind-stupefying phrases, new-fangled
> words, and unheard-of notions, the absurdities of which are called specu-
> lative and transcendental, then it becomes a parody of philosophy, and
> brings it into discredit; such has been the case in our day. (*Über die*
> *Universitätsphilosophie* [1850], in *Sämtliche Werke*, Vol. IV: *Parerga und*
> *Parilipomena I*, Darmstadt, 1963, pp. 236f.; *Parerga and Paralipomena:*
> *Short Philosophical Essays*, trans. E. F. J. Payne, 2 vols, Oxford University
> Press, 1974, vol. 1, pp. 194–5)

Lecture 12

1   In the transcription of this lecture (Vo 5818) there is a lacuna in the
middle of the opening sentence where the person responsible for tran-
scribing the tape recording has written 'inaudible'. The entire sentence
as given here is a conjectural reconstruction by the editor.

2   'The more everything changes, the more it remains the same.' See also
NaS IV.13, p. 238; *History and Freedom*, Livingstone, p. 171.

3   Adorno is referring to a journal of 1800/01 that was indeed entitled the
Journal of Speculative Physics, and in which Schelling published, amongst
other things, his essay 'An Exposition of My System of Philosophy' in
1801.

4   Johann Wilhelm Ritter (1776–1810), along with Novalis and Friedrich
Schlegel, belonged to the Jena circle of the early German romantics and
was one of the most important contributors to the genre of the 'frag-
ment' in German literature. He was the founder of electro-chemistry
and authored *Fragments from the Literary Remains of a Young Physicist:*
A Little Book for the Friends of Nature (Heidelberg, 1810). The 'forgotten Preface' to Ritter's *Fragments* was described by Walter Benjamin
as 'the most significant piece of confessional prose amongst the German
romantics' and as a text which effectively 'revealed what romantic eso-
tericism actually means'. Ritter was first rediscovered for a broader literary readership in Ricarda Huch's book *Die Blütezeit der Romantik* of
1899 and in the first volume of her work *Die Romantik* of 1908. Benjamin ascribed a significant role to Ritter's reflections on the philosophy
of language in his book *Der Ursprung des deutschen Trauerspiels* of
1928 (*The Origin of German Tragic Drama*, trans. John Osborne, Verso,
1998; see pp. 10, 13, 213–15).

5   Adorno is almost certainly referring to Georg Simmel, *Der Konflikt der modernen Kultur: Ein Vortrag*, Munich, 1918.
6   See Ernst Bloch's *Erbschaft dieser Zeit* (Zurich, 1935, pp. 217f.), where he has this to say about Heidegger:

> Certain psychological requirements, and also a stolid peasant seriousness, strangely unite with the desire to describe it, to make it really discoverable in words; Heidegger has the anxiety even as he lectures on it. This seriousness is strangely upheld by a pedantic nature rambler, who is joined by a professor of anxiety and care, as if this were a subject like others too. There thus arises a kind of learned lecture-desk sorrow which, although it has subjectivized 'consciousness in general', does not cease to be pure conceptual vision. (*The Heritage of Our Times*, trans. Neville Plaice and Stephen Plaice, Polity, 1991, p. 280)

When Adorno suggests that Bloch had eventually become more sympathetic to ontology he may be alluding to the fact that, in 1960, the latter had delivered a lecture in Tübingen and Heidelberg entitled 'On the Ontology of the Not-Yet', a text that was subsequently included in a book of the same title (E. Bloch, *Philosophische Grundfragen I: Zur Ontologie des Noch-Nicht-Seins: Ein Vortrag und zwei Abhandlungen*, Frankfurt am Main, 1961).

7   On the use of the word *Anliegen* or 'concern', see *Jargon der Eigentlichkeit*, GS 6, pp. 465f. passim; *Jargon of Authenticity*, Tarnowski and Will, pp. 79f.
8   See *Being and Time*, §6: 'The Task of a Destruction of the History of Ontology', Stambaugh, p. 19.
9   The concept of a 'conservative revolution', originally developed in opposition to the French Revolution of 1789, was later taken up in and after the period of the First World War by writers such as Thomas Mann, Rudolf Borchardt and Hugo von Hofmannsthal and was exploited politically in ways that eventually led, albeit indirectly, towards German fascism. It was not for nothing that Hitler was able to describe himself in 1936 as 'the most conservative revolutionary in the world' (see R. Konersmann, the article 'Revolution, konservative', in *Historisches Wörterbuch der Philosophie*, Vol. 8, Basel, 1992, col. 984). After the end of the Nazi regime the concept was popularized once again by Arnim Mohler, the student of Carl Schmitt and secretary of Ernst Jünger, in particular through the dissertation written under Karl Jaspers which was entitled *Die Konservative Revolution in Deutschland 1918–1932: Grundriß ihrer Weltanschauungen* (Stuttgart, 1950). Max Rychner's critique of Mohler's imposing collection of relevant material is more interesting than the work in question. Rychner's discussion, along with the article by Konersmann, provides all the information which is required on this concept (see Max Rychner, *Sphären der Bücherwelt: Aufsätze zur Literatur*, Zurich, 1952, pp. 184ff.).

10 In his lecture 'On the Current State of German Sociology', delivered in 1959, Adorno described National Socialism as 'both pseudo-revolutionary and pseudo-conservative' (GS 8, p. 501).

11 See Martin Heidegger, *Platons Lehre von der Wahrheit: Mit einem Brief über den 'Humanismus'*, 2nd edn, Bern, 1954, p. 75: 'The arrival of beings rests in the sending of being.' In his references to Heidegger's *Letter on 'Humanism'* (1946) Adorno mistakenly refers to *Plato's Doctrine of Truth*. According to Heidegger, the latter text was delivered as a lecture in 1930/31 and was first published in 1942, whereas the *Letter on 'Humanism'* first appeared as an 'appendix' in a 1947 Swiss edition of *Plato's Doctrine of Truth*. Adorno appears to have regarded these two texts as a single work, which is neither philologically nor philosophically justifiable.

12 See Lecture 4 above, pp. 32–3.

13 Karl Reinhardt (1886–1958); see the two essays on Reinhardt by Gadamer in his *Gesammelte Werke*, Vol. 6, *Griechische Philosophie II*, Tübingen, 1985, pp. 278ff. and 285ff. In a letter to Reinhardt on the occasion of the latter's seventieth birthday, dated 16 February 1956, Adorno wrote:

> You know that today, for me, you are still the same as you were when I first heard you lecture – though I am no longer sure whether this was the series on Plato or on the pre-Socratics – when you were the young scholar far and indeed doubly superior to everything merely academic. Doubly superior because you were always more scholarly than the scholars and because you were always so much more than merely scholarly. Words cannot fully capture what you have meant for me, for my entire intellectual development, and while a sense of decency, which is certainly a great category of Greek thought, would indeed usually forbid one to express these things so openly, perhaps for once this might be permitted on this day.

14 Reading *jugendbewegte* for *jugendbewegungshafte* (Vo 5822).

15 See the words of Mephistopheles in *Faust Part Two*: 'Go, my original, your glorious way! – / How truth would irk you, if you really sought it: / For who can think of truth or trash to say, / But someone in the ancient world has thought it? / And yet this fellow puts us in no danger, / For wait a few more years and things will mend: / The vat may hold a ferment strange and stranger, / There'll be some wine to bottle in the end.' Goethe, *Sämtliche Werke*, ed. Friedmar Apel, Vol. 7.1, p. 277; *Faust Part Two*, trans. Philip Wayne, Penguin, 1987, p. 98 (line 6807).

16 Hitler joined the German Workers' Party in Munich in September 1919 (with the membership number of 555). 'He was not, as he always claimed, the seventh member ... "but at best the seventh member of the committee"', which Anton Drexler, the first leader of the party, had invited him to join as 'recruitment director'. See Ian Kershaw, *Hitler 1889–1936: Hubris*, Allen Lane, 1998, p. 127. According to the terms of the Versailles Treaty, the German Army was not permitted to exceed 100,000

men and the German Navy was not permitted to exceed 15,000 men. In order to get round these restrictions the German military entered into an understanding with the various regional administrations in the country which allowed for a clandestine remilitarization on the part of the so-called Black Reichswehr – i.e. secretly trained reserve formations of the army – which thus fundamentally contravened the provisions of the Versailles Treaty (in which they were also covertly supported by the Soviet Union).

17   It has not been possible to identify such a passage.

18   In an entry in his journal from the year 1846 Kierkegaard writes: 'In relation to their systems most systematizers are like a man who has built a vast palace for himself while he lives nearby in a barn; they themselves do not live in the vast systematic edifice. But in matters of the spirit this is and remains a decisive objection. Spiritually, a man's thoughts must be the building in which he lives – otherwise it's wrong' (Søren Kierkegaard, *Papers and Journals: A Selection*, trans. Alastair Hannay, Penguin, 1996, p. 212).

19   See the second German edition of Adorno's *Kierkegaard: Construction of the Aesthetic*, which was published by Suhrkamp in 1962 and also included his lecture on 'Kierkegaard's Doctrine of Love' (from 1940).

20   Reading *implizite Ontologie* for *explizite Ontologie* here.

21   See the title of chapter II of the second section of Part Two of the *Concluding Unscientific Postscript*, where we read: 'Truth is subjectivity'. Kierkegaard, *Concluding Unscientific Postscript to 'Philosophical Fragments'*, trans. H. V. Hong and E. H. Hong, Princeton University Press, 1992, Vol. I, p. 189. See also Adorno, GS 2, p. 167; *Kierkegaard: Construction of the Aesthetic*, Hullot-Kentor, p. 118.

22   Heidegger's claim regarding the priority of the question is expressed in almost all of his later writings. Thus in the essay *On the Question of Being* he writes:

> I write all this in the form of questions; for, as far as I can see, thinking can today do more than to continually ponder what is evoked in the said questions. ... *But the question concerning the essence of being dies off if it does not relinquish the language of metaphysics, because metaphysical representation prevents us from thinking the question concerning the essence of being.* ... Is it due to 'being' ... that our saying falls in a telling manner in its response, remaining what is all too readily suspected as so-called 'mysticism'? ... These are questions that are scarcely beginning to become worthy of question in such a way that we could find ourselves at home in them and never again let them go, even at the peril of having to relinquish old and established habits of thinking in the sense of metaphysical representation and of being accused of disdain for all sound reasoning. These are questions that, in our passing 'over the line', still display a particularly acute character; for such passage moves within the realm of the nothing. (*Zur Seinsfrage*, Frankfurt am Main, 1956, pp. 26 and 29; *On the Question of Being*, trans. William McNeill, in *Pathmarks*, McNeil, pp. 306 and 309)

23 'If God held fast in his right hand the whole of truth and in his left hand only the ever-active quest for truth, albeit with the proviso that I should constantly and eternally err, and said to me: "Choose!", I would humbly fall upon his left hand and say: "Father, give! For the pure truth is for you alone!"' See Gotthold Ephraim Lessing, *Werke und Briefe*, ed. Wilfried Barner et al., Vol. 8: *Werke 1774–1778*, Frankfurt am Main, 1989, p. 510 (*Eine Duplik*); Lessing, *Philosophical and Theological Writings*, trans. H. B. Nisbet, Cambridge University Press, 2005, p. 98 (*A Rejoinder*).

24 See Kierkegaard, *Concluding Unscientific Postscript*, Hong, Vol. I, 'Something about Lessing', pp. 61f.

25 Reading *Kierkegaard* as the referent for *er* here (Vo 5830).

Lecture 13

1 See Lecture 12, p. 125.

2 Adorno is referring to *The Moment*, a journal published by Kierkegaard himself, which was mentioned in Lecture 12, p. 124.

3 Edmund Husserl, *Logische Untersuchungen*, Vol. I, *Prolegomena zur reinen Logik*, now in *Gesammelte Schriften*, Vol. 2; *Logical Investigations*, trans. J. F. Findlay, Humanities Press, 1970, Vol. 1: *Prolegomena to Pure Logic*, ch. 7: 'Psychologism as Sceptical Relativism', especially §§34–8.

4 See Goethe's poem 'Parabolisch': 'Poems are painted window panes, / Peer from the market into the church / And all is dark and gloomy ... / Yet only step inside! / And greet the sacred chapel / Then all is light and colour, / Suddenly old story and adornment gleam, / A noble semblance works its meaning; / Learn this, God's children: / Be edified and feast your eyes!' (Goethe, *Sämtliche Werke*, Part I, Vol. 2, p. 542).

5 It was not possible to trace this saying back to Voltaire, although Adorno also cites and alludes to it elsewhere (GS 17, p. 261, and GS 7, p. 466; see *Aesthetic Theory*, Hullot-Kentor, p. 397).

6 The expression appeared specifically in the title of Helmut Schelsky's book *Die skeptische Generation. Eine Soziologie der deutschen Jugend*, Düsseldorf and Cologne 1957. For Adorno's view of the text in question see GS 8, p. 527f.

7 See the words of Baron Ochs auf Lerchenau in Act II of *Rosenkavalier*: 'Ich selber exkludier mich nicht' (Hugo von Hofmannsthal, *Lustspiele I*, ed. Herbert Steiner, Stockholm, 1947, pp. 351f.).

8 See Adorno's remarks in the *Metakritik der Erkenntnistheorie*, in the section entitled 'Phenomenology Attempts to Break Out' (GS 5, pp. 193ff.; *Against Epistemology*, Domingo, pp. 189f.).

9 By 'later terminology', Adorno means the terminology used by Schelling. See GS 6, p. 275; *Negative Dialectics*, Ashton, p. 279. But see also note 17 to Lecture 22 below.

10 The crucial passage on 'acosmism' in Kierkegaard is to be found in his doctoral dissertation *The Concept of Irony*:

> When Fichte infinitized the I in this way, he advanced an idealism beside which any actuality turned pale, an acosmism in which his idealism became actuality even though it was Docetism. In Fichte, thought was infinitized, subjectivity became the infinite, absolute negativity, the infinite tension and urge. Because of this, Fichte has significance for science and scholarship. His *Wissenschaftslehre* [theory of knowledge] infinitized knowledge. But he infinitized it negatively, and thus instead of truth he obtained certainty, not positive but negative infinity in the I's infinite identity with itself; instead of positive striving, that is, happiness, he obtained a negative striving, that is, an ought. (Kierkegaard, *The Concept of Irony with Continual Reference to Socrates*, trans. H. V. Hong and E. H. Hong, Princeton University Press, 1989, p. 273)

11 An evident allusion to the late work by Max Scheler, *Die Stellung des Menschen im Kosmos* [Man's Place in the Cosmos], Darmstadt, 1928; now in Scheler, *Gesammelte Werke*, Vol. 9, Bonn, 1995.

12 The passage which Adorno is referring to is to be found in 'The Doctrine of the Method of Pure Practical Reason' in the second *Critique*: 'Now, if these concepts are to become subjectively practical they must stop short with objective laws of morality, to be admired and esteemed with reference to humanity: the representation of them must be considered in relation to human beings and to the individual human being.' Kant, *Werke in sechs Bänden*, ed. Wilhelm Weischedel, Vol. IV: *Schriften zur Ethik und Religionsphilosophie*, Darmstadt, 1963, p. 295; *Critique of Pure Practical Reason*, trans. Mary J. Gregor, in *Practical Philosophy*, Cambridge University Press, 1996, p. 266.

Lecture 14

1 This sentence has been amended from the transcript by the editor (Vo 5845).

2 Compare the passage from *Either/Or* which Adorno cites in his book on Kierkegaard: 'The failing of the mystic is that by his choice he does not become concrete for himself, nor for God either; he chooses himself abstractly and therefore lacks transparentness' (GS 2, p. 47; *Kierkegaard*, Hullot-Kentor, pp. 30–1). See also the following passage quoted from *Sickness unto Death*: 'The devil's despair is the most intense despair, for the devil is sheer spirit, and therefore absolute consciousness and transparency; in the devil there is no obscurity that might serve as a mitigating excuse, his despair is therefore absolute defiance' (GS 2, p. 82; *Kierkegaard*, p. 56). Adorno interprets these ideas as follows:

> The centrality of the category of transparentness in Kierkegaard's doctrine of existence has been recognized by Guardini: 'To be "transparent" to

oneself. For Kierkegaard the word has the greatest significance. It means ingenuous, free of all obscurity, manifestly authentic.' Clearly, Guardini's commentary is a Catholic interpretation of Kierkegaard's 'transparentness': for him, nature has been atoned for by the sacrifice of Christ, whereas for the Protestant, Kierkegaard, a sinful-ambiguous nature stands ever again in need of rescue. (GS 2, p. 104; *Kierkegaard*, p. 72)

3   The affinities between Lukács and Heidegger may be rather more complex than Adorno was able to recognize here. In the late 1920s and early 1930s both men defended radically contrasting positions and almost forced the intelligentsia who were not already committed to one creed or another to choose between these two thinkers. In this regard, *History and Class Consciousness* and *Being and Time* alike broke with the perspective of merely theoretical considerations and effectively occupied a space which is often described, inadequately enough, in terms of competing 'world-views'. But there is no question that both of these books confront their readers with claims and demands that go beyond those usually associated with philosophical works and almost border on theological concerns in spite of the atheistic form of argument explicitly adopted by both thinkers. In earlier times we would probably have spoken of 'prophetic works' in this connection. In the case of Adorno, and Benjamin too, it was the earlier writings of Lukács which made the strongest impression on their thought, although from the very beginning both proved completely immune to the seductive power that was exercised by Heidegger on so many intellectuals of his generation. However strongly Adorno always emphasized his opposition to the later Lukács, who ended up defending the cultural policies of the Soviet Union in the Stalinist period, his proximity to the thought of the Hungarian philosopher during the 1920s has not been sufficiently recognized. For this reason it is worth considering the following report of his first personal encounter with Lukács, as documented in a letter dated 17/18 June 1925 which Adorno dispatched from Vienna to his friend Kracauer:

Immediately after my return something sensational happened: [Soma] Morgenstern called me up and invited me to meet Lukács, whom he had already got to know through a rather dubious Hungarian writer called [Béla] Balazs. On Saturday I was standing outside his place, all on my own, in Hütteldorf, Isbarygasse 12, where he occupies a pointedly primitive room on the ground floor. He immediately made a deep and powerful impression upon me; a small, delicate, and unkempt fair-haired Eastern European Jew with a Talmudic nose and wonderfully deep unfathomable eyes. He looked quite the scholar in his linen sporting jacket, yet there was also an entirely unconventional or deathly mild and lucid atmosphere about him which almost betrays a shy personality behind it all. He embodies the ideal of inconspicuousness and indeed also an idea of intangibility. I immediately sensed that he also lay beyond any possible merely human relationship, and in the three or more hours of conversation which ensued I conducted myself accordingly in a very reticent fashion. So the discussion was really more like an interview than a conversation. I am in the process of writing up what was said and will send you the result in due course. Since I am so busy today and can write to you only briefly, here are a just couple of points in this regard. He began by thoroughly disavowing his theory of the novel, claiming that it was 'idealist and mythological' in character. In contrast, he emphasized the 'substantive' understanding of history provided by the Marxian dialectic. When I objected that this too is idealism (which he did not really grasp), he responded by saying 1) that the object is 'taken up and produced in its being in and for itself' precisely through this dialectic (something which I shall never understand); and 2) that true nature is something that will only be revealed in the 'classless society.' He emphatically rejects Bloch's interpretation of his 'agnosticism'; what Bloch sees as 'the shell' is the whole world for him. He endorsed Feuerbach's anthropomorphism, apart from its neglect of Hegel's 'logic of appearance'; in other words, the fact that God has proved influential as a historical factor means that he is 'actual' (an appalling thought!). Finally he indulged in a violent polemic against Kierkegaard against whom he says he has written a book which somehow got lost in Hungary. He claims the latter's critique of Hegel strikes the 'Hegel who misunderstood himself in panlogistic terms' but not the thinker who has been clarified in Marxian terms. He thinks Kierkegaard does not recognize history or objective reality, that he never attains what is really concrete, that his Calvinistic God is nothing but a 'black abyss of despair', and (becoming malicious in the usual way here) that he is the ideological representative of the dying bourgeois world. In this polemic against Kierkegaard he also turned against you (I had indicated our shared intellectual outlook right at the beginning) on account of Bloch's critique, which particularly irks him. And then again later against both of us: he thinks the question of 'personality' arises from 'private problems' with which 'history does not concern itself'.

At one point he really shocked me: when he announced that in his conflict with the Third International his critics are right, concretely speaking, and what is required, in dialectical terms, is only his own absolute commitment to dialectic. It is in this madness that his human greatness and the tragic reversal consist. He expresses reluctantly terrible things about Tolstoi, perhaps not without implicit reference to himself.

In 1949 Adorno wrote a polemical piece directed against the essay 'Heidegger redivivus' which Lukács had published in East Germany (Adorno's polemic, which was not actually published in his lifetime, can be found in GS 20.1, pp. 251ff.). Adorno here interprets Lukács's critique of Heidegger as a 'textbook example of quite inadequate transcendent critique'. Instead of attempting

> to unfold the social-political implications of the fascistic cult of 'being', the hierarchical articulation of 'origins', ... by exploring and defining the immanent inconsistencies here, Lukács forgets the problematic of reification, to which such an analysis should be referred, and takes up a reified standpoint himself, namely a position where the categories of being and consciousness simply appear as given in a quite unmediated way, as if all talk of dialectic in Marxism were never seriously meant in the first place. (Ibid., p. 252)

As a result,

> we are faced with the rather grotesque situation that it is the bourgeois
> thinker Heidegger who critically applies the category of reification in
> relation to those we call the great thinkers, and to the 'legacy' of Plato
> and Aristotle, albeit with a rather displaced emphasis, while the Marxist
> Lukács shrinks from such critique because it appears to pay insufficient
> honour to the history of spirit and ultimately to real humanity. However
> suspect Heidegger's mythologizing attempt to get 'back to origins' remains
> – something incidentally that he also shares with phenomenology as a
> whole – there is unquestionably a truth moment to this very critique of
> the great philosophical tradition which Lukács ultimately appears to have
> missed. And this is the idea that these thinkers, exponents of an urban-
> bourgeois civilization, certainly already reveal aspects of that reification
> of consciousness and associated processes of domination which are grounded
> in the relations of production themselves, and which only a very short-
> sighted historicist perspective could date back to the seventeenth century
> at the earliest. (Ibid., p. 253)

One of the few commentators who had a genuine sense for the 'affinity'
between Heidegger and Lukács was Lucien Goldmann, who relatively
early on interpreted *Being and Time* as a polemical response to *History
and Class Consciousness* (see Goldmann, *Mensch, Gemeinschaft und
Welt in der Philosophie Immanuel Kants*, Zurich, 1945; *Immanuel Kant*,
trans. Robert Black, New Left Books, 1971). Goldmann had planned
a specific work on Lukács and Heidegger which would have explored
the relationship between their two principal early books, but the text
in question never advanced beyond the 'Introduction'. This was published
posthumously along with a series of related lectures by Goldmann from
1967–8 (Goldmann, *Lukács et Heidegger: fragments posthumes établis
et présentés par Youssef Ishaghpour*, Paris, 1973). Yet when Goldmann
attempts to place Adorno in relation to the constellation of Lukács and
Heidegger the results are somewhat bizarre or even unintentionally comic.
We are told that

> Adorno ends up with the idea of a purely negative dialectic, with an
> attitude of rejection which requires [!] an impoverishment of content, a
> rejection and impoverishment which would find its ideal expression in
> Beckett. In terms which are almost reminiscent of Heidegger – whom he
> once so vigorously criticized – Adorno now repudiates everything con-
> nected with popular consciousness and any accommodation with popular
> consciousness, and thus ends up, by virtue of this critique, defending
> positions which are rather conservative. (Ibid., p. 169)

Perhaps it should be pointed out on Goldmann's behalf that these obtuse
observations derive from a transcription which was based on tape recordings and which he may well have been unwilling to publish in this form.
4   It was not possible to identify precisely such a passage in Nietzsche,
but see his remarks in section 12 of *The Antichrist*: 'I except a few

skeptics – the decent type in the history of philosophy: the rest are simply unaware of the most basic requirements of intellectual honesty. All these great enthusiasts and prodigies behave like our little females: they consider "beautiful sentiments" adequate arguments, regard a heaving bosom as the bellows of the deity, and conviction a *criterion* of truth' (F. Nietzsche, *Sämtliche Werke*, Vol. 6: *Der Fall Wagner u. a.*, Munich, 1988, p. 178; *The Antichrist*, trans. Walter Kaufmann, in *The Portable Nietzsche*, p. 578).

5   See Lecture 11 above, p. 108.

6   Adorno is probably thinking of the following passage from §47 of *Being and Time*:

> Yet, the no-longer-being-in-the-world of the deceased (understood in an extreme sense) is still a being [*ein Sein*] in the sense of the mere objective presence [*Nur-noch-vorhandensein*] of a corporeal thing encountered ... The *end* of the being qua Dasein is the *beginning* of this being [*Seienden*] qua something merely [*bloßen*] present ... Even the objectively present corpse is, viewed theoretically, still a possible object for pathological anatomy whose understanding is oriented toward the idea of life. (*Sein und Zeit*, p. 238; *Being and Time*, Stambaugh, p. 229)

7   Quintilian's example of a paradoxical derivation of one word from another (*Institutio oratoria*, I, 6): *lucus*, a (dark) grove where no 'light' penetrates. See Ernst Robert Curtius, *Europäische Literatur und lateinisches Mittelalter*, 2nd edn, Bern, 1954, p. 487.

8   See Ludwig Rubiner, *Der Mensch in der Mitte*, Berlin, 1917.

9   A book with this precise title has not been identified, although two brochures with the (same) title *Man at the Centre of the Social Order* did appear in 1953. Compare Adorno's very similar remarks in *The Jargon of Authenticity*:

> To characterize the change in function of the word 'man', we need only consider two titles which resemble one another. At the time of the German November Revolution, there appeared a book by the pacifist Ludwig Rubiner, *Man in the Middle*; in the fifties, a book called *Man at the Center of the Business Operation*. Thanks to its abstractness, the concept [of man] lets itself be squirted like grease into the same machinery it once wanted to assail. Its pathos, meanwhile evaporated, still echoes in the ideology which holds that business, which must be operated by human beings, exists for their sake. This means that the organization has to take care of its workers so that their productivity will climb. (GS 6, p. 454; *The Jargon of Authenticity*, Tarnowski and Will, pp. 61–2)

10 The meaning of this phrase, which the editor was unable to find in the writings of Karl Kraus, appears to have been strangely misinterpreted by Adorno in this context, as if he had forgotten his own earlier reference to it in his essay 'Aldous Huxley and Utopia':

> An order which does away with the irrationality in which commodity production is entangled but also satisfies needs will equally do away with

the practical spirit, which is reflected even in the non-utilitarianism of bourgeois *l'art pour l'art*. It would abolish not merely the traditional antagonism between production and consumption, but also its most recent unification in state capitalism, and it would converge with the idea that, in the words of Karl Kraus, 'God created man not as consumer or producer but as man.' (GS 10.1, p. 113; in *Prisms*, trans. Samuel Weber and Shierry Weber, Spearman, 1967, p. 110)

Lecture 15

1 The opening sentence of the lecture is missing in the transcription (see Vo 5858) and has been reconstructed by the editor.

2 See the Preface to Hegel's *Philosophy of Right*: 'When philosophy paints its grey in grey, then has a shape of life grown old. By philosophy's grey in grey it cannot be rejuvenated but only understood. The owl of Minerva begins its flight only with the falling of dusk' (Hegel, *Werke*, Vol. 8: *Grundlinien der Philosophie des Rechts oder Naturrecht und Staatswissenschaft im Grundrisse*, p. 28; *Outlines of the Philosophy of Right*, trans. T. M. Knox, Oxford University Press, 2008, p. 16).

3 Adorno discusses de Maistre in NaS IV.13, p. 37; *History and Freedom*, Livingstone, p. 24.

4 For Simmel's thesis on 'life', see the lecture which Adorno delivered in 1940 in the sociology seminar of Robert MacIver at Columbia University in New York: 'On the Problem of Individuality and Causality in Simmel', in *Frankfurter Adorno Blätter* VIII, 2002. And on Simmel's 'philosophy of life' generally, see, in particular, Hans-Joachim Lieber, 'Kulturkritik und Gesellschaftstheorie im Denken Georg Simmels', in Lieber, *Kulturkritik und Lebensphilosophie: Studien zur Deutschen Philosophie der Jahrhundertwende*, Darmstadt, 1974, pp. 67ff.

5 See Heidegger, *Kant und das Problem der Metaphysik*, pp. 157ff.; *Kant and the Problem of Metaphysics* (§§32–4).

6 Adorno discussed the loss of historical consciousness on several occasions. In particular see his lecture of 1959, 'The Meaning of Working through the Past':

> Hermann Heimpel has on several occasions spoken of the how the consciousness of historical continuity is atrophying in Germany, a symptom of that societal weakening of the ego Horkheimer and I had already attempted to derive in the *Dialectic of Enlightenment*. Empirical findings, for example, that the younger generation often does not know who Bismarck and Kaiser Wilhelm I were, have confirmed this suspicion of the loss of history. (GS 10.2, p. 557; *Critical Models: Interventions and Catchwords*, trans. H. W. Pickford, Columbia University Press, 1998, p. 91)

He expressed such thoughts even more pointedly perhaps in his essay 'In Memory of Eichendorff' of 1957:

> The break in the continuity of historical consciousness that Hermann Heimpel saw results in a polarization: on the one hand, cultural goods

that are antiquarian, and perhaps even shaped for ideological purposes; and on the other, a contemporary historical moment that, precisely because it is lacking in memory, is ready to subscribe to the status quo, even by mirroring it where it opposes it. The rhythm of time has become distorted. While the streets of philosophy are echoing with the metaphysics of time, time itself, once measured by the steady course of a person's life, has become alienated from human beings; this is probably why it is being discussed so feverishly. (GS 11, p. 69; *Notes to Literature*, trans. Shierry Weber Nicholsen, Columbia University Press, 1991, Vol. 1, p. 55)

7   Goethe offered a similar diagnosis in 1827 in his 'Zahme Xenien', albeit with a contrary emphasis: 'You have it better / Than our old continent. / You have no ruined castles / You are not inwardly disturbed / In living time with / Useless memories / And fruitless strife' (Goethe, *Sämtliche Werke*, Part I, Vol. 2, p. 739).

8   Adorno cites the same phrase in NaS IV.15, p. 248, and translates it into German: '"History belongs in the garbage," as we could freely render it.' And he continues, as if he wanted to correct the Goethe quotation cited in the previous note with Goethe himself, by saying: 'The same formulation was basically already anticipated in the last great speech of Mephistopheles at the end of *Faust* where we learn of all that was and no longer is "that it were better had it never been."'

9   See *Genesis* 25: 7–8: 'And these are the days of the years of Abraham's life which he lived, an hundred threescore and fifteen years. / Then Abraham gave up the ghost, and died in a good old age, an old man, and full of years; and was gathered to his people.'

10 On the concept of substance in Kant's philosophy, see NaS IV.4, pp. 301ff.; *Kant's Critique of Pure Reason*, Jephcott, pp. 107ff.

11 The passage in question is actually to be found in the *Groundwork*: 'In the kingdom of ends everything has either a *price* or a *dignity* [*Würde*]. What has a price can be replaced by something else as its *equivalent*; what on the other hand is raised above all price and therefore admits of no equivalent has a dignity' (*Werke*, Vol. IV, pp. 67f.; *Groundwork of the Metaphysics of Morals*, trans. Mary J. Gregor, in Kant, *Practical Philosophy*, Cambridge University Press, 1996, p. 84).

12 On the theme of the 'disenchantment of the world', see NaS IV.13, pp. 269 and 443, n. 285; *History and Freedom*, Livingstone, pp. 195 and 318, n. 7.

13 See Martin Heidegger, *Aus der Erfahrung des Denkens*, Pfullingen, 1954, pp. 6f., 10f., 12f., 18, 22 and 27; the essay from which Adorno quotes here, 'The Thinker as Poet', is included in Heidegger, *Poetry, Language, Thought*, trans. Albert Hofstadter, New York, 1971, pp. 3–14.

14 The Swabian poet Cäsar Flaischlen (1864–1920) also wrote a number of plays and novels, the latter including *Martin Lehnhardt* (1895) and *Jost Seyfried* (1905). He was also the author of the poem 'Hab Sonne im Herzen', which was once extremely popular with the educated classes. Max Jungnickel (1890–1945, lost in action in the Soviet Union), poet and writer, author of titles such as *Der Himmels-Schneider* (1913), *Ins*

Blaue hinein (1917) and *Brennende Sense* (1928), was an active supporter of the Nazis. Adorno had already invoked Jungnickel in relation to Heidegger on other occasions (see GS 6, p. 448; *The Jargon of Authenticity*, Tarnowski and Will, p. 52). See also GS 11, p. 13: 'Wherever philosophy imagines that by borrowing from literature it can abolish objectified thought and its history – what is commonly termed the antithesis of subject and object – and even hopes that Being itself will speak, in a *poésie* concocted of Parmenides and Jungnickel, it starts to turn into a washed-out cultural babble' (*Notes to Literature*, Nicholsen, Vol. 1, 'The Essay as Form', p. 6).

Lecture 16

1   Adorno is alluding to the physician and philosopher Alfons Bilharz (1836–1925), author of *Metaphysik als Lehre vom Vorbewußten* (Wiesbaden, 1897) and *Philosophie als Universalwissenschaft* (Wiesbaden, 1912). In the collection to which Adorno refers, Bilharz presented a poem entitled 'Sum ergo cogito' [I am therefore I think] which contained echoes of the first stanza of Goethe's poem *Gefunden* of 1813. In his poem Bilharz attempted to capture the experience that transformed him from 'a scientist into a philosopher': 'Once in a wood I strolled content, / To look for nothing / My sole intent. / Struck by light from heavenly heights / At earth's own centre I felt I stood / The rays of light my thought did turn / Disclosed for me the sacred truth. / The truth revealed not Thought as Being / but Being as Thought in simple union' (*Die Philosophie der Gegenwart in Selbstdarstellungen*, ed. Raymund Schmidt, Vol. 5, Leipzig, 1924, pp. 2f.).

2   Adorno had already made this point with obvious reference to Heidegger in 1958 – even before the *The Jargon of Authenticity* – in 'The Essay as Form'. See GS 11, p. 14; *Notes to Literature*, Nicholsen, Vol. 1, p. 7.

3   For a discussion of Scotist ontology, see Karl Heinz Haag, *Der Fortschritt in der Philosophie*, pp. 51f., and Günther Mensching, *Das Allgemeine und Besondere: Der Ursprung des modernen Denkens im Mittelalter*, Stuttgart, 1992, pp. 210ff.

4   Adorno offers a similar interpretation in NaS IV.13, p. 18; *History and Freedom*, Livingstone, p. 11.

5   On the increasingly 'static character which is beginning to reveal itself in society', see Adorno's lecture 'Über Statik und Dynamik als soziologische Kategorien', GS 8, pp. 217ff.

6   A mistake on Adorno's part since he had not actually mentioned this earlier.

7   See Paul Ludwig Landsberg, *Die Welt des Mittelalters und wir. Ein geschichtsphilosophischer Versuch über den Sinn eines Zeitlaters*, Bonn, 1923.

8   The exponents of 'critical theory' had always regarded this 'feeling' as a criterion for the misconceptions perpetrated by modern ontology.

See, for example, the observations in Karl Heinz Haag's post-doctoral dissertation (1960): 'The question is whether the ontological structures exist in their own right, Φύσει [by nature], or whether they are mere products of thought, θέσει [by convention] ... If we assume ... this question has already implicitly been answered – as if it were indeed a desirable thing to possess an ontology once more at last – we already thereby come to a decision regarding the truth or untruth of ontology' (*Kritik der neueren Ontologie*, p. 47. See also Lecture 22, p. 230).

9 Originally presented as a lecture in Frankfurt on 25 October 1958; first published in *Archiv für Philosophie*, Vol. 9, nos 1–2 (1959), pp. 67ff.; now in GS 5, pp. 295ff.

10 See NaS IV.14, pp. 148 and 269, n. 173; *Metaphysics: Concept and Problems*, Jephcott, pp. 94 and 174.

11 See especially NaS IV.4, pp. 132ff.; *Kant's Critique of Pure Reason*, Livingstone, pp. 85ff.

12 It can hardly be said that the political intention behind Adorno's critique of Heidegger or, indeed, his critique of Heidegger's thought as a whole have attracted the attention or exercised the effect which they deserve. In this regard it is symptomatic that an enormous 965-page volume by Dieter Thomä on the textual history and reception of Heidegger, which appeared with Adorno's publisher Suhrkamp in 1990, makes almost no mention of Adorno's critique, even though a central concern of the book is supposed to be the question 'What is the relationship between Heidegger's philosophy and his engagement with the Nazis?' While the author discusses in some detail the most recent minor philosopher to have voiced his thoughts on this matter, he has absolutely nothing to say about the fact that Adorno dedicated two substantial discussions to this very question, namely the chapters which constitute the first part of Adorno's principal work, *Negative Dialectics*. In Thomä's view Adorno adopts a 'position which does not see Heidegger in terms of his own theoretical development but already treats him as a representative of a particular orientation or tendency', and such an approach 'ultimately leads to a non-philosophical explanation of his philosophy'. And this supposedly devastating judgement, as we have just indicated, is based not on the critique advanced in *Negative Dialectics* but merely on *The Jargon of Authenticity* – and perhaps indeed not even on that text, but on a resumé of his critical views which Adorno happened to provide in a letter (see Dieter Thomä, *Die Zeit des Selbst und die Zeit danach: Zur Kritik der Textgeschichte Martin Heideggers 1910–1976*, Suhrkamp, 1990, p. 486).

13 Alfred Rosenberg (1893–1946), one of the most important ideologists of the Nazi movement, from 1923 editor of the *Völkischer Beobachter*, and from 1933 the leading figure in the NSDAP responsible for elaborating the Nazi 'world-view'. During the Second World War he was involved in confiscating and appropriating works of art and other cultural

assets, and from 1941 he was the Minister for the Occupied Regions of Eastern Europe. At the Nuremberg Trials he was condemned to death as a war criminal. Rosenberg published his book *Der Mythus des 20. Jahrhunderts* in 1930:

> The 'Myth of the Twentieth Century' is the myth of blood. It claims that the highest human values arose and flourished on the basis of the Nordic way of life. Culture emerged wherever the Nordic races set foot. It was Nordic man that blessed the land of India, Persia, Greece, and Rome, and Nordic man was the inspired benefactor who was destined to rule. His achievements only decline when subhuman man, especially 'Eastern-Syrian' man, gains ground, when Nordic man consents to miscegenation and abandons his heritage to bastard offspring. ... Rosenberg's 'Myth of the Twentieth Century' is a philosophy for hardy souls; it persuades them that everything is a matter of blood. Thus it perfectly sets the mood for a situation of civil war: Rosenberg's mysticism of blood is the philosophical reflection of the Fascist thirst for blood. (Ernst Niekisch, *Das Reich der niederen Dämonen*, Berlin, 1957, pp. 92 and 95)

14 Adorno is alluding to Schelling's *System of Transcendental Idealism* of 1800.
15 Adorno is referring to Husserl's *Ideas for a Pure Phenomenology and Phenomenological Philosophy* of 1922.
16 Adorno is alluding to the supplementary text 'On the Phenomenological Constitution of Judgement', which was included in Husserl's book *Formal and Transcendental Logic* of 1929.
17 René Descartes, *Meditations on First Philosophy*, trans. E. S. Haldane and G. R. T. Ross, in *Philosophical Works of Descartes*, Dover, 1955, Vol. I, pp. 145–6:

> At the same time I must remember that I am a man, and that consequently I am in the habit of sleeping, and in my dreams representing to myself the same things or sometimes even less probable things, than do those who are insane in their waking moments ... But in thinking over this I remind myself that on many occasions I have in sleep been deceived by similar illusions, and in dwelling carefully on this reflection I see so manifestly that there are no certain indications by which we may clearly distinguish wakefulness from sleep that I am lost in astonishment. And my astonishment is such that it is almost capable of persuading me that I now dream.

18 See *Faust I*, verse 382: 'what inwardly holds the world together'.
19 Heidegger, *Platons Lehre von der Wahrheit*, pp. 84f.; *Letter on 'Humanism'*, in *Pathmarks*, McNeill, p. 257.
20 The word *enthalten* [contain] has been inserted in the German text by the editor. Otherwise the preceding preposition *in* would have to be deleted and *Being and Time* would then effectively be equated with the trash by Rosenberg, which was hardly Adorno's intention.

Lecture 17

1   Adorno had not actually employed the expression 'myth of the nineteenth century' earlier in the lectures. In this connection it may be that he was thinking of one of the principal works of anti-Semitic literature, namely Houston Stewart Chamberlain's book *The Foundations of the Nineteenth Century* ([1899] 1911).

2   See the report of Hippolytos quoted in NaS IV.14, p. 271, n. 179; *Metaphysics: Concept and Problems*, Jephcott, p. 175. For a conspectus of the cosmological and theological theories of Epicurus and his successors, see A. A. Long and D. N. Sedley, *The Hellenistic Philosophers*, Cambridge University Press, 1987.

3   The only expression 'mentioned' specifically by Heidegger in this connection seems to be 'the famous Epicurean warning λάθε βιώσας' [live in obscurity] (Martin Heidegger, *Vorträge und Aufsätze*, p. 262).

4   See Walter Benjamin, *Gesammelte Schriften*, Vol. II.1, 2nd edn, Frankfurt am Main 1989, p. 175; also Vol. I.1, 3rd edn, 1990, p. 138.

5   See Lecture 9, p. 84.

6   *hendiadys* – 'one thing by two': a technical term in classical rhetoric for naming one thing with two distinct terms.

7   When he speaks of the 'Protestant side', Adorno is referring primarily to the theology of Rudolf Bultmann. In this connection, see Adorno's correspondence with Paul Tillich regarding the hermeneutic 'Word of God' theology that was heavily influenced by Heidegger: quoted in NaS IV.14, p. 280, n. 213; *Metaphysics: Concept and Problems*, Jephcott, pp. 181–2, n. 4.

8   See, for example, the following passage from Heidegger's letter to 'German students' published in the Freiburg student newspaper on 3 November 1933: 'It is not principles or "Ideas" that must furnish the rules of your being. The Leader [*Führer*] himself and he alone *is* today and in future the German reality and its law. Learn to know this ever more deeply: From now onwards every single thing demands decision and every act responsibility. Heil Hitler!' (Cited in Guido Schneeberger, *Nachlese zu Heidegger: Dokumente zu seinem Leben und Denken*, Bern, 1962, pp. 135f.)

9   See the various texts collected in Guido Schneeberger's *Nachlese*, the most important of which is Heidegger's rectoral address 'Die Selbstbehauptung der deutschen Universität: Rede, gehalten bei der feierlichen Übernahme des Rektorats der Universität Freiburg i. Breslau am 27.5.1933, Breslau o. Jahr'. The text has been reprinted in a new edition (Frankfurt am Main, 1983) along with Heidegger's reflections on the subject from 1945: *Das Rektorat 1933/4: Tatsachen und Gedanken* (pp. 21ff.). Many of these texts and materials are translated in R. Wolin (ed.), *The Heidegger Controversy: A Critical Reader*, MIT Press, 1993. See also Heidegger, *Nature, History, State 1933–1934*, trans. and ed. Gregory Fried and Richard Polt, Bloomsbury Academic, 2015.

10   See Karl Löwith, *Heidegger: Denker in dürftiger Zeit*, now in *Sämtliche Schriften*, Vol. 8, Stuttgart, 1984, pp. 124ff.
11   See Heinrich Zimmer, *Maya: Der indische Mythos*, Stuttgart, 1939.
12   See Max Scheler, *Der Formalismus in der Ethik und die materiale Wertethik*.
13   But see NaS IV.4, pp. 338ff., and especially pp. 409ff., n. 293; *Kant's Critique of Pure Reason*, Livingstone, pp. 224ff., and 277f., n. 14.

Lecture 18

1   See especially GS 5, pp. 190ff; *Against Epistemology*, Domingo, pp. 186ff.
2   See, however, Adorno's remarks on the idea of the contingent a priori in contrast to the formal a priori in Husserl: NaS IV.14, pp. 255f., n. 110; *Metaphysics: Concept and Problems*, Jephcott, p. 164, n. 6.
3   For a relevant discussion of the problem of universals in medieval philosophy, see Karl Heinz Haag, *Kritik der neueren Ontologie*, pp. 10ff.; the same author's *Der Fortschritt in der Philosophie*, pp. 37ff.; Günther Mensching, *Das Allgemeine und das Besondere*, pp. 59ff.; Rolf Tiedemann, *Studien zur Philosophie Walter Benjamins*, 2nd edn, Frankfurt am Main, 1973, pp. 18ff.
4   In this regard, the thematic index to Elisabeth Ströker's edition of Husserl's *Gesammelte Schriften* refers only to §39 of the *Ideas for a Pure Phenomenology and Phenomenological Philosophy*.
5   Adorno's most extensive discussion of the concept of 'categorial intuition' is found in the final chapter of his *Metakritik*: GS 5, pp. 190ff.; *Against Epistemology*, Domingo, pp. 186ff.
6   Adorno developed this argument most fully in *Negative Dialectics*, especially in the chapter entitled 'Being and Existence' (GS 6, pp. 104ff.; *Negative Dialectics*, Ashton, pp. 97–131).
7   See note 4 to Lecture 8 above.
8   See, for example, Heidegger's essay 'The Question concerning Technology' of 1953: 'Since man drives technology forward, he takes part in ordering as a way of revealing. But the unconcealment itself, within which ordering unfolds, is never a human handiwork [*Gemächte*], any more than is the realm through which man is already passing every time he as a subject relates to an object' (*Vorträge und Aufsätze*, p. 26; *The Question concerning Technology*, Levitt, p. 18). While the nominalized form *Gemächte* (meaning 'fabrication' or 'handiwork', and related to the verb *machen*) is extremely rare, it seems highly unlikely Heidegger was aware that it has survived to this day as a word for male genitalia (deriving from the Old High German form *gimath*). See Grimm's *Wörterbuch*, Vol. 5, 1984 reprint, col. 3148).
9   This is Adorno's terminology. He is referring to the tendency to divide absolutely everything simply in terms of true or false, black or white, yes or no. See GS 3, p. 333: 'It [i.e. the hieroglyphic meaning of the

consumer of mass culture] articulates all phenomena down into their most subtle nuances in accordance with the simple two-valued logic of do and don't, and through this reduction of precisely what is alien and unintelligible it overtakes the consumers of culture.'

10   See Genesis 2: 17 to 3: 22.

11   Jean Beaufret (1907–1982), a French follower of Heidegger and addressee of Heidegger's *Letter on 'Humanism'*.

12   Adorno later attempted to fulfil this demand in the section of *Aesthetic Theory* dedicated to the question of natural beauty (GS 7, pp. 97ff.; *Aesthetic Theory*, Hullot-Kentor, pp. 81ff.).

Lecture 19

1   At this point Adorno begins to read from his Paris lecture 'The Ontological Need', and specifically from p. 17 of the typescript (= Ts 13606). The chapter of *Negative Dialectics* which bears the same title was elaborated in 1965 on the basis of this fourth version of that lecture. The material presented in the present lecture corresponds to GS 8, pp. 83–94; *Negative Dialectics*, Ashton, pp. 76–87.

2   See *Sein und Zeit*, p. 38; *Being and Time*, Stambaugh, pp. 35–6.

3   In relation to Adorno's following remarks, see the section of *Negative Dialectics* entitled 'Unsuccessful Realism': GS 6, pp. 86f.; *Negative Dialectics*, Ashton, p. 78.

4   See Lecture 18, p. 191, and note 8 to Lecture 18.

5   The German Youth Movement of the early twentieth century represented a kind of cultural revolution in which significant numbers of bourgeois youth tried to break free of the Wilhelminian world of their parents, yet they proved entirely unable to withstand the most reactionary tendencies, namely the nationalism and anti-Semitism, which were carried over from the pre-war period. The beginnings of the Youth Movement go back to the founding of the *Wandervogel* Association in 1898, a group which was effectively dominant until about 1910, when leadership of the movement passed to the so-called *Freideutsche Jugend*. Walter Benjamin played a certain role in this latter group up until the outbreak of war in 1914, when he completely severed his relations with the Youth Movement for good. In the subsequent period the *Bündische Jugend* became ever more influential and eventually led over large parts of the Youth Movement to the Nazi cause in 1933. In contrast, the Youth Movement never seemed to have held any attractions whatsoever for Adorno, who was a full eleven years younger than Benjamin. Adorno may also have been immunized against this influence by his experience of the musical activities and tendencies of the Youth Movement. And indeed he would mount a sustained polemic against such activities and tendencies in the period after the Second World War as well (see GS 14, pp. 67ff.). The sharpest expression of his critical attitude to the German Youth Movement can be found in his childhood reminiscences of Amorbach (GS 10.1, p. 307).

6   See Heidegger, *Einführung in die Metaphysik*, p. 155: 'In contrast, to go expressly up to the limit of Nothing in the question about Being, and to take Nothing into the question of Being – this is the first and only fruitful step toward the true overcoming of nihilism' (*Introduction to Metaphysics*, Fried and Polt, p. 226).

7   See the opening section of Hegel's *Logic*: 'Being, the indeterminate immediate, is in fact *nothing*, and neither more than less than nothing' (Hegel, *Werke*, Vol. 5, p. 83; *Science of Logic*, Miller, p. 82).

8   See Adorno's reference to Heidegger's *Introduction to Metaphysics* in *Negative Dialectics* (GS 6, p. 86; *Negative Dialectics*, Ashton, p. 79).

9   See Karl Heinz Haag, *Kritik der neueren Ontologie*, p. 73.

10   In relation to the following, compare the section 'On Categorial Intuition' in *Negative Dialectics* (GS 6, pp. 87ff.; *Negative Dialectics*, Ashton, pp. 80ff.).

11   It was not possible to identify the use of this expression in Husserl; but see GS 5, p. 209; *Against Epistemology*, Domingo, p. 207.

12   In the corresponding passage in *Negative Dialectics*, Adorno inserted the phrase (absent from the typescript: Ts 12616) 'as Günther Anders observed' (GS 6, p. 90; *Negative Dialectics*, Ashton, p. 83).

13   The expression 'administered world' – not so much a specific category as an expressive catchphrase – was invariably used by the leading exponents of critical theory after their return to Germany when referring to the almost seamlessly organized character of modern society (in the meantime we would now probably speak of the completely 'marketized' character of contemporary social and economic life). In this respect, the principal issue for Adorno – who sometimes claimed that such expressions were coined or introduced by Critical Theory, although he was not sure whether it was he himself or Horkheimer who first used the expression 'administered world' – was 'what the administered world makes of its compulsory members' (GS 6 p. 51; *Negative Dialectics*, Ashton, p. 41), which was the liquidation of individuals and their freedom: 'the administered world has the tendency to choke all spontaneity' (GS 10.2, p. 351). Administrative behaviour, which had become an independent force in its right and was now pursued for its own sake, had already begun to exercise profound effects on all aspects of the superstructure in Adorno's lifetime and had deeply damaged the fields of art and theory which once stood for critique and contestation: 'In the administered world neutralization is universal' (GS 7, p. 339; *Aesthetic Theory*, Hullot-Kentor, p. 299). Yet Adorno did not want to demonize the administered world in an abstract way. He attempted to offer a dialectical approach which might disclose the possibility of something quite different harboured within it rather than simply posited against that world. Thus in 'Culture and Administration', an essay from 1961, Adorno writes:

> If the administered world is one where every little corner is disappearing, it might still be able, through the insights and capacities of those on which it can draw, to create centres of freedom which merely blind and unconscious processes of social selection only destroy. That irrationality which

finds expression in the independent power assumed by administration in
relation to society is the refuge of what is not exhausted in culture itself.
It finds its *ratio* solely through divergence from the prevailing rationality.
(GS 8, p. 145)

14 In relation to the following, see the section of *Negative Dialectics* entitled
    'Being θέσει' (GS 6, pp. 90ff.; *Negative Dialectics*, Ashton, pp. 83ff.).
15 See note 9 to Lecture 12.
16 For Heidegger's understanding with fascism, see Elisabeth Lenk, 'Das
    verborgene Sein', in Theodor W. Adorno und Elisabeth Lenk, *Briefwechsel
    1962–1969*, ed. Elisabeth Lenk, Munich, 2001, pp. 182ff.
17 See the section of *Negative Dialectics* entitled 'The Meaning of Being'
    (GS 6, pp. 93ff.; *Negative Dialectics*, Ashton, p. 85).
18 According to Adorno, the new ontological movements basically attempt
    to restore the old *intentio recta* – namely a direct relation to the object
    – which was defended by scholastic philosophy: 'the faithful trust in an
    external world given as it is, prior to critical reflection, an anthropologi-
    cal condition devoid of self-consciousness which is merely crystallized
    in the context of the relation of the act of knowing to the object known'
    (GS 10.2, p. 746). In traditional 'philosophical terminology', the process
    of reflection 'would go by the name of *intentio obliqua*' (ibid., p. 742),
    namely an indirect relation to the object which is mediated by
    subjectivity.
19 Heidegger's 'What is Metaphysics?', his inaugural address at the Uni-
    versity of Freiburg in 1929, concludes with what he described as 'the
    fundamental question of metaphysics': 'Why are there beings at all, and
    why not far rather Nothing?' (Heidegger, *Was ist Metaphysik?*, p. 38;
    What is Metaphysics?, trans. David Farrel Krell, in Heidegger, *Pathmarks*,
    McNeill, p. 96). See also *Einführung in die Metaphysik*, p. 1 passim;
    Introduction to Metaphysics, Fried and Polt, pp. 1ff.).
20 See Gottfried Wilhelm Leibniz, *Principes de la nature et de la grace,
    fondés en raison*: 'Given that principle [i.e. the principle of sufficient
    reason], the first question we can fairly ask is: *Why is there something
    rather than nothing?*' (*The Principles of Nature and Grace, founded in
    Reason*, in G. W. Leibniz, *Principles of Nature and Grace based on
    Reason*, trans. J. Bennett, p. 4 (2006), retrieved from: earlymoderntexts.com/
    assets/pdfs/leibniz1714a. See also Schelling's remarks in his *Philosophy
    of Revelation*: '… if I try and reach the limit of all thinking, then I must
    also recognize that it is possible that nothing at all existed. The ultimate
    question is always: why is there anything at all, why is there not nothing?
    I cannot answer this question by abstracting from actual being' (F. W.
    J. Schelling, *Philosophie der Offenbarung*, Munich, 1954, p. 242).
21 At the corresponding point in *Negative Dialectics* Adorno refers to his
    book *Hegel: Drei Studien* (Frankfurt am Main, 1963, pp. 127ff.; now
    in GS 5, pp. 343ff.; *Hegel: Three Studies*, Nicholsen, pp. 110ff.).
22 An expression which Adorno used on several other occasions. In his
    lecture on 'The Idea of Natural History', he ascribed it to Hegel, although

it does not appear in this precise form in Hegel's published writings: 'if philosophy wished to remain nothing beyond the registering of this shock, the shock that history presents itself just as much as nature – then indeed, as Hegel reproached Schelling, this would simply be a night of indifference in which all cats are gray. How do we escape this night?' (GS 1, p. 361; 'The Idea of Natural History', in: *Telos* 60 (1984), p. 122). See also GS 6, p. 290; *Negative Dialectics*, Ashton, p. 294; GS 13, p. 125; and GS 20.1, p. 80. In Hegel's *Phenomenology*, the expression in question appears in a slightly different form as 'the night in which, as the saying goes, all cows are black' (*Phenomenology of Spirit*, Miller, p. 9).

Lecture 20

1 At this point some sentences are fragmentary or missing in the transcript (Vo 5926). A hand-written note which has been added here reads: 'impossible to understand'.

2 The text follows the typescript (Ts 13621) from the point where Adorno had broken off at the end of the previous lecture. See the parallel passage in GS 6, p. 94; *Negative Dialectics*, Ashton, pp. 86–7.

3 After German troops had overrun Holland and Belgium, Winston Churchill (1874–1965), who had been prime minister since 10 May 1940, delivered his first speech in that capacity in the House of Commons on 13 May:

> In this crisis I hope I may be pardoned if I do not address the House at any length today. I hope that any of my friends and colleagues, or former colleagues, who are affected by the political reconstruction, will make all allowance for any lack of ceremony with which it has been necessary to act. I would say to the House, as I said to those who have joined this Government: 'I have nothing to offer but blood, toil, tears, and sweat.' We have before us an ordeal of the most grievous kind. We have before us many, many long months of struggle and of suffering. (*Into Battle: Speeches by Winston S. Churchill*, compiled by Randolph S. Churchill, London, 1941, p. 208)

4 For what follows, see the section of *Negative Dialectics* entitled 'Ontology Prescribed' (GS 6, pp. 94ff.; *Negative Dialectics*, Ashton, p. 87).

5 An allusion to Schiller's poem 'Lied der Glocke': 'Sacred order, most blessed / Daughter of Heaven, who binds / All that is equal / In freedom, lightness and joy, / Who granted the building of cities / Who from your groves / Called unto the savage breast, / Entered the huts of men, / Brought them to gentler manners, / And wove the dearest bond of all / The feeling for the Fatherland!' (Friedrich Schiller, *Sämtliche Werke*, ed. Gerhard Fricke und Herbert S. Göpfert, Vol. 1. *Gedichte, Dramen I*, 4th edn, Munich, 1975, p. 438).

6 The 'tremendous power of institutions' is one of the forms in which the administered world finds tangible expression and reveals its inner

tendency towards an oppressive social order where freedom has become nothing but ideology. Arnold Gehlen, in his book *Urmensch und Spät-kultur* (1956), developed a theory of institutions which found an implicit but resolute opponent in Adorno. Gehlen claimed that social institutions are supposed to protect and 'relieve' individuals of otherwise unsup-portable tasks and burdens, that the stability of society is strictly pro-portional to the stability of its institutions, and that the dissolution or even the challenging of institutional structures in modern society could only lead to what he calls an 'exaltation of subjectivity': to excessive or exaggerated demands on individuals and their contingent inner capaci-ties and characteristics. According to Gehlen, this development may well have led to considerable innovations and achievements in the field of modern art but, ultimately, threatens to have disastrous results for contemporary society. Adorno insists, on the contrary, that social insti-tutions reveal an immanent tendency to restrict the freedom of human beings, and that the crucial determining institutions of society, and espe-cially the economic sphere, possess a coercive character which has long undermined, at least in the administered world, those who imagine they are sustained in the alleged sense by social institutions. Adorno claims that, 'even if we concede the indescribable power and significance of institutions in human life' and that

> this power and significance is greater than it has ever been before, we must also recognize that this involves something which is not entirely compatible with the idea of mature and responsible human beings, namely human beings who are capable of deciding things by appeal to their own reason; and that to the extent that human beings do become mature and responsible they also outgrow their need for institutions in this regard. And I would say that the task of education, in the important and emphatic sense of the word, consists in raising human beings to be mature and responsible and in actually reducing institutions to the role which Kant ascribed to them, which is simply that of ensuring that the freedom of no human being threatens the freedom of another. (From a conversation between Adorno, Gehlen and Alexander von Cube on the subject of 'Freedom and Institutions', recorded by West German radio on 3 June 1967)

7 Adorno is alluding to a famous formulation of Heidegger's: '*Da-sein* means: being held out into the nothing' (*Was ist Metaphysik?*, p. 33; *What is Metaphysics?*, in *Pathmarks*, McNeill, p. 91.

8 Adorno, by contrast, offered a defence of 'isms' in *Aesthetic Theory* (GS 7, pp. 43ff.; *Aesthetic Theory*, Hullot-Kentor, pp. 31ff.).

9 For what follows, see the section of *Negative Dialectics* entitled 'Protest against Reification' (GS 6, pp. 97ff.; *Negative Dialectics*, Ashton, p. 89).

10 See Lecture 16, p. 166, and note 7 to Lecture 16 above.

11 Adorno is referring to the first volume of Husserl's *Logical Investiga-tions*, which appeared in 1900. On the problem of relativism, see Lecture 13, pp. 131ff. above.

12   See *Faust Part One*, verse 860 onwards; also quoted in NaS IV.13, p. 387, n. 37; *History and Freedom*, Livingstone, p. 275, n. 7).

13   Both the typescript version which Adorno uses in the lecture here and the text of *Negative Dialectics* refer to the Frankfurt edition of 1949, p. 42 and p. 47.

14   The typescript version which Adorno uses in the lecture here refers to the *Kritik der reinen Vernunft*, ed. Theodor Valentiner, Leipzig, 1913, p. 133. In *Negative Dialectics* he refers to the Academy edition of Kant's works, Vol. IV [it should actually be Vol. III], p. 95 (i.e. B 110).

15   The typescript of Adorno's lecture 'The Ontological Need' ends at this point. For the corresponding passage in *Negative Dialectics*, see GS 6, p. 99; *Negative Dialectics*, Ashton, p. 92.

16   See note 2 to Lecture 8 above.

17   See Lecture 2, p. 12 and p. 19.

18   In what follows Adorno relies on the second Paris lecture on 'Being and Existence' and begins from Ts 1359. It corresponds to the section of *Negative Dialectics* entitled 'Copula' (GS 6, pp. 107ff.; *Negative Dialectics*, Ashton, p. 100).

19   That is to say, not self-signifying but co-signifying. See GS 5, p. 75; *Against Epistemology*, Domingo, p. 68. Here Adorno draws on Oscar Kraus's 'Introduction' to the first volume of Franz Brentano's *Psychologie vom empirischen Standpunkt*, p. XIXf. Kraus also uses these concepts in a note to his edition of Brentano's *Ursprung sittlicher Erkenntnis*, Leipzig, 1921, pp. 48f.

20   According to Husserl, these are expressions which are only fully meaningful in relation to the circumstances of their utterance or a particular act of perception: 'Genuinely occasional expressions have no doubt a meaning which varies from case to case, but in all such changes a common element is left over, which distinguishes *their* ambiguity from that of a casual equivocation' (Edmund Husserl, *Gesammelte Schriften*, Vol. 4, *Logische Untersuchungen*, Vol. 2, Part II, pp. 552f.; *Logical Investigations*, trans. J. N. Findlay, Vol. 2, p. 683).

Lecture 21

1   In what follows Adorno repeats almost word for word what he had already read out from his second Paris lecture on 'Being and Existence' at the end of the previous lecture and then continues with the same text (Ts 13959). The corresponding passages in *Negative Dialectics* are to be found in the sections entitled 'Copula' and 'No Transcendence of Being' (GS 6, pp. 107ff.; *Negative Dialectics*, Ashton, pp. 100ff.).

2   Adorno may have been thinking of §16 from Hegel's *Propaedeutic*, which he had already discussed in one of his seminars:

   1. The beginning of Science is the immediate and indeterminate concept of *being*. – 2. On account of its complete lack of content this is the same

as *nothing*. This nothing, as the thought of that emptiness, is itself being and on account of its purity is the same as the former. – 3. There is therefore no distinction in it, for what it is is simply the positing of both as distinct and the disappearance of each into its opposite, or it is pure *becoming*. (G. W. F. Hegel, *Werke*, Vol. 4, *Nürnberger und Heidelberger Schriften 1808–1817*, p. 13)

See also the beginning of Hegel's *Logic*, especially the 'Remarks' in the opening chapter on 'Being', *Werke*, Vol. V, pp. 84ff.; *Science of Logic*, Miller, pp. 83ff.

3   The text of the Paris lecture refers to Walter Benjamin, *Schriften I*, Frankfurt am Main, 1955, pp. 366ff. and 426ff.; the corresponding references in Benjamin's *Gesammelte Schriften* are Vol. I.2, pp. 471ff. and 605ff.

4   Adorno is alluding to the Goddess Freia in scene 2 of Wagner's *Rheingold* who dispenses everlasting youth to all the Gods and Goddesses: 'Golden apples grow in her garden; she alone knows how to tend them; the taste of the fruit confers on her kinsfolk endlessly never-ageing youth' (Richard Wagner, *Dichtungen und Schriften*, Vol. 3, p. 29).

5   For what follows, see the section of *Negative Dialectics* entitled 'The Child's Question' (GS 6, pp. 116ff.; *Negative Dialectics*, Ashton, p. 110).

6   An expression used by Hegel in the *Encyclopaedia Logic*:

> Thinking that produces only *finite* determinations and moves among them is called *understanding* (in the more precise sense of the word). More specifically, the *finitude* of the thought-determinations is to be construed in this double sense: the one, that they are *merely subjective* and are in permanent opposition to the objective; the other, that due to their *limited content* generally they persist in opposition to each other and even more so to the absolute. To provide a more detailed introduction and in order to explicate the importance and the standpoint here given to logic the *positions of thought towards objectivity* will here be studied. (G. W. F. Hegel, *Werke*, Vol. 8, p. 91; *Encyclopedia of the Philosophical Sciences*, Part I: *Science of Logic*, Brinkmann and Dahlstrom, §25, p. 66)

Adorno appropriated this expression and liked to use it in a variety of contexts. See GS 5, pp. 52 and 296 (*Against Epistemology*, Domingo, p. 45, and *Hegel: Three Studies*, Nicholsen, p. 54); GS 7, pp. 13, 364 and 420 (*Aesthetic Theory*, Hullot-Kentor, pp. 4, 320 and 363); GS 13, p. 174 passim.

7   See Hermann Schweppenhäuser, 'Studien über die Heideggersche Sprach-theorie', *Archiv für Philosophie*, Vol. 7, nos 3–4 (1967), p. 304; also available in book form, as *Studien über die Heideggersche Sprachtheorie*, Munich, 1988, pp. 35ff.

8   In *Negative Dialectics* Adorno inserted the words 'in Scholem's phrase' in the corresponding passage (GS 6, p. 118; *Negative Dialectics*, Ashton, p. 112).

9   Adorno provides a decisive formulation of this thought in *The Jargon of Authenticity* (Tarnowski and Will, p. 28): 'Nihilism turns into farce, into mere method, as has already happened to Cartesian doubt. The question – a favourite prerequisite of the jargon – must sound all the more radical the more loyally it directs itself to the kind of answer which can be everything except radical.' The category of doubt – of *dubitatio* or *doute* – in Descartes and Cartesianism had come to compete with the notion of wonder or θαυμάζειν in Plato (see note 11 below) and thus initiated an experimental mode of thought which was methodologically ready to doubt a whole range of propositions precisely in order to establish a set of propositions which could no longer be doubted. In the *Discours de la méthode* Descartes tells us that, 'because in this case I wished to give myself entirely to the search after Truth, I thought that it was necessary for me ... to reject as absolutely false everything as to which I could imagine the least ground of doubt, in order to see if afterwards there remained anything in my belief that was entirely certain' (*Philosophical Works of Descartes*, Haldane and Ross, Vol. 1, pp. 100–1). The very radicality with which Cartesian doubt establishes itself as a method and claims universal validity is exposed by Adorno as an ideological illusion:

> The procedure was so planned from the beginning that nothing outside its sequence of stages could disturb it. Hence the imperviousness of method to everything from Cartesian doubt right up to Heidegger's respectful destruction of the philosophical legacy. Only specific and never absolute doubt joins of itself in the parade through the goal of method, which is once again to be produced out of method itself ... Doubt simply shifts judgement to preparing for assuming the vindication of pre-critical consciousness scientifically in secret sympathy with conventional sensibility [*Menschenverstand*]. At the same time, however, method must constantly do violence to unfamiliar things, though it exists only so that they may be known. It must model the other after itself. This is the original contradiction in the construction of freedom from contradiction in the philosophy of origins. (GS 5, pp. 19f.; *Against Epistemology*, Domingo, pp. 11–12)

10 For what follows, see the section of *Negative Dialectics* entitled 'The Question of Being' (GS 6, pp. 118ff.; *Negative Dialectics*, Ashton, p. 112).

11 The experience of θαυμάζειν (of 'wonder' or 'amazement') has been regarded as the origin of philosophy, and often also as its ultimate meaning, since the time of Plato's *Theaetetus* (155 d), even if the Stoics considered the contrary stance of *Nihil admirari*, the freedom from amazement, as the ideal attitude for the philosopher (and thereby still indirectly related back to *admiratio*). Throughout the entire history of philosophy we encounter the return of this idea of 'wonder', along with its periodic rejection by certain thinkers. Thus Hamann, for example, bluntly declared that 'nihil admirari must always remain the foundation of philosophical judgement' (Johann Georg Hamann, *Sämtliche*

Werke, ed. Josef Nadler, Vol. II, Vienna, 1950, p. 164). Schopenhauer, on the other hand, claimed that the 'philosopher … always confronts a perplexity which he seeks to escape and which is none other than the θαυμάζειν of Plato, who calls it a μάλα φιλοσοφικὸν πάθος. But this is what distinguishes the spurious philosophers from the genuine ones. For the latter this perplexity arises when they behold the world itself, while for the former it only comes from a book' (A. Schopenhauer, *Sämtliche Werke*, Vol. I, p. 68). Adorno rediscovered something of this ancient idea of wonder in Ernst Bloch's book *The Spirit of Utopia*. In the essay 'The Handle, the Pot, and Early Experience' he described Bloch's thought as

> a philosophy that could hold its head high in front of the most advanced literature … If, as Plato said, philosophy originated in amazement and – one drew the conclusion spontaneously – allayed that amazement through its further course, then Bloch's volume, a folio in quarto, protests the nonsensical state of affairs, frozenly taken for granted, in which that philosophy pompously cheats itself of what it ought to be. Bloch's philosophy did not merely begin with amazement: it was intended to open out onto the amazing. Mystical and *hochfahrend* in the double sense of explosive and ascending, it wanted to do away with the ceremonials of intellectual discipline that prevent it from achieving its goal; fraternally, it allied itself with the boldest aspects of contemporary art and would have preferred to transcend them by extending them through intellectual reflection. (GS 11, p. 557; *Notes to Literature*, Nicholsen, Vol. 2, p. 212)

Later in his *Aesthetic Theory*, a text which he did not live to complete, Adorno suggested that the experience of θαυμάζειν had effectively passed from philosophy to the domain of art:

> Art becomes an enigma because it appears to have solved what is enigmatical in existence, while the enigma in the merely existing is forgotten as a result of its own overwhelming ossification. The more densely people have spun a categorical web around what is other than subjective spirit, the more fundamentally have they disaccustomed themselves to the wonder of that other and deceived themselves with a growing familiarity with what is foreign. Art hopes to correct this, though feebly and with a quickly exhausted gesture. A priori, art causes people to wonder, just as Plato once demanded that philosophy do, which, however, decided for the opposite. (GS 7, p. 191; *Aesthetic Theory*, Hullot-Kentor, p. 167)

12 See NaS IV.14, p. 231, n. 3; *Metaphysics: Concept and Problems*, Jephcott, p. 147, n. 3.
13 See Karl Jaspers, *Die geistige Situation der Zeit*, 5th edn, Berlin, 1960. There is an English translation under the title *Man in the Modern Age*, trans. Eden Paul and Cedar Paul, New York, 1957.
14 Ludwig Klages (1872–1956), philosopher and graphologist, originally a member of the circle of Stefan George, who came to defend an essentially irrationalist and anti-Semitic philosophy of life. His principal work

was *Der Geist als Widersacher der Seele* [Spirit as Antagonist of the Soul], 3 vols, Leipzig, 1929–32. Adorno himself has been 'situated' rather bizarrely by certain later would-be representatives of the Frankfurt School somewhere in the vicinity of Klages and his thought (see, for example, Albrecht Wellmer, *Zur Dialektik der Moderne und Postmoderne. Vernunftkritik nach Adorno*, Frankfurt am Main, 1985, pp. 10f. and 45). Yet Adorno always emphatically attacked Klages as a 'zealous apologist of myth and sacrifice' (GS 3, p. 68; *Dialectic of Enlightenment*, Jephcott, p. 260, n. 6). As early as his inaugural address Adorno had already presented his own programme for a philosophy of historical images as 'instruments of human reason' and had drawn an unmistakable contrast with the way that Klages and others like him also appealed to images. Adorno's images here 'are essentially different from the primordial mythic and archaic images in the form that psychoanalysis finds them, in the form that Klages hopes to preserve them as categories of human knowledge. However much they may seem to resemble one another, they go their different ways where the latter assume their fateful course above the heads of human beings' (GS 1, p. 341). Thus Adorno welcomed the fact that as 'early as 1902 Hofmannsthal recognized the bizarre inconsistency between the pedantic sobriety and the dogma of intoxication which Klages' philosophy unceasingly disavows and compares it to the masked-ball of Alfred Schuler' (GS 10.1, p. 217; *Prisms*, trans. Samuel Weber and Shierry Weber, London, 1967, p. 208). For Adorno, the 'agitatory cult of primordial powers' which George shared with Klages anticipated the 'fateful tendencies of National Socialism. The mythologists unceasingly destroy what they take to be the substance through the act of naming. They heralded the sell-out of allegedly primal words like "death", "inwardness" and "genuineness" which subsequently was consummated in the Third Reich' (GS 10.1, p. 215; *Prisms*, p. 206). The fact that Adorno revealed a significant interest in Klages in his correspondence with Horkheimer – that is to say, in private documents not intended for publication – should really be regarded as an indication of his objective opposition to the chthonic tendencies of the thought of Klages. Adorno suggested as much in a letter to Benjamin of 5 December 1934, when he emphasized how 'sharply opposed' Benjamin now was to Scheler. He continued in the same spirit:

And it is indeed only in this sense that I can imagine any relationship to Jung, or Klages for example (whose doctrine of 'phantoms' in the section 'The Actuality of Images' from his *Spirit as Antagonist of the Soul* lies closest of all, relatively speaking, to our own concerns). Or to put it more precisely still: it is exactly here that the decisive distinction between archaic and dialectical images really lies, or ... this is the place for a materialist doctrine of ideas. (*Theodor W. Adorno / Walter Benjamin. Briefwechsel 1928–1940*, ed. Henri Lonitz, 2nd edn, Frankfurt am Main, 1995, p. 84; *The Complete Correspondence 1928–1940*, trans. Nicholas Walker, Polity, 1999, p. 61)

15 From the Te Deum, a Latin hymn dating from the fifth/sixth century CE and used in the Roman Catholic liturgy. It was translated into German by Martin Luther for use in the Protestant hymnbook and has been set by numerous composers, from Orlando di Lasso to Zoltán Kodaly, including Bach, Mozart, Berlioz, Verdi and Bruckner. The final verses of the hymn draw on the Vulgate version of Psalm 30 and Psalm 70: 'In te Domine speravi non confundar in aeternum' – 'In thee, O Lord, have I put my trust, let me not be confounded.' Adorno often cites the phrase *non confundar*, usually in connection with art and the utopian promise it bears. See GS 6, p. 119; *Negative Dialectics*, Ashton, p. 113; GS 7, pp. 199 and 200; *Aesthetic Theory*, Hullot-Kentor, pp. 174 and 175; GS 11, p. 214; *Notes to Literature*, Nicholsen, Vol. 1, p. 184; GS 16, p. 320; *Quasi Una Fantasia: Essays on Modern Music*, trans. Rodney Livingstone, London, 1998, p. 77.
16 Heidegger, *Sein und Zeit*, p. 11; *Being and Time*, Stambaugh, p. 10.

Lecture 22

1 On account of lacunae in the transcription (Vo 5949) the editor has reconstructed the opening of this sentence.
2 Namely the second Paris lecture on 'Being and Existence' (Ts 13971ff.). For what follows, see the section of *Negative Dialectics* entitled 'Volte' (GS 6, pp. 121ff.; *Negative Dialectics*, Ashton, p. 115).
3 The corresponding sentence in *Negative Dialectics* alludes to the famous 'Postscript' which Heidegger later added to his essay 'What is Metaphysics?' Originally Heidegger had said: 'if indeed it belongs to the truth of being that being *indeed* prevails in its essence without beings, that a being never is without being', but in later editions he seems to say the opposite: 'if indeed it belongs to the truth of being that being *never* prevails in its essence without beings, that a being never is without being' (*Was ist Metaphysik?*, p. 41; *Postscript to 'What is Metaphysics?'*, in *Pathmarks*, McNeill, p. 233; see GS 6, pp. 122f. [translation slightly amended]; *Negative Dialectics*, Ashton, pp. 115f.).
4 Heidegger, *Platons Lehre von der Wahrheit: Mit einem Brief über den Humanismus*, p. 68; *Letter on 'Humanism'*, in *Pathmarks*, McNeill, p. 248: 'However, here the opposition between *existentia* and *essentia* is not what is at issue, because neither of these metaphysical determinations of being, let alone their relationship, is yet in question.'
5 *Platons Lehre von der Wahrheit*, pp. 78f.; *Pathmarks*, McNeill, p. 249: 'The sentence the human being "ek-sists" is not an answer to the question of whether the human being actually is or not; rather, it responds to the question concerning the "essence" of the human being.'
6 *Platons Lehre von der Wahrheit*, p. 68; *Pathmarks*, McNeill, pp. 248f.
7 Herbert George Wells (1866–1946) wrote *The Time Machine*, one of the earliest examples of science fiction, in 1895. In this story he describes an invention which permits travel in the fourth dimension both into the

future and into the past. The inventor of the machine, the so-called time traveller, disappears at the end along with his machine and leaves the narrator to wonder in the Epilogue: 'It may be that he swept back into the past, and fell among the blood-drinking hairy savages of the Age of Unpolished Stone; into the abysses of the Cretaceous Sea; or among the grotesque saurians, the huge reptilian brutes of the Jurassic times. He may even now – if I may use the phrase – be wandering on some plesiosaurus-hunted Oolitic coral reef, or beside the lonely saline lakes of the Triassic Age' (Wells, *The Time Machine*, London, 2017, p. 144).

8   Heidegger, *Platons Lehre von der Wahrheit*, p. 75; *Pathmarks*, McNeill, p. 252: 'The advent of beings lies in the destiny [*Geschick*] of being.'

9   For what follows, see the section in *Negative Dialectics* entitled 'Function of the Concept of Existence' (GS 6, pp. 128ff.; *Negative Dialectics*, Ashton, p. 122).

10 Karl Jaspers, *Philosophie*, Vol. I: *Philosophische Weltorientierung*, Berlin, 1956, p. xx.

11 The allusion is to the *doctor subtilis*, a name traditionally ascribed to the medieval philosopher Duns Scotus.

12 The second Paris lecture (Ts 13977) here refers to Jaspers's *Philosophie*, p. xxiii (note 10 above), and to Heidegger's *Über den Humanismus* (Frankfurt am Main, 1949), pp. 17f.

13 For what follows, see the section in *Negative Dialectics* entitled '"Dasein in Itself Ontological"' (GS 6, pp. 130ff.; *Negative Dialectics*, Ashton, pp. 124ff.).

14 See note 14 to Lecture 9 above.

15 Heidegger, *Sein und Zeit*, p. 12; *Being and Time*, Stambaugh, p. 11.

16 *Sein und Zeit*, p. 13; *Being and Time*, Stambaugh, p. 12.

17 Adorno otherwise ascribed the concept of 'egoity' [*Egoität*] to Schelling: 'The moment of human singularity – what Schelling described as "egoity" – cannot be thought away from any concept of the subject; and the subject would lose all meaning if it failed to remember this moment' (GS 10.2, p. 741; also GS 6, p. 275; *Negative Dialectics*, Ashton, p. 279). It may, however, have originated with Hegel, who used the word a number of times in his essay *Faith and Knowledge*, although not in Adorno's sense: 'The supreme abstraction of this absolutized negation is the Ego-concept [*Egoität*], just as the thing is the highest abstraction pertaining to position. Each of them is only a negation of the other. Pure being like pure thinking – an absolute thing and absolute Ego-concept – are equally finitude made absolute' (Hegel, *Werke*, Vol. 2: *Jenaer Schriften 1801–1807*, p. 301; *Faith and Knowing*, trans. Walter Cerf and H. S. Harris, New York, 1977, p. 66).

18 For what follows, see the section of *Negative Dialectics* entitled 'Existence Authoritarian' (GS 6, pp. 132ff.; *Negative Dialectics*, Ashton, pp. 127ff.).

19 Jaspers, *Philosophie* (note 10 above), p. 264.

20 For what follows, see the section in *Negative Dialectics* entitled 'Historicality' (GS 6, pp. 134ff.; *Negative Dialectics*, Ashton, pp. 128ff.).

21 Although 'the moment' is one of Kierkegaard's basic theological-philosophical concepts, Adorno is alluding here to the journal *The Moment*, which Kierkegaard himself wrote and published in 1854–5. He was 'trying to exercise an influence through journalistic means precisely to bring out the momentary character of this influence for the sake of the eternal "moment"' (Hayo Gerdes, in Kierkegaard, *Werkausgabe II*, Düsseldorf, 1971, p. 589).

22 For Adorno's critique of the concept of historicity, see Lecture 9, p. 87, and note 4 to Lecture 9.

23 Adorno's original lecture 'Being and Existence' (Vo 13983) here includes the remark: 'Karl Löwith has emphasized this aspect of Heidegger's view of history (see Karl Löwith, *Heidegger, Denker in dürftiger Zeit*, Frankfurt am Main 1953, p. 49).'

24 Adorno was mistaken in citing Plato's dialogue *Gorgias* here. He was probably thinking of the *Meno* (73c-d), where Socrates questions the boy Meno, who is a disciple of Gorgias: 'Seeing then that they all have the same virtue, try to remember and tell me what Gorgias and you, who share his opinion, say it is. – Meno: It must simply be *the capacity to govern men*, if you are looking for one quality to cover all the instances ... – Socrates: And here is another point. You speak of "capacity to govern". Shall we not add, "justly but not otherwise"? – Meno: I think we should, for justice is virtue' (Plato, *The Collected Dialogues*, ed. Edith Hamilton and Huntington Cairns, Princeton University Press, 1963, p. 356).

25 At this point Adorno begins to read out parts of his third Paris lecture 'On Negative Dialectics', the fourth version of which seems to have been completed on 16 July 1961 (Ts 16715–16752). In *Negative Dialectics*, this lecture was incorporated into Part II of the book *Negative Dialectics: Concept and Categories* (GS 6, pp. 140ff.; *Negative Dialectics*, Ashton, pp. 134ff.).

26 For what follows, see the section in *Negative Dialectics* entitled 'The Need for the Substantive' (GS 6, pp. 140ff.; *Negative Dialectics*, Ashton, pp. 136ff.).

27 'God governs the world: the content of his governance, the fulfilment of his plan, is world history. Philosophy seeks to understand this plan: for only what is fulfilled according to that plan has reality; what is not in accord with it, is but a worthless existence [*faule Existenz*]' (Hegel, *Werke*, Vol. 12, p. 53; *Introduction to the Philosophy of World History*, trans. Leo Rauch, Hackett, 1988, p. 39).

28 For what follows, see the section of *Negative Dialectics* entitled 'Peephole Metaphysics' (GS 6, pp. 142ff.; *Negative Dialectics*, Ashton, pp. 137ff.).

Lecture 23

1 See the deployment of this concept in *Negative Dialectics*, where Adorno provides the ultimate formulation of this idea: 'Except amongst the

heretics, all Western metaphysics has been peephole metaphysics. The subject – a mere limited moment – was locked up in its own self by that metaphysics, imprisoned for all eternity to punish it for its deification. As through the crenels of a parapet, the subject gazes upon a black sky in which the star of the idea, or of "being", is said to rise' (GS 6, p. 143; *Negative Dialectics*, Ashton, pp. 139–40).

2   At this point Adorno returns to his Paris lecture 'On Negative Dialectics' (Ts 16721ff.). See the section in *Negative Dialectics* entitled 'Non-Contradiction not to be Hypostasized' (GS 6, pp. 144ff.; *Negative Dialectics*, Ashton, pp. 139ff.).

3   For what follows, see the section of *Negative Dialectics* entitled 'Relation to Left Hegelianism' (GS 6, pp. 146f.) and 'Materialism Imageless' (GS 6, pp. 204ff.; *Negative Dialectics*, Ashton, pp. 143ff. and 204ff.).

4   In the 'Introduction' to the *Phenomenology* Hegel writes:

> But not only is a contribution by us superfluous, since concept and object, the criterion and what is to be tested, are present in consciousness itself, but we are also spared the trouble of comparing the two and really *testing* them, so that, since what consciousness examines is its own self, all that is left for us to do is simply to look on. For consciousness is, on the one hand, consciousness of the object, and on the other, consciousness of itself; consciousness of what for it is the True, and consciousness of its knowledge of the truth. (Hegel, *Werke*, Vol. 3: *Phänomenologie des Geistes*, p. 77; *Phenomenology of Spirit*, Miller, p. 54).

5   The theory of knowledge as a kind of 'mirroring' or 'reflection' of reality became the official epistemology of institutionalized Marxist-Leninism, which showed no qualms about describing itself as 'Diamat'. For Adorno it was evident that 'Marx, disgusted with academic squabbles, went rampaging through the epistemological categories like the proverbial bull in a china shop; and he scarcely put much weight on terms such as "reflection" [*Widerspiegelung*]' (GS 6, p. 206; *Negative Dialectics*, Ashton, p. 206). Adorno's critique of this epistemic theory of reflection, according to which knowledge is supposed to copy or reflects objective reality within human consciousness, can be expressed in a nutshell as follows: 'The theory of knowledge as a mirroring denies the spontaneity of the subject, a *movens* of the objective dialectics of the productive forces and relations. If the subject is bound to mirror the object in mulish fashion – inevitably doing injustice to the object, which only opens itself to the subjective excess of thought – the result is the disquieting spiritual stillness of total administration' (GS 6, p. 205; *Negative Dialectics*, Ashton, p. 205). For a defence of the reflection theory of knowledge on a rather sophisticated level, see Thomas Metscher, 'Ästhetik als Abbildtheorie. Erkenntnistheoretische Grundlagen materialistischer Kunsttheorie und das Realismusproblem in den Literaturwissenschaften', in T. Metscher, *Kunst und sozialer Prozess: Studien zu einer Theorie der ästhetischen Erkenntnis*, Cologne, 1977, pp. 150ff.

6   On Epicureanism and its theory of 'images' (εἴδωλα), see the letter of
    Epicurus to Herodotos (in A. A. Long and D. N. Sedley, *The Hellenistic
    Philosophers*).

7   This is perhaps Adorno's first explicit formulation of the theory of the
    priority of the object which would prove so central in his thought. See
    the section in *Negative Dialectics* entitled 'Priority of the Object' (GS
    6, pp. 184ff.; *Negative Dialectics*, Ashton, p. 183; see also NaS IV.4,
    pp. 412ff., n. 296; *Kant's Critique of Pure Reason*, Livingstone, p. 279,
    n. 17.

8   A formulation of Kant's. See the 'Deduction of the Pure Concepts of
    the Understanding' in the second edition of the first *Critique*, §16, on
    'The Original-Synthetic Unity of Apperception': 'It must be possible for
    the "I think" to accompany all my representations; for otherwise some-
    thing would be represented in me which could not be thought at all,
    and that is equivalent to saying that the representation would be impos-
    sible, or at least would be nothing to me' (*Critique of Pure Reason*,
    Kemp Smith, pp. 152–3 (B 131f.).

9   According to the transcript of the lecture (Vo 5965). The text of the
    Paris lecture, on the other hand, reads: 'But the mediation of the subject
    and the mediation of the object are not the same' (Ts 16743).

10 In the transcript someone has mistakenly added: 'This can already be
    found in the Introduction to the Critique of Pure Reason.' The corre-
    sponding passage in *Negative Dialectics* refers to the table of categories:
    'See Kant, *Critique of Pure Reason*, WW III, Academy Edition, Berlin
    1911, p. 93f.' (i.e. B 106f.).

11 For what follows, see the section of *Negative Dialectics* entitled 'Reversal
    of the Subjective Reduction' (GS 6, pp. 178ff.; *Negative Dialectics*,
    Ashton, p. 176).

12 In *Negative Dialectics* Adorno added the sentence: 'Alfred Sohn-Rethel
    was the first to point out that in this principle, in the general and neces-
    sary activity of the mind, social labour is ineluctably involved' (GS 6,
    p. 178; *Negative Dialectics*, Ashton, p. 177). Sohn-Rethel arrived at a
    decisive formulation of his ideas only at a late stage of his career, in his
    book *Geistige und körperliche Arbeit. Zur Theorie der gesellschaftlichen
    Synthesis*, Frankfurt am Main, 1970. For the relationship between Adorno
    and Sohn-Rethel, see *T. W. Adorno und Alfred Sohn-Rethel: Briefwechsel
    1936–1969*, ed. Christoph Gödde, Munich, 1991.

13 In the Paris lecture and in *Negative Dialectics*, Adorno adds the refer-
    ence: 'See Marx, Kritik der Gothaer Programms, Auswahl und Einleitung
    von Franz Borkenau, Frankfurt a. Main 1956, pp. 199ff.' See also GS
    5, pp. 270f.; *Hegel: Three Studies*, Nicholsen, pp. 23f.

14 For the following, see the section in *Negative Dialectics* entitled 'Inter-
    preting the Transcendental' (GS 6, pp. 180f.; *Negative Dialectics*, Ashton,
    p. 178).

15 'Unaquaeque res, quantum in se est, in suo esse perseverare conatur'
    [Each thing, so far as it can by its own power, strives to persevere in
    its being] (*Ethics*, Bk III, prop. 6, in *The Collected Works of Spinoza*,

Curley, Vol. 1, p. 498). As Adorno puts it elsewhere: 'Self-preservation, the Spinozist *sese conservare*, is truly a law of nature for all living beings' (GS 6, p. 342; *Negative Dialectics*, Ashton, p. 349). But, for the specific historical fate of this law of nature, see Max Horkheimer, 'Vernunft und Selbsterhaltung', in *Gesammelte Schriften*, Vol. 5: *Dialektik der Aufklärung und Schriften 1940–1950*, ed. Gunzelin Schmid Noerr, Frankfurt am Main, 1987, pp. 320ff; see also GS 3, p. 28 passim; *Dialectic of Enlightenment*, Jephcott, p. 8 passim.

16 See Husserl, *Cartesianische Meditationen*, in *Gesammelte Schriften*, Vol. 8, p. 26.

17 For what follows, see the section of *Negative Dialectics* entitled 'Transcendental Illusion' (GS 6, pp. 182ff.; *Negative Dialectics*, Ashton, p. 180).

18 A fairy tale by Wilhelm Hauff tells how the bewitched son of a shoemaker became cook to the duke but was unable to prepare the most delicious pie of all because he was unfamiliar with the special herb required. It was only with the help of an equally bewitched goose that the spell that bound him was broken by the herb in question and he 'escaped from the palace happy and unrecognized, along with the goose' (Hauff, *Romane, Märchen, Gedichte*, ed. Hermann Engelhard, Stuttgart, 1961, pp. 693ff.). The significant role played by the author of *The Singer* in the mental world of Adorno can be gathered from an essay on concertgoing he wrote in 1937, where he speaks simply of 'the great Wilhelm Hauff' (GS 16, pp. 279f.).

19 See also NaS IV.14, p. 100, and the quotation from Schelling (n. 124); *Metaphysics: Concept and Problems*, Jephcott, p. 63 and p. 166, n. 2.

INDEX

acosmism 136
appearance/essence 224
art/philosophy 112–13
being 4, 5, 78–9
being, concept of 5–6
being, doctrine of 4
civil society 137
concepts 39, 43
critique 167–8, 249
determinate negation 241,
    253n6
dialectic 69, 74, 136, 237, 241,
    242
essence xv, xvi, 8, 85
existence 270n2
Fall 193
givenness 200
Idea 124
Kierkegaard on 90–1, 107–8,
    181–2
knowledge 193
labour 98
man 150
nature 111, 127
objectivity 98
philosophy of nature 111
pure becoming 218
pure being 199
and Schopenhauer 107–8
thought 193
transience 240
truth 232
works
    Encyclopaedia Logic 298n6
    Phenomenology of Spirit 203,
        305n4
    Philosophy of Right 109,
        285n2
    Propaedeutic 297–8n2
    Science of Logic 4, 26, 85, 86,
        170, 253–4n9
    System of Philosophy 115
Heidegger, Martin 75–6, 82–3, 89,
    168–9, 183, 186–9
    From the Experience of Thinking
        160–1

Holzwege xix
Introduction to Metaphysics
    77–8, 198
Letter on 'Humanism' 80, 82,
    91, 121, 172, 182–3, 229
On the Essence of Ground 6,
    212
On the Question of Being
    278n22
'Plato's Theory of Truth' 169
poems 160–1, 162, 194–5
'The Question concerning
    Technology' 291n8
'What is Metaphysics?' 294n19,
    302n3
What is Metaphysics? 25,
    257n4
see also Being and Time
Heidegger: Thinker in a Barren
    Time (Löwith) 101
Heimat (homeland) 178, 179
Helms, Hans G. 272n12
hendiadys 290n6
Heraclitus 23–4, 25, 76, 218
Herder, Johann Gottfried 212
heresies 119, 120
hermeneutics 35, 258n5
heteronomy xiv, 33–4, 102, 209
hierarchy 131, 151, 165–6, 182,
    210, 211, 248, 282
Hippolytus 290n2
historicity 179–80, 234, 304n22
history
    homeland 179
    irreversible 164
    loss of 156
    mythology 179–80
    ontologized xv, 180, 234
    philosophy 25, 236
    thinking 99, 230
History and Class Consciousness
    (Lukács) 281–3n3
history of philosophy 25, 71, 90–1,
    108–9, 115, 132, 236
Hitler, Adolf 123, 169–70, 210,
    277–8n16